Ethnicity, Race, and Crime

D0556765

SUNY Series in New Directions in Crime and Justice Studies
Austin T. Turk, Editor

Ethnicity, Race, and Crime

Perspectives across
Time and Place

Edited by
Darnell F. Hawkins

NATIONAL UNIVERSITY
LIBRARY

STATE UNIVERSITY OF NEW YORK PRESS

Published by
State University of New York Press, Albany

© 1995   State University of New York

All rights reserved

Printed in the United States of America

No part of this book may be used or reproduced
in any manner whatsoever without written permission
except in the case of brief quotations embodied in
critical articles and reviews.

For information, address State University of New York
Press, State University Plaza, Albany, N.Y., 12246

Production by E. Moore
Marketing by Theresa A. Swierzowski

Library of Congress Cataloging-in-Publication Data
Ethnicity, race, and crime : perspectives across time and place /
    Darnell F. Hawkins, editor.
        p.   cm. — (SUNY series in new directions in crime and justice
    studies)
    Includes bibliographical references and index.
    ISBN 0-7914-2195-3 (acid free). — ISBN 0-7914-2196-1 (pbk. : acid
free)
    1. Criminal justice, Administration of—United States.
2. Discrimination in criminal justice administration—United States.
3. United States—Race relations.   4. United States—Ethnic
relations.   I. Hawkins, Darnell Felix, 1946–   . II. Series: SUNY
series, New directions in crime and justice studies.
HV9950.E87   1995
364.2'56—dc20   94-10968
                                                                        CIP

10 9 8 7 6 5 4 3 2 1

Modern European and American History is centered around the effort to gain freedom from the political, economic, and spiritual shackles that have bound men. The battles for freedom were fought by the oppressed, those who wanted new liberties, against those who had privileges to defend. In the long and virtually continuous battle for freedom, however, classes that were fighting against oppression at one stage sided with the enemies of freedom when victory was won and new privileges were to be defended.

—Erich Fromm, *Escape From Freedom*

For when you domesticate a member of your own species, you reduce his output, and however little you may give him, a farmyard man finishes by costing more than he brings in. For this reason the settlers are obliged to stop the breaking-in halfway; the result, neither man nor animal, is the native.

—Frantz Fanon, *The Wretched of the Earth*

Crime became real, for example—for the first time—not as *a* possibility but as *the* possibility. One would never defeat one's circumstances by working and saving one's pennies; one would never, by working, acquire that many pennies, and besides, the social treatment accorded even the most successful Negroes proved that one needed, in order to be free, something more than a bank account. One needed a handle, a lever, a means of inspiring fear. It was absolutely clear that the police would whip you and take you in as long as they could get away with it, and that everyone else—housewives, taxi drivers, elevator boys, dishwashers, bartenders, lawyers, judges, doctors and grocers—would never, by the operation of any generous human feeling, cease to use you as an outlet for his frustrations and hostilities.

—James Baldwin, *The Fire Next Time*

Contents

MARVIN E. WOLFGANG

Foreword

As a criminologist who has written about race, ethnicity, and crime—sometimes hesitantly or even fearfully—I can write candidly and with historical experience that this volume edited by Darnell Hawkins is the most luminous I have read on these topics for many years. There is a boldness here of thought, theory, concepts. There is depth and comprehensiveness. The authors in this collection illuminate the meaning of racism in ways that go beyond sheer advocacy. The scientificity (an audibly crunching but truthful term) of these chapters is abundantly and fortunately clear.

This volume has been produced during the days of concern for, and challenges of, *political correctness, multi-culturalism, cultural diversity.* None of these authors has written with undue attention to the buzz words of the moment. I believe their analyses will endure over time and ideological challenges.

A Foreword is not the place to summarize chapters or contributions. The editor has done this task well. I do wish, however, to express my special respect and admiration for the intellectual quality of the editor's remarks, especially his review of selected studies in the first chapter, and for the scientific integrity of the works he solicited.

I think this collection will become a classic. A classic is a book that is timeless, or nearly timeless, in its insightful perception, one that endures beyond the usual decade of disappearance, one that teachers of crime and justice will be assigning for young minds of more than one generation to read.

I agreed to consider the task of writing this foreword before I saw the manuscript. Now that I have read it, I am honored to have this word before the excellent text.

DARNELL F. HAWKINS

Introduction

In anticipation of the intergroup conflict that characterized the world-wide struggle against European colonials, W. E. B. DuBois observed in 1903 that "the problem of the twentieth century is the problem of the color-line,—the relation of the darker to the lighter races of men in Asia and Africa, in America and the islands of the sea" (DuBois, 1961:23). Consistent with his prediction, considerations of color and race have shaped the world's history for much of this century. In the United States where European colonialism took the form of Indian Wars, black chattel slavery, and permanent white homesteading, DuBois's statement has been particularly prophetic. The dilemma posed by the nation's *race problem* has left its mark on all aspects of its institutional and social life (Myrdal, 1944).

As the twentieth century draws to a close, there are grim reminders that race still matters in the United States and other parts of the postcolonial world. The black majority in South Africa has only recently achieved the right to vote. Native nonwhite populations in Brazil, Peru, Australia, the United States, New Zealand, and other countries struggle against dominant majorities to maintain their cultural heritages. And in the United States the police beatings of black motorists Rodney King in Los Angeles and Malice Green in Detroit have highlighted the inequality of justice and the persistence of racial bigotry. The color line remains an integral part of American society (Farley and Allen, 1987; Jaynes and Williams, 1989)

On the other hand, only a social analyst with the sleep habits of Rip Van Winkle could fail to observe that many of the most barbarous, inhumane, and globally disruptive events of the century did not always pit the darker and lighter races against each other. Instead, they arose from ethnic and nationality cleavages within populations of similar skin color. Europe witnessed two major interethnic wars, the genocide of millions of Jews and other "outsiders," and the rise of a cold war militarism that curbed civil liberties and promoted armed struggle for a half-century. This century has also seen Japanese expansionism and imperialism directed at its Asian neighbors, continuing

1

military conflict between dominant Chinese populations and ethnic minorities within and outside China, and interethnic conflicts in much of Africa.

Indeed, with the seeming collapse of many of the hegemonic nation-states that were erected in response to the cold war or to divide Europe's former African and Asian colonial empires, it appears likely that interethnic struggles will see a worldwide increase. As the twentieth century was characterized by the color line, the twenty-first may be characterized by dividing lines based on ethnic differences. Ongoing interethnic wars and armed conflicts in Northern Ireland, Ethiopia, Sudan, Indonesia, and the former nation of Yugoslavia illustrate the salience of ethnic differences during the late twentieth century. Though underanalyzed by social scientists, intergroup competition and conflict based on ethnic differentiation has been a fact of life throughout human history.

While these global events are often considered peripheral to traditional investigations of crime in society, they are vital for an understanding of the social dynamics that underlie the studies of ethnicity, race, and crime included in this volume. Whether formed as a result of colonialism or the cold war, the multiethnic, multiracial nation-states of the twentieth century are characterized by the existence of a well-acknowledged set of interrelationships among ethnicity, race, the production of criminal law, and the sanctioning of criminal behavior. This collection of essays was designed to explore those interconnections by providing discussions that are grounded not only in the criminological literature but also in the sociological study of intergroup relations. Though most analyses are limited to the United States, the themes explored in this collection arise from and are responsive to the global events described above. The volume fills a relative void in the social science and criminological literatures, since few edited collections or authored works have examined the linkage among ethnicity, race, crime, and the administration of justice.

VOLUME OVERVIEW

The sixteen chapters in this volume were selected to provide varying approaches to the study of crime and its relationship to ethnicity and race. They are almost equally divided among those that provide historical perspectives and those that explore contemporary phenomena. Though diverse in their approaches, the chapters share a common theme: the author's attempt to explain why some ethnic and racial groups appear to be more likely than others to be sanctioned for involvement in crime.

The volume begins with an effort to outline the major theoretical currents that have guided research and writing on ethnic and racial differences in the level of crime and punishment in modern societies. To this end, Darnell Hawkins critically reviews the work of eight authors, writing between 1899 and 1970, who have made significant contributions to this area of inquiry. Included in his analysis is a discussion of how the political and social volatility of the question of ethnic and racial differences in the level of involvement in criminal activity has shaped both public and scholarly discourse on the subject. The competing explanations for intergroup differences advocated and criticized by the eight authors included in this review are to be found in various forms in most of the other chapters included in the volume.

Thomas Regulus raises issues similar to those of Hawkins in his review of sociobiological perspectives on ethnic, race, and class differences in the rate of involvement in crime. The growing acceptance of *new* biological determinist views of the etiology of crime and other social behavior is noted. Regulus cites both the seeming potential of sociobiological theory and research findings for devising crime control strategies, and the perhaps greater threat of racial and class bias in the attempted application of research. This chapter makes a particularly valuable contribution to the volume, since most of the other chapters utilize more traditional sociological approaches to the study of crime in society. And as both Regulus and Hawkins note, these traditional approaches have increasingly come to be seen as inappropriate or inadequate as many prominent modern analysts of crime—for example, Wilson and Herrnstein (1985)—begin to link group differences in the rate of involvement in crime to sociobiological factors.

The second part of the volume contains six articles, all of which provide historical perspectives on crime and crime control in the United States. Chapters by Joan McCord, M. Craig Brown and Barbara D. Warner, and Eric Monkkonen explore issues of ethnic differences in crime and punishment that emerged with the immigration of Europeans to America during the nineteenth and early twentieth centuries.

Monkkonen's work is significant because it is one of only a few studies, either historical or contemporary, that move beyond a simple black-white dichotomy to compare crime rates and punishment of African-Americans to those of specific white ethnic/nationality groups. Though hampered by data availability constraints, Monkkonen finds that New York City experienced a relatively high rate of fatal interpersonal aggression between 1800 and 1874. However, he finds that African-Americans were not significantly more likely than recently arrived white immigrants to be involved in such violence. Given current perceptions of black criminality, his study illustrates the value of longitudinal investigations and intergroup comparisons based on disaggregated ethnic/racial data.

McCord, Brown and Warner also have an interest in examining the crime patterns of white ethnics in America's large cities during the last century. Their goal is to offer an explanation for the reportedly high rates of crime found among these groups during that period. Both chapters raise doubts regarding traditional accounts of the relationship among nationality, ethnicity, immigrant status and crime in the United States. McCord does so by suggesting that there has been misspecification of how crime is related to immigration, ethnicity, and religion. She argues that the failure of earlier analysts to control for the economic condition of various groups led to unwarranted views of the importance of cultural difference or other ethnic traits as contributors to criminality. Brown and Warner propose that the politics of law enforcement and interethnic competition must be factored into the study of crime etiology in turn-of-the-century America. In support of conflict perspectives, they find that the police were used by dominant ethnic groups to target ethnic subordinates and that such targeting was a major cause of the imbalance in arrests and other indices of criminality.

The theme of crime and criminality as indices of intergroup competition, inequality, and social control is further developed in the chapters by E. M. Beck and Stewart Tolnay and Martha Myers. Both sets of authors seek to account for patterns of crime and punishment (both formal and informal) in the post–Civil War south. Like Brown and Warner, Beck and Tolnay use a "threat" hypothesis and a model of economic competition to explain variations in rates of social control. For Beck and Tolnay, such control is measured by lynch mob activity directed toward African Americans between 1882 and 1930. Myers turns her attention to the treatment of blacks within both the formal and informal criminal justice systems of the late nineteenth- and early twentieth-century south. In an examination of the punishment of rape offenders, she argues that the specter of black criminality was an integral feature of race relations during this period. Like Beck and Tolnay, Myers finds that shifts in local economic conditions affected the rate and severity of formally administered punishment.

The nine chapters in the concluding section of the volume all examine late twentieth-century patterns of crime and social control. The first six of these explore in various ways the question of the disproportionate presence of African Americans among those processed through the American criminal justice system. The authors are not unanimous in their conclusions regarding the causes of such disproportionality.

The chapter by Gary LaFree is both a call for future researchers to face more squarely the existence of racial differences in the rate of reported crime in the United States and a useful analysis of post–World War II crime rate patterns. Many may challenge the accuracy of LaFree's view that the link between race and crime has been ignored. For example, arguments and questions not unlike those posed by LaFree can be found in the works of the authors reviewed by Hawkins in the introduction to this volume. Like these earlier analysts, LaFree notes the sizable racial gap in the arrest rates for serious crime in the United States. He concludes on the basis of a review of recent literature that neither deterrence, social disorganization, nor economic distress perspectives fully explain postwar rates and trends. He proposes that the absence of a viable explanation argues for a bringing to the fore the relationship between race and crime. Although there is arguably some basis for LaFree's contention that neither of the three aforementioned perspectives fully explains the black-white crime rate gap, some may question the extent to which the data he reports fully support his conclusions.

Robert Crutchfield and Dorothy Lockwood and her colleagues respond to LaFree's call for attentiveness to and explanations for the connection between race and reported crime. Crutchfield uses the National Longitudinal Surveys of Youth Labor Market Experience to examine the relationship among race/ethnicity, access to work, and involvement in crime. While Crutchfield finds no single overriding correlate or cause of racial differences in the rate of involvement in crime among youth today, he takes exception to LaFree's seeming conclusion that economic factors are not important. Like the authors who conducted the historical studies included in this volume, Crutchfield argues that a complete understanding of race and crime must include a consideration of the importance of the distribution of jobs, and labor and market inequalities. He suggests that both crime and urban unrest are the result of economic disadvantage, isolation, and marginality.

Dorothy Lockwood, Anne Pottieger, and James Inciardi probe the issues raised by LaFree and Crutchfield through an examination of crack cocaine-related crime and consumption in Miami, Florida, between 1987 and 1991. Responding partly to media accounts of crack use and related crime as primarily a problem for African-Americans, the researchers find that the relationships among crime, crack use, and ethnicity are complex. Patterns of involvement in use/crime were found to vary by age, gender, and treatment status, as well as ethnicity. In the same way that McCord suggested that prior researchers failed to consider the socioeconomic conditions under which new immigrants to the United States were forced to live during the last century, Lockwood, Pottieger, and Inciardi argue that the media have failed to consider the significance of such conditions when proposing a link between race and crack cocaine.

Compared to the three chapters discussed above, the following two chapters in this section by William Chambliss and Coramae Richey Mann are more solidly grounded in the arguments of the conflict perspective. Their explanations for contemporary racial differences in the rate of reported crime closely resemble the historical accounts of Brown and Warner, Beck and Tolnay, and Martha Myers. Chambliss, whose earlier writings helped establish the credibility of conflict-oriented views of crime and justice, here tackles the problem of the disproportionate imprisonment of persons of African ancestry in the United States today. To explain extant levels of racial disproportionality, he argues that between 1964 and 1990 the activities of a collection of diverse social and political interest groups created a "moral panic" about crime in the United States. These interests included conservative legislators, law enforcement agencies, the media, and social scientists. In the same way that Brown and Warner attributed the disproportionate arrest of certain white ethnic groups during the turn of the century to the politics of social control, Chambliss traces the politics and ideology of racially motivated policing in modern America. He provides a thoroughly documented and persuasive account of the effects of this *moral panic* and attendant overpolicing and over-incarceration on poor African-American communities.

Coramae Mann builds upon and extends many of the arguments made by Chambliss. Her focus is on an examination of how socioeconomic inequality has contributed to the generation and persistence of *moral panics* aimed at the social control of all peoples of color in the United States. In addition to arguing that unequal social control is a *cause* of racial differences in rates of reported crime, Mann links *institutionalized racism* to crime through her discussion of its role in fostering those criminogenic social conditions often mentioned by traditional, positivistic analysts of the etiology of crime. That is, she sees a comparatively high rate of black crime as an "understandable" consequence of the substandard living conditions and consequent pathology created by racism. Her discussion echoes arguments made by Bonger (1916) who explored the social misery that contributes to the criminality of the poor. For Mann, higher rates of crime among peoples of color in the United States are a social reality that stems from both their economic misery and their greater risk of social control.

Theodore Chiricos and Charles Crawford provide an interesting test of the hypotheses proposed by both Chambliss and Mann. Sharing Chambliss's concern for the high rates of imprisonment experienced by African-Americans, Chiricos and Crawford assess the evidence of racial bias in the decision to incarcerate. Their evidence consists of thirty-eight studies of race and imprisonment conducted since 1975. They conclude that after controlling for prior record and crime seriousness, blacks are disadvantaged at the point of in/out decisions. Bias is amplified for studies conducted in the south, in places where blacks comprise a significant percentage of the population, in rural areas, and in places with significant unemployment.

In her discussion of minority injustice in the United States, Coramae Mann cited the plight of Native Americans. This theme is explored further in the chapter written by Zoann Snyder-Joy. She provides an informative sketch of the effects of European colonialism on American Indian self-determination and confronts many of the classic questions now associated with the study of ethnicity, race, and crime. After noting the disproportionate representation of Indians among those arrested for crime in the United States, she ponders the extent to which systematic discrimination, higher criminality, or other influences account for the Indian-white difference.

The final two chapters explore the interrelationship among ethnicity, race, and crime through the study of two western European societies—Germany and France. These analyses raise questions very similar to those raised in the study of the experiences of white ethnics in the United States during the last century and of nonwhites in the country today. Since World War II both Germany and France have seen increases in ethnic and racial diversity as their governments have allowed and sometimes encouraged the immigration of workers. As recent events in these countries have shown, animosity against the foreign-born has become more evident. Roland Chilton, Raymond Teske, and Harald Arnold note interesting parallels and differences between Germany and the United States in the response of government to the rising crime rates of ethnic and racial minorities. Their discussion of the effects of subordinate group status on involvement in crime and punishment for it is supportive of conflict theories of social control. And, like Mann, they note the effects of economic and political disadvantage on the production of crime among ethnic minorities in Germany.

Pamela Irving Jackson's depiction of the mobilization of law enforcement in France in response to minority threat mirrors Brown and Warner's findings regarding the policing of immigrant populations at the turn of the century in the United States. Her assertion that economic competition was the basis for social control efforts is also similar to arguments made by Beck and Tolnay and Myers about antiblack violence in the American south. Like Chilton, Teske, and Arnold, Jackson notes the parallels between the treatment of African Americans and European racial/ethnic minorities. She observes that, as in the United States, criminal justice agencies in France are increasingly expected to handle the problems of inner city disorganization resulting from the growth of minority populations in a stagnant economy. I was particularly impressed by the author's ability to place issues of crime and punishment within the larger political and social contexts from which they emerge.

Considered as a group, the papers prepared for this volume make a valuable contribution to the efforts of social scientists to understand the effects of ethnic/racial diversity and conflict on crime and social control. Much remains to be studied. Much remains to be learned. The recent controversy at the National Institutes of Health surrounding the question of racial differences in the rate of involvement in interpersonal violence illustrates the sensitivity and volatility of discussions of ethnicity, race, and crime. Many of the issues raised in this volume have the potential to evoke similar controversy and concern. As during the past, the public and scholarly discourse on the subject of ethnicity, race, and crime itself can be used to justify ethnocentrism, bigotry, and discriminatory policies and practices. Such discourse can also lead to the eradication of myth, pseudo-science, and stereotypes, a goal shared by all contributors to this volume.

REFERENCES

Bonger, Willem A. 1916. *Criminality and Economic Conditions*. Boston: Little Brown.

DuBois, W. E. B. 1961. *The Souls of Black Folk*. New York: Fawcett World Library.

Farley, Reynolds, and Walter R. Allen. 1987. *The Color Line and the Quality of Life in America*. New York: Russell Sage Foundation.

Jaynes, Gerald D., and Robin M. Williams (eds.). 1989. *A Common Destiny: Blacks and American Society*. Washington, D.C.: National Academy Press.

Myrdal, Gunnar. 1944. *An American Dilemma: The Negro Problem and Modern Democracy*. New York: Harper.

Wilson, James Q., and Richard J. Herrnstein. 1985. *Crime and Human Nature*. New York: Simon and Schuster.

Part I

Theoretical and Conceptual Issues

DARNELL F. HAWKINS

1

Ethnicity, Race, and Crime:
A Review of Selected Studies

In an early contribution to the sociology of knowledge, DeGre (1955) observed that all science, including those disciplines not involved in the study of human society, are

> part of the tertiary institutions of a culture, being influenced by the larger constellation of stresses and strains, cultural values, technological accomplishments and needs, and overall-definitions of life goals that characterize the social group, society and world situation in which they are operative. (p. 3)

The accuracy and relevance of this observation are nowhere more evident than in the attempt by social scientists to explain ethnic and racial differences in the rate of involvement in crime and criminal punishment during the last century in the United States and other western societies.

Contemporary social scientists who study crime have been accused of failing to boldly confront the question of the extent to which ethnic and racial groups differ. This oversight has been said to be particularly evident among researchers who examine the etiology of criminal behavior, as compared to those who study the administration of justice where ethnic and racial disparities are said to be more widely noted. While there does appear to be a relative paucity of theory-based investigations, several thoughtful and provocative examinations of the subject have been published during the last century. This chapter summarizes and critically reviews ten seminal works that have explored conceptual, theoretical, and empirical dimensions of the relationship among ethnicity, race, and crime during this period: DuBois (1899, 1904); Sellin (1928,1938); Sutherland (1924,1934); Shaw (1929); Shaw and McKay (1942); Bonger (1943); and Wolfgang and Cohen (1970).[1]

Though the earliest of these studies was conducted nearly a century ago, contemporary debate on the subject of ethnic and racial difference in crime and punishment centers around many ideas first presented by these investigators. Therefore, a critical assessment of these works is vital to our understanding of this important area of criminological research. Let us begin that assessment by situating these investigations and the overall study of ethnicity, race, and crime within the larger social scientific tradition of which they are a part.

RESEARCH ON RACE AND ETHNIC RELATIONS AND INEQUALITY

The documentation and analysis of ethnic and racial differences in social behavior and status have been the mainstay of modern social science. Given its origins as a paradigmatic challenge to notions of biological determinism, modern social science has had an almost singular goal—the refutation of many commonly held notions of human *nature* and its relationship to social behavior. Since race and ethnicity have figured so prominently in this nature versus nurture discourse, a major part of this research tradition has been the study of race and intergroup relations.

Pettigrew (1980:xxi, citing Vander Zanden, 1973:32) reported that the race relations work of American sociologists since 1895 has centered around three basic themes: (1) a description and documentation of Black disadvantage within American life, (2) an attack on racist notions of black biological inferiority, and (3) an interpretation of black disadvantages as derived from white prejudice and discrimination. Pettigrew (1980:xxx) suggests that these themes are indicative of the degree to which late nineteenth- and early twentieth-century race relations literature in the United States was dominated by a "liberal political tone and assumptions."

Pettigrew notes that this liberal and reformist orientation has led to many contradictions and analytic biases that have been the source of criticism from both the right and left in recent decades. The tendency of researchers to focus on these themes is said by Pettigrew to have resulted in three forms of analytic bias: (1) by documenting black and minority disadvantages, liberal race relations research has emphasized *static* description far more than dynamic process; (2) it has stressed the reactive and *pathological* features of black life more than its proactive, healthy features; and (3) it has focused on the *individual* level and such phenomena as prejudiced personalities at the expense of the societal levels and such critical phenomena as group discrimination (1980:xxxi).[2]

Similar foci and biases characterize the study of American ethnic relations—for instance, see Steinberg (1989). Attempts by eugenicists and social Darwinists to restrict the immigration of eastern and southern Europeans to the United States during the years preceding and following the turn of the century were based on notions of inferiority not unlike those used to label blacks (see Gould, 1981; 115). These efforts and the public debate they engendered led to a social scientific defense of these white ethnic groups using arguments similar to those noted by Vander Zanden. Commentary regarding the foreign-born was as commonplace as discussions of blacks during the late 1800s and early twentieth century.

It is my contention that the study of ethnicity, race and crime embodies the analytic and ideological biases described by Pettigrew. My examination of each of the criminological studies listed above is designed to illustrate how these biases are manifested and how they contribute to both the strengths and limitations of these important works. By also presenting the specific sociohistorical context within which each investigation emerged, I attempt to show how the themes and conclusions evident in all the studies illustrate DeGre's view of the social construction of social science.

THE LEGACY OF SLAVERY AND ITS AFTERMATH: DUBOIS ON CRIME AMONG AFRICAN-AMERICANS

I begin with two of the earliest, but most frequently overlooked, discussions of race and crime conducted within the tradition of modern social science. While W. E. B. DuBois's political activism and studies of African-American life have received much notice and acclaim, his work on crime and justice among blacks has been less widely noted. His turn-of-the-century studies of black crime in Philadelphia and in the American south were among the first to confront the task of explaining the disproportionate presence of blacks among these charged with the violation of the criminal law. Since many of the most virulently racist, social Darwinist critiques of black life were published during the period in which he wrote, DuBois was also among the first to provide a retort to their arguments in the tradition of liberal race relations research and criminology.

Both DuBois and the social Darwinists were attentive to several observations made by various social analysts of that period and later: (1) evidence of comparatively higher rates of arrest, conviction, and imprisonment among the black population than among whites; (2) an apparent increase in the rate of crime among blacks after the abolition of slavery; and (3) apparently higher rates of black crime in urban than in rural areas and in the north as compared to the south.

In response to these observations, late nineteenth-century advocates of biological determinism bemoaned the end of slavery and the social control it was said to have exerted on the *natural* criminal tendencies of blacks. As proof of the inherent criminality of blacks and the problems posed by their emancipation, many scholars and political leaders of the period cited the higher rates of crime among free, northern blacks as compared to both southern blacks and northern whites, (see Otken [1894:228–29] and Hoffman [1896: 217–34]. In comparing the crime rates of the black population before and after slavery, Hoffman says:

> During slavery the negro committed fewer crimes than the white man, and only on rare occasions was he guilty of the more atrocious crimes, such as rape and murder of white females. (p. 217)

DuBois's commentary on black crime in Philadelphia (1899) and in Georgia and the south (1904) responded to these biological determinist views. Rather ironically, some of the criminal justice data presented by DuBois were consistent with that presented by Hoffman, Otken, and others who shared their views. For example, he noted an apparent rise in the rate of black crime after the abolition of slavery during the late 1700s in Pennsylvania and in the south after the Civil War.

DuBois's examination of public documents in Philadelphia revealed little consistent concern for black crime until after slavery was abolished by Pennsylvania in 1780. He interpreted such lack of concern to be some indication of a relatively low rate of black crime before 1780. After 1780, freed blacks came to Philadelphia in relatively large numbers from elsewhere in Pennsylvania and other states. This influx of migrants was accompanied by a rise in the city's crime rate. By 1809 black churches united in an effort to suppress criminal activity. The efforts met with little success, largely due to the effects of a series of race riots and the disenfranchisement of blacks by the Pennsylvania state legislature in 1837. The latter was initiated largely out of the increasing fear of blacks among whites after the Nat Turner rebellion. DuBois reports that these changes in black-white relations led to the increasingly disproportionate representation of blacks among persons sentenced to the state penitentiary between 1830 and 1850. The level of racial disproportionality in rates of imprisonment and arrest declined after 1850, but showed a return to earlier levels around 1895 (1899:237–48).

DuBois's study of black life in Philadelphia provided the first insight into the plight of what is now labeled the black urban underclass. Along with the emerging Chicago school of sociology, his work also was among the first to note the effects of (im)migration, both from Europe and from within the United States, on the rate of crime in northern cities. In his 1904 study DuBois and his associates continued this line of analysis by comparing arrest, conviction, and imprisonment rates for blacks and whites in a number of southern and nonsouthern states and cities for the period between 1858 and 1900.

Unlike some later analysts, DuBois and his associates saw little need to question the accuracy of data showing the overrepresentation of blacks among those arrested and sentenced for crime. They recognized the role that racial discrimination played in the administration of justice during this period, but their concern was with the etiology of criminal conduct rather than bias. After analyzing national imprisonment data, DuBois and associates say:

> It seems fair to conclude that Negroes in the United States, forming about one-eighth of the population were responsible in 1890 for nearly one-fifth of the crime. (1904:13)

Commenting on city crime rates, Monroe N. Work notes:

> It is recognized that the crime rate of Negroes is greater than that of whites. In 1900 the rate of Negro arrests and commitments was from one and a half to ten times greater than that of whites. . . . The peculiar conditions of the Negro, past and present, tend to keep his crime rate high. (1904:20)

DuBois and others saw their task to be that of providing *social* explanations for the comparatively high rate of black crime. For DuBois the overinvolvement of Philadelphia blacks in crime was a *natural* product not of their genetic makeup but of the degradation and social disruption caused by slavery:

> From his earliest advent the Negro, as was natural, has figured largely in the criminal annals of Philadelphia. . . . Crime is a phenomenon of organized social life, and is the open rebellion of an individual against his social environment. Naturally then, if men are suddenly transported from one environment to another, the result is lack of harmony with the new conditions; lack of harmony with the new physical surroundings leading to disease and death or modification of physique; lack of harmony with social surroundings leading to crime. (1899:235)

Noting the role played by the social upheaval that resulted from the ending of slavery and the rural to urban migration that ensued, DuBois observed:

Throughout the land there has been since the war a large increase in crime, especially in cities. This phenomenon would seem to have sufficient cause in the increased complexity of life, in industrial competition, and the rush of great numbers to the large cities. It would therefore be natural to suppose that the Negro would also show this increase in criminality and, as in the case of the lower classes, that he would show it in greater degree. . . . The Negro began to rush to the cities in large numbers after 1880, and consequently the phenomena attendant on that momentous change of life are tardier in his case. His rate of criminality has in the past two decades risen rapidly, and this is a parallel phenomenon to the rapid rise of the white criminal record two or three decades ago. (1899:240–41)

In his ensuing discussion of the causes of crime and poverty, DuBois noted further parallels in trends of criminality among whites and blacks:

A study of the statistics seems to show that the crime and pauperism of the Negroes exceeds that of whites; that in the main, nevertheless, it follows in its rise and fall the fluctuations shown in the records of whites, i.e., if crime increases among the whites it increases among Negroes, and vice versa, with this peculiarity, that among the Negroes the change is always exaggerated—the increase greater, the decrease more marked in nearly all cases. (1899:282)

In these observations are themes that have resounded in the literature on race and crime for nearly a century. Included among these are: (1) the synchronicity of changes in rates of crime among blacks and whites, (2) the effects of urban life on the genesis of criminal conduct among all racial or ethnic groups, (3) the contribution to black criminality of the *peculiar* condition of servitude that marked their entry into the United States, and (4) the relationship between economic deprivation and criminality. These were themes that would guide later work on black crime, as well as the work of those who explored the etiology of crime among America's white ethnic populations.

IN DEFENSE OF THE FOREIGN-BORN: SUTHERLAND AND SELLIN ON ETHNIC AND RACIAL DIFFERENCES IN CRIMINALITY

As previously noted, the social Darwinist critique that prompted the development of a liberal race relations tradition and criminology in the

United States was aimed at not only blacks but also various groups of white ethnics. While DuBois and his associates were preoccupied with explaining crime among blacks, other social scientists of the period analyzed crime patterns among those populations. Some of this research and commentary was concerned specifically with ethnic and nationality differences in the rate of involvement in crime. But most often researchers compared the criminality of the foreign-born (of all nationalities and ethnic heritages) to that of native whites. Two early contributors to this research tradition were the noted criminologists Edwin Sutherland and Thorsten Sellin.

In his pioneering 1924 textbook, *Criminology,* Sutherland included sections on immigration and race as part of his discussion of correlates and causes of criminal behavior. These sections were expanded somewhat in his 1934 volume, *Principles of Criminology.* Though somewhat brief, these early observations had a great impact on later analysts such as Sellin (1928, 1938) who further developed many of Sutherland's ideas. Both Sutherland and Sellin questioned data and public commentary of the period that purported to show higher rates of crime among foreign-born immigrants than among the native-born. They also investigated racial differences in the rate of involvement in crime, looking at the crime of not only blacks but also other American nonwhites.

To a greater extent than DuBois, Sutherland urged caution in concluding that the *actual* rate of crime among blacks was greater than that of whites. For example, after providing statistics showing that blacks during the 1920s and 1930s were arrested, convicted, and committed to prisons three times as frequently as native-born whites, Sutherland (1934:111) argues:

> These statistics probably reflect a bias against the Negro because of the prejudice against that race. . . . Even if the statistics are completely reliable, they involve a comparison of groups that differ economically, educationally, and socially, as well as racially.

Sellin shared Sutherland's cautionary views but his conclusions mirror those of DuBois. In his 1928 note on black crime, Sellin acknowledged the role that race prejudice plays in the production of black-white crime rate disparities, but concluded:

> Nothing in the above pages points to a conclusion that the Negro's *real* criminality is lower or as low as the white's. . . . It would be extraordinary, indeed if this group were to prove more law-abiding than the white, which enjoys more fully the advantages of a civilization the Negro has helped to create. The assumption that the Negro presents the

higher rate of *real* criminality is, therefore, no indictment of the Negro race. (p. 64, emphasis in the original)

But both Sutherland and Sellin were less willing to accept the then popular view that the crime of the foreign-born was excessive. Sutherland (1924:97) suggested that statistics purporting to show foreign-born versus native differences were "misleading unless the differences in ages, rural-urban distribution, and sex are taken into account and this cannot always be done satisfactorily." He noted that in 1910 only 5.7 percent of the foreign-born were under fifteen years of age as contrasted with 26.6 percent of native-born whites. He also suggested that given higher rates of crime in urban than in rural areas, "immigrants have higher rates because they live in cities rather than because they are immigrants" (1924:98). Indeed, Sutherland asserts that once these errors of specification are corrected, native-born whites are shown to have higher rates than foreign-born immigrants. Further, native-born rates were said to exceed those of the foreign-born for both minor and serious offenses.

In both 1924 and 1934, Sutherland notes the tendency of second generations of immigrant groups to have higher rates of crime than the first generations. In 1934, he also cites a study by Taft (1933) who reported that immigrants to America had higher rates of serious crime than their counterparts at home. He also noted that immigrants who arrived in the United States in childhood had higher rates of imprisonment than immigrants who arrived when adults (1934:113–14). Sellin made similar observations in his study of culture conflict and crime (1938:74–107).

But while confidently dismissing arguments that native-born whites were less criminal than recent immigrants, Sutherland and Sellin found the question of nationality and ethnic differences among whites more difficult to address. Like black-white comparisons, comparisons among national and ethnic/cultural groups raised the specter of the kind of biological determinism these and other liberal analysts of the period were seeking to counter. Yet, practical, ideological, and scientific considerations led both Sutherland and Sellin to pay some attention to evidence of crime rate differences across national and ethnic groupings.

Among practical considerations was the public debate of the period that resulted from the reporting of the country of origin and the foreign-born status of criminals in various governmental documents—for example, the 1911 report of the United States Immigration Commission and the 1931 report on crime of the foreign-born (Wickersham Report). The data from these reports were widely used by political conservatives of the period to argue for the restriction of the immigration of southern and eastern Europeans. Like DuBois's study of black crime in Philadelphia, Sutherland's 1924 analysis of nationality differences in criminal involvement presented data that many conservatives may have found to be supportive of their immigration restriction goals. For example, Sutherland used findings from Laughlin (1922:740,790–92) to conclude:

> There is abundant evidence that certain nationalities have a large excess of particular offenses. Laughlin reports that if 100 is taken as the rate of commitment to state and federal penal institutions for all groups, the persons born in the Balkan states would have a rate of 294, those from southern and eastern Europe 141, those from northwestern Europe 38. (1924:99)

In his 1934 discussion of differences among national groupings, Sutherland writes:

> The several immigrant groups differ widely among themselves in their general rate of arrest and imprisonment. The rate of imprisonment to all types of prisons in 1910 and 1923 was five times as high for persons of Irish nativity as for persons of German nativity. National groups differ widely also in the comparative frequencies of different crimes. Some immigrant groups have high rates for drunkenness and other misdemeanors, and low rates for felonies. Persons of Irish nativity were committed to state prisons for major offenses in 1923 about one-fifth as frequently as persons of Italian nativity, while they were committed to jails and workhouses more than twice as frequently. (p. 114)

He provides similar discussion of the comparative rate of arrest and imprisonment for other national groupings, including Finns, Greeks, and Swedes.

Culture Conflict and Conflict of Norms

How does one explain apparent differences in the rate of involvement in crime across national groupings such as those identified by Sutherland, Sellin, and others? Given the obvious potential for a clash between the cultural heritages of immigrants with the dominant American culture, Sutherland (1934) proposed a notion of *culture conflict* as a potential explanation for such differences. In response to the seeming nationality differences in the rate of involvement across specific types of crimes, Sutherland (1934: 114–15) says: "Thus the traditions of the home country are transplanted to America and determine the relative positions of the immigrant groups with reference to the types of crime."

Sellin (1938) further explored this theme through his conceptualization of a conflict of norms. Sellin's need to devise such a theory at first appears inconsistent with his view of the criminality of the foreign-born—namely, his assertion that they come into contact with the law less frequently than the native-born (1938:74). Yet, his theory seems ideally suited for explaining the widely reported disproportionate crime among recently arrived immigrant populations as compared to earlier settled groups. A careful reading of his work, however, indicates that his concern is less with the foreign-born than with later generations of immigrants. In addition, he argues that his theory was intended to explain ethnic differences *among* the foreign-born.

Because of his emphasis on culture as a criminogenic factor, Sellin recognized the obvious irrelevance of many of the indices of nationality used in governmental reports and studies of the period. He notes, for example, that immigrants labeled as Russian included such diverse groups as Jews, Czechs, Slovaks, Germans, and others. He then adds:

In order words the population statistics on the foreign-born hide completely the existence of different cultural groups and cut across culture areas, which are more important to the sociologist than are political divisions. (1938:72)

Despite this and other reservations regarding the utility, accuracy, and validity of comparisons across national groupings, Sellin judges some findings from the 1931 Wickersham Commission Report to be worth sociological scrutiny. He echoes Sutherland's earlier view by noting:

The data presented here and the findings of a number of other studies show that while most foreign-born groups do not come into contact with the law as frequently as the native-born, some have much higher rates than the latter. Furthermore, even when the rates may be low for most offenses attributable to a group, they may be extremely high for a few crimes. . . . We might add that those European nativity groups which show extraordinary high rates—the Greek, the Lithuanian, the Polish, the Austrian, and the Italian—should be studied most intensely and the same holds true for the Mexican and the Oriental groups. The latter seem curiously enough to have received the attention of the scholar more than the others. (1938:78)

Sellin proceeds to construct a theory designed to show how criminal conduct might emerge as a result of the clash of norms drawn from unrelated or distinctly different cultures such as Anglo-Saxon versus Slavic traditions (*primary* culture conflicts). He also links differential rates of crime to *sec-*

ondary cultural conflicts, those "conflicts that grow out of the process of social differentiation which characterizes the evolution of our own culture" (pp. 104–5). He proposed that these two types of conflict might be useful to explain the criminal conduct of newly arrived immigrants (of all ethnic/racial backgrounds) and their offspring, as well as indigenous cultural groups such as African Americans. Although reference is seldom made nowadays to his theory, Sellin's 1938 essay, along with the work of Clifford Shaw and Henry McKay, provided the underpinnings for modern notions of subculture as it has been used in the study of ethnicity, race and crime.

THE TRIUMPH OF SOCIAL DISORGANIZATION THEORY: SHAW AND MCKAY'S URBAN STUDIES

Sellin (1938) believed that the delinquency area studies of Clifford Shaw (1929) provided evidence of the effects on criminal behavior of those conflicts of norms he labeled as *secondary*. Sellin suggested that the socioeconomic and environmental conditions described by Shaw

> give rise to social attitudes which conflict with the norms of the law. While Shaw stresses the fact that these areas are, in the cities he has studied, largely inhabited by European immigrants, this fact would appear to be of minor importance, since he has shown that no matter from what country these immigrants came, the delinquency rates of their children ultimately approach each other after exposure to the conditions mentioned. It is likely that in large European cities with homogeneous populations, the same conditions breed high delinquency. (pp. 62–63)

Shaw's 1929 study and his later work with Henry McKay (1942) both made major contributions to the study of ethnicity, race, and crime as part of the Chicago school of American sociology. Their studies introduced the notion of *social disorganization* as an explanation for varying rates of crime and other forms of sociopathology in American cities.

In many ways the work of Shaw and his associates represents a significant innovation in the study of race and ethnic differences in the rate of involvement in crime. Earlier analysts of American crime patterns, including those reviewed in this chapter, tended to insist on the uniqueness of blacks in comparison to white immigrants or the white native-born. Therefore, they offered different explanations for the high level of crime reported among blacks as compared to groupings of whites.[3] Although DuBois noted the parallelism between black and white rates of crime, he and his associates also noted the *peculiar* condition of blacks in American society. Sutherland reminded us that black and white comparisons involved groups that differed along socioeconomic dimensions, "as well as racially." Sellin stressed the caste-like status of the black population. To the contrary, Shaw and his associates noted the similarities among not only *disorganized* white ethnic groups, but also between those groups and blacks. The following statement from Shaw's 1929 study of Chicago illustrates this view:

> This study has indicated that school truancy, juvenile delinquency, and adult crime rather than being distributed uniformly throughout the city of Chicago are largely concentrated in certain areas. . . . Moreover, many of the people who come into the deteriorating section are European immigrants or southern Negroes. All of them come from cultural and social backgrounds which differ widely from the situations in the city. In the conflict of the old with the new the former cultural and social controls in these groups tend to break down. This, together with the fact that there are few constructive community forces at work to re-establish a conventional order, makes for continued social disorganization. (pp. 204,205)

Even more arguments for the causal parallelism of black and white ethnic crime and delinquency distribution are provided by Shaw and McKay (1942). After observing that overall rates of delinquency were highest for those areas with high concentrations of blacks and foreign-born, they emphasize caution in assuming a causal link between these attributes and delinquent behavior:

> First, comparisons indicate that the white as well as the Negro, the native as well as the foreign-born, and the older immigrant nationalities as well as the recent arrivals range in their rates of delinquency from the very highest to the lowest. No racial, national, or nativity group exhibits a uniform, characteristic rate of delinquents in all parts of Chicago. . . . Within the same type of social area, the foreign-born and the natives, recent immigrant nationalities, and older immigrants produce very similar rates of delinquents. (pp. 152–54)

Shaw and McKay believed, therefore, that the correlation they found between rates of delinquency and concentrations of foreign-born or black heads of families was due to attributes of communities, not some unmeasured traits of individuals that arise from their race or nativity. Their observations and conclusions have had a profound effect on the study of ethnicity, race and crime. Many contemporary analysis acknowledge their indebtedness to these two investigators. However, during the years following the publication of their first study, the Nazi terror in Europe once again highlighted the salience of ethnic and racial distinctions, as opposed to class status, in the study of society.

BONGER: RACE AND CRIME IN EUROPE AND AMERICA

Willem Bonger's 1943 study, *Race and Crime,* was written largely in response to specific arguments made by advocates of biological determinism. In this instance the setting is not early twentieth-century America, but Europe during the rise of fascism. The targets of his critique are advocates of Nordic supremacy. Bonger was a leading sociological criminologist in the Netherlands and a major actor in the movement to internationalize the study of criminology. In comparison to the works of DuBois, Sutherland, Sellin, Shaw, and McKay, Bonger's analysis of the relationship among ethnicity, race, and crime shows a deeper grounding in the then emerging anthropological critique of the concept of race that is best symbolized by Ruth Benedict's *Race: Science and Politics* (1940).

Given this orientation, Bonger begins by questioning the social significance of commonly accepted notions of race and ethnicity, and their usefulness as a means of classifying human populations. On considering extant views of the relationship between race and criminal behavior, Bonger noted that few of the major European schools of criminological thought during his era or earlier had specifically examined the relationship between race and crime. And he challenged the scientific basis for the few assertions about the relationship made by advocates of these schools.

Bonger attributes both the slight theoretical consideration given and the inaccuracy of earlier attempts to examine the nature of the connection between race and crime to

> the fact that too little account is taken of what "crime" really is. The impression is given that crime is a quality like the possession of blue eyes, a dark skin, musicality, and so forth. If this were so, then criminality would appear in all the individuals of a certain race, and in none of another race. To express the problem in this way, however, is quite wrong. Criminality is not a characteristic. It is comparable neither to a physical quality such as the possession of blue eyes, nor to a spiritual one such as musicality. No one comes into the world with "criminality," in the way in which one is born with a certain color of eyes, and so forth. Crime is something completely different. (p. 27)

Bonger goes on to stress the subjectivity of the criminal label and the role of the state in defining and punishing crime, themes systematically pursued only by Sellin among the analysts reviewed to this point. While recognizing the law as an indicator of the interests of the community and criminality as a form of antisocial conduct, Bonger notes that "it is certainly great nonsense to speak of criminal and non-criminal races" (p. 28). While discounting notions of criminal versus noncriminal races, Bonger was left with the task of explaining the possibility and reality of varying levels of reported crime across racial groupings. In doing so, he raises the possibility that some racial groups may be more predisposed to crime than others:

> Do the races differ quantitatively in their elementary inclinations? Though these inclinations in themselves have nothing to do with crime, still, *under certain circumstances* they can acquire an antisocial character. Thus the persons who have these inclinations in stronger degree than others are more predisposed to crime. And do the races differ in temperament, for instance in emotionalism? Not that temperament, in itself, has anything to do with crime, but again *under certain circumstances* it can increase the intensity of desire and therefore increase the urgency for its expression. And do the races also differ in the power and readiness of their restraints (moral restraints and those of self-interest)? By the nature of things, the answer can be of great, even decisive importance in our case. Indeed, the differences in predisposition to crime among the individuals of one race lie chiefly in this field. (pp. 28–29)

Bonger never provides a definitive answer to this question. Consequently much of his ensuing analysis of race differences in crime reflects the kind of ambivalence evident in the passage above. In an attempt to explore the relevance of racial predispositions, he first examines crime for the major racial groupings. Data for the Chinese and Japanese, collected primarily in the United States, were said to reveal only a slight tendency toward crime among them. Using data from studies of Filipinos, Indonesians, Sudanese, Malaysians, and Mediterraneans he concludes that the kind of race differences alluded to in the quote above do not appear to account for the criminality of "the dark-skinned races" (pp. 29–38).

Despite this conclusion, Bonger displays a seeming fascination with the idea of a possible link between crime and certain race/ethnic characteristics. Of particular interest to Bonger is the question of whether racial traits explain the comparative criminality of nonwhites versus whites and disparities in crime rates among groups of Europeans. After examining data from an earlier study showing whites to have lower rates of imprisonment than blacks and Indians in South Africa, he reports:

> In considering these figures, one must take into account the fact that whites, for numerous reasons (better legal defense, etc.) are less fre-

quently sentenced than the others. The greater criminality of both last-mentioned groups, as well as the nature of their crimes, is connected with their greater impulsivity and limited mental development. The authors do not go further with the question as to how far these qualities are inherent, racial characteristics. (p. 38).

Citing the greater availability of reliable crime data and studies on crime among African Americans, Bonger suggests that we are well informed as to the level and patterns of their criminality. Hence, among his case studies of the connection between race and crime, black American "criminality forms the *pièce de résistance*" (p. 38).

Along with his case study of crime among blacks in the United States, Bonger examines the criminality of Jews, Mediterranean and Alpine groups, Nordics, Urgo-Finns, and residents of the eastern Baltic countries. Arguing that reliable data were available only to examine the criminality of American blacks and Jews, only a limited analysis is made of the criminality of the other groups. While acknowledging the part played by racial bigotry in elevating the level of reported crime for blacks, he concludes:

> Crimes committed by Negroes are more frequently prosecuted than those committed by whites. Negroes are less well able to defend themselves legally, they are less often in a position to secure a good lawyer, and they are more promptly sentenced to prison. . . . These figures leave no room for doubt: crime among the Negroes is significantly higher than among the whites. It is three to four times higher among the men, and four or five times higher among the women. To me, this appears to eliminate the idea that actual criminality among the Negroes is no greater than among whites—even if the above-mentioned causes make it appear greater than it is. (p. 43)

Since he relies heavily on the ideas of American social scientists, including Sellin, Sutherland, Monroe Work, and others, it is not surprising that his explanations for the high rate of crime among blacks are similar to theirs: socioeconomic disadvantage, political powerlessness, underemployment, undereducation, the legacy of slavery, and so forth. However, unlike many of the liberal American commentators, Bonger's list of potential explanations includes ideas seemingly more compatible with social Darwinist views than the "enlightened" perspective he purports to represent. Among these *explanations* are various race traits. Though he acknowledges a lack of evidence linking such traits to crime, he cites the work of observers who have described blacks in various ways, many of which are quite uncomplimentary and stereotypical (pp. 48–51).

The analysis of Jewish crime in Europe was patterned after that of blacks in the United States. Bonger reported that Jews had lower rates of reported crime than non-Jews in Germany, Austria, Hungary, Poland, and the Netherlands. The data were described as "favorable" for Jews in comparison to other groups. Only for commercial misdemeanors was there evidence of a comparatively high rate of Jewish offending. Bonger did note that since much of their involvement was with economic crimes, economic crises sometimes led to sharp increases in Jewish crime rates. He also noted that in areas where Jews lived in poverty, they showed a significant "poverty criminality" (pp. 51–59). While suggesting that Jewish crime patterns likely reflected less any racial trait or predisposition than their occupational choices and patterns of residence (for example, urban), as in his discussion of blacks Bonger provides a listing of racial/ethnic characteristics and traits of Jews cited by various analysts. Again, as in the discussion of black criminality, Bonger suggests that we have no reason to believe that these sometimes uncomplimentary traits, if inherent, are linked to criminal conduct.

WOLFGANG AND COHEN: CONFRONTING NEO-SOCIAL DARWINISM IN AN ERA OF URBAN UNREST AND CIVIL RIGHTS REFORM

In contrast to earlier statements on this subject, the observations of Marvin Wolfgang and Bernard Cohen were made during a period in which the criminality of white ethnic immigrants is no longer a topic of public or scholarly debate. They write when a series of political, legal, and social reforms are contributing to the hope that the *peculiar* social status of blacks within American society will finally be significantly altered. Juxtaposed with this newfound optimism were the urban riots and continuing evidence of racial disproportionality in rates of crime and punishment. Both sets of events served to heighten public and scholarly interest in the criminality of African Americans. In their introduction, Wolfgang and Cohen cited a recent NORC nationwide survey, which indicated that crime and race were two of the most widely discussed and important issues of the day (1970:1–2). The authors made it clear from the outset that their aim was to refute many of the common public misconceptions regarding the relationship between race and crime.

The authors began their critique by examining the meaning of race from genetic and social/legal points of view. Like many race relations researchers of the post–World War II era, they adhere to the anthropological statements of the biological equality of various races embodied in UNESCO documents of the 1950s and 1960s. Their discussion of the social relevance of race categories is a critique of the then current genetic views of black-white difference, most notably the widely publicized work of Arthur Jensen (1969) on race and intelligence. In discounting genetic interpretations of race difference, the authors say:

> Resort to racism through a false genetic explanation of differences in mental abilities, personality or conduct, is universally discredited by scholars in genetics who perceive racial differences principally in terms of the history of man's physical movements and cultural change.

The authors' argument throughout the remainder of their book is that genetic views of racial differences are worthless as an explanation for criminal conduct. Like previous analysts they note: (1) the extent to which the making of the criminal code includes certain group interests while excluding others; (2) the problem of unrecorded and undetected crime; and (3) the inaccuracy of recorded crime data. Having noted these biases, the authors provide Uniform Crime Report data for 1967 and other statistics that show a sizable racial gap in the rate of reported crime. Also noted are relatively high rates of crime among Mexican Americans and Puerto Ricans. As previous investigators had done, the authors urged caution in interpreting these data:

> It should be kept in mind, however, that none of these figures demonstrates that Negroes as a race are more prone to crime. They do demonstrate that the average black citizen is more likely than the average white citizen to be exposed to a plethora of conditions that result in being arrested, convicted and imprisoned. Most of these conditions are inherent in the social structure and are not subject to control by an individual. (p. 34)

Their questioning of the seeming link between race and crime also addressed other problems. They noted the role that racial discrimination and bias may play in the administration of justice and called for further research on this topic. They also observed that the lower clearance rates for certain crimes—for example, various property offenses—produce statistics that underestimate crime rates for both blacks and whites, with the underestimate being greater for whites than blacks. And in an interesting challenge to both the validity of crime statistics and to genetic views of race and crime, Wolfgang and Cohen note (citing Korn and McCorkle, 1959; and Herskovits, 1930) the mixed African and European ancestry of many persons labeled as blacks in the United States. They suggest that such mixed ancestry among blacks make it difficult to ascribe their criminality solely to their nonwhite genes. After noting that perhaps 40 percent of the black population, including black offenders, are either half or more than half white, they observed:

Any correction of the totals of Negro offenders toward greater conformity with the genetic distribution would have the effect of redistribut-
ing a very considerable number of criminals from the Negro to the
white side of the ledger. The percentage "transferred" by this procedure would be large enough to reduce the presently "unfavorable" picture of Negro crime drastically. (p. 37, from Korn and McCorckle,
1959:231)

The remainder of the book represents a conscious effort by the authors
to dispel other popular misconceptions about race and crime, many of which
were the subject of intensive public debate during this period. These included: (1) views of black crime and criminality that were said to overemphasize its interracial character and frequently lead to white fear of
victimization by blacks as a result of ordinary street crime or rioting. (2) De-
pictions of black criminality as more "dangerous" and more "excessive"
than that of whites, including white immigrants of the past. And (3) the belief
that black-white crime rate differences could no longer be attributed to bias,
since due to legal reforms, most of the gross injustices of the past had been
eliminated.

Particularly significant is the author's discussion of the similarities and
dissimilarities between blacks and white ethnic immigrants. Responding to
arguments of some American white ethnics during the period that blacks
should be able to rise out of poverty "by their own bootstraps," Wolfgang
and Cohen make several arguments. They cite a then recent report of the U.S.
Riot Commission that suggested there is a tendency among middle-class
whites to exaggerate how quickly they became a part of the middle class. The
report noted that only after three generations were some of these groups finally able to move into the American mainstream.

Wolfgang and Cohen also note that the economic and social conditions
faced by late 1960s urban black populations are much less favorable to their
upward mobility than those faced by white immigrants. Among the significant differences noted by the authors are: (1) the ability of whites to gain a
foothold in a nonmechanized economy that sorely needed unskilled labor and
the attempted mobility of blacks during an era of increased mechanization;
(2) blocked opportunities for blacks resulting from racial prejudice that is
more virulent than the discrimination and bias faced by white ethnics; (3) the
use of political machines, now replaced by new political structures, by white
ethnics to gain political and economic advantage; and (4) a legacy of slavery
and racial oppression that may have led to less motivation and ambition to
succeed among blacks than among more optimistic European immigrants
(pp. 62–63).

Two chapters of the book are devoted to analyses of bias in the administration of justice. To a large extent these chapters merely echo the observations and conclusions of several earlier federal governmental reports. But they do offer additional evidence in support of the authors' earlier claim that such bias may continue to play a significant sole in producing black-white crime rate disparities.

Like analysts who preceded them, the authors, after a thoughtful and careful analysis of statistical data, and an attempt to correct misconceptions, are left with the more difficult task of telling the reader what can reasonably be concluded about the relationship between race and crime. This task is tackled in the final two chapters of the book. Retracing the themes explored in the book's introduction, Wolfgang and Cohen depict their study as an effort to counter those "voices in the wilderness of ignorance or prejudice who contend that the non-white, by reason of his biology alone, is a predisposed criminal" (pp. 89–90). Again much of their ire is directed against the I.Q. studies of Jensen (1969). Like Bonger, Wolfgang and Cohen challenge conceptions of both race and criminality in their critique of Jensen's brand of neo-social Darwinism. They observe:

> Rates of criminality, as has been shown, are also strongly influenced by environmental differences. What we know about genetically determined traits suggests that they are specific; that is, we inherit hair and eyes of specific color and perhaps certain specific psychological potentialities. But criminal behavior is not specific, for there are almost as many kinds of crime as differences in behavior. According to Mendel's rule of inheritance of specific traits, if criminality, were genetically determined, we should inherit specific tendencies for embezzlement, burglary, forgery, etc. And if we inherited specific *criminal* forms of behavior, and some of us were genetically destined to be burglars or stock embezzlers, rapists or check forgers, we would also have to inherit specific *non-criminal* occupations, which means some of us would be as genetically destined to become police officers or truck drivers or school teachers, as to have red hair. (p. 92)

Wolfgang and Cohen are unconvinced as to the soundness of Bonger's (1943) speculation regarding the possible link between genetically determined behavior traits and criminality. They assert:

> Nor can it be argued that Negroes or whites or any group of people have personality and behavioral traits that genetically predetermine them toward *general* criminality. This position not only ignores the fact that the definition of crime is not stable in time or place, it also fails to

recognize that most criminals obey most laws—indeed are extremely careful to do so in order to avoid drawing police attention. A valid genetic theory would have to explain why criminals observe most laws and only break some laws some times. (p. 92)

Reminiscent of the arguments of Shaw and McKay (1942), Wolfgang and Cohen insist that "instead of asking why a Negro becomes delinquent or criminal, we should ask why *anyone* does" (p. 94). Among the theories they consider to be most useful for explaining the criminality of all groups are those that emphasize the importance of subculture, relative deprivation, and differential opportunity. However, by emphasizing the role that racial prejudice plays in restricting the life chances of blacks, Wolfgang and Cohen also recognize some aspects of the *peculiarity* of the plight of blacks as compared to similarly deprived whites. In concluding, they propose that a statement by Hill (1959) best expresses their view of the causes of observed levels of black delinquency. Hill is said to have observed:

Negroes who live in blighted areas suffer deeply from discrimination, rejection and the lack of integration rather than by processes of social disorganization. An increase in juvenile delinquency is likely to occur most frequently when and where aspirations of youth persist under conditions of limited and prescribed opportunities. Under such conditions, access to success goals by legitimate means is seldom available to Negro youth in cities. They do not have opportunities for internalization of acceptable and respectable norms of conduct. (p. 97, from Hill, 1959:84)

ETHNICITY, RACE, AND CRIME: THE STRENGTHS AND WEAKNESSES OF THE LIBERAL CRIMINOLOGICAL TRADITION

In this concluding section of the chapter, I assess the strengths and weaknesses of the studies included in my review. As my discussion of these works has suggested, each study was a product of its historical period and each author was inevitably affected by the social *stresses* and *strains* that marked the decades in which they wrote. The immediate concerns of DuBois and his associates were quite different from those reflected in the work of Wolfgang and Cohen. Those immediate concerns greatly affected the content and tone of their investigations. Such differences aside, however, these eight have produced a remarkably uniform body of research on ethnicity, race, and crime. They share a common objective—an attempt to account for ethnic and racial disparities in the rate of reported crime. Together they make a valuable contribution to our knowledge of this important area of social research.

Berger (1963) described sociology as a form of consciousness that differs from other ways of viewing human beings and the social world. The consistency of that sociological or social scientific imagination is quite evident in all the studies reviewed above. Further, to the extent that this consistency stems from their grounding in a *liberal* race relations research tradition and positivist social science and politics (Fay, 1975), their work also reflects the biases and weaknesses inherent in those worldviews.

It is my contention that a careful reading of these studies reveals some common threads that derive largely from their authors' grounding in a liberal research tradition. At least four major sets of shared attributes, central tendencies, or themes can be identified:

1. In general, these commentators tend to adhere to positivist notions of scientific method and functionalist views of the etiology of crime. These minimize a consideration of the extent to which the criminal justice system operates as a mechanism of individual and group social control and subordination.
2. As advocates of social change in eras marked by repeated episodes of ethnic and racial conflict, liberal criminologists were sensitive to the social and political divisiveness inherent in discussions of ethnic and racial difference in criminal conduct. While this sensitivity is evident in their discussions of nonwhite-white difference, it is perhaps most apparent for the examination of differences among white ethnics.
3. While not always completely developed in their own studies, the ideas of these authors regarding the etiology of crime and ethnic and racial differences have significantly affected contemporary thinking on these issues. They and their followers have largely succeeded in replacing biological determinism with conceptualizations based on the effects of social or environmental forces.
4. Criminologists of all orientations have been far from successful in devising a holistic theory to explain ethnic and racial differences in the exposure to the criminal justice system. The persistently high rates of officially reported crime for black Americans has posed something of a dilemma for both liberal social scientists and those in the conflict tradition. Evident in some of the earlier attempts to explain racial difference has been a tendency toward a *moralistic* view of the criminal conduct of racial minorities and members of lower socioeconomic groups. Though less moralistic in their tone, more recent analysts have often tended to overemphasize the *sociopathology* and *normlessness* found among blacks. *In some instances, these social determinist views may contribute as much to the promulgation of racist and ethnocentric biases as the biological determinist views they replace.*

In providing such a listing I do not mean to set up these analysts as "straw men" or to oversimplify their work. Each of the studies was selected because it provides a comprehensive discussion of the relationship among race and/or ethnicity and crime. In each instance the authors have provided complex, well-developed, and often contradictory lines of analysis and argument. Like many such evaluations in social science, I base the listing on what I consider to be evidence of *central tendencies,* emphasis, or patterns of omission in the works, considered both individually and as a whole. My observations are not new, of course. Since their initial advocacy, liberal criminological perspectives have been criticized by adherents to both more radical and more conservative views. I begin my own critique with one of the now standard comparisons—the distinction between liberal criminology and the conflict perspective.

LIBERAL CRIMINOLOGY AND THE STUDY OF SOCIAL CONTROL

The discussion in these studies of the effects of social stratification and inequality on crime and punishment provides an illustration of both their uniformity and their narrowness when viewed from the perspective of the late twentieth century. Given their grounding in the reformist ideology that undergirds the liberal race relations/criminology tradition, each work is explicit in its recognition of the fact that social inequality, race and class oppression, and discrimination within the criminal justice system greatly affect racial and ethnic differences in the rate of crime and punishment. As shown above, the authors all also stress the role that economic deprivation appears to play in the etiology of criminal behavior and ethnic and racial differences. On the other hand, the effects of inequality on punishment, as opposed to the etiology of criminal conduct, appear to be a secondary concern for most of the authors reviewed. While each study includes an almost *mandatory* discussion of the effects of bias on ethnic/racial differences in punishment and social control these observations generally fail to provide the kinds of insights now commonly associated with advocates of the conflict perspective in criminology—for example, Turk (1969), Quinney (1970), Chambliss and Seidman (1971).

Instead, as a group the authors' works tend to reflect theoretical views now commonly associated with social evolutionist or functionalist views of society and positivistic approaches to its study. One manifestation of this orientation is their focus on crime as an index of *misconduct* rather than a measure of social control. In comparison to the work of conflict theorists, that of liberal criminologists reflects a perennial quest for a measure of *actual* or *real* criminality. Official data are routinely challenged to the extent that they do not encompass *le chiffre noir* of undetected and unreported offending. For liberal criminologists this lack of a precise measure of crime raises obvious *scientific* concerns; it also affects their reformist ideals. Liberal criminologists tend to share the hope that once *real* crime has been isolated and measured, its *causes* can be identified and solutions can be devised. In such a research tradition, arrest rates, rates of conviction or imprisonment, and sentencing measures are important only to the extent to which they can be used to estimate the "true" incidence of criminal conduct.

Most of the research reviewed above is an exercise in this perennial quest for a measure of *real* crime. Criminal justice system data are rejected as a measure of ethnic and racial differences in the rate of crime because they reflect the bias inherent in an economically, ethnically, and racially stratified society. And, of course, alternative data are unavailable or themselves raise questions of accuracy. As many of the quotes from the studies reviewed above indicate, the quest for a measure of *real* crime often leaves researchers in the position of never being able to reach definitive conclusions regarding the relationship among ethnicity, race, and crime. Consider, for example, the following quotes from several of the studies reviewed above:

> The value of such figures is lessened by the varying efficiency and diligence of the police, by discrimination in the administration of law, and by unwarranted arrests. (DuBois, 1899:242, discussing black versus white arrests in Philadelphia, 1864–1896)

> The relation of immigration to crime in the United States is a problem of first-rate importance from the point of view of a theory of criminality and of legislative and administrative policies. Many research studies have been conducted on this problem. These studies have yielded certain statistical conclusions and other less definite conclusions. The statistical conclusions are supported by a large mass of data, but the data are criminal statistics which are relatively unreliable as indexes of crime. (Sutherland, 1934:112–13)

> We do not know with certainty the actual amount of crime among whites, Negroes, Puerto Ricans or any other group. We do know that persons of all groups commit many offenses that are unrecorded. . . . Only from arrests do we know the race of offenders, yet arrests in any year represent only about 30 per cent of the index crime recorded. (Wolfgang and Cohen: 100)

Though Sellin, Shaw and Mckay, and Bonger were all willing to acknowledge a seemingly high rate of crime among blacks and perhaps some white ethnics, all voiced similar reservations. It is not that these observations regarding the accuracy and validity of data are untrue or do not represent valid concerns. Rather, I use them to illustrate the centrality of the concern of these researchers for accurately measuring criminal conduct as opposed to explaining varying levels of criminal punishment.

Conflict theorist and others who emphasize the importance of *social control* show little interest in the intricacies of counting *real* crime. Indeed, conduct is important only to the extent that it is sanctioned. What liberal criminologists consider to be only imprecise counts of *real* misconduct (arrest, convictions, imprisonment, or executions), conflict theorists consider to be the only meaningful phenomena for measurement and study. And while the former tend to view all these as potential indices of wrongdoing, the latter see them only as evidence of social control. To a much greater extent than the authors of the studies reviewed, conflict analysts have chosen to study how the criminal justice system is used by dominant ethnic and racial groups to maintain their status. The level of the contact that subordinate white ethnics or blacks have had with the American criminal justice system is less a product of their conduct than their social standing.

As I have previously noted, my criticism should not be taken to imply that these types of perspectives are completely absent from the studies reviewed in this chapter. DuBois (1899) described black crime as a *rebellion* against racism and inequality. Significantly, both Sutherland (1949) and Sellin (1976), in their later studies of white-collar crime and the slavery-penology link, developed theories of crime and punishment that reflect some of the basic tenets of conflict theory. But these insights are only marginally evident in their earlier studies of ethnicity, race, and crime. That is, they are not the primary focus of these investigations.[4]

BALANCING SCIENCE AND POLITICS: THE EFFECTS OF INTERGROUP CONFLICT ON THE STUDY OF ETHNICITY, RACE, AND CRIME

All the authors discussed above noted the scarcity at the time of their writing of studies that had examined the relationship among ethnicity, race, and crime. As late as 1970, Wolfgang and Cohen observed: "There are enormous problems in understanding the meaning of these terms, race and crime, let alone their interaction. Many scholars have devoted their lives to research on each; fewer have examined the two together" (p. 2). Much the same can be said of the study of ethnicity and crime. Despite substantial public debate on the question of ethnic and nationality differences in the rate of crime during the last century and more, American scholars have provided surprisingly few studies of the subject. The researchers included in this review are among only a handful of social scientists who have provided systematic study and discussion of such differences.

Following DeGre's observation that science reflects the tenor of its time and place, I propose that study of ethnicity, race and crime during the last century reflects a balancing of the scientist's need to know with the politics of race and ethnicity in the United States. The work of the authors in this chapter and that of other analysts has been affected as greatly by social and political realities as by the canons of scientific inquiry. These political and social forces have led to the relative absence of studies of race, ethnicity and crime, as noted by Wolfgang and Cohen. They have also greatly affected the nature of the findings, interpretations and conclusions reached by those who have chosen to investigate the subject.

CAUTION AND RETICENCE

Social scientists, like all scientists, are encouraged to be cautious in their interpretations of data and in the conclusions they reach. The effects of positivistic ideals on the social research of the period represented by these studies further contributed to the kind of caution seen in the works reviewed. As noted, all the observers questioned the validity of official statistics, whether imprisonment statistics can be used to estimate the rate of crime, the importance of acceptable definitions of race, nationality, or ethnicity, and the like. Such questioning is the hallmark of the scientific method they were seeking to develop.

On the other hand, it appears that the authors' discussions of the crime rates of blacks versus whites, foreign-born versus natives, and nationality versus nationality, illustrate both a respect for the rules of science *and* the *politics* of intergroup relations in the United States. Numerous examples of that dual tension can be seen in the above-cited quotes from their works. Their discussions of both ethnic and racial difference in rates of criminal conduct are interspersed with caveats, exceptions, and warnings. The studies of DuBois (1899, 1904) and Sellin (1928) reveal somewhat less of this tendency, but their works too show aspects of this pattern. *One result of such reticence is a tendency of the researchers to downplay the finding that some ethnic and racial groups do have comparatively higher rates of officially reported crime. Obversely, in some instances researchers appear to underemphasize the fact that officially reported rates for other groups are comparatively low.*

Those researchers reviewed in this chapter were acutely aware of the extent to which their work may itself have contributed to the stereotypes, misconceptions, and biases they initially sought to counter. When combined with the caution inherent in positivistic scientific analysis, the conscious effort of these analysts to avoid an exacerbation of intergroup tensions sometimes led to a reluctance to draw conclusions from the data they analyzed. This reluctance was heightened by the presumption of liberal criminologists that their main concern should be the etiology of criminal behavior rather than varying levels of social control.

During the late twentieth century, caution and reticence of the kind described above has been generally associated with the study of crime among African Americans or Hispanics. The political and social volatility of discourse on the relationship between crime and race has been noted by many observers, including authors of chapters in this volume. On the other hand, my reading of the works reviewed in this chapter and other studies written during the period under review suggests that researchers appear somewhat more willing to acknowledge racial than ethnic and nationality differences in the rate of presumed involvement in crime. In particular, researchers were more nearly unanimous in their belief that blacks and some nonwhites have had higher rates of involvement in crime than they were in their belief that some white ethnics have had higher rates of involvement than others. This does not apply equally to all of the works reviewed, but a tendency in this direction does seem to be evident.

To what do we attribute this tendency? To the extent that researchers could rely upon earlier, quantitative studies of crime, such investigations may themselves have provided more evidence of racial than of ethnic differences. The scarcity of studies of ethnic crime patterns has been linked to the lack of official census, crime and punishment data for ethnic groupings as compared to data that allow black-white comparisons (see Hawkins, 1993). On the other hand, Sellin (1938) was among those who examined such ethnic differences and who argued that the relative inattention he noted to the study of crime among them could not be attributed solely to these data/methods concerns.

Though Sellin forcefully argued against the tendency of some earlier analysts to confuse nationality, country of origin, and ethnicity in their discussions of crime and punishment, upon reviewing data from the 1931 Wickersham Commission Report he did note high rates of crime among persons of Greek, Lithuanian, Polish, Austrian, and Italian ancestry. He advocated greater study by scholars of the reasons for these differences and seemed to suggest the influence of racism on scholarly research when he noted that the crime of Orientals in the United States had been studied more extensively than the crime of these white national groupings. Other comments also imply that the lack of official data alone does not explain the inattentiveness to differences in reported rates of crime among whites.[5]

Many of the studies of Oriental crime reviewed by Sellin did not involve the use of national or state crime data. Instead they were case studies of local areas, the most common type of research method utilized by sociologists during this period and earlier. Many of the studies of black crime conducted during the period involved the study of cities or neighborhoods (see DuBois [1904]). Sellin suggested that given the concentration of white ethnics in enclaves located throughout urban America during the period, local studies of their crime patterns might answer many of the questions posed by researchers and politicians. To what other factors can we attribute a seeming lack of interest in the study of crime among white ethnics?

The paucity of studies on the crime of white national and ethnic groupings and a tendency to *downplay* ethnic differences in social research may stem from other sociopolitical realities of the late nineteenth and early twentieth centuries in the United States. The first is the sensitivity of researchers to the continuing efforts of eugenicists and others to restrict the immigration of southern and eastern Europeans. Many of the governmental reports on the crime of the foreign-born during the period arose from the efforts of anti-immigration groups. As previously noted, much of the social research of the period was designed to counter these anti-immigration arguments.

Second, both social science and larger public opinion of the era were undoubtedly affected by the growing political influence of those groups that were targeted by anti-immigrationists. Through their vote and other political activity, these groups were beginning to influence and often dominate the political machines that controlled urban politics and the administration of criminal justice. On the other hand, for much of the period covered by these studies (1899–1970) blacks and other nonwhites exercised little political clout. In contrast to earlier decades (1830s–1860s) when the Irish were a relatively powerless minority and were the target of frequent ethnic violence, by the turn of the century they and other more recent arrivals were a political force of some significance. The relative lack of overrepresentation of the Irish among those immigrants listed in the 1911 and 1931 federal governmental reports was no doubt a reflection of both their growing economic success and their subsequent entry into many of the important decision-making positions within the criminal justice system—for example, police, prosecutors, and judges. By the 1920s Italians, Greeks, and other relative newcomers were among those most likely to be labeled criminal by the government and public opinion (Claghorn, 1923:102–20).

Many of the political tactics used by these less advantaged white ethnics vis-à-vis the criminal justice system during the early 1900s were similar to those of blacks in the 1960s. For example, Claghorn (1923:197–99) noted that Italians in Boston during 1919 accused the Irish and Jews of dominating the courts. The editorials in the city's Italian newspaper during that year encouraged the appointment of more Italian-American judges. It is my contention that by 1931 when the Wickersham Commission report appeared, researchers were responsive to these social changes and were consequently more cautious about studying or commenting on the high rates of crime among Italians, Greeks, and other groups. This greater sensitivity during the period to divisive ethnic comparisons based on crime rates is similar to the scholarly reaction to the study of black-white differences that emerged after the legal and political success of blacks during the 1970s. In each instance despite the seeming persistence of group differences in official measures of crime, these differences were less likely than they were in earlier periods to become a scholarly *pièce-de-résistance* (Bonger, 1943).

CRIME, MORALITY, AND SOCIOPATHOLOGY: VIEWS OF THE BLACK CRIMINAL

Given the willingness of researchers to conclude that the evidence warrants a finding that the *real* criminality of blacks in the United States is higher than that of whites, all the analysts reviewed have been confronted with the task of explaining the black crime rate. Each of the authors whom I have discussed paid considerable attention to the causes of black criminality. I suggest that attempts by these writers to explain black criminality also reveals some of the essential weaknesses of liberal criminology and of the studies reviewed. One of these shortcomings has to do with the tendency of many writers to view all criminal conduct as evidence of individual or group *pathology*. It has been observed that DuBois was quite adamant in his belief that black-white crime rate differences could not be attributed solely to bias in the administration of justice. While providing considerable insights, many of which remain relevant even today, DuBois's explanations and his descriptions of black criminality often lapse into a *moralistic* critique of the lifestyles of lower-class blacks. In describing poor blacks in Philadelphia, DuBois speaks of their "ignorance, lack of discipline and moral weakness" and their need for "moral encouragements" (1899:284). Frank Sanborn, a DuBois associate, spoke of crime as evidence of "human depravity" and "vice" (1904:1–2). Proctor and Work linked high rates of black crime in Atlanta and Savannah, Georgia, to "demoralizing agencies" such as "low dance houses" (1904:49–51). Drunkenness and gambling were said to contribute to more serious vice and crime.[6]

Though Bonger skillfully denies any linkage between the racial and ethnic characteristics he describes and criminality, his listing of black American racial traits contains many unflattering stereotypes and descriptions of the black lifestyle (1943:48–51). Labels of sociopathology, *moral failing,* and racial deficiency are a well-documented part of the legacy of public opinion toward blacks and the poor in the United States. Unfortunately, all too often they are also part of the liberal social scientific view of the criminality of poor blacks and other racial and ethnic minorities. DuBois depiction of black lower-class life was similar to that used by other analysts of the period and earlier to describe the Irish, the Italians, and other immigrants.

Sellin, Sutherland, and Shaw and McKay appeared especially sensitive to the images of deficiency and moral failing that often accompanied discussions of the crimes of blacks and white ethnics. Given their defense of the foreign-born, it was precisely such images of white ethnic groups that they were seeking to counter. Thus, these researchers were careful to avoid the most blatantly stereotypical images of immigrants or blacks and their lifestyles that were so popular during the time that they wrote. Sellin, quoted above, noted that a high rate of crime among blacks was no indictment of the black race. On the other hand, while they successfully avoided stereotype and obvious moral blame, their avoidance of a fully developed conflict perspective has led to subsequent interpretations of their work that are sometimes consistent with the images of black crime more graphically presented by DuBois and his associates.

For example, given the failure of blacks to achieve the same measure of improved social status as white ethnics and to reduce their contact with agents of the criminal law, the more moralistic DuBoisian and pre-DuBoisian images of black lower-class life have remained a part of the liberal criminological research tradition. So perhaps has the race traits imagery of blacks alluded to by Bonger. The persistence of these images has become more evident in the late twentieth century as researchers seek to explain high rates of black crime in a post–civil rights era (see Hawkins, 1993).

While the grossest of these images have been removed from *polite* conversation, liberal criminology may have contributed to social determinist views of the criminality of blacks that incorporate images of black life not unlike those liberal social science has sought to avoid. Such images, or the potential for them, can sometimes be found in ecological and sociological studies of slums, ghettoes, gangs, the disadvantaged, inner cities, and the urban underclass. These images may be indicative of Pettigrew's (1980) charge that liberal race relations research has stressed pathological features of black life. Such images appear to be embedded in most *theories* designed to explain the etiology of crime, since many of these were devised largely in response to the disproportionate crime rates found among both racial and ethnic minorities. These include criminological theories that have been devised during the last half-century and posit notions of subculture, differential association, social disorganization, social learning, and social-control.

While a critical examination of those theories is beyond the scope of this paper, several observations regarding them can be made in light of my review of the studies above. Like the labeling of individuals (Becker,

1965), some of these social theories tend to merely label groups rather than explain their social behavior and often serve only to blame the victims of societal injustice (Ryan, 1971). While the authors reviewed in this chapter were careful to avoid victim blame in its most conspicuous form, their lack of a well-articulated conflict perspective often leads to the kind of scientific ambivalence that allows readers to drift toward group inadequacies as a potential *cause* of ethnic and racial differences in the level of contact with the criminal justice system.

This (mis)reading of liberal criminological research has been made more likely as a result of recent developments within American society and the study of crime. More than during the past, late twentieth-century researchers in the liberal criminology tradition have become increasingly convinced that criminal justice system bias does not account for continuing high rates of crime among blacks. Hindelang's (1978) comparison of victimization and official arrest data is frequently cited as proof that the *real* crime rate of blacks is disproportionate in comparison to that of whites. And, despite periodic instances of bias, such as the Rodney King incident in Los Angeles, many believe that changed times have resulted in less discrimination in the administration of justice in the U.S.A.

Further, because liberal criminology sets for itself the unreachable goal of measuring *real* crime and criminality, and eschews a fully developed conflict orientation, it leaves itself vulnerable to the arguments of supporters of biological determinism. Its proponents must inevitably rely on official crime data—data that increasingly are taken as evidence of *real* crime rate differences across social groups. In the absence of plausible explanations for group differences, the study of ethnicity, race, and crime in the late twentieth-century among liberal criminologists has become little more than a *cataloging* of group differences in the rate of officially recorded crime. Wilson and Herrnstein (1985) illustrate the extent to which liberal criminology is vulnerable to accusations of documenting but failing to adequately explain higher rates of *real* crime for some racial and ethnic groups than others.

CONCLUSION

I believe that the researchers whose work is reviewed in this chapter have made invaluable contributions to the study of ethnicity, race, and crime. Their studies, despite shortcomings that are much more evident in retrospect, constitute individual and collective acts of courage. Public discourse about both race and crime in the United States has always been an ideological and political mine field. But, as my review has illustrated, there is much to be learned, and there remains a potential for both social good and harm in examining this controversial and difficult subject.

Much work remains to be done to continue the work begun by these analysts. Future researchers must extend rather than completely abandon the themes found in the work of the researchers reviewed in this chapter. Events during the years since the last study reviewed here (1970), indicate the correctness of DuBois's observation that the major problem of the twentieth century is "the problem of the color line." Recent global events also illustrate the salience of ethnic differences. Social science has shown that it has much to contribute to the study and solution of the problems that stem from both ethnic and racial misunderstanding and intolerance.

I remain firmly convinced that biological/genetic research, despite its increasing sophistication and renewed popularity today, offers little in terms of understanding group differences in the rate of contact with the criminal law. Race, crime, and criminality are social constructs. Social researchers must not replace the quest for a measure of *real* crime with a renewed search for the *real* criminal. A more promising approach may lie in the construction and utilization of theoretical paradigms that combine ideas from both liberal criminology and various conflict perspectives. After all, the basic tenets of the conflict perspective represent a synthesis and elaboration of many ideas related to the administration of justice and intergroup relations first found in the work of each of the authors reviewed in this chapter.

NOTES

1. There are, of course, other notable studies or commentaries on the subject of ethnicity, race, and crime that appeared during this period. Among these were Taft (1936), Branham and Kutash (1949), Frazier (1957), Korn and McCorkle, and Pope (1979). The present studies were selected for review because of their comparatively comprehensive coverage of the major issues surrounding this topic and because their work has been widely cited by subsequent analysts. I exclude from my review the numerous empirical studies of ethnicity, nationality, race, and crime that were conducted during this period. Coramae Mann (1993) has also provided an excellent discussion of the themes explored in this chapter and in this volume. Unfortunately, it did not appear in print in time to be critically reviewed in the present essay.

2. With the publication of Gunnar Myrdal's classic, *An American Dilemma*, in 1944 race relations researchers began to focus on the study of the opinions and attitudes of whites. This was largely due to Myrdal's insistence that whites were largely responsible for the race *problem* in the United States.

3. It appears that for both Sutherland and Sellin, the kind of oppressor-oppressed, privileged-underprivileged, high caste-low caste dichotomies used to explain black-white differences were not applicable to either the foreign-born or various white nationalities. Thus, while the authors do note the subordinate social status of

these groups, they (unlike the Chicago school) do not stress the centrality of that status as a factor in the etiology of crime among them.

4. The lack of a fully developed conflict orientation obviously cannot be attributed solely to the effects of the *times* in which the studies were undertaken. Especially during the earlier years of the period covered by these studies, researchers were keenly aware of both legal and extralegal miscarriages of justice that give credence to the arguments of conflict theorists. In addition, many of indices of crime during these years provide much prima facie support for the arguments of the conflict perspective. Blacks sometimes comprised 80 to 90 percent of persons confined in southern prisons during many of the years covered by the research of DuBois.

5. The attention paid to the study of Chinese and Japanese criminality likely reflected efforts to restrict their immigration after 1882 and 1908. The attention is somewhat surprising given the relatively small size of these populations in the U.S.A. The criminality of the Chinese was of considerable concern. DuBois (1904:11) reported Chinese-Americans to have an imprisonment rate exceeding that of blacks in 1890. Of course, their rate, like that of the foreign-born, may have reflected the large number of males in the population.

6. The sometimes harsh evaluations by DuBois and associates of the morals and lifestyles of the black poor reflected the rhetoric of the times as it applied to all the poor. But it also has elements of the *race improvement* themes that were prominent in the comments of black social activists of that period and even today.

REFERENCES

Becker, Howard. 1973. *Outsiders: Studies in the Sociology of Deviance.* New York: Free Press.

Benedict, Ruth. 1940. *Race: Science and Politics.* New York: Viking Press.

Berger, Peter L. 1963. *Invitation to Sociology: A Humanistic Perspective.* New York: Doubleday.

Bonger, Willem A. 1943. *Race and Crime.* New York: Columbia University Press.

Branham, Vernon C., and Samuel B. Kutash. 1949. "The Negro in Crime." Pp. 267–77 in *Encyclopedia of Criminology.* New York: Philosophical Library.

Chambliss, William J., and Robert B. Seidman. 1971. *Law, Order and Power.* Reading, Mass.: Addison-Wesley.

Claghorn, Kate Holladay. 1923. *The Immigrant's Day in Court.* New York: Harper and Brothers.

DeGre, Gerard. 1955. *Science as a Social Institution.* New York: Random House.

DuBois, W. E. Burghardt. 1899. *The Philadelphia Negro: A Social Study.* New York: Benjamin Blom.

DuBois, W. E. Burghardt. 1904. (editor) *Some Notes on Negro Crime, Particularly in Georgia—Proceedings of the Ninth Atlanta Conference for the Study of Negro Problems.* Atlanta: Atlanta University. Reprinted: New York: Octagon Books, 1968.

Fay, Brian. 1975. *Social Theory and Political Practice.* London: George Allen and Unwin.

Gould, Stephen J. 1981. *The Mismeasure of Man.* New York: W. W. Norton.

Hawkins, Darnell F. 1993. "Crime and Ethnicity" pp. 89–120. In Brian Forst (ed.). *The Socio-Economics of Crime and Justice.* New York: M. E. Sharpe.

Herskovits, Melville J. 1930. *The Anthropometry of the American Negro.* New York: Columbia University Press.

Hill, Mozell. 1959. "The Metropolis and Juvenile Delinquency Among Negroes." *Journal of Negro Education* 28:277–85.

Hindelang, Michael J. 1978. "Race and Involvement in Common Law Personal Crimes" *American Sociological Review* 43:93–109.

Hoffman, Frederick L. 1896. *Race Traits and Tendencies of the American Negro.* New York: Macmillan.

Jensen, Arthur R. 1969. "How Much Can We Boost I.Q. and Scholastic Achievement?" *Harvard Educational Review* 39 (winter):1–123.

Korn, Richard R., and Lloyd W. McCorkle. 1959. *Criminology and Penology.* New York: Henry Holt.

Laughlin, H. H. 1922. *Analysis of America's Melting Pot.* Hearings before the Committee on Immigration and Naturalization, House of Representatives, 67th Congress, Third Session, November 21, 1922, Serial 7-C.

Mann, Coramae Richey. 1993. *Unequal Justice: A Question of Color.* Bloomington: Indiana University Press.

Myrdal, Gunnar. 1944. *An American Dilemma.* New York: Harper and Row.

National Commission on Law Observance and Enforcement. 1931. *Report on Crime and the Foreign-Born.* Washington, D.C.: U.S. Government Printing Office.

Otken, Charles H. 1894. *The Ills of the South: Or Related Causes Hostile to the General Prosperity of a Southern People.* New York: Putnam.

Pettigrew, Thomas F. (ed.). 1980. *The Sociology of Race Relations: Reflection and Reform.* New York: Free Press.

Pope, Carl E. 1979. "Race and Crime Revisited." *Crime and Delinquency,* July:347–57.

Proctor, H. H. and M. N. Work. 1904. "Atlanta and Savannah." pp. 49–52. In W. E. Burghardt DuBois (editor) *Some Notes on Negro Crime; Particularly in Georgia—Proceedings of the Ninth Atlanta Conference for the Study of Negro Problems.* Atlanta: Atlanta University. Reprinted. New York: Octagon Books, 1968.

Quinney, Richard. 1970. *The Social Reality of Crime.* Boston: Little Brown.

Ryan, William. 1971. *Blaming the Victim.* New York: Pantheon.

Sanborn, Frank B. 1904. "The Problem of Crime". Pp. 1–2. In W. E. Burghardt DuBois (editor). *Some Notes on Negro Crime, Particularly in Georgia— Proceedings of the Ninth Atlanta Conference for the Study of Negro Problems.* Atlanta: Atlanta University. Reprinted: New York: Octagon Books, 1968.

Sellin, Thorsten. 1928. "The Negro Criminal: A Statistical Note." *Annals of the American Academy of Political and Social Science* 140:52–64.

———. 1938. *Culture Conflict and Crime.* New York: Social Science Research Council.

———. 1976. *Slavery and the Penal System.* New York: Elsevier.

Shaw, Clifford R. 1929. *Delinquency Areas.* Chicago: University of Chicago Press.

———, and Henry D. McKay. 1942. *Juvenile Delinquency and Urban Areas: A Study of Rates of Delinquents in Relation to Differential Characteristics of local Communities in American Cities.* Chicago: University of Chicago Press.

Steinberg, Stephen. 1989. *The Ethnic Myth: Race, Ethnicity and Class in America.* Boston: Beacon.

Sutherland, Edwin H. 1924. *Criminology* Philadelphia: Lippincott.

———. 1934. *Principles of Criminology.* Chicago: Lippincott.

———. 1949. *White Collar Crime.* New York: Holt, Rinehart and Winston.

Taft, Donald R. 1933. "Does Immigration Increase Crime?" *Social Forces* 12 (October):69–77.

———. 1936. "Nationality and Crime." *American Sociological Review* 1(October):724–36.

Turk, Austin T. 1969. *Criminality and the Legal Order* Skokie, Ill.: Rand McNally.

United States Immigration Commission. 1911. "Immigration and Crime." Vol. 36. Washington, D.C.: U.S. Government Printing Office.

Vander Zanden, James W. 1973. "Sociological Studies of American Blacks." *Sociological Quarterly* 14:

Wilson, James Q., and Richard J. Herrnstein. 1985. *Crime and Human Nature.* New York: Simon and Schuster.

Wolfgang, Marvin, and Bernard Cohen. 1970. *Crime and Race; Conceptions and Misconceptions.* New York: Institute of Human Relations Press.

Work, Monroe. 1904. "Crime in Cities." Pp. 18–32. In W. E. Burghardt DuBois (editor). *Some Notes on Negro Crime, Particularly in Georgia—Proceedings of the Ninth Atlanta Conference for the Study of Negro Problems.* Atlanta: Atlanta University. Reprinted: New York: Octagon Books, 1968.

2

Race, Class, and Sociobiological Perspectives on Crime

Black and lower-class populations have the highest rates of *street* and index crime involvement in the United States (Blumstein et al., 1986:24–26, 47–49; Hindelang, 1981; Wolfgang, Figlio, and Sellin, 1972). Sociological theories argue that location and experiences in the social environment are responsible for these differences in crime involvement (Cloward and Ohlin, 1960; Elliott, Huizinga, and Ageton, 1985; McCord and McCord, 1959; Sampson, 1987). Psychological explanations propose that crime involvement is related to personality attributes of offenders that occur independently of the social environment (Eysenck, 1977; Huesmann, Lefkowitz, and Walder, 1984). These theories would assign race and social class differences in crime involvement to differences in personality.

Biological and biosociological perspectives of criminality take the psychological view a step further. They attribute personality traits associated with criminal offending to innate genetic, biochemical, and neurological characteristics of offenders (see Fishbein, 1990; Mednick, 1981; Moffitt, 1990; and Wilson and Herrnstein, 1985, for reviews). Research on the biological correlates of racial and class differences in offending is virtually absent, but by inference biological and biosocial perspectives suggest that they have sources in the biological constitutions of these groups (see Wilson and Herrnstein, 1985). They also suggest that the social environment has a weaker causal role than sociological explanations admit.

In this chapter, the biological and biosociological perspectives are briefly outlined and their implications for race and class differences in of-

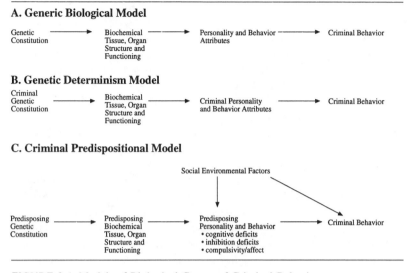

FIGURE 2.1 Models of Biological Causes of Criminal Behavior

fending are discussed. A causal role for biology is plausible, but its relative importance compared to social factors in crime causation is questioned. In this discussion, the terms biocriminal and biocriminological are used interchangeably to refer to both the biological and biosociological views of crime causation.

THE BIOLOGICAL AND BIOSOCIAL PERSPECTIVES

Biological and biosocial studies assess four levels of biological organization. These are: the structure of genetic and organic molecules, the functioning of neurons and cellular tissues, the biochemistry of hormones, neurotransmitter, and enzymes, and the functioning of specialized neurological organ systems—that is, the brain (Ellis, 1990: 4–5). Biocriminal researchers share the assumption that structural and functional differences in one or more of these levels of biological organization occur among noncriminal and criminally prone individuals (Ellis, 1990; Wilson and Herrnstein, 1985). Chronic offenders and some serious offenders are most likely to possess the defective biological constitutions and hyper or hypo functioning biochemical and neuropsychological conditions assumed to be criminogenic (Fishbein, 1990; Goldstein, 1987; Moffitt, 1990) [Fig. 2.1—A].

Two categories of biocriminal causation are advanced. Genetic determinism implies that criminality and crime involvement are substantively transmitted through the genetic makeup of individuals. Genetic determinism is not widely advocated but is implicit in studies of XYY and XXY chromosomes abnormalities (Jacobs et al., 1965; Witkin et al., 1976), and studies of identical twins (Christiansen, 1977) and adoption (Hutchings and Mednick, 1977; Mednick and Hutchings, 1978; Mednick, Gabrielli, and Hutchings, 1984, 1987). Hypothetically, criminality among possessors of extra Y chromosomes and the concordance in criminal behavior among identical twins and among adopted offsprings and their criminal biological parents occurs because of their genetic constitutions. See Figure 2.1—B. The XYY and XXY theory has been largely discredited (Cloninger et al., 1982), but twin and adoption studies continue to provide the central empirical evidence used to support a genetic determinant in the biocriminal relationship.

The biosocial category of causation attributes criminality to biological predispositions. Genetic and developmental aberrations cause hyper and hypo functioning biological processes, which in turn are believed responsible for neuropsychological conditions, which increase individual potential or predispositions for criminal behavior. Biological predispositions endow individuals with personality and behavioral tendencies that increase their risk for crime involvement. Three biological conditions underlie biocriminal predispositions.

Cognitive deficiencies associated with brain dysfunctions, low global intelligence, lower verbal compared to nonverbal intelligence, and psychopathology (Andrew, 1982; Buikhuisen, 1987, 1988; Hare, 1980; Moffitt and Silva, 1987) represent one group of predispositional conditions. Cognitive deficits limit capacity for learning right from wrong, to retain the connection between negative consequences for negative behavior, and to discern important aspects of the social environment in selecting between criminal and noncriminal behavior. Slow autonomic nervous system functioning, a second crime predisposing condition, contributes to inadequately developed moral conscience, insensitivity to others, and low fear responses. The absence of these inhibitors leads to inappropriate behavior (Mednick, 1981; Siddle, 1977). A final condition includes neuropsychological tendencies for compulsive, heightened emotional affect, aggressive or violent and antisocial styles of behavior. Biological sources of these include brain damage, hyperactivity-attention deficit disorder syndrome, heightened or low hormone and neurotransmitter levels, and more generally genetic constitution (Farrington, 1991; Gove and Wilmoth, 1990; Moffitt, 1990).

The biosocial perspective includes a role for the social environment (Fishbein, 1990; Moffit, 1990; Rowe, 1986; Rowe and Osgood, 1984). Predisposing biological conditions increase the potential of individuals for crime involvement, but factors in the social environment—that is, poor parenting and social learning experiences—trigger and translate them into criminal behavior, Figure 2.1—C. In spite of the inclusion of social environmental effects, equal or greater importance is given to predisposing biological conditions in crime causation (Fishbein, 1990; Rowe and Osgood, 1984).

Backed by research reporting links between biological traits and criminal behavior, biological and biosocial perspectives have a seductive appeal in their simplistic location of criminality in the genetic and biological predispositions of individuals. They appear to have potential as explanations for race and class differences in crime involvement. However, a review of this research leads to a different conclusion. Any effects of biological factors on race and class differences in offending are small and secondary to those of social environmental factors. I outline my reasoning for this conclusion in the following pages.

CRIMINALITY AND CHRONIC OFFENDING

Criminality refers to personality and behavioral predispositions to engage in criminal behavior. Predisposing traits of criminality include compulsivity, impulsivity, or lack of self-control, orientations for immediate gratification, a propensity for risk-taking and excitement, insensitivity to others, a lack of moral constraint, and a lack of concern for consequences in the satisfaction of self interests (Farrington, 1991; Hirschi and Gottfredson, 1986; Venables and Raine, 1987).[1] Chronicity of offending, on the other hand, refers to actual offense history defined by a combination of offense frequency, seriousness, and longevity of offense careers (Blumstein et al., 1986; Chaiken and Chaiken, 1982, 1985; Greenwood, 1982; Hamparian et al., 1978; Petersilia, Greenwood, and Lavin, 1977; Wolfgang et al., 1972). Theoretically, predisposing traits of criminality should be strongly correlated with chronicity of offending. Sociologically, predisposing criminality leading to chronic offending is a product of socialization, social learning, culture, and social structural dislocation (Cloward and Ohlin, 1960; Elliott, Huizinga, and Menard, 1989; Miller, 1958; Sampson, 1987). Biocriminal points of view attribute persistent and stable differences in criminality to genetic and neuropsychological dysfunctions (Gove and Wilmoth, 1990; Mednick et al., 1987; Venables and Raine, 1987) or a combination of biological and social factors (Buikhuisen, 1988; Hirschi and Gottfredson, 1986; Moffitt, 1990).

If criminality is a product of biological dysfunctions, predisposing biological traits should be disproportionately found among chronic offenders. Individuals with low biological predispositions for criminality should rarely be found among chronic offenders. Biocriminal studies of twins, families, and adoption often support the direction of this relationship, but the size of the relationship varies among studies (Wilson and Herrnstein, 1985; p. 93, Table 1; Walters, 1992; Tables 1, 2, and 3). The proportion of individuals with high predicted biological criminality who are not chronic offenders and the percentage of those with low predicted biological criminality who are chronic offenders differ across studies. Walters' (1992) metaanalysis of these studies concludes that the biocriminal relationship is modest or "less favorable to the gene crime hypothesis."

SELECTED AND REPRESENTATIVE SAMPLES

Inconsistency in the size of the biological trait and crime involvement relationship is partially due to differences in type of samples used. Studies using selected or nonrepresentative samples of delinquents, prisoners, and other persons referred for intervention are particularly troublesome. Membership in these groups occurs not only because of the high prevalence of an assortment of problems among them, but also because of other disguised social selection processes influenced by their minority and low social status characteristics. The biocriminal relationship reported for selected samples may be artificially inflated by selection processes that determine who does and does not become counted among official problem populations.

Better estimates of the biocriminal and social environmental relationships should rely on representative samples of populations or cohorts. Gottfredson and Hirschi's (1990: 53–61) review of Mednick's cross-fostering adoption studies provides insights on this issue. Cross-fostering studies attempt to separate the biological effects of natural parents and the social environmental effects of adoptive parents on the criminal behavior of adopted children (Hutchings and Mednick, 1977; Mednick, Gabrielli, and Hutchings, 1984; Van Dusen, Mednick, and Gabrielli, 1983). Gottfredson and Hirschi find that the biological parents' effect on adopted children's criminal histories reported in Hutchings and Mednick's pilot study (1977) is weaker and closer to zero in Mednick's (1984) larger 14,000 adoptee subject cohort replication.

Gottfredson and Hirschi conclude that Mednick's work shows that the effects of genetic factors in the transmission of criminality are small or zero. Their review is relevant because the Mednick studies approximate comparison of the biocriminal relationship in a representative population (the cohort adoptee study) to that in a selective adoption population (the pilot study). It suggests that the biocriminal relationship is weaker in the general population than in selected samples because selection biases are minimized.

The use of representative samples will be critical in assessments of the biocriminal bases of race and class differences in offending. The prevalence of lower measured IQ, hyperactivity-ADD, asocial and aggressive personality traits, mental illness, and other hypothesized biocriminal traits (Dohrenwend and Dohrenwend, 1969; McLeod and Shanahan, 1993; Osborne and McGurk, 1982; Scarr, 1981) and the prevalence of offending are high among black and lower-class populations. A substantial biological trait and offending correlation should be expected among these populations, but it would probably be stronger in selected samples than in representative samples. Representative samples would provide estimates that approximate the real strength of the biological trait and offending relationship.

General population assessments would also allow comparative estimates of the biocriminal relationship between race and class groups. I suspect, for example, that the percentage of white and middle-class persons possessing the assumed biocriminal traits who are chronic offenders is much smaller than the percentage of black and lower-class persons with these traits who are chronic offenders. Findings like this would undermine notions that biological factors are important sources of race and class differences in offending, in spite of a larger biocriminal association for black and lower-class groups. The absence of a consistent biocriminal effect across races and social classes among those with the hypothesized predisposing traits would weaken assumptions that these factors are critical sources of differences in offending. Social environmental variables are implicated as the probable sources of those differences.

MEASUREMENT AND CONCEPTS IN BIOCRIMINAL CAUSATION

Some researchers assign an equal or larger role to biological factors than to social environmental factors in crime causation (Fishbein, 1990; Hirschi and Hindelang, 1977; Rowe and Osgood, 1984). In twin studies, common intrafamily socialization among siblings is believed to be experimentally controlled so that the larger correlation in crime involvement among identical twins over that of fraternal twins and nontwin siblings is interpreted as an indication of stronger genetic contributions to criminality. In adoption studies, since the only contributions adoptive parents can have on adopted youths' behavior is through socialization, the stronger association of biological parent and adopted youth criminality is interpreted to mean genetic effects are more important. Adoption, twin, cohort, and representative studies that explicitly include social environmental variables in their analyses report the relative weight of their effects as smaller than the included biological variables (for social class, see Hirschi and Hindelang, 1977; Mednick et al., 1987; Mofitt, 1988; Moffitt, Gabrielli, and Mednick, 1981; for family and parenting variables, see Moffitt, Gabrielli, and Mednick, 1981; for peer group effects, see Rowe and Osgood, 1984).

Selected sample biases as discussed above contribute to findings of some studies supporting this position. Denno (1990) using a selected sample of black youths referred for clinical treatment reports different results. In this study, both social and biological factors have strong direct and indirect effects on subsequent adult criminal behavior. However, Denno found that social variables collectively had the strongest associations to adult criminal behavior among sample members. Denno's use of multiple, rather than single, social environmental measures probably contributed to these results.

Other measurement and conceptual issues also contribute to the underestimation of social environmental effects and the inflation of biological effects. Biocriminal research tests relationships at the individual level (Wilson and Herrnstein, 1985) using biological variables that are specific and individualistic in both their conceptual meaning and measurement. The same is not true of social variables, which are more aggregate in measurement and/or global in conceptual meaning. Social class or status, family structure, quality of parenting, and delinquent peer associations represent averaged nominal and ordinal differences between groups rather than unique attributes of individuals and their environments. While members of the lower-class share some average differences from members of the middle class, the specific class attributes and experiences of each member of the lower-class are unique. Rowe and Osgood's (1984) discussion of the distinction between the effects of shared environments and specific (individual) environment addresses this issue. Using aggregate or average social variable measures to represent individual social attributes results in truncated and weak social environment effect estimates in individual level studies. Decomposition of social variables to measure unique social differences among individuals could improve their empirical strength compared to the effects of biological variables.

Social class, family structure, and other social variables used in biocriminal research may also have weak and truncated effects on delinquency and offending because of poor conceptual selection and measurement of these variables. For instance, social class and social status are overlapping but different conceptually. An assortment of measures are used to represent these concepts—that is, family income, father's occupation, SES of census trait of residence—as well as the personal income, education, and/or occupation of sample members. These do not have the same implications as measures of social class and social status, and their relationships to offending differ for juveniles versus adults and for offending measured by official compared to self-report data (Thornberry and Farnworth, 1982). Similar conceptual and measurement problems occur with family-parenting variables (Loeber and Stouthamer-Loeber, 1986; Mercy and Steelman, 1982; Van Voorhis et al.,

1988), peer, and other social variables. Biocriminal research as a body has not paid attention to nuances in the conceptual meaning and predictiveness of alternative measures of these social concepts. Some truncation of social variable effects can be attributed to this problem.

The truncation of unique attributes of individuals associated with the use of aggregate and macro social variables does not mean they should not be used in tests of the relationship between biological and social traits with crime involvement. They are useful when interpreted as mediators of associations between other aggregate and individual level variables and behavior (McCord, 1990; Sampson, 1987; Sampson and Wilson, 1992). For instance, poverty is associated with crime, but the relationship is not consistent across all those who are poor. Sampson and Wilson have shown that poor urban black Americans are more likely to live in extremely economically depressed and more densely poor communities lacking in stable middle-class institutions than are poor urban whites. The relationship between poverty and social adjustment is exaggerated for poor urban blacks compared to poor urban whites because of differences in the aggregate social contexts of their communities.

Similarly, the distribution of employment, income, and educational attainment has different relationships to aggregate white and black crime. These opportunity variables have an inverse relationship to criminality and crime rates in cross-sectional studies, but they are stronger for blacks than whites. LaFree, Drass, and O'Day (1992) find that these relationships change in analysis of aggregate longitudinal data for the United States. Overtime, the opportunity and crime relationship tends to be positive for blacks but remains inverse for whites. The relationship between opportunity variables and crime for racial groups are neither simple nor are they necessarily straightforward. Analyses that do not control for social contextual effects—that is, community differences—and that do not anticipate that the social dynamics of crime causation may differ from group to group in different forms of analyses are subject to flawed conclusions about the effects of those variables.

The individual and aggregate contributions of social factors to crime causation are underestimated in biocriminal research because of incorrect levels of measurement and simplistic interpretation of their conceptual effects. The lack of appropriate controls for aggregate social structural variables like the social contexts of communities also handicaps assessment of social environmental influences in crime causation. Social variable effects on crime involvement are deflated and biological trait effects inflated because of these issues. Biocriminal studies ought to decompose social variables so that the unique individual level effects of these variables are measured and ought to develop models that assess both individual and aggregate social environmental sources of crime causation.

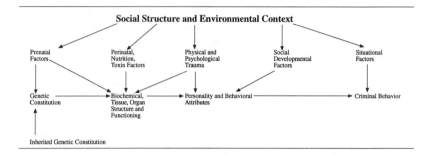

FIGURE 2.2 Multiple Environmental and Biological Effects Model of Criminal Behavior

SPECIFYING MULTIPLE SOCIAL SOURCES
OF BIOCRIMINAL RISK

Biosocial studies depict social variable effects in crime causation as direct or interactions with predisposing personality traits triggering crime involvement, Figure 2.1—C. This implies that genetic constitution and biological predispositions for criminality exist prior to and independently of social environmental influences (Rowe and Osgood, 1984). The effects of social environmental factors are more complex and are sometimes responsible for altering biological constitution and functioning at various points along the biocriminal causal sequence (Buikhuisen, 1988; Capron and Duyme, 1989; Fishbein, 1990; Moffitt, 1988, 1990). As illustrated in Figure 2.2, prenatal, perinatal, and postnatal problems, nutrition, exposure to environmental toxins, and various forms of trauma, among other factors are influential in biological development and functioning. These are rarely included in empirical models estimating the biocriminal relationship.

Multiple social environmental determinants of genetic constitution and biological dysfunctions must be included in biocriminal models to equitably separate the influences of biological and social factors in crime causation. Multiple-social-factor models will be critical in assessments of race and class differences in criminality, because differences in exposure to health and biologically altering environments effect the distribution of biocriminal traits among these groups. Table 2.1 shows that black infants and children have rates of low birth weight, infant mortality, and child deaths that are one and one-half to more than two times those of white infants and children (Center for the Study of Social Policy, 1992). These health risk differences are substantially associated with living in impoverished environments, 44 percent of the black compared to 15 percent of the white children in the United States live in poverty.

TABLE 2.1   Four Indicators of White and Black Child Well Being in The United States, 1989.

Indicator	White Children	Black Children
Percent low birth weight babies	5.7	13.2
Infant morality rate (per 100,000 live births)	8.2	17.7
Child death rate: ages 1–14 (per 100,000 children)	29.4	48.4
Percent children in poverty	14.7	43.6

Source: Center for Social Policy, 1992: p. 21.

TABLE 2.2   Percentage of Six Months of Five Year Old Children Estimated to Exceed Blood Lead Levels of 15 MG PER 100 ML of Blood, all U.S. SMSA's, 1984.

Family Income	White	Black
<$6000	27% (1,039,600)	62% (698,300)
$6000–14,999	16% (2,666,300)	46% (793,300)
≥$15,000	7% (7,643,900)	31% (991,800)

Source: U.S. Department of Health and Human Services, 1988: I-12, Table I-2.

Exposure to environmental chemical hazards like head poisoning is associated with depressed cognitive development, hyperactivity-ADD, and mental retardation (Needleman et al., 1979, 1984). All these are predisposing conditions for criminality according to the biocriminal perspective, and black and lower-class populations are at greater risk for this problem. Table 2.2 shows that among households with incomes of less than $6,000 annually, 62 percent of the black children compared to 27 percent of the white children exceed the lowest permissible level of lead in their blood. As household income increases, the percentages of children with lead poisoning decreases, but large racial differences remain. In households with $15,000 or more income, the percentage of children at risk for lead poisoning is still significantly larger for blacks, 31 percent, compared to 7 percent for whites. Similarly, prenatal maternal substance abuse (Bower, 1989; Stimmel, 1985; Streissgath, Barr, and Sampson, 1989), poorer prenatal, perinatal and postnatal care, higher levels of nutritional deficiencies, and emotional and physical trauma are factors contributing to the higher levels of underdeveloped cognition and dysfunctional biochemical and neuropsychological problems among the black and poor populations.

Biocriminal studies that do not control for the multiple locations and forms of social environmental determinants of biological dysfunctions will report stronger biological effects on race and class differences in criminality and offending than justified. This occurs because antecedent effects of social environmental determinants of biological dysfunctions are not removed. Since biologically altering and criminogenic social factors occur in the same social environments for many black and lower-class offenders populations, some of the observed biological trait associations with criminality is spurious. Controls for the multiple social environmental sources of biocriminality will minimize this potential spuriousness in biological trait effects.

RACE, BIOLOGY, AND CRIME: AN EXAMPLE

Disputes over how much of measured intelligence is a product of individual genetic constitution versus environmental influences (Capron and Duyme, 1989; Jencks, 1992) directly bear on biocriminal and sociological assumptions about crime causation. Biocriminologists emphasize the genetic component of intelligence as a precursor to criminality as discussed above. Social explanations argue that group and some individual differences in IQ are more dependent on effects the social environments has on the development of genetic potentials. Sociologists also maintain that intelligence has no direct effect on delinquency. Rather delinquency is a reaction to frustrations with schooling and other social experiences mediated indirectly by intelligence.

An examination of the intelligence and delinquency controversy provides an illustration of some of the issues discussed above regarding weaknesses in biocriminal perspectives as explanations for race and class differences in offending. Data presented in the second Philadelphia cohort study (Tracy, Wolfgang, and Figlio, 1990) are used for this purpose. Tracy et al. (1990, Table 5.1, p. 39) show that the prevalence of official[2] delinquency and chronic delinquency is greater among nonwhite than white youths. In this cohort, 41 percent of the nonwhite youths and 23 percent of the white youths are delinquent. Eleven percent of the nonwhite youths are chronic delinquents compared to slightly more than 3 percent of the white youth cohort.

Table 2.3 is an adaptation of one of the Tracy et al. (1990) analyses and shows that the above noted racial differences in delinquency are related to differences in academic achievement, where achievement scores are used as surrogate measures of intelligence.[3] The marginal totals in the table show that the 3.2 average quartile achievement of white youths is higher than the 2.1 mean quartile achievement of nonwhite youths (third column total in Table 2.3). The 2.7 average quartile achievement of nondelinquents is also higher than the 2.1 average of delinquents (third row total in Table 2.3). The cross-classification of race and delinquent status shows that low achievement scores are related to delinquency within and across racial groups. The average achievement quartile score is 2.2 for nonwhite nondelinquents and 1.9 for nonwhite delinquents. The mean quartile achievement score for white non-

TABLE 2.3   Average Quartile Achievement Level by Delinquent Status and Race

Race	Nondelinquent	Delinquent	Total
White	3.3 (N = 1948)	2.7 (N = 507)	3.2 (N = 2455)
Nonwhite	2.2 (N = 2788)	1.9 (N = 1516)	2.1 (N = 4304)
Total	2.7 (N = 4736)	2.1 (N = 2023)	2.5 (N = 6759)

Source: Adapted from Tracy et al. 1990, Table 5.8, p. 50. Tracy et al. (1990) present this table as a frequency distribution across four quartiles of national achievement scores for nondelinquents and delinquents among white and black members of their 1958 cohort. This table summarizes their table by computing the mean quartile achievement for each race and delinquent status group.

delinquents is 3.3 and 2.7 for white delinquents. A biological effect on delinquency for both white and nonwhite youths is implied to the extent that intelligence as measured by achievement scores is attributed to genetic endowment. Furthermore, it may appear that the intelligence-genetic effect is stronger for nonwhite youths who tend to have the lowest average achievement scores and are more likely to be delinquent. Thirty-four percent of the black youth cohort (1516\4304) have delinquency records compared to 21 percent of the white youth cohort (507\2455).

It should be obvious though that something more influences the distribution of race, achievement, and delinquency data in Table 2.3. Achievement is not consistently related to delinquency within or across racial groups. There is a smaller difference in the average quartile achievement of nonwhite nondelinquents and delinquents (2.2 to 1.9, a difference of .3 quartiles) than occurs between white nondelinquents and delinquents (3.3 to 2.7, a difference of .6 quartiles). Why is the size of the average achievement scores distinguishing between delinquency status of the white and nonwhite groups different? The larger difference in achievement between delinquent and nondelinquent white youths suggests that intelligence is a more crucial determinant of white than nonwhite delinquency.

More peculiar, the average quartile achievement of nonwhite nondelinquents, 2.2, is lower than that of white delinquents, 2.7. Why are white youths with higher average intelligence more prone to delinquency than nonwhite nondelinquents with lower average intelligence? It is unlikely that these racial differences in the associations of achievement with delinquency are inherent in the causal properties of intelligence or its genetic source.

Attributing these observations to genetic factors oversimplifies and ignores important irregularities in the intelligence and delinquency relationship within and between racial groups. These irregularities are exhibited by other data also (see Hirschi and Hindelang, 1977). Unmeasured social factors would probably tell a more interesting and perhaps critical story about these racial differences in intelligence and delinquency. If there is a causal race, intelligence, and crime relationship, then social environmental variables mediate and specify the relationship. Differences in unique and aggregate social environmental variables that impact individuals within and across racial groups provide more plausible explanations for the achievement and delinquency associations revealed in Table 2.3 than do arguments emphasizing the biology of intelligence. Models that appropriately measure and conceptualize social variables as well as take into account the different types and locations of social variable effects would significantly reduce the empirical implications of genetic sources of intelligence as a cause of delinquency.

DISCUSSION

In this paper, I express skepticism about the importance of biological factors in crime causation and race class differences in offending. Skepticism is based on several empirical and theoretical characteristics of existing research. Empirical support for a biological, criminality, and chronic offending relationships based on studies of selective samples are predictably biased in favor of biological effects. Comparative review of cross-fostering adoption studies (Gottfredson and Hirschi, 1990) and metaanalysis of family, twin, and adoption studies (Walters, 1992) show that the biology-crime relationship is modest or small at best.

Furthermore, if there are real biological effects on criminality and crime involvement, the relationships between biological traits and crime are overestimated compared to those of social environmental factors. Research reporting equal or larger effects of biological traits may be artifacts of social variable truncation. Truncation partially results from the use of aggregate variables, which mask unique differences among individuals, and from poor attention to conceptual and measurement issues in selecting social variables included in empirical models. Where the inclusion of aggregated or macrosocial environmental variables might be informative in biological and biosociological research, omitted is consideration is of how their relationships to the behaviors of different social groups may not be the same. In addition, social environmental determinants (that is, lead poisoning, prenatal and perinatal trauma) of genetic, biochemical, neuropsychological, personality, and behavioral predispositions associated with criminality are not included in empirical models and most theoretical statements. Because these social determinants of biocriminal conditions are absent, analyses give greater weight to innate biological conditions than would occur if the effects of their social environmental sources were separated out.

At this juncture, sociological explanations of criminal behavior should continue to provide the more theoretically important accounts of crime causation, and for race and class differences in crime involvement. Simple correlations between hypothesized biocriminal traits and crime involvement should be larger for black and lower-class persons than white and middle-class individuals, but this is probably more coincidence than causal. Appropriate controls and specifications of social environmental variables in biocriminal models as discussed in examples are expected to show that social variables largely account for race and class differences in the biology and crime relationship.

Differences in the causal implications of biological and social environmental factors have different consequences for policy and intervention. Should biocriminal views prove valid, they will be reflected in public policies emphasizing some forms of biomedical engineering and manipulation for social control. These will be disproportionately applied to black and lower-class groups according to their disproportionate involvement in crime. Objectively, this might seem appropriate to biocriminologists, but it would be politically troublesome. Skepticism leads me to believe that the validation of significant and large biocriminal causes of crime that are applicable to the vast majority of crimes, offenders, and chronic offenders will not occur. In this event, the greater problem is the potential for the mystification and the rhetoric of biocriminality to lead to policies of biomedical crime control over and above its substantive importance. In such a case, black and lower-class offenders and populations would be subject to these interventions without objective and theoretical justification. Biocriminological research deserves acknowledgment as a legitimate arena of study and should be evaluated objectively on it merits. Racist and classist potentials of the way these perspectives might be translated into public policy also merit continued scrutiny and criticism.

NOTES

1. Criminality has been defined as a unique personality trait and as a subpattern of a more general propensity for problem and risky behavior. For example, Gottfredson and Hirschi (1990) embraced the concept of ''self-control'' as a general asocial orientation that may be expressed in many ways. Criminality is one among several patterns of asocial behavior that may occur among those with a lack of self-control.

2. The cohort offending patterns represented by this data omits those crimes and delinquencies that did not come to official attention. The analysis presented might differ if self-report data on crime and delinquent involvement for the cohort are used.

3. The quartile rank of cohort member scores on the California Achievement Test is used as a proxy for intelligence. Based on standardized national norms, achievement scores of cohort youths are divided into four ranked groups or quartiles.

The first quartile includes those whose scores ranked in the lowest 25 percent. The fourth quartile includes those with scores ranking in the highest 25 percent of national norms for youths.

REFERENCES

Andrew, June M. 1982. "Memory and Violent Crime Delinquents." *Criminal Justice and Behavior* 9: 364–71.

Blumstein, Alfred, Jacqueline Cohen, Jeffrey A. Roth, and Christy A. Visher, ed. 1986. *Criminal Careers and Career Criminals,* vol. 1. Washington, D.C.: National Academy of Press.

Bower, Bruce. 1989. "Drinking While Pregnant Risks Child's IQ." *Science News* 135 (February 4): 68.

Buikhuisen, Wouter. 1987. "Cerebral Dysfunction and Persistent Juvenile Delinquency." In *The Causes of Crime: New Biological Approaches,* edited by Sarnoff A. Mednick, Terrie E. Moffitt, and Susan A. Stack. Cambridge: Cambridge University Press, pp. 168–84.

———. 1988. "Chronic Delinquency: A Theory." In *Explaining Criminal Behavior: Interdisciplinary Approaches,* edited by Wouter Buikhuisen and Sarnoff A. Mednick. Leiden, Netherland: E.J. Brill, pp. 27–47.

Capron, Christiane, and Michel Duyme. 1989. "Assessment of Effects of Socioeconomic Status on IQ in a Full Cross-fostering Study." *Nature* 340 (August 17): 552–54.

Center for the Study of Social Policy. 1992. *Kids Count Data Book.* Washington, D.C.

Chaiken, Jan M., and Marcia R. Chaiken. 1982. *Varieties of Criminal Behavior: Summary and Policy Implications.* Santa Monica, Calif.: Rand Corporation.

Chaiken, Marcia R., and Jan M. Chaiken. 1985. *Who Gets Caught Doing Crime?* Washington, D.C.: U.S. Department of Justice, Bureau of Justice Statistics (Discussion Paper).

Christiansen, Karl O. 1977. "A Preliminary Study of Criminality Among Twins." In *Biosocial Bases of Criminal Behavior,* edited by Sarnoff A. Mednick and Karl O. Christiansen. New York: Gardner Press, pp. 89–108.

Cloninger, C. Robert, Soren Sigvardsson, Michael Bohman, and Anne Liis Von Knorring. 1982. "Predisposition to Petty Criminality in Swedish Adoptees: II. Cross-Fostering Analysis of Gene-Environment Interaction." *Archives of General Psychiatry* 39: 1242–47.

Cloward, Richard A., and Lloyd E. Ohlin. 1960. *Delinquency and Opportunity: A Theory of Delinquent Groups.* Glencoe, Ill.: Free Press.

Denno, Deborah W. 1990. *Biology and Violence: From Birth to Adulthood.* Cambridge: Cambridge University Press.

Dohrenwend, Bruce P., and Barbara S. Dohrenwend. 1969. *Social Status and Psychological Disorder: A Causal Inquiry.* New York: Wiley-Interscience.

Elliott, Delbert S., David Huizinga, and Suzanne S. Ageton. 1985. *Explaining Delinquency and Drug Use.* Newbury Park, Calif.: Sage Publications.

Elliott, Delbert S., David Huizinga, and Scott Menard. 1989. *Multiple Problem Youth: Delinquency, Substance Use, and Mental Health Problems.* New York: Springer-Verlag.

Ellis, Lee. 1990. "Introduction: The Nature of the Biosocial Perspective." In *Crime in Biological, Social, and Moral Contexts,* edited by Lee Ellis and Harry Hoffman. New York: Praeger, pp. 3–17.

Eysenck, Hans J. 1977. *Crime and Personality.* 3d ed., rev. and enl. London: Routledge and K. Paul.

Farrington, David P. 1991. "Antisocial Personality from Childhood to Adulthood." *Psychologist* 4: 389–94.

Fishbein, Diana H. 1990. "Biological Perspectives in Criminology." *Criminology* 28:27–72.

Goldstein, Gerald. 1987. "Neuropsychiatry: Influences between Neuropsychology and Psychopathology." *Clinical Neuropsychologist* 1: 365–80.

Gottfredson, Michael R., and Travis Hirschi. 1990. *A General Theory of Crime.* Stanford: Stanford University Press.

Greenwood, Peter W. 1982. *Selective Incapacitation.* Santa Monica, Calif.: Rand Corporation.

Gove, Walter, and Charles Wilmoth. 1990. "Risk, Crime, and Neurophysiologic Highs: A Consideration of Brain Processes Which May Reinforce Delinquent and Criminal Behavior." In *Crime in Biological, Social, and Moral Contexts,* edited by Lee Ellis and Harry Hoffman. New York: Praeger, pp. 261–93.

Hamparian, Donna M., Richard Schuster, Simon Dinitz, and John P. Conrad. 1978. *The Violent Few: A Study of Dangerous Juvenile Offenders.* Lexington, Mass.: Lexington Books.

Hare, Robert D. 1980. "A Research Scale for the Assessment of Psychopathy in Criminal Populations." *Personality and Individual Differences* 1: 111–19.

Hindelang, Michael. 1981. "Variations in Sex-Race-Age Specific Incidence Rates of Offending." *American Sociological Review* 46: 461–74.

Hirschi, Travis, and Michael Gottfredson. 1986. "The Distinction Between Crime and Criminality." In *Critique and Explanation: Essays in Honor of Gwynne Nettler*, edited by Timothy F. Hartnagel and Robert Silverman. New Brunswick, N.J.: Transaction Books, pp. 55–69.

Hirschi, Travis, and Michael J. Hindelang. 1977. "Intelligence and Delinquency: A Revisionist Review." *American Sociological Review* 42:571–87.

Huesmann, L. Rowell, Monroe M. Lefkowitz, and Leopold O. Walder. 1984. "Stability of Aggression over Time and Generations." *Developmental Psychology* 20: 1120–34.

Hutchings, Barry, and Sarnoff A. Mednick. 1977. "Criminality in Adoptees and Their Adoptive and Biological Parents: A Pilot Study." In *Biosocial Bases of Criminal Behavior*, edited by Sarnoff A. Mednick and Karl O. Christiansen. New York: Gardner Press, pp. 127–41.

Jacobs, Patricia A., Muriel Brunton, Marie M. Melville, R. P. Brittain, W. F. McClemont. 1965. "Aggressive Behavior, Mental Sub-normality, and the XYY Male." *Nature* 208: 1351–52.

Jencks, Christopher. 1992. *Race, Poverty, and the Underclass*. Cambridge, Mass.: Harvard University Press.

LaFree, Gary, Kriss A. Drass, and Patrick O'Day. 1992. "Race and Crime in Postwar America: Determinants of African-American and White Rates, 1957–1988." *Criminology* 30: 157–88.

Loeber, Rolf, and Magda Stouthamer-Loeber. 1986. "Family Factors as Correlates and Predictors of Juvenile Conduct Problems and Delinquency." In *Crime and Justice: A Review of Research*, vol. 7, edited by Michael Tonry and Norval Morris. Chicago: University of Chicago Press, pp. 29–149.

McCord, Joan. 1990. "Crime in Moral and Social Contexts, The American Society of Criminology 1989 Presidential Address." *Criminology* 28: 2–26.

McCord, William, and Joan McCord with Irving K. Zola. 1959. *Origins of Crime: A New Evaluation of the Cambridge-Somerville Youth Study*. New York: Columbia University Press.

McLeod, Jane D., and Michael J. Shanahan. 1993. "Poverty, Parenting, and Children's Mental Health." *American Sociological Review* 58: 351–66.

Mednick, Sarnoff A. 1981. "Biosocial Bases of Morality Learning." In *New Directions in the Rehabilitation of Criminal Offenders*, edited by Susan E. Martin, Lee B. Sechrest, and Robin Redner. Washington, D.C.: National Academy Press, pp. 289–303.

Mednick, Sarnoff A., William F. Gabrielli, Jr., and Barry Hutchings. 1984. "Genetic Influences in Criminal Convictions: Evidence from an Adoption Cohort." *Science* 224: 891–94.

Mednick, Sarnoff A., William F. Gabrielli, Jr., and Barry Hutchings. 1987. "Genetic Factors in the Etiology of Criminal Behavior." In *The Causes of Crime: New Biological Approaches*, edited by Sarnoff A. Mednick, Terrie E. Moffitt, and Susan A. Stack. New York: Cambridge University Press, pp. 74–91.

Mednick, Sarnoff A., and Barry Hutchings. 1978. "Genetic and Psychophysiological Factors in Asocial Behavior." *Journal of the American Academy of Child Psychiatry* 17: 209–23.

Mercy, James A., and Lala Carr Steelman. 1982. "Familial Influence on the Intellectual Attainment of Children." *American Sociological Review* 47: 532–42.

Miller, Walter. 1958. "Lower Class Culture as a Generating Milieu of Gang Delinquency." *Journal of Social Issues* 14(3): 5–19.

Moffitt, Terrie E. 1988. "Neuropsychology and Self-reported Early Delinquency in an Unselected Birth Cohort: A Preliminary Report from New Zealand." In *Biological Contributions to Crime Causation*, edited by Terrie E. Moffitt and Sarnoff A. Mednick. Dordrecht, Netherlands: Martinus Nijhoff, pp. 93–117.

———. 1990. "The Neuropsychology of Juvenile Delinquency: A Critical Review." In *Crime and Justice: A Review of Research*, vol. 12, edited by Michael Tonry and Norval Morris. Chicago: University of Chicago Press, pp. 99–169.

Moffitt, Terrie E., and Phil A. Silva. 1987. "WISC-R Verbal and Performance IQ Discrepancy in an Unselected Cohort: Clinic Significance and Longitudinal Stability." *Journal of Consulting and Clinical Psychology* 55: 768–74.

Needleman, Herbert L., Charles Gunnoe, Alan Leviton, Robert Reed, Henry Peresic, Cornelius Maher, and Peter Barrett. 1979. "Deficits in Psychological and Classroom Performance of Children with Elevated Dentine Lead Levels." *New England Journal of Medicine* 300: 689–95.

Needleman, Herbert L., Michael Rabinowitz, and Alan Leviton. 1984. "The Relationship between Prenatal Exposure to Lead and Congenital Anomalities." *Journal of the American Medical Association* 251: 2956–59.

Osborne, R. Travis, and Frank C. J. McGurk. 1982. *The Testing of Negro Intelligence*. Volume 2. Athens, Georgia: Foundation for Human Understanding.

Petersilia, Joan, Peter W. Greenwood, and Marvin Lavin. 1977. *Criminal Careers of Habitual Felons*. Santa Monica, Calif.: Rand Corporation.

Robins, Lee N. 1966. *Deviant Children Grown Up: A Sociological and Psychological Study of Sociopathic Personality*. Baltimore: Williams and Wilkins.

Rowe, David C. 1986. "Genetic and Environmental Components of Antisocial Behavior: A Study of 265 Twin Pairs." *Criminology* 24: 513–32.

Rowe, David C., and D. Wayne Osgood. 1984. "Heredity and Sociological Theories of Delinquency: A Reconsideration." *American Sociological Review* 49: 526–40.

Sampson, Robert J. 1987. "Urban Black Violence: The Effect of Male Joblessness and Family Disruption." *American Journal of Sociology* 93: 348–82.

Sampson, Robert J., and William Julius Wilson. 1993, Forthcoming. "Toward a Theory of Race, Crime, and Urban Inequality." In *Crime and Inequality*, edited by John Hagan and Ruth Peterson. Stanford: Stanford University Press.

Scarr, Sandra. 1981. *Race, Social Class, and Individual Differences in IQ*. Hillsdale, N.J.: Lawrence Erlbaum Associates.

Siddle, David A. T. 1977. "Electrodermal Activity and Psychopathy." In *Biosocial Bases of Criminal Behavior*, edited by Sarnoff A. Mednick and Karl O. Christiansen. New York: Gardner Press, pp. 199–211.

Stimmel, Barry, editor. 1985. *The Effects of Maternal Alcohol and Drug Abuse on the Newborn*. Hawthorn Press.

Streissguth, Ann P., Helen M. Barr, and Paul D. Sampson. 1989. "IQ at Age 4 in Relation to Maternal Alcohol Use and Smoking During Pregnancy." *Developmental Psychology* 25: 3–11.

Thornberry, Terence P., and Margaret Farnworth. 1982. "Social Correlates of Criminal Involvement." *American Sociological Review* 47: 505–18.

Tracy, Paul E., Marvin E. Wolfgang, and Robert M. Figlio. 1990. *Delinquency Careers in Two Birth Cohorts*. New York: Plenum.

U.S. Agency for Toxic Substances and Disease Registry. 1988. *The Nature and Extent of Lead Poisoning in the United States: A Report to Congress*. Atlanta: U.S. Department of Health and Human Services.

Van Dusen, Katherine T., Sarnoff A. Mednick, and William F. Gabrielli, Jr. 1983. "Social Class and Crime in an Adoption Cohort." *Journal of Criminal Law and Criminology*, 74 (spring): 249–69.

Van Voorhis, Patricia, Francis T. Cullen, Richard A. Mathers, and Connie Chenoweth Garner. 1988. "The Impact of Family Structure and Quality on Delinquency: A Comparative Assessment of Structural and Functional Factors." *American Sociological Review* 26: 235–61.

Vandenberg, Steven G., Sandra M. Singer, and David L. Pauls. 1986. *The Heredity of Behavior Disorders in Adults and Children*. New York: Plenum Medical Book Company.

Venables, Peter H., and Adrian Raine. 1987. "Biological Theory." In *Applying Psychology to Imprisonment: Theory and Practice*, edited by Barry J. McGurk, David M. Thornton, and Mark Williams. London: Her Majesty's Stationery Office Books, pp. 3–27.

Walters, Glenn D. 1992. "A Meta-Analysis of the Gene-Crime Relationship." *Criminology* 30: 595–613.

Weiss, Gabrielle, and Lily T. Hechtman. 1986. *Hyperactive Children Grown Up: Empirical Findings and Theoretical Considerations.* New York: Guilford Press.

Wilson, James Q., and Richard J. Herrnstein. 1985. *Crime and Human Nature.* New York: Simon and Schuster.

Witkin, Herman A., Sarnoff A. Mednick, Fini Schulsinger, Eskild Bakkestrom, Karl O. Christiansen, Donald R. Goodenough, Kurt Hirschborn, Claes Lundsteen, David R. Owen, John Philip, Donald B. Rubin, and Martha Stocking. 1976. "Criminality in XYY and XXY Men." *Science* 193: 547–55.

Wolfgang, Marvin E., Robert M. Figlio, and Thorsten Sellin. 1972. *Delinquency in a Birth Cohort.* Chicago: University of Chicago Press.

Part II

Historical Perspectives

JOAN McCORD

3

Ethnicity, Acculturation, and Opportunities: A Study of Two Generations

The number of cities in the United States with populations of at least ten thousand people rose from five, in 1800, to 345, in 1890, marking the beginning of a transition from a rural to an urban society (Weber, 1899/1963; Thernstrom, 1964/1970). After a brief hiatus, brought about by water shortages and crop infestations at the end of the nineteenth century (Hicks, 1931/1961), another 14.5 million people arrived in the United States. Three quarters of them settled in cities (Axinn and Levin, 1975). For the first time, in 1920, census figures showed an urban population greater than the rural population.

Typically, immigrants lived in the poorest urban areas. Adding to Jeffersonian attitudes attributing virtue to farming and sin to urban life, settlement patterns of the newer immigrants contributed to anti-immigrant sentiments. Ethnic identities were sometimes forged and often maintained through newspapers written in native tongues of the immigrants (Gans, 1962/1982; Park et al., 1925/1967; Suttles, 1968; Warner, 1962). The crowded, demoralizing conditions in pockets of urban poverty where many immigrants settled also provided conditions for frequent drunkenness and persistent crime (Hawes, 1971; Hogan, 1985; Menninger, 1947; Shaw and McKay, 1942/1972; Tarde 1897/1969; Ward, 1989; Weber, 1899/1963).

Despite evidence showing that immigrants were not particularly prone to crime or drunkenness (Abbott, 1915; Powell, 1966; Taft, 1936; van Vechten, 1941), the long-standing belief that they were fed arguments favoring prohibition and promoting restrictions on immigration (Board of State Charities of Massachusetts, 1872; Hofstadter, 1955; Panunzio, 1932; Sinclair, 1951; Ward, 1989).

Congress established the forerunner of the Federal Bureau of Immigration in 1891 in a bill that excluded carriers of contagious diseases and "immoral" people. President Cleveland vetoed a law approved by Congress in 1893 that was designed to exclude most immigrants from eastern and southern Europe through a literacy test. The Emergency Quota Act of 1921 restricted the number of immigrants from any country to 3 percent of the United States population in 1910 who were from that country. The Johnson Immigration Act of 1924 squeezed even more tightly by limiting the number of immigrants from any country to 2 percent of the United States population in 1890 who were from that country.

Theories linking immigration to crime postulate that immigrants and their children turn to illegitimate activities when success through legitimate routes appears unattainable (Baltzell, 1964; Bell, 1960; Cloward and Ohlin, 1960; Glazer and Moynihan, 1963; Hartshorne, 1968; Hawkins, 1993; Nelli, 1969). The relation between mobility and crime, some believe, rests partly on the inability of immigrants to cope with the different environment they find in the cities where they settle (Park et al., 1925/1967). Under such circumstances parents may be unable to provide adequate control for their acculturating children (Gordon, 1964; Lukoff and Brook, 1974).

Theories that immigrants lack the ability to supervise and guide their children in a foreign culture complement those suggesting that living in unfamiliar environments blocks opportunities for success. Both associate crime with immigration.

Suggestions that frustrated desires for success lead to crime have been linked with assumptions that immigrants note their relative status. Yet whether immigrants feel deprived partially depends on the comparisons they make. If poor immigrants compare their conditions to those of middle-class Americans, they might be expected to feel deprived. If, on the other hand, immigrants compare their conditions to those they left behind, they might feel less deprived than the similarly situated native-born. Children of immigrants may be more likely than their parents to compare themselves with native-born Americans.

Despite perceived links between crime and immigration, the data are ambiguous. For example, comparative data show that although immigrants accounted for a disproportionate amount of crime in Boston for the year 1914, in Chicago native-born residents were more likely to be criminal (Gault, 1932). Crime rates in Philadelphia did not increase during periods of high immigration (Hobbs, 1943), and with the exception of Italians, homicide rates among immigrants were *lower* than those among native-born

Americans (Lane, 1979). Additionally, a United States Immigration Commission report showed highest criminal rates among Americans of native parentage and higher criminal rates among children of immigrants than among immigrants (Park et al. 1925/1967).

Unfortunately, much of the information about how crime is related to ethnicity and nativity has depended on police records. These records as sources of evidence about ethnicity and immigration are likely to embody the prejudices of police and the self-interest of arrested individuals. To discern how immigration is related to crime, sources of information about crime should be independent of those for immigration and ethnicity.

The purpose of the present study is to investigate the relationship of crime to ethnicity, nativity, and religion. Information about ethnicity, nativity, and religion was gathered as part of an elaborate procedure for identifying families that would become part of an intervention program designed to help youths at risk for becoming delinquents. The background information is completely independent of data regarding crime.

DESCRIPTION OF A STUDY OF IMMIGRANTS

The study focuses on two generations of men residing in Cambridge and Somerville between 1935 and 1945. The sample was selected because the families lived in overcrowded, rundown neighborhoods. High-crime rates, poverty, and obvious property deterioration had been grounds for selecting neighborhoods. Criminal records for the men of both generations were traced until the men died or reached at least the age of forty.

The project originally included 506 boys from 466 families. To avoid duplication of families, only one son per family was included. To assure correct ethnic identification of the sons, only families in which the natural parents had been described were included (N = 409). Because information was lacking regarding the religion of thirty fathers, these families too were omitted from analyses. The twenty-eight blacks (only seven of whom were born in the United States), five agnostics, four Jews, three Protestant Italians, and three Protestant Portuguese were also dropped because there were too few for separate analyses and they did not fit criteria for typical ethnicity. The remaining 366 pairs of fathers and sons provided data for analyses.

The sample included 76 Italian Catholics, 33 Portuguese Catholics, and a mixture of 94 pairs from such places as Greece (N = 6), Ireland (N = 18), French Canada (N = 11), and eastern Europe (N = 14). Among the mixed group, 58 pairs were Catholic and 36 pairs were Protestant. There were 133 father-son pairs in which the fathers were born in the United States of apparently Yankee heritage. Among them were 74 pairs of Catholics and 59 pairs of Protestants.

TABLE 3.1   Fathers' Immigration and Fathers' Education* (Percent)

	Immigrant		Native-Born	
	Catholic (N = 117)	Protestant (N = 29)	Catholic (N = 97)	Protestant (N = 51)
Through 8th Grade	25.6	55.2	66.0	74.5
Less than Grammar School Graduate	74.4	44.8	34.0	25.5
	100.0	100.0	100.0	100.0

*Numbers do not total 336 because information on education was not available for 42 fathers.

Fathers were born between 1872 and 1908, with a mean in 1896. The 173 immigrant fathers had been born an average of 4.5 years before the 163 native-born fathers (t = 5.9, p = .0000). Sons were born between 1926 and 1934. The sons of immigrants had been born an average of five months before the sons of native-born men (t = 2.5, p = .0130).

Few of the fathers had graduated from high school. Therefore, those who had graduated from eighth grade (grammar school) were considered to have had a relatively good education. The fathers' educations were related both to immigration (F = 20.15, p = .0000) and religion (F = 8.5, p = .003), but not to the interaction between immigration and religion. Catholic immigrants were the least educated and native-born Protestants were the most educated. The proportions who graduated from grammar school are shown in Table 3.1.

Fathers were classified in terms of the highest status occupation reported on any record available through 1948. Having been selected because of residence in congested urban areas, the sample was skewed toward blue-collar occupations. Nevertheless, differences in the fathers' occupations reflected both religion (F = 6.3, p = .04) and the interaction between religion and immigration status (F = 8.17, p = .02). Catholic immigrants were most likely to be unskilled laborers. Protestant immigrants were most likely to be skilled or semiskilled workers. Protestants born in the United States were most likely to hold white-collar positions. Table 3.2 shows the relation of fathers' occupations to these dimensions of ethnicity.

Information about the sons' occupations was collected in 1980. As can be seen in Table 3.3, the sons had risen in occupational status compared with that of their fathers, with a higher proportion holding white-collar jobs regardless of the nativity of their fathers. The father's religion (F = 7.3, p = .03), but not his immigration status or the interaction between religion and immigration, was significantly related to son's occupational status. As found for their fathers, Catholics were less likely than Protestants to have

TABLE 3.2   Fathers' Immigration and Fathers' Occupations* (Percent)

	Immigrant		Native-Born	
	Catholic (N=113)	Protestant (N=27)	Catholic (N=88)	Protestant (N=49)
White-Collar	14.2	7.4	10.2	32.7
Skilled or Semi-skilled	51.3	81.5	67.0	55.1
Unskilled	34.5	11.1	22.7	12.2
	100.0	100.0	99.9[1]	100.0

*Numbers do not total 336 because information on occupation was not available for 59 fathers.
[1]Column does not sum to 100 due to rounding.

TABLE 3.3   Fathers' Immigration and Sons' Occupations* (Percent)

	Immigrant		Native-Born	
	Catholic (N=135)	Protestant (N=35)	Catholic (N=100)	Protestant (N=55)
White-Collar	31.9	48.6	28.0	38.2
Skilled or Semi-skilled	45.2	45.7	56.0	50.9
Unskilled	23.0	5.7	16.0	10.9
	100.1[1]	100.0	100.0	100.0

*Numbers do not total 336 because information on occupation was not available for 11 sons.
[1]Column does not sum to 100 due to rounding.

white-collar occupations. Conversely, Catholics were more likely to be unskilled workers.

Overall, then, the immigrant families seemed to be at a slight (though statistically reliable) disadvantage in terms of education and occupational status. Cross-generational improvements in occupation were slower among Catholics than among Protestants. Although few Irish Catholics appeared in the sample, the pattern of advancement in the suburbs was similar to that found in Boston (Thernstrom, 1973).

CRIMES, NATIVITY, RELIGION, AND GENERATION

Analyses focused on four types of crimes. Personal crimes of violence included those crimes against persons listed in the Federal Bureau of Investigations Index—for example, assault, attempted assault, kidnapping, robbery, rape, murder, and attempted murder. Property crimes included such crimes on the F.B.I. index as larceny, arson, larceny of auto, breaking and entering, attempted larceny, receiving stolen property, and theft. Crimes of drunkenness included public drunkenness and driving under the influence of alcohol. Misdemeanors consisted in nuisance crimes of business (for example, unlicensed hack, unlicensed sale of liquor), victimless sex crimes, trespass, gambling, contributing to the delinquency of a minor, and other misdemeanors against order or ordinances.

The first two, violent crimes and property crimes, are typically considered to be serious crimes. Theories explain their occurrence in relation to poverty, relative deprivation, anomie, frustration, differential association, and inappropriate home management. Each of these dimensions had been used to explain putatively higher crime rates among immigrants than among native-born.

Because of the impoverished conditions under which the families were living, the present analyses control effects of economic conditions. Without such controls, one might easily confuse effects of poverty with effects of immigration, ethnicity, or religion.

Drunkenness was part of the stereotype attributed to the newer immigrants in arguments favoring prohibition. Convictions for crimes of drunkenness and for misdemeanors could be expected to reflect both cultural differences and concurrent police policies.

Measures of prevalence were based on the CATMOD procedure provided in SAS 6.0 (1990). Because of redundancy, a saturated model could not be tested. Instead, for each crime, predictions were made by a model in which main effects of father's nativity, culture, religion, and generation were introduced together with three interactions: father's nativity by father's religion, culture by generation, and father's nativity by generation. Relations were considered to be significant if the probability for obtaining them by chance was less than .05.

No significant differences were found for any of the main effects or interactions in relation to the prevalence of criminals convicted for violent crimes. It is clear, however, that neither the immigrant fathers nor their sons were more likely to have been convicted for these violent crimes than were the native-born fathers and their sons. Among the immigrant fathers, 10.9 percent had been convicted for violent crimes as had 14.7 percent of the native-born fathers; 11.6 percent of the sons of immigrants and 13.5 percent of the sons of native-born fathers had been convicted for violent crimes.

Nativity ($X^2_{(1)} = 8.08$, p = .0045), generation ($X^2_{(1)} = 5.89$, p = .0152), and their interaction ($X^2_{(1)} = 4.63$, p = .0314) were related to property crimes. Immigrant fathers were least likely to be convicted for property crimes, with 4 percent convicted as compared with 18 percent of their sons, 15 percent of the native-born fathers, and 23 percent of the sons of native-born fathers.

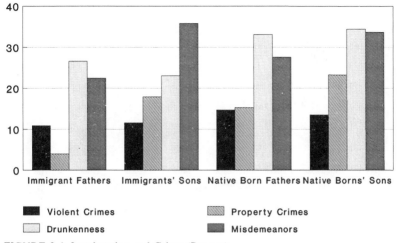

FIGURE 3.1 Immigration and Crime (Percent)

The prevalence of drunkenness crimes reflected ethnicity (as the term has been defined in this research). In ascending order, the rates of conviction were 14.5 percent of the Italians, 28.8 percent of the Portuguese, 33.5 percent of the *other* ethnics, and 34.6 percent of the Yankees were convicted for at least one drunkenness crime ($X^2_{(3)} = 15.35$, p = .0015).

Prevalence of misdemeanors reflected generational differences, with sons more likely than their fathers to be convicted for these crimes against order and ordinances ($X^2_{(1)} = 4.27$, p = .0387). Within the immigrant families, 22.5 percent of the fathers and 35.8 percent of the sons had been convicted for misdemeanors. Within the native-born families, 27.6 percent of the fathers and 33.7 percent of the sons had been convicted for misdemeanors.

None of the comparisons showed that immigrants or their sons were more likely to be convicted for crimes than were native-born men and their sons. The distributions are shown in Figure 3.1.

The prevalence of different types of crimes across ethnic groups is shown in Figure 3.2.

Although crime was not more prevalent among immigrant families than among native-born families, differential frequencies in convictions could account for a perception that immigrants were prone to crime. The general linear models procedure, SAS 6.0 (1990), was used to test this possibility for each of the four types of crime. Due to the redundancy of classes, a fully saturated model could not be used, so three sequential models were used instead. The first tested main, two-way, and three-way interacting effects of father's nativity, culture, and generation. The second tested main, two-way, and three-way interacting effects of father's nativity, father's religion, and generation. The third tested main effects of father's nativity, culture, and fa-

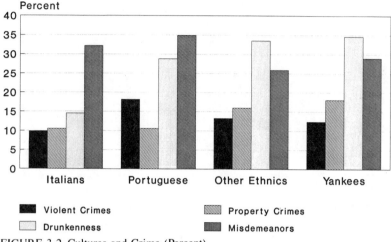

FIGURE 3.2 Cultures and Crime (Percent)

ther's religion, and generation together with the interacting effects of father's nativity by father's religion, culture by generation, and father's nativity by generation. Relations were considered to be significant if the probability for obtaining them by chance was less than .05.

The first model showed no significant relations with violent crimes. The second indicated that father's religion by generation was related to violent crimes ($F = 5.87$, df $= 1$, p $= .0156$), with Catholic fathers and Protestant sons convicted more frequently. The third model suggested an additional interaction between father's nativity and generation ($F = 4.68$, df $= 1$, p $= .0308$). Catholic native-born fathers and Protestant sons of immigrants had the highest crime rates for violence. These complex relations are shown in Table 3.4.

A somewhat different picture emerged in relation to property crimes. The first model revealed a main effect for generation ($F = 19.18$, p $= .0001$) and an interaction effect for culture by generation ($F = 2.82$, df $= 3$, p $= .0382$). The second and third models showed significant effects only for

TABLE 3.4   Fathers' Immigration and Religion: Mean Number of Convictions for Violent Crimes

	Immigrant		*Native-Born*	
	Catholic ($N = 137$)	*Protestant* ($N = 36$)	*Catholic* ($N = 104$)	*Protestant* ($N = 59$)
Fathers	0.20	0.08	0.40	0.10
Sons	0.15	0.31	0.17	0.14

TABLE 3.5 Fathers' Immigration and Culture: Mean Number of Convictions for Property Crimes

	Immigrant Fathers			Native-Born Fathers		
	N	Fathers	Sons	N	Fathers	Sons
Italians	69	0.03	0.25	7	0.57	0.57
Portuguese	27	0.15	0.15	6	0.33	0.17
Other Ethnics	77	0.04	0.87	17	0.18	0.47
Yankees	—	—	—	133	0.23	0.58

TABLE 3.6 Fathers' Immigration and Religion: Mean Number of Convictions for Drunkenness Crimes

	Immigrant		Native-Born	
	Catholic (N = 137)	Protestant (N = 36)	Catholic (N = 104)	Protestant (N = 59)
Fathers	0.94	0.97	4.05	1.02
Sons	0.67	1.00	1.69	0.64

generation. As can be seen in Table 3.5, the sons of Italian and *other* ethnic immigrants were likely to commit more property crimes than their fathers. Except for the sons of *other* ethnics, sons of immigrants were not likely to be convicted for more property crimes than were other similarly situated members of their generation. Immigrants had exceptionally low conviction rates.

Crimes of drunkenness had complex relationships involving the father's nativity, generation, and the father's religion. Statistics for the third model showed father's nativity ($F = 12.21$, $df = 1$, $p = .0005$), father's religion ($F = 12.78$, $df = 1$, $p = .0004$), and generation ($F = 5.99$, $df = 1$; $p = .0146$) to be significant predictors of rates for drunkenness crimes. As shown in Table 3.6, Catholic native-born fathers had the highest rates of conviction for drunkenness and sons of native-born Protestants had the lowest conviction rates.

Crime rates for misdemeanors reflected only a three-way interaction among father's nativity, culture, and generation ($F = 3.17$, $df = 2$, $p = .0428$). Among immigrants, Portuguese fathers had the highest rates; but their sons had no higher rates than did sons of Italian or other ethnic immigrants. Conviction rates for misdemeanors are shown in Table 3.7.

SUMMARY AND DISCUSSION

A broad range of theories draws support from the belief that, historically, immigrants contributed disproportionately to crime in America. Evi-

TABLE 3.7   Fathers' Immigration and Culture: Mean Number of Convictions for Misdemeanors

	Immigrant Fathers			Native-Born Fathers		
	N	Fathers	Sons	N	Fathers	Sons
Italians	69	0.33	0.62	7	1.57	0.42
Portuguese	27	1.18	0.62	6	0.00	0.83
Other						
Ethnics	77	0.35	0.69	17	0.59	0.59
Yankees	—	—	—	133	0.62	0.71

dentiary support has seemed to come from some studies that confounded socioeconomic conditions with nativity. Some theorists argue that immigrant groups lived in poverty when they came to America and that they were therefore temporary members of the *dangerous class*. As time passed and they became assimilated (the story goes), their conditions improved and they began to practice more socialized behavior. Variations of the theory have turned on whether the benefits of assimilation occur through decreased anomie accompanying increasing acceptance of middle-class norms or through successful participation in the competition for what is commonly believed to be the American style of achieving success. The present study raises questions about the fundamental claim on which these theories rest.

The study used official court records to ascertain criminality. Classifications of nativity, ethnicity, and religion came from independent records. Generation was controlled in the analyses. All the families had resided in impoverished areas of Cambridge and Somerville, Massachusetts.

The analyses showed that immigrants were *not* more likely than similarly situated native-borns to commit crimes of violence or property crimes. Nor were they more likely to be convicted for crimes related to drunkenness. The proportion of sons of immigrants who were convicted for misdemeanors was only slightly, and not reliably, greater than that of the same generation in native-born families. Among the fathers, immigrants were slightly, and not reliably, less likely to be convicted.

These results suggest that there has been misspecification of how crime is related to immigration, ethnicity, and religion. Differences in the frequencies of offending could provide a reasonable basis for the misspecification. Sons of Protestant immigrants had relatively high frequencies for crimes of violence; such was not the case for sons of Catholic immigrants. Sons of *other* ethnic immigrants had relatively high frequencies for crimes against property; such was not the case for sons of Italian or Portuguese immigrants. Immigrants themselves were less frequently convicted for both types of crime than were fathers born in the United States.

Of course what was true for Cambridge and Somerville may not be true for other locations. Nevertheless, correct identification of the causes relating phenomena turn upon finding those descriptions under which the relationships can be considered invariant across conditions. At least among those living in disordered, crowded, rundown areas considered in this study, neither immigrants nor their offspring were particularly likely to commit crimes.

Parallels have been drawn between the experiences of immigrants from Europe and the experiences of blacks who have migrated to northern cities. Arguments resting on such parallels have claimed that time will heal the wounds now festering in urban areas. The analogy on which this argument is based appears to rest on mistaken assumptions, so the conclusions should carry little weight.

It seems plausible that attributions of crime to immigrants has been a result of confusion and prejudice. The fact that immigrants lived in crowded, run-down, impoverished areas and that crime was rampant in such areas could lead to an assumption that immigrants were responsible for the crime. The ecological fallacy represented by such errors has been documented for other phenomena. Another form of confusion could occur because the immigrant criminals might be more memorable, thus seeming to account for a higher proportion of the disorders reported by contemporary observers. And finally, of course, the belief that immigrants were responsible for many of the ills of the city would be a not unexpected outcome of the widespread prejudices found with incoming foreigners seen as "babbling in alien tongues and framed by freakish clothes" (Barth, 1980, p. 15).

Unfortunately, what appears to be a false premise lies at the foundation of many *strong* theories. It remains to be seen whether a reexamination of the premises will lead to greater tolerance of differences or more accurate assessments of the current problems besetting American cities.

REFERENCES

Abbott, G. 1915. "Immigration and Crime." *Journal of Criminal Law and Criminology* 6, 4, 522–32.

Axinn, J., and Levin, H. 1975. *Social Welfare: A History of the American Response to Need.* New York: Dodd, Mead.

Baltzell, E. D. 1964. *The Protestant Establishment: Aristocracy and Caste in America.* New York: Vintage Books.

Barth, G. 1980. *City People.* New York: Oxford University Press.

Bell, D. 1960. *The End of Idealogy.* Glencoe, Ill.: Free Press.

Board of State Charities of Massachusetts. 1872. *Eighth Annual Report.* Boston: Board of State Charities of Massachusetts.

Cloward, R. A., and Ohlin, L. E. 1960. *Delinquency and Opportunity.* New York: Free Press.

Gans, H. T. 1962/1982. *The Urban Villagers.* New York: Free Press.

Gault, R. H. 1932. *Criminology.* Boston: D. C. Heath.

Glazer, N., and Moynihan, D. P. 1963. *Beyond the Melting Pot.* Cambridge: M.I.T. Press.

Gordon, M. M. 1964. *Assimilation in American Life: The Role of Race, Religion, and National Origin.* New York: Oxford University Press.

Hartshorne, T. L. 1968. *The Distorted Image: Changing Conceptions of the American Character since Turner.* Cleveland: Press of Case Western Reserve University.

Hawes, J. M. 1971. *Children in Urban Society: Juvenile Delinquency in Nineteenth-Century America.* New York: Oxford University Press.

Hawkins, D. (1993). "Crime and Ethnicity." pp. 89–120 In Brian Forst (ed.), *The Socio-Economics of Crime and Justice.* New York: M. E. Sharpe.

Hicks, J. D. 1931/1961. *The Populist Revolt: A History of the Farmers' Alliance and the People's Party.* Lincoln: University of Nebraska Press.

Hobbs, A. H. 1943. "Criminality in Philadelphia: 1790–1810 compared with 1937." *American Sociological Review* 8, 198–202.

Hofstadter, R. 1955. *The Age of Reform: From Bryan to F.D.R.* New York: Alfred A. Knopf.

Hogan, D. J. 1985. *Class and Reform: School and Society in Chicago, 1880–1930.* Philadelphia: University of Pennsylvania Press.

Lane, R. 1979. *Violent Death in the City.* Cambridge: Harvard University Press.

Lukoff, I. F., and Brook, J. S. 1974. "A sociocultural exploration of reported herion use." In C. Winick (ed.), *Sociological Aspects of Drug Dependence* (35–59). Cleveland: CRC.

Menninger, W. C. 1947. "The role of psychiatry in the world today." *American Journal of Psychiatry* 104(Sept.), 155–63.

Nelli, H. S. 1969. "Italians and Crime in Chicago: The Formative Years, 1890–1920." *American Journal of Sociology* 74, 4, 373–91.

Panunzio, C. 1932. "The Foreign Born and Prohibition." *Annals of the American Academy of Political and Social Science* 163, 147–54.

Park, R. E., Burgess, E. W., and McKenzie, R. D. 1925/1967. *The City.* Chicago: University of Chicago Press.

Powell, E. H. 1966. "Crime as a function of anomie." *Journal of Criminal Law, Criminology, and Police Science* 57, 161–71.

SAS Institute. 1990. Cary, North Carolina: Author.

Shaw, C. R., and McKay, H. D. 1942/1972. *Juvenile Delinquency and Urban Areas.* Chicago: University of Chicago Press.

Sinclair, A. 1951/1962. *Prohibition, The Era of Excess.* Boston: Little, Brown.

Suttles, G. D. 1968. *The Social Order of the Slum: Ethnicity and Territory in the Inner City.* Chicago: University of Chicago Press.

Taft, D. R. 1936. "Nationality and crime." *American Sociological Review* 1, 724–36.

Tarde, G. 1897/1969. "Criminal youth." In T. N. Clarke (ed), *On Communication and Social Influence: Selected Papers.* Chicago: University of Chicago Press.

Thernstrom, S. 1964/1970. *Poverty and Progress: Social Mobility in a Nineteenth Century City.* New York: Atheneum.

———. 1973. *The Other Bostonians: Poverty and Progress in the American Metropolis, 1880–1970.* Cambridge, Mass.: Harvard University Press.

van Vechten, C. C. 1941. "Criminality of the foreign-born." *Journal of Criminal Law and Criminology* 32, 139–47.

Ward, D. 1989. *Poverty, Ethnicity, and the American City, 1840–1925.* New York: Cambridge University Press.

Warner, S. B., Jr. 1962. *Streetcar Suburbs: The Process of Growth in Boston, 1870–1900.* Cambridge: Harvard University Press.

Weber, A. F. 1899/1963. *The Growth of Cities in the Nineteenth Century: A Study in Statistics.* Ithaca: Cornell University Press.

M. CRAIG BROWN
BARBARA D. WARNER

4

The Political Threat of Immigrant Groups and Police Aggressiveness in 1900*

Not unlike the 1960s, the turn of the century was a period of cultural and political upheaval in urban America. Immigrants swelled the size of America's cities creating the potential for economic, cultural, and political conflict between immigrant and native-born Americans. In this study we examine police aggressiveness as a response to this potential conflict, much like previous studies have examined policing as a response to the threat of racial conflict in American cities during the latter half of the twentieth century. We focus on police aggressiveness in arrests for drunkenness, a crime with considerable police discretion and one directly associated with immigrant social life at the turn of the century.

We also go beyond much of the previous literature by examining the political dimensions of the conflict between minority and majority groups and their consequences for policing. The decades around the turn of the century were the era of the great urban political machines. Machine politicians built their organizations by attending to the interests of the immigrant community, mobilizing votes of the foreign-born, and seeking to control urban government agencies like the police. In response, native-born Americans, attempting to maintain cultural hegemony and political power, fought bitterly to reduce the influence of ethnic machines by supporting reform candidates and attempting to implement reform structures like merit systems in urban government.

We examine the impact of two dimensions of the foreign-born population on political structure and policing. First, we examine the relative size of the foreign-born population in a city as an indication of the threat posed by immigrants. Second, we analyze the diversity in national origins of the immigrant community. Although a large immigrant population may have been unsettling to native-born citizens, immigrants who did not share a common culture or language were unlikely to form the durable political coalitions necessary to get power and influence. While most immigrants may have been sympathetic to the appeals of machine politicians, each group had its own political favorites and some ethnic groups felt enough enmity toward their fellow immigrants to forge political ties with the native-born (Meagher, 1985; Kolesar, 1989). Therefore, we explore how the relative size and diversity of the foreign-born population influenced urban politics and, in turn, police aggressiveness in the fifty largest American cities in 1900.

THEORETICAL BACKGROUND

The Threat Hypothesis

The theoretical roots of most research on variations in crime control due to differences in the relative size of a minority group population can be traced to Blalock's (1967) *threat hypothesis.* The threat hypothesis suggests that as minority group membership grows, majority members will intensify their efforts to maintain dominance. In her recent work based on the threat hypothesis, Jackson (1989) argues that "minority group threat is based on fear of losing dominance to a culturally dissimilar group. It is influenced by minority size because social disorganization, cultural differences, and sociopolitical dominance questions are more pressing where the subordinate group is larger" (p. 5).

It is often argued that the crime control apparatus is one key resource the majority group has at its disposal to combat minority threat. As the state's first line of crime control, the police have thus become the central subjects of threat research. Researchers have examined the effects of the percentage nonwhite on police force size (Greenberg, Kessler, and Loftin, 1985; Liska, Lawrence, and Benson, 1981; Jacobs, 1979), municipal expenditures on policing (Jackson and Carroll, 1981; Jackson, 1989), arrest rates (Liska and Chamlin, 1984), and police use of deadly force (Liska and Yu, 1992). The evidence strongly suggests that, controlling for the actual level of crime, policing is positively related to the percent nonwhite. Thus, in contrast to public choice theorists and functionalists who argue that police size and police activity are directly driven by the public's demand to control crime, these studies show that the size of the minority population explains an increment to the variance in policing beyond the level of crime.

Nonetheless, the generality of the relationship between minority group size and policing is questionable in three ways. First, almost all these studies address only one historical period (the latter half of the twentieth century), and only the relationship between whites and nonwhites.[1] Second, the specific nature of the *threat* and the mechanisms through which it operates have seldom been examined. Blalock's development of the threat hypothesis actually involves two types of threats, one related to power and one to economic competition. The distinction between these types of threats is seldom made. Most studies simply use the minority percentage of the population to globally define the level of threat, neither specifying nor measuring the political or economic arrangements threatened by increases in minority group size. Third, because they have not specified mechanisms, most studies have examined only the *potential* for change in social control implied by threat, and have only peripherally addressed the actual impact of minority group threat on political change. By focusing on the *political* threat of immigrants, a turn-of-the-century minority group, and the mediating role of urban political structure and culture in aggressiveness of policing, the present study redresses many of the weaknesses of earlier crime control research.

The Political Nature of Minority Group Threat

Blalock's (1967) presentation of the threat hypothesis includes an explicitly political dimension: the power threat to the majority group's political stability. Blalock argues that "the 'power threat' factor can be interpreted as representing a fear of *political* power in the hands of the minority" (p. 147, emphasis in original). He also suggests that as the minority group percentage increases, the majority group's discriminatory behavior should increase at an increasing rate.

The political nature of minority group threat has rarely been investigated. One of the earliest threat studies used the level of civil rights activities by blacks as a specific indicator of political unrest and therefore political threat (Jackson and Carroll, 1981). They suggested that "civil rights mobilization activity—although it was nonviolent and noncriminal—might have been threatening to whites because it threatened to change the role of a subordinate group in local politics" (p. 294). Their findings show that both threat variables (percent black and civil rights mobilization activities) were positively related to municipal policing expenditures. Nonetheless, though they suggest that political change is the mechanism translating threat into action, this claim is not explicitly tested.

Jackson and Carroll, however, do provide additional support for Blalock's formulation of the threat hypothesis, reporting a nonlinear relationship between percent black and police expenditures. This result indirectly demonstrates the political nature of the threat of minority groups since low but increasing levels of percent black are associated with increasing expenditures until blacks constitute a majority, translate their numbers into political power, and decrease expenditures.

Jackson's (1989) recent longitudinal study of city police expenditures during the 1970s further explores the political nature of crime control. By examining structural characteristics of cities and newspaper articles related to crime and policing, she explains changes in police expenditures and police-community relations. Detroit provides an interesting example. Changes in Detroit's demographic makeup during the 1970s resulted in a city where blacks were the majority (63 percent) by the end of the decade. At this point Detroit had also elected a black mayor and, according to newspaper coverage, police community relations had improved and budgetary cuts in policing were subsequently made. Jackson states:

> As the city's demographic profile changed, tipping the balance to majority black, city residents assumed greater control over the police, especially over citizen complaint procedures. The perceived value of police officers in terms of citizen safety and the overall crime rate was being recalculated and reduced in light of the city's budget deficit. (p. 74)

Police strength became less of a priority because "political control of the city had been resolved" (p. 75).

The political nature of minority group threat has also been studied in relationship to urban political culture and structure. Brown and Warner (1992) found that the percentage of foreign-born in cities at 1900 was positively related to arrest rates for drunkenness. The results also show that political machines decreased arrest rates while reform institutions like civil service increased arrest rates. Indeed, the impact of percent foreign-born was largely explained by controls for political variables. Hence, in turn-of-the-century American cities, political culture and structure mediated minority group threat.

This paper extends our previous research by considering an additional dimension of the foreign-born population of cities in 1900 and further exploring the mechanisms mediating threat and crime control. We analyze how the size and diversity of the foreign-born population influence political control and, in turn, police aggressiveness. The power threat hypothesis suggests that the majority group is threatened by the potential of a growing minority group to mobilize their political clout and dominate elections. We argue that the extent to which immigrants represented a viable political threat was not solely due to their relative numbers but also dependent upon their homogeneity. Immigrants, regardless of their numbers, were not monolithic in interests or actions. Therefore, understanding the political threat posed by foreign-born groups requires consideration of both size and diversity.

Hypotheses

We translate the general threat hypothesis into several specific hypotheses involving immigrants at the turn of the century. First, we expect that the relative size of the foreign-born population will positively affect the arrest rate for drunkenness, controlling for the level of drinking and the number of police. We also examine diversity in national origins as an inverse measure of the minority group's capacity for mobilization, hypothesizing that the diversity of the immigrant community will undercut the ability of immigrants to organize politically and increase the power of the dominant native-born group to influence police and maintain high arrest rates.

We further hypothesize that political variables mediate the impact of immigrant group size and mobilization capacity on the dominant group's policing response. Specifically, we hypothesize that the presence of a political machine represents a decrease in the power of the heretofore dominant native-born group and therefore should decrease the arrest rate. In contrast, reform institutions in city government should embody the values of the native-born group that championed their adoption and are therefore hypothesized to increase arrest rates. Further, we hypothesize that the effect of the size of the foreign-born population will diminish once these political variables are added to the equation. Finally, we believe that the diversity of the foreign-born population is central to their mobilization capacity and consequently their ability to gain political control and control of policing. As a result, low levels of diversity in the immigrant community should increase the probability that a political machine will gain control and decrease arrest rates.

DATA AND MEASURES

The Rate of Arrests for Drunkenness

Police aggressiveness is measured by the number of arrests for drunkenness per ten thousand population for each of the fifty largest cities in 1900.[2] Included in this arrest category are the following offenses: "common drunk," "drunk and disorderly," and "all cases where drunkenness in any form was the primary cause of arrest" (U.S. Department of Labor, 1900, p. 919). Public drunkenness is a behavior allowing for much discretion in judging the presence or degree sufficient to warrant arrest. Studying the policing of activities with high levels of police discretion is important, because in these cases police behavior tends to directly reflect departmental policies (see, for example, Wilson, 1968). Harring (1983) argues that departmental policy on such issues was "strongly influenced by bourgeois and petty-bourgeois demands and enforced through political channels, including the mayor, the city council, and such interest groups as chambers of commerce and boards of trade, and through such opinion makers as local newspapers" (p. 151). Thus, arrest rates for drunkenness make for an ideal test of how police policies and actions responded to the political threat posed by immigrants. In the average city, arrests for drunkenness were made at the rate of about 156 per 10,000 population. The fifty cities ranged from 27.8 to 432.9 per 10,000.

Immigrants

The potential for political change, or *threat* variable, is measured by the percentage foreign-born of each city's population (U.S. Census Office, 1902a, pp. 103–5). It is the percent foreign-born, reflecting the element of the city least assimilated to American culture, that probably best indicates the threat represented by immigration. However, we test this assumption by comparing the association between percent foreign-born and arrests and that between the percent foreign-parent in a city—ethnics who were native-born but had foreign parents (U.S. Census Office, 1901, pp. 866–69)—and the rate of arrests for drunkenness. Percent foreign-parents represents the threat of ethnics who were one generation away from immigrant status. The percentage of foreign-born averaged nearly 23 percent and ranged from less than 3 percent to nearly 48 percent. Percent foreign-parent averaged about 32 percent and ranged from 5 percent to over 51 percent.

Foreign-Born National Diversity

The diversity of the immigrant community is measured with a heterogeneity index that takes into account the distribution of the immigrant population among ten principal ethnic groups defined by national origins. The ten national origins used in the diversity measure were: Austria, Bohemia, and Hungary; Canada; Denmark, Norway, and Sweden; England, Scotland, and Wales; Germany; Ireland; Italy; Poland; Russia; and other. For the typical city, the first nine categories comprised 92 percent of the foreign-born population.[3] The diversity index is calculated by subtracting from 1 the sum of the squared proportions of immigrants in each group ($1-\Sigma p_i^2$). With ten categories, the maximum diversity would therefore be .9—that is, if each of the ten national origins comprised 10 percent of the ethnic population. The diversity index averaged .76 and ranged from .52 to .85 across the fifty cities in our sample.

Urban Politics

We examine the political culture and structure of a city with two variables: the presence or absence of a political machine controlling the city government, and the number of years since the adoption of a merit system governing employee appointments and promotions. Machine politics involves political mobilization based on patronage, favoritism, or other material inducements and grassroots political organization in a city's neighborhoods (Scott, 1969; Wolfinger, 1972; Shefter, 1976; Guterbock, 1980). Our measure is based on historical descriptions of the cities in our sample. (For a more complete discussion of our coding methods, see Brown and Halaby, 1984, 1987; Brown and Warner, 1992.) A city was classified as having a citywide machine if descriptions identified a political machine that controlled the mayor's office and a majority on the city council for successive elections. Other cities included a few having no machines in 1900 and many cities with machines of a neighborhood (that is, less than citywide) scope. Seven cities had citywide machines. Five of the fifty cities were coded as missing because historical documentation was too thin to permit coding.[4]

The second political variable is an indicator of reform. An important goal of structural reformers was to replace the particularism of machine politics with *merit* considerations—universalistic appointment and advancement criteria for public employment. The institutionalization of merit system reform in each city in 1900 was captured by the number of years (expressed in log terms to compensate for skewness) that *at least* the city police department had been covered by a merit system. The year in which the merit system was implemented is based on a survey of city personnel departments. Dates were verified by obtaining either a copy of the enabling legislation or the first civil service rules. Thirty-four percent of the cities had merit systems in 1900. Among cities adopting merit systems, the average merit system had been in place for a little more than ten years. The range was from a low of one year, for cities that had just adopted a merit system as the turn of the century approached, to a high of sixteen years.

Control Variables

The analyses in this study control for two additional variables: police force size and the level of alcohol consumption. Because cities in 1900 varied widely in the number of police per capita (Harring, 1983), the number of police per ten thousand population is included in all models (U.S. Department of Labor, 1900). Cities ranged from about five police per 10,000 population to about twenty-seven. The average was 12.6.

The second control variable is a proxy for the level of alcohol consumption in each city. Since cities with higher levels of alcohol consumption can be expected to have higher levels of drunkenness and therefore higher arrest rates, it was necessary to include a control for this variable. Although no data exist on the actual prevalence of drunkenness, we were able to devise two proxies. From information on the local brewing industry, the per capita value of malt liquor produced in each city was computed (U.S. Census Office, 1902b, pp. 1069–70). This variable is a reasonable proxy for consumption because technical limitations in preservation and distribution at the turn of the century meant that breweries "served a strictly local market" (Timberlake, 1963, p. 103). In the average city, $10.42 worth of beer and ale was brewed per citizen. The low was zero in dry cities and the maximum was $48.72. The number of saloons per ten thousand population was also computed for each city (U.S. Department of Labor, 1900, pp. 934–35). Cities averaged about thirty-one bars per 10,000 population and ranged from zero to nearly eighty-eight. These two variables ($r = .501$) were standardized and summed to create one overall proxy for the level of alcohol consumption.

RESULTS

Table 4.1 reports ordinary least squares estimates of the equations that test the logic of our theoretical arguments. Throughout, we assume that the foreign-born segment of the urban population best represents the threat of ethnics in turn-of-the-century American cities. We tested that assumption by comparing the association between percent foreign-born and arrest rates for drunkenness ($r = .32$) and that between percent foreign-parent, the percentage of ethnics who were native-born but had foreign parents, and the rate of arrests for drunkenness ($r = .006$). These associations[5] provide some support for the idea that the percent foreign-born is the most sensitive threat variable. Natives with foreign-born parents were well on the road to cultural assimilation and may well have moved to parts of the city less associated with an immigrant lifestyle and less likely to attract the attention of the police. Immigrants were clustered in the central-city neighborhoods favored by machine politicians, associated with social disorganization, and aggressively patrolled by the police.

Equations 1 and 2 estimate the net impact of the variables describing the foreign-born community and urban politics, respectively. Equation 1 considers the percent foreign-born and diversity variables along with the basic control variables. The percent foreign-born variable is positive and significant, with each percentage point increase adding a little less than two and one-half arrests per 10,000 population. As predicted, the diversity variable is positive and more than twice its standard error. The scale of the diversity variable, from zero to nearly one, means that its coefficient, 322.396, can be

TABLE 4.1   Unstandardized Ordinary Least Squares Coefficients for Selected Regressions: U.S. Cities, 1900

	Equation/Dependent Variable				
	1	*2*	*3*	*4*	*5*
	Arrest Rate	*Arrest Rate*	*Years/Since*		*Arrest Rate*
	for	*for*	*Adoption of*	*Citywide*	*for*
Independent Variable	*Drunkenness*	*Drunkenness*	*Merit System*	*Machine*	*Drunkenness*
Alcohol	-17.671*	-13.287	-0.058	0.071*	-10.817
consumption	(6.761)	(7.552)	(0.091)	(0.031)	(7.377)
Police per 10,000	10.282*	10.075*	0.044	0.007	9.726*
population	(2.294)	(2.309	(0.031)	(0.010)	(2.204)
Percent foreign-born	2.442*		0.045*	-0.002	1.097
	(1.012)		(0.014)	(0.004)	(1.100)
National diversity	322.396*		-1.845	-1.520*	377.065*
	(147.700)		(1.979)	(0.710)	(166.401)
Years since adoption		32.309*			28.302*
of merit system		(10.145)			(11.112)
Citywide machine		-79.407*			-48.884
		(35.376)			(35.905)
Constant	-276.242*	16.089	0.569	1.284*	-294.619*
	(114.982)	(31.134)	(1.541)	(0.564)	(132.817)
R²	0.492	0.523	0.242	0.290	0.589
Number of cities	50	45	50	45	45

*Coefficient more than twice its standard error.
Notes: Arrest rates are per 10,000 population.
Years since adoption of merit system are in natural log terms.
Numbers in parentheses are standard errors.

interpreted as the net impact on arrests of a full-range change in diversity—that is, a change of one—from complete homogeneity to maximum heterogeneity. It therefore appears that the organizational capacity of the immigrant community, as indicated by the degree of ethnic diversity, plays an important role in the rate at which arrests for drunkenness were made. Net of the level of alcohol consumption, the size of the police force, and the magnitude of the political threat represented by the relative size of the foreign-born population in a city, communities with foreigners drawn from a diversity of national origins had much higher arrest rates. At this stage of the analysis we can only presume that cities with less diversity were more capable of political organization and were able to turn that capacity into lower arrest rates, but we examine this issue further in Equations 4 and 5.

In keeping with prior theorizing and research, we performed functional form experiments allowing percent foreign-born to have linear, quadratic, and cubic terms. We also examined scatterplots between drunkenness and diversity, and estimated a model with just the control variables and the diversity variable in linear and quadratic forms. These experiments came to very little. With respect to percent foreign-born, there was at least some indication of a curvilinear pattern similar to the one reported by Jackson and Carroll (1981). However, the scatterplot suggested that most of the curvilinearity was due to a few extreme cases, and indeed the exclusion of one city (Atlanta) reduced the higher order terms to nonsignificance. Atlanta had a very high arrest rate for drunkenness but very few immigrants, the high arrest rate apparently stemming from another *threatening* group—poor blacks (Watts, 1973).[6] When it came to the diversity variable, there were no results supporting a curvilinear pattern at all.

We also performed another kind of functional form experiment by allowing an interaction term for percent foreign-born and diversity. We hypothesized that the effect of diversity may be conditional on the size of the foreign-born population. That is, the effect of the diversity of the immigrant community on arrest rates might vary depending on the size of the foreign-born population. However, this interaction term did not even approach significance, leaving the additive model involving percent foreign-born and ethnic diversity as the most successful to this point. To capture the joint effects of these two variables it is apparently not necessary to invoke more complicated models.[7]

Equation 2 estimates the net impact of the political variables on arrest rates for drunkenness. Because it was not possible to determine the turn-of-the-century politics of five of the cities, this equation is based on forty-five cities. Both political variables have coefficients greater in magnitude than twice their standard errors. The coefficient of the merit system variable is positive, indicating higher arrest rates for drunkenness where bureaucratic reforms were institutionalized in urban government. In contrast, the presence of a political machine in control of city government meant fewer arrests: net of other variables, the police in cities controlled by a machine averaged nearly 80 fewer arrests per 10,000 population than police in other cities. It is noteworthy that the coefficient of the variable measuring alcohol consumption is no longer more than twice its standard error in Equation 2, due mainly to a strong association between alcohol consumption and the presence of a citywide machine ($r = .45$) and empirically demonstrating the close tie between politics and the production and selling of alcohol in turn-of-the-century cities. It appears that machines paid their debts to immigrants, and to the producers and sellers of alcohol, by using their influence to set lenient policies toward the policing of alcohol.

Equations 3 and 4 explore the connections between the political variables and the size and diversity of the foreign-born population. If the political variables act as mediators in the link between foreign-born threat and police aggressiveness, they themselves must be related to the variables describing variations in the immigrant community. Equation 3 regresses years since the adoption of a merit system on the immigration variables and the usual controls for alcohol consumption and the number of police. Only the percent foreign-born has any impact on the institutionalization of merit system reform. Because the merit system variable is expressed in log terms, the coefficient of the foreign-born variable means that for every one percentage point increase in the relative size of the foreign-born population, merit system reform will be institutionalized about one-half of one percent longer. The threat of a large immigrant population therefore did translate into reform effort. The structural residues of reform—government and police bureaucracies—were a major byproduct of the immigrant threat. Whether this bureaucratization of the police in turn translated into more aggressive policing will be addressed in Equation 5.

Equation 4 regresses the presence or absence of a citywide political machine on the immigration and control variables. Two variables have an impact on the probability of machine control in 1900. First, the level of alcohol consumption increases the probability of machine control, demonstrating the tie between machine politicians and alcohol entrepreneurs. Second, as predicted, increases in the diversity variable decrease the probability of machine control. This suggests that machine politicians had an easier time consolidating control in cities with only a small number of significant ethnic groups and that machine control may have carried the impact of ethnic homogeneity to policing.

Because the citywide machine variable was dichotomous, the OLS version of Equation 4 was in reality a linear probability model. In such circumstances a logistic regression is often a better functional form (Hosmer and Lemeshow, 1989). As a result, we reestimated Equation 4 with a maximum likelihood logistic regression routine. The results were replicated, but the coefficients for the alcohol consumption and diversity variables were only about one and one-half their standard errors, suggesting caution in the interpretation of these effects. Nonetheless, the results are at least suggestive for a small sample size of forty-five cities.

Equation 5 estimates the combined effect on the arrest rate for drunkenness of all the elements: immigrants, politics, and control variables. Several key findings emerge. The merit system variable is positive and significant, sustaining the political hypotheses discussed above. Merit systems tended to increase aggressive policing resulting in higher arrest rates. Second, the coefficient of the percent foreign-born variable drops to less than half its magnitude in Equation 1 and much less than twice its standard error. In light of the results of Equation 3, where only percent foreign-born was linked to merit system institutionalization, this means that merit system reform mediates the political threat represented by immigration. The bureaucratization of police departments was at least in part a response to immigration and apparently had the effect intended by reformers: a degree of political insulation and the rationalization of policing meant higher arrest rates for a lifestyle crime like drunkenness.

Third, the diversity variable continues to be positive and significant, showing the direct impact of the organizational capacity variable in shaping the behavior of agencies like the police. Fourth, in contrast to Equation 2, in Equation 5 the political machine variable, still negative, drops to about half its former magnitude and somewhat less than twice its standard error. However, if the two weakest variables (alcohol consumption and percent foreign-born) are trimmed from the equation, the coefficient of the machine variable once again becomes significant.

Therefore, foreign-born diversity has both direct and indirect effects on arrest rates for drunkenness. High diversity in the immigrant community meant that it was difficult for machine politicians to form durable winning coalitions; low diversity meant easier mobilization of the few prominent ethnic groups and a higher probability of winning control of urban politics and policing. Once achieved, machine control of city government meant a more lenient attitude toward lifestyle issues related to the immigrant community. Of course, the direct effect of diversity on arrests means that not all the impact of that variable was carried through political machines. Other unmeasured variables, some political and some not, must be specified in further research.

These results extend our previous political interpretation of the aggressiveness with which turn-of-the-century police made arrests for drunkenness (Brown and Warner, 1992). Large immigrant populations presented a political threat to native-born Americans, and they responded with structural reforms in urban politics like merit systems and increased arrest rates. But where the foreign-born community was not ethnically diverse, there was a better opportunity for machine politicians to gain city power. The interests of the immigrant community in freeing itself from the regulation of lifestyle issues by the police, and the support of producers and sellers of alcohol, translated into a liberal outlook by machine politicians toward drinking and consequentially decreased arrest rates.

DISCUSSION

Turn-of-the-century American cities provide a rich environment in which to explore issues related to the threat of a minority group, urban politics, and the aggressiveness of the police in making arrests for a lifestyle crime like drunkenness. Immigrants were drawn to the opportunities in an increasingly urban and industrial America. Their numbers and customs made them a threat to established cultural, economic, and political arrangements, and created considerable potential for conflict with native-born Americans. Politicians and the police were at the center of these conflicts. Machine politicians tended to support the interests of immigrants while reform-oriented politicians reflected middle-class positions. The behavior of the police, particularly with regard to sensitive issues like public drunkenness, was in part the result of these two political forces.

And though we have pursued the political linkages much further than earlier research, the broad outlines of what we have found are consistent with what has been found in different times, different places, and with different threatening groups. Our findings therefore substantiate the view that social control is not entirely driven by levels of crime, but is in part a response to potentially threatening groups. Further, these findings demonstrate some of the political variables mediating threat and social control.

Our research has focused on the political aspect of threat. Although we believe the two political variables examined here were instrumental in shaping police policy, we do not mean to suggest an oversimplistic view of the political process. Other political variables, such as the ethnic and social class composition of city councils and linkages between government and the police, should also be investigated. The extent to which policing was centralized may also have affected the extent to which police actually carried out departmental policy. This research is also limited in that it examined only two dimensions of the minority group: size and diversity. Other dimensions of the minority community that may affect their ability to obtain political power or make policy reflect their interests should also be investigated.

Finally, this historical analysis raises questions about the politics of policing in contemporary America. Like foreign-born immigrants in the beginning of this century, today's growing black and Hispanic urban populations may be viewed as threats to established cultural, economic, and political arrangements, creating a political perception of a need for increased levels of aggressive policing. For example, some authors (Livingston, 1992, pp. 37–43) have suggested that political cries for "law and order" in the 1980s were in reality symbolic statements attempting to maintain "a racially unjust society."

Although the literature examining the relationship between percent nonwhite and policing tends to show that the effect of the racial variable has decreased in recent decades (Liska et al., 1981; Greenberg et al., 1985; Jackson, 1989), the political mechanisms through which this decrease may have come about have rarely been examined (Jackson, 1989, remains an exception). To what extent have recent gains in the control of urban politics by blacks and Hispanics affected the use of formal social control? What are the political structures in contemporary society for which control by *minority* groups may affect levels and aggressiveness of policing? These questions of contemporary connections between urban demographic makeup, political structure and control, and police behavior remain significant questions for the rest of this century and beyond.

NOTES

*The authors contributed equally to this chapter and appear in alphabetical order.

1. Jackson's (1989) inclusion of Hispanics is one recent exception to this.

2. The cities were Albany, Atlanta, Baltimore, Boston, Buffalo, Cambridge, Camden, Chicago, Cincinnati, Cleveland, Columbus, Dayton, Denver, Detroit, Fall River, Grand Rapids, Hartford, Indianapolis, Jersey City, Kansas City, Los Angeles, Louisville, Lowell, Memphis, Milwaukee, Minneapolis, Nashville, Newark, New Haven, New Orleans, New York, Omaha, Paterson, Philadelphia, Pittsburgh, Portland (Oregon), Providence, Reading, Richmond, Rochester, San Francisco, St. Joseph, St. Louis, St. Paul, Scranton, Seattle, Syracuse, Toledo, Wilmington, Worchester.

3. Analyses were also done using twenty-three ethnic categories for the diversity variable, but the results were the same as those using the smaller number of categories.

4. Dayton, Hartford, Newark, St. Paul, and Syracuse remain undocumented.

5. We also did regression analyses, finding percent foreign-parent to be a consistently unproductive variable. These results and the high correlation between percent foreign-born and percent foreign-parent ($r = .79$), especially in light of the small sample size, deterred us from using the two in one equation as twin candidates for threat variables.

6. For a more complete discussion of this issue and a related one discussing the larger role of percent black as another threat indicator in southern cities in 1900, see Brown and Warner (1992).

7. Equation 1 also shows that the number of police per 10,000 population exerts a powerful positive influence on arrests. As expected, the larger the police force size, the greater the city's capacity to make arrests. Surprisingly, however, the coefficient for alcohol consumption in Equation 1, although significant, is negative. Several explanations for the inverse relationship are possible. First, one could argue that the causal relationship is reversed and that vigorous policing of alcohol consumption decreased the public forms of consumption most likely to result in arrest. However, the historical evidence that the police were unable or unwilling to effectively regulate saloons and public drinking undermines this explanation. Second, it is possible that high

levels of alcohol consumption may have overwhelmed the capacity of the police to deal with the problem leading to a decreased arrest rate, a phenomenon termed *system overload* (Geerken and Gove, 1975, 1977) or *system strain* (Logan, 1975). Third, the negative relationship between alcohol consumption and arrests may indicate that the businessmen behind the large-scale production and distribution of alcohol, anxious to influence politicians and the police (Duis, 1983), were successful. In our opinion, this is the most likely explanation (Brown and Warner, 1992).

REFERENCES

Blalock, Hubert. 1967. *Toward a Theory of Minority-Group Relations.* New York: John Wiley.

Brown, M. Craig, and Charles N. Halaby. 1984. "Bosses, Reform, and the Socio-economic Bases of Urban Expenditure, 1890–1940." Pp. 69–89 in *The Politics of Urban Fiscal Policy,* edited by Terrence J. McDonald and Sally K. Ward. Beverly Hills, Calif.: Sage.

————.1987. "Machine politics in America, 1870–1945." *Journal of Interdisciplinary History* 17, 587–612.

Brown, M. Craig, and Barbara D. Warner. 1992. "Immigrants, urban politics, and policing in 1900." *American Sociological Review* 57:293–305.

Duis, Perry. 1983. *The Saloon: Public Drinking in Chicago and Boston, 1880–1920.* Champaign-Urbana: University of Illinois Press.

Geerken, Michael R., and Walter R. Gove. 1975. "Deterrence: Some theoretical considerations." *Law and Society Review* 9:497–513.

————.1977. "Deterrence, overload, and incapacitation: An empirical evaluation." *Social Forces* 56:424–47.

Greenberg, David F., Ronald C. Kessler, and Colin Loftin. 1985. "Social inequality and crime control." *Journal of Criminal Law and Criminology* 76:684–704.

Guterbock, Thomas M. 1980. *Machine Politics in Transition: Party and Community in Chicago.* Chicago: University of Chicago Press.

Harring, Sidney L. 1983. *Policing a Class Society: The Experience of American Cities, 1865–1915.* New Brunswick: Rutgers University Press.

Hosmer, David W., and Stanley Lemeshow. 1989. *Applied Logistic Regression.* New York: John Wiley.

Jackson, Pamela Irving. 1989. *Minority Group Threat, Crime, and Policing.* New York: Praeger.

Jackson, Pamela Irving, and Leo Carroll. 1981. "Race and the war on crime: The sociopolitical determinants of municipal police expenditures in 90 non-Southern U.S. cities." *American Sociological Review* 46:290–305.

Jacobs, David. 1979. "Inequality and police strength: Conflict theory and coercive control in metropolitan areas." *American Sociological Review* 44:913–25.

Kolesar, Robert J. 1989. "The politics of development: Worcester, Massachusetts, in the late nineteenth century." *Journal of Urban History* 3–28.

Liska, Allen E., and Mitchell B. Chamlin. 1984. "Social structure and crime control among macrosocial units." *American Journal of Sociology* 90:383–95.

Liska, Allen E., Joseph J. Lawrence, and Michael Benson. 1981. "Perspectives on the legal order: The capacity for social control." *American Journal of Sociology* 87:413–25.

Liska, Allen E., and Jiang Yu. 1992. "Specifying and testing the threat hypothesis: Police use of deadly force." Pp. 53–68 in Allen E. Liska's (ed.) *Social Threat and Social Control*. Albany: State University of New York Press.

Livingston, Jay. 1992. *Crime and Criminology*. Englewood Cliffs, N.J.: Prentice-Hall.

Logan, Charles. H. 1975. "Arrest rates and deterrence." *Social Science Quarterly* 56:376–89.

Meagher, Timothy J. 1985. " 'Irish all the time:' Ethnic consciousness among the Irish in Worcester, Massachusetts, 1880–1905." *Journal of Social History* 19:273–303.

Scott, James C. 1969. "Corruption, Machine Politics and Political Change." *American Political Science Review* 63:1142–58.

Shefter, Martin. 1976. "The emergence of the political machine: An alternative view." Pp. 14–44 in *Theoretical Perspectives on Urban Politics*, by W. Hawley et al. Englewood Cliffs, N.J.: Prentice-Hall.

Timberlake, James H. 1963. *Prohibition and the Progressive Movement, 1900–1920*. Cambridge: Harvard University Press.

U.S. Census Office. 1902a. *Abstract of the Twelfth Census of the United States*. Washington, D.C.: U.S. Government Printing Office.

————1902b. *Twelfth Census of the United States Manufacturers, Part II*. Washington, D.C.: U.S. Government Printing Office.

U.S. Department of Labor. 1900. *Statistics of Cities*. Vol 5. Washington, D.C.: U.S. Government Printing Office.

Watts, Eugene J. 1973. "The police in Atlanta, 1890–1905." *Journal of Southern History* 39:165–82.

Wilson, James Q. 1968. *Varieties of Police Behavior.* Cambridge: Harvard University Press.

Wolfinger, Raymond, 1972. "Why political machines have not withered away and other revisionist thoughts." *Journal of Politics* 34:365–98.

ERIC MONKKONEN

5

Racial Factors in New York City Homicides, 1800–1874

It is important to examine issues of race, ethnicity, and violence in a historical setting so that we may establish a perspective from which to view contemporary problems.[1] We may look back to a time when guns were rarer, when poverty was more widespread, and when racial discrimination was more intense, and ask what differences this made. There is more than an antiquarian interest that propels this quest: Gurr (1989) has surveyed a large body of research that indicates that our current high homicide rates and rates of other criminal violence are a relatively recent phenomenon. He shows how there is good evidence to believe that homicide and violent crime rates have been declining since the middle ages. Some European scholars argue that there has been a more general transition over the past six-hundred years from crimes of violence to theft (Soman, 1980)—known as the *violence au vol* thesis.

Lane's research on Philadelphia suggests that these patterns were not the same for African-Americans. After the Civil War, white homicide rates declined, while black homicide rates increased (1981, 1986, 1992). Lane shows how racial discrimination created what was a structurally different city for blacks, as opposed to the one for whites, including immigrants. He argues that these structural features account for the crime differences.

In particular, we can compare various newly arrived immigrants to African-Americans. We know that African-Americans faced increasing hostility from immigrants around the time of the Civil War and that all evidence points to their declining opportunities in the late 1850s (Hodges, 1986).[2]

Although the data limitations frustrate fine-grained analyses, a historical analysis makes clear some of the differences between the nineteenth and twentieth centuries. These differences serve to remind us that broad historical change affects interpersonal behavior and conflict. That they are affected suggests that such patterns can continue to change, that a criminal offense sometimes considered to be beyond the reach of social control is not beyond the reach of social and historical circumstance. In some ways, the exact nuances of change are less significant than that there is change at all.

The data base used here, constructed for an ongoing quantitative study of homicide in New York City, provides us with an opportunity to examine race, ethnicity, and homicide in the nineteenth century. When possible, I will compare race and ethnic groups drawn as finely as possible, but as the discussion of the data explains, when the data seem too fragmentary, I then generalize to a more aggregated level.

SETTING

It is essential to understand some of the relevant features of nineteenth-century New York City even before describing the data. Though very important, New York has never been a typical American city. In the first three quarters of the nineteenth century, it grew dramatically from a city of about sixty-thousand to become a metropolis of over a million. This astonishing growth made it America's largest metropolis, with a polyglot immigrant population after 1840. Its early size alone makes the city worth studying, for while atypical, it was by any kind of definition, the major American metropolis.

Because most of the homicides analyzed below occurred after the 1830s—95 percent in the half-century between 1834 and 1874—this description will focus on this mid-century period. By 1834, the city's population had reached a quarter-million, but it would not be until the last years of the 1840s that the transforming demographic event occurred: the flood of immigration from Ireland and Germany. In 1850, the city reached a half-million, and on the eve of the Civil War, over 800,000.

It may have had a foreign-born population as high as 20 percent in the 1820s, according to Rosenwaike (1972). In 1845, when the census began reporting birthplace tallies, the city had 135,000 foreign-born residents, about one-third of its population. By 1850 the figure had reached over a quarter-million; in 1860 it grew again to well over a third of a million—almost one-half the city was foreign-born.

Yet for the city's African-American population, there was a very different history—one of declension in size from 16,000 in 1840, to about

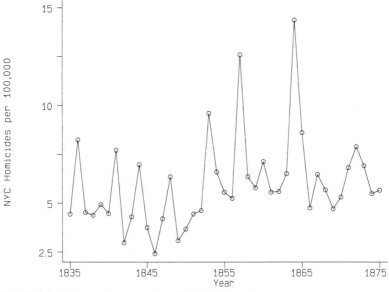

FIGURE 5.1 Homicides per capita, 1835–1875

12,000 in 1860, and to perhaps less than 10,000 in 1865. New York state had abolished slavery by 1827. Thus, by mid-century, less than 2 percent of the city's population was black. This demographic trajectory, so different for the rest of the city's people, tells us much. Traditionally, African-American men had worked on the city's docks, in its shipyards, and in various service occupations. The new immigrants competed vigorously, and sometimes violently, for these jobs.

This story had a tragic culmination in 1863, in the New York City draft riots. No matter how one interprets these riots, they always contain a base element of racism.[3] Triggered by the efforts to draft poor and immigrant workers, the city's white immigrant youth quickly turned their initial political protest into a race war against African-Americans. A large but never reliably established number died—many victims of vicious public lynchings. Not too surprisingly, after the riots, the city's black population decreased even faster. Even though we can outline this demographic history of black New Yorkers, we cannot yet establish precise population measures, and it is clear that census enumerations might be highly inaccurate. Thus, constructing at risk denominators is extremely difficult.

The personal violence of the riots horrified New Yorkers. But personal violence had been an increasing feature of city life well before 1863. The estimated per capita homicide rate had been increasing for several decades, reaching heights that would not again be reached until 1970. This grim feature of the nation's largest metropolis went undiscussed in the nineteenth-century media.[4] Figure 5.1 establishes the increasing violence of New York City in the mid-nineteenth century.

Data and Sources

The data consist of 1,559 murder cases. Ninety-five percent of these cases occurred after 1831 and before 1874. The small number (76) of pre-1831 cases are a result of fewer real homicides and more fragmentary sources. Variables include weapon, relationship of the killer to victim, and subsequent outcomes affecting the killer—arrest to execution. For both killer and victim, variables include gender, age, and race or ethnicity. Seemingly obvious inferences have been avoided, which has created more missing variables: for instance, a person mentioned as a *youth* has not been assigned an age, or seemingly ethnic names have not been given an ethnic code. The reason for this seemingly excessive caution is that Lane's Philadelphia study used German names to indicate ethnicity, when it was equally possibly that in Pennsylvania the person could have been fifth-generation American born. The one place I have made an interpretive leap is for some Irish-named people who were involved with other Irish born.

The data sources used here required detailed discussion, as their provenance suggests where the biases may lie. The data used for this study have been generated in the context of a long-term, comparative study of annual homicide rates in New York, Liverpool, and London. Outside Massachusetts, nineteenth-century vital statistics for the U.S.A. are very poor. There are no *official* sources. The closest to such would be the coroner's reports, which begin with detailed annual reports in 1866. Even these annual reports are fugitive sources, and for this reason were gathered in a single place as a research project on mortality by medical researcher Haven Emerson (1941, 1955).

The coroner was required to investigate and call a jury to examine all nonnatural deaths. These individual reports are available in the city archives. Prior to about 1823, they are fragmentary. Homicides comprise only a tiny part of these reports. After 1866, the summaries of these investigations were available in annual reports. The coroner's jury played a major role in determining how the deaths were reported. When the jury decided that the cause of death was not one man hitting another in a bar, but rather the fall to the floor or that the victim had a weak heart, the case would be tallied in the annual reports as an accidental death or as due to heart failure.

Juries were prone to do so in a society that still accepted physical violence between men as an ordinary part of social discourse. Few remember today that prior to his election to the presidency, Andrew Jackson had murdered one man in a gun fight, and that he had tried to murder others in violent attacks. In his day, these were understood as justified and exemplary of his manly virtues, virtually required because his honor and that of his wife had been slighted. In this world, gun murder could be interpreted as a duel; the beating to death of a senator as a *caning*. Coroners' juries reflected their world, and as a result, they found no murder where juries today would.

To gather data on homicide then, requires supplementing the coroners' reports. An initial check on the completeness of the 1866 homicide counts compared with those reported in the *New York Times* indicated some discrepancies, and further name comparisons have shown that for the pre-1870 years, the lists of homicide victims in the newspapers and in the coroner's records overlap but do not match completely. There was, in other words, an undercount by the coroner. The original manuscripts for the coroner are preserved in the New York City Archives in relatively complete form back to 1823, and sporadically for twenty-five years before that. The genealogist Kenneth Scott has transcribed essential details for all existent years prior to 1849 (1973, 1988, 1989, 1991).

Most of the data analyzed here have come from newspapers. After the 1820s and prior to the late 1870s, the press of New York City reported homicides with some vigor, if not with the constancy we might have wished. Typically there would be a notice of a fight or killing, which gave some detail of the event, the weapon, and the people involved. The media reported minor killings from elsewhere in the United States as well, giving some confidence that local events would not go unreported. In fact, the use of language tended to result in overreporting: *fatal* or *mortal* did not mean that a person had died, only that it seemed like they might die. All the killings reported here are those in which the newspaper report stated as a fact that the person was dead.

The newspapers of the day were particularly frustrating in the failure to follow stories that they had begun. Hundreds of reports involved a wounding where the conclusion was that the victim "surely will die." Did they die? We will never know because this conclusion often became a nonsequitur. Similarly, dozens of stories about killings, and subsequent murderers' arrests, never drew to a close. Was there a trial? a conviction? Did those sentenced to die, die?

Using the newspapers is complicated by several other factors as well. While by far the most consistent and reliable newspaper, the *New York Times*, began publication only in 1853. Compared to other papers, the *Times* exhibited less race bias than was typical for the era, in part because of its Republican leanings. For the era between the late 1820s and the 1850s, there are several newspapers that daily reported local news, like homicides: these included the *Daily-Tribune*. Prior to the mid-1820s, the reporting of what we called news was practically nonexistent. Newspapers served as means of financial communication for elites. Even so, careful searching has revealed homicide mentions do occur, and so my research continues to scan these early newspapers, including the *Commercial Advertiser, Evening Post,* and *Daily Citizen.*

Some supplemental information is available: for executions, a data set of all known executions in the U.S.A. was compiled by Watt Espy, so that for those few murderers executed, we are able to complete the stories (Espy, 1987). Aggregate data on those convicted of murder are also available through state reports, so that we can compare numbers of homicides to numbers convicted, but this cannot be done by name, at least not yet.

There is with these data a question that has plagued all criminologists: unreported offenses.[5] While we know today that murders are the crime most often cleared by arrest, we are treading on more speculative ground in the past. For instance, far more people die accidentally than by murder. As a port city in an era when swimming was a rare skill and bath tubs even rarer, New York had hundreds of drownings every year. How many of those "found drowned" were victims of murder? Forensic science was nonexistent, so the person "found drowned" was almost never called a murder victim (Johnson, forthcoming). Is it likely that hundreds of clever killers simply pushed their victims into the water, and that the data reported here only touch the dry land killings? I hope not. What is known about the killings that did get reported lends substantial plausibility to this hope. Simply put, most killers knew their victims, did not try very hard at all to run away, and exhibited no wisdom or cleverness in their behavior. It is almost impossible to imagine that they would bother to lure a victim to the docks, especially when a fight and subsequent killing so seldom resulted in trial or punishment.

A more difficult issue remains the nonreporting of details of importance to us today: race, ethnicity, and age. For the analysis below, I have used differing assumptions, as appropriate, about the nature of missing information. In each case I make these clear and try to indicate how the biases might run. Moreover, the data reported on here should be regarded as those generated by a work in progress. Probably when the newspapers or coroner failed to note ethnicity, the person was most often native born-white. But this *most often* could still have been half the time, so that the undercount of other white ethnics could have been very high. Sometimes historians have been forced to guess at ethnicity by names, but I have avoided that here, except when there is a very strong contextual as well as textual probability that the person's ethnicity can be inferred. Such a case would occur when an Irish-named person was involved in a conflict with another, and the second person, in another article, was identified as Irish.

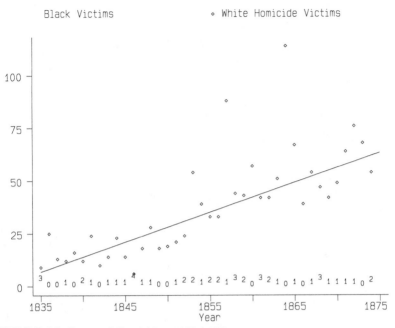

FIGURE 5.2 Counts of Homicides, 1830–1875

Trends—Fundamental Outlines

Although we cannot yet contrast the percapitized rates of black and nonblack homicides for lack of reliable population denominators, we can examine crude trends. Simply correlating the counts is not completely appropriate, because of the relative rarity of homicides. (Pearsonian correlation is .25, positive, but not very big.) Counts vary dramatically from one time period to another. For a small population, like the African-Americans, many years may elapse between homicides. One or two missing observations can make the difference between a perceived crime wave and feelings of security. Therefore, I have used the regression lines to construct slopes.[6] These are not percapitized: the slopes are of actual counts. Given that the black population was steady or declining over these years, the white population zooming upward the scatter looks about right, especially for the fitful occasions of black homicides.

Race and Ethnicity

A question of initial interest is the nature of interracial homicides. These can give some insight into race relations and the nature of social relationships in nineteenth-century New York. In must be noted that even here relationships

TABLE 5.1   Killer and Victim Races

| Victim Race | Killer Race | | Total |
	White	Black	
White	1405	27	1432
Black	23	27	50
Total	1428	54	1482

Pearson chi2 = 373.7290 Pr = 0.000 likelihood-ratio chi2(1) = 126.8062
Pr = 0.000

TABLE 5.2   Ethnic and Race Identities

| Victim's Ethnicity | Killer's Ethnicity | | | | | | Total |
	Black	U.S. white	Irish	German	Italian	Other	
Black	27	2	1	1	1	0	32
U.S. white	6	8	7	3	3	1	28
Irish	7	6	95	18	7	3	136
German	1	3	3	39	0	0	46
Italian	0	0	1	0	9	0	10
Other	3	4	7	9	1	6	30
Total	44	23	114	70	21	10	282

Pearson chi2(25) = 402.2995 Pr = 0.000

cannot be unambiguously inferred: a low level of interracial violence could simply be the result of high degrees of social segregation. Killer and victim races can first be examined under the assumption that all African-American killers or victims were noted as such, while native-born whites, or persons who appeared to be, would likely go unnoted. Beginning with this least restrictive definition of race and ethnicity, Table 5.1 tabulates by those identified as black versus all others, the assumption being that blacks would be more likely to be noted. Less than 4 percent of all killers or victims were black. The table shows that black victims were as likely to be killed by blacks as whites, while black killers were slightly more likely to kill blacks. This suggests some degree of racial motivation in the killings of blacks, dealt with further below.

In order to look more closely at ethnic and race relations between killer and victim, those victims and killers with ethnicity or race identified have been paired. Missing information reduces the total number of cases to 282 or about 20 percent of all killings. Table 5.2 displays the relationship: the diagonal shows that some ethnic/race pairing was common across the range of murders.

These figures can be interpreted several ways, but the most straightforward has to do with opportunity—killers and victims usually knew one another, were relatives, friends, workmates, or casual acquaintances. Even an interracial killing, the murder on Oct. 20, 1844, of James Chapple (probably white) by Samuel Riley (black), is best understood this way: Chapple was a sailor and Riley the cook on board the docked brig the *Francis P. Beck.* The most clustered, the Irish, had 83 percent of their victims from the same ethnic group, blacks had 61 percent from their group, Germans 56 percent, and Italians 42 percent. Irish killers and victims cluster strongly, suggesting their stronger degree of ethnic clustering. And, in this context, African-Americans were no different from other sociocultural groups.

At-Risk Populations

While the data analyzed here include over eighty years of New York City's history, 1750–1874, three-fourths of the cases are for the two decades 1854–1874. During these years, the city's population grew from about 600,000 to just over a million. Its African-American population, on the other hand, grew only slightly from 13,000 to about 14,000. If we take an imaginary population figure at the mid-point, about 800,000 and 13,500, we can contrast the homicides black and white in the ratio to populations—the black homicide rate equaling about twice the white one. (This ratio is based on the assumption that all black victims were reported as such, and that victims without racial identification were white.) By narrowing assumptions and defining the population at-risk more appropriately, these figures may be refined.

The corresponding mid-point estimates of native-born whites, Irish, Germans, and Italians are 414,000, 160,000, 109,000, and 1000.[7] Assuming that native-borns were the least likely to be so noted in homicide reports, in contrast to the foreign-born and blacks, a crude ratio of homicides by group at-risk setting native-born whites to 1, yields .8 for the Irish, .9 for the Germans, 2 for the African-Americans, 15 for Italians, and .7 for all foreign-born.[8] The foreign-born ratio to the native-born white ratio is almost certainly a vast underestimate, the foreign-born white homicide victims simply not being noted in the sources. The best both sets of comparative at-risk estimates can give us is a sense that the black homicide rates probably ranged from 1.6 to 2 times the white homicide rate.

Even this range of estimates may need to be modified by the notion of population at-risk, for homicide was both gender and age asymmetrical. Of the 1,397 nonblack victims where sex is mentioned, 78 percent were men: for blacks alone, the figure is 90 percent (for both killers and victims). Of the 555 victims where age is mentioned, 90 percent were between the ages of 17 and 50, 50 percent between 23 and 40: for 18 blacks alone, the figure is similar, 90 percent between the ages of 22 and 51, 50 percent between 26 and 40, although the low numbers of reported ages may bias these values.

The 1860 census of population reported age and sex distributions by race for New York county. Of the whites, 23.5 percent were males between 20 and 49; as contrasted with 23.3 percent of the black population. Yet one wonders about the believability of these data: by the 1910 census, 25.2 percent of the total white population were males between 20 and 49 years old, as compared to 30.9 percent of the black population. The 1910 age/sex distribution makes a notable difference: it alone would reduce the ratio of black to white homicides from 2 to 1.4. Changes of similar magnitude could occur for the other ratios. For the 1860 data, the question occurs of whether the decreasing population had been young men, or whether they had been miscounted. Recent studies suggest why the population counts might be biased. First, Margo Anderson's history of the U.S. Census establishes how volatile the issue of the black population was on the eve of the Civil War—especially the proportion of free versus enslaved blacks. Second, a recent issue of *Social Science History* devoted to the question of historical census undercounts shows that there were sometimes large count errors (Parkerson, 1991). Third, the controversy over counting the very poor and racial minorities in recent censuses emphasizes how even today the proper enumeration of the poor is difficult (Anderson, 1988).

Finally, Roger Lane's detailed study of *William Dorsey's Philadelphia* casts particular doubt on the 1860 census's accuracy in enumerating the African-American population. Characterizing the census's enumeration in Philadelphia as "crudely unreliable," Lane argues that the census was a "barometer" of race relations, "an especially suspect enterprise from the black perspective." He points out that the northern city was a place for escapees to hide, that the Fugitive Slave Act certainly made free blacks afraid to give information to white officials, and public discussion of forced emigration to Africa added even more threat to any census. Lane shows, for example, that of twenty prominent black Philadelphians in 1870, six are missing from the census (Lane, 1991, 59–60).

Given that the homicide rate is sensitive to how the population at-risk is defined and measured, the demographic composition of the New York City African-American population remains an important, unresolved, and perhaps even insoluble, issue.

Race and Weapons

Homicide notices often mentioned weapon type. Because their high cost and low quality no doubt cut down on their prevalence, guns were used far less often than today. The Civil War caused a step upward in the using of guns, though compared to today, guns were still relatively rare in homicides. Of the 1,323 cases with information on weapon, 18.7 percent were gun murders and

TABLE 5.3   Race and Weapon

Weapon	Killer Race		Total
	White	*Black*	*Total*
Gun	241	6	247
Knife	328	24	352
Poison	33	0	33
Other	671	20	691
Total	1273	50	1323

27 percent knife murders. Dividing these cases at 1861 gives 634 post-1861 cases; 25 percent were gun murders and 26 percent knife murders; the pre-1861 gun percentage drops to 13.

Race also made a difference in weapon use, as shown in Table 5.3. Twelve percent of black killers used guns, and 48 percent used knives. For whites the figures were 19 percent and 26 percent. Most interesting is the Civil War impact: prior to 1862, no black killers used a gun; all six incidents occurred after 1862. These differences suggest that blacks were less likely to own handguns, possibly due to cost.

Race and Gender

As in the examination of race and age, our understanding of race and gender relations depends in some part on the population at-risk. That is, should the gender ratio of the African-American population differ dramatically from that of, say, the Germans, then this alone might account for differences in homicide.

Although there is no clear warrant to say so, I hypothesize that the African-American population was more adult and more male than the white population. This would result in more black victims and killers being men. Interestingly, this was the case for victims but not for killers. For killers, the race/gender distributions were similar enough to show no statistical significance. For victims, the differences were statistically significant: 90 percent of the black victims were men, as opposed to 77 percent of the white victims (see Table 5.4). Given the small numbers of black victims with relevant information, this means that six more of the victims would have been women had the race differences not obtained.

Aside from the plausibility of differing but unmeasured at-risk populations, which would still leave unaccounted the differences between victims and killers, other possibilities can only be raised as questions. Were African-American men more in public than women? Did their work on and near the docks put them at-risk relative to African-American women, who worked in

TABLE 5.4   Race and Gender

	Victim Race		
Victim Sex	*White*	*Black*	*Total*
Male	1044	43	1087
	78%	90%	78%
Female	304	5	309
	22%	10%	22%
Total	1348	48	1396
	100%	100%	100%

Pearson chi2(1) = 3.9603 Pr = 0.047
likelihood-ratio chi2(1) = 4.6544 Pr = 0.031

	Killer Race		
Killer Sex	*White*	*Black*	*Total*
Male	1116	46	1162
	94%	90%	94%
Female	74	5	79
	6%	10%	6%
Total	1190	51	1241
	100%	100%	100%

Pearson chi2(1) = 1.0547 Pr = 0.304
likelihood-ration chi2(1) = 0.9204 Pr = 0.337

safer locations? Did white men attack spouses and women companions more? Were there cultural differences in the tolerance of violence against women?

A cross-tabulation shows no statistically meaningful differences by killer's race and whether or not the victim was a spouse (see Table 5.5). But a comparison of noted ethnicity and race of men who killed women shows some apparent differences: 21 percent (10) of the victims of black offenders were women, as opposed to 39 percent (45) of Irish, 32 percent (24) of German, and 15 percent (3) of Italian. Note that all the cautions apply to interpreting these data: gender balance, the probable underreporting of ethnicity versus the probable higher reporting of race. The results nearly disappear when all killer victim relationships are examined: 24 percent (296 of the 1,211 pairs where gender is positively known) of all killings were a man killing a woman. We are left with a conundrum—Was there in fact a cultural difference, did the apparently lesser degrees of femicide reflect demography and opportunity, or is the difference a consequence of poor reporting?

Racial Attacks

At least three killings of blacks could be identified in the media as having possible racial motivations. These exclude the dozens of racially motivated killings during the draft riot of 1863. One was in Brooklyn, which was not

TABLE 5.5   Spousal Violence

Relationship	Killer's Noted Race or Ethnicity						
	US	Black	French	British	Irish	(Irish?)	Total
Other	50	48	5	12	86	40	241
Spouse	3	8	2	1	40	12	66
Total	53	56	7	13	126	52	307
Victim	Male Killer's Noted Race or Ethnicity						
	US	Black	French	British	Irish	(Irish?)	Total
Men	35	38	6	10	69	35	193
Women	12	10	1	1	45	14	83
Total	47	48	7	11	114	49	276

yet part of New York City, but a separate municipality, but I include it to supplement the descriptions. These three cases were identified by examining, where possible, the twenty-two cases where the victim was black and the killer was not identified as black. It is easy enough to guess that these cases are not representative, but I present them to give an idea of the information available.

An example from "Battle Row" in Brooklyn (hence does not enter the formal analysis here) in which race may have played a part is the August 25th murder of Charles H. Rodgers by a "rowdy white gang, without apparent cause of provocation" (*New York Times* 8/29/1866). This case typifies the interpretive difficulties encountered. Rodgers was stabbed in front of his house at 9 P.M. by one from the "skylarking group," which included Charles Kelly, Michael Quirk, Joseph Kelly, George Rampen, John Kennedy, and Frederick Miller. A witness stated that she heard the men say, "Show me the black s___ of a b___ who struck me and I will cut his d___ guts out, or shoot him." Someone said, "There is the black s___ of a b___; let's give it to him." The men were arrested. Had there been an earlier fight? Was this a race murder?

The first of the probable race murders in New York City took place on August 8, 1847, when an unknown person murdered a sailor named James Steele, who was returning to his barge. Although absolutely no mention is made of possible racial motives, one cannot help but wonder. Six years later, on December 22, 1853, James Crumsley murdered 29-year-old Edward Matthews. This happened when "a terrible conflict took place in the Fifth Ward, between a party of white men, who are of notorious character, and a gang of colored persons." This "riot" occurred after an African-American had been assaulted by three of the white men, took shelter in a black oyster and liquor saloon run by Matthews, from whence a group of blacks returned to avenge his injuries. According to the paper, Matthews "was a sort of leader among the colored residents of the Fifth and Eighth Wards, in consideration of his pugilistic abilities" (*New York Times* 12-22-1853).

Ten years later, many race murders occurred during the draft riots. An article describing the arrest of John McAlister, a 40-year-old Irish laborer for the murder of a sailor, William Williams, indicates the nature of these murders. The tone of the article, entitled "Fiendish Murder of a Negro," captures the horrific incident. McAlister bashed in the head of Williams with a twenty-pound paving black in front of a crowd of "men, women and children, who coolly witnessed the fiendish act" (*New York Times* 8-1-1863). Police caught and arrested McAlister two weeks later.

In 1867 William Higgins and a gang of white men murdered Christian Bostwick in Higgins's liquor store (*New York Times* 7-24-1867). Higgins testified that Bostwick, a cook on a coastal steamer, refused to leave the store, so he beat him. According to the article, Bostwick was well known among the "numerous colored population in the Eighth Ward." Police arrested Higgins.

All of these cases carry in common the elements of a racial attack. Typically, the killers were backed up by other white men, and typically victim's noted occupations hint that there could have been latent conflicts over occupations involved. Since all the secondary literature for this era indicates how job "turf" formed an important part of antiblack aggression in northern cities, these incidents seem to support that notion. On the other hand, the high number attacks that did not carry racial overtones requires that we be very cautious. In Table 5.1, above, the dichotomized race distribution of victims and killers contains little to support a strong pattern of race-motivated killings. Therefore, I conclude that race motivation played a secondary role in homicides. Yet in such a small black community, the impact of even a few unpredictable racial attacks must have been very deep. These occasional yet lethal attacks, followed by the awful events in the draft riot, imply that New York City's black residents always had to be alert to sudden attacks.

An Issue of Justice

The study of the role played by racial bias in the justice system is fraught with complexity, even in the present era. During the period under examination here, New York City changed from a slave to a nonslave to a fairly vigorous pro-Reconstruction political atmosphere. But ethnic and racial hostility ran high, and most New Yorkers were white, especially after the antiblack draft riots.

Immigrants, particularly the Irish and Germans, were more heavily involved in homicides than their numbers warrant, but as the city continued to fill with immigrants in the post–Civil War era, homicides per capita decreased.

The ways in which race mattered were complex and shifting, and my discussion here is based on the assumption that while ethnicity (and class) played a highly important role, the experience of blacks contrasted with all nonblacks is a fundamental starting point. Here the question is about treatment by the justice system: Were there differences in arrest, trial, and punishment of blacks and nonblacks?

The Appendix reports the results of logit analyses of the likelihood of arrest, trial, and execution for blacks versus all others. These analyses were done with two different assumptions about missing information: one, that cases with missing information on race or ethnicity should be dropped from the analysis, and second, that African-Americans would be more likely to be noted than others, so that when unreported, a person's race was probably white.

Blacks had about the same likelihood of arrest and trial for homicides as nonblacks (see Appendix, Tables 5.7 and 5.8). It is possible that missing information about trails—quite common—biases these results, just as it is possible that there was an underreporting of murders by nonblacks. The data collection strategy for this research, using all suspicious deaths, whether or not called a homicide by a coroner's jury, was deliberately designed to overcome such events, however.

A precise analysis of the past is even more difficult, although one can guess that a society with fewer claims to evenhanded justice might have less to hide. Because we have good records on executions, it is possible to examine at least the outlines of the role race played in the heaviest and rarest punishment meted out to killers in nineteenth-century New York. For this portion of the analysis, the data on the beginning and end of the individual level processes are better than those on the middle. That is, the original counts of murder and any executions are more accurate than are arrests, trials, and sentences.

Nineteenth-century New Yorkers tended to be against capital punishment, in contrast to our perception of that era. Out of over 1,560 murderers, only 2 percent, 31 were executed for their crime. And the proportion being executed was diminishing over time—every year between 1800 and 1875 decreased the probability of execution by 3 percent. Even though a high proportion of arrests was made, there was erratic follow-up. Basically, it was easy to get away with murder, in part because when cases came to trial, juries were apt to give the offenders the benefit of the doubt. In a city filled with bars, rowdiness, and a good deal of physical violence, the all important coroner's juries often placed themselves in the offender's situation and found the deaths to be accidental, the result of a friendly fight. Beginning in the decade of the 1820s, the loosely parallel relationship between executions and homicides ended—executions remaining at the same level, even as homicides spiraled upward. It is possible that this represents a measurement problem, that the further back in time, the more difficult the recovery of homicides with no punished killer.

The one exception to such leniency for capital offenses came for African-American offenders, who were twice as likely to be hanged as their white compatriots. Surprisingly, the race of their victims did not seem to matter much, however. And even this clearly biased system allowed 90 percent of the black offenders (51 of 58) to escape the gallows. Executions became substantially less frequent every year (see Appendix for a fuller discussion).

CONCLUSION

There are several conclusions to be drawn from this probe, based on still fragmentary data. New York was a violent city, even if not as violent as today. Perhaps more important is what was not: a city with violence coming from people of color. It was a violent city of principally white persons, many of them recent immigrants. Had guns been as prevalent as today, how much more violent would this city have been?

The rate at which homicides occurred fluctuated considerably through this period, but it is important to note that it often dropped as precipitously as it rose: immigrants did not necessarily produce violence, as though by some law of pressure cooking. Persons of color participated in this violent society. In the few specifically racial incidents, African-Americans were the victims of racially motivated attacks. None of these incidents compared to the draft riots, of course, but they do illustrate that African-Americans were in a dangerous city.

Finally, there are two broader implications to be drawn. First is a message of hope: rates of violence can come down, even if we cannot yet identify mechanisms causing that to happen. Second is a message about research: we can learn a great deal from the past that will help us think about the present, if we are willing to commit the energy to the task. It is worth doing. Coming to grips with contemporary crises as complicated and as ancient as interpersonal violence means coming to grips with a long human history.

APPENDIX

Logit Analyses of Increased Probability Racial Differences in Treatment of Murders

Below are various logit estimations predicting whether or not a killer was arrested, tried, and executed. They test various assumptions about missing information (concerning race) and about undiscovered homicides.

TABLE 5.6   Arrests (N = 1182 chi2(2) = 14.10 Pseudo R2 = 0.0086)

Arrested	Coefficient	Standard Error	t	P>|t|	[95% Confidence Interval]	
Killer Black	.938	.2951	3.181	0.002	.3597	1.517
Year died	.0069	.0037	1.843	0.066	-.0004	.0142
Constant	-12.83	6.94	-1.848	0.065	-26.45	.7901

TABLE 5.7   Trials (N = 1182 chi2(2) = 15.23 Pseudo R2 = 0.0159)

Tried	Coefficient	Standard Error	t	P>|t|	[95% Confidence Interval]	
Killer Black	1.192	.2942	4.054	0.000	.615	1.77
Year died	.0064	.0057	1.119	0.263	-.0048	.0176
Constant	-13.76	10.60	-1.298	0.195	-34.57	7.046

Table 5.6 estimates whether or not the killer's race affected probabilities of arrest, no assumptions about the killer's race being made. Because victims are not included in the equations, about 70 percent of the known homicides are used for the estimates. A coefficient of less than one for the killer's race indicates that being black reduced the probability of an event occurring, in this case arrest. Table 5.6 shows that race made little difference. Again, the assumption here is that the nearly 400 missing observations made no difference. If we assume that all black killers were identified, then the first coefficients for Tables 5.6 and 5.7 become negative.

In Table 5.7 the affect of offender's race on the likelihood of being tried is examined: here the coefficient is positive, but as the standard error and the 95 percent confidence intervals both indicate, the amount greater than one is slight.

Table 5.8A is the first of several examining executions. Though infrequent as punishment, the existence of a separate data set on executions, in addition to the high probability of being reported, makes these data more complete and reliable than those on arrests and trials, where the possibility of an overlooked trial or arrest is much more likely. The separate data set is known as the Espy file, the results of years of work by Watt Espy, now archived at the Inter University Consortium for Political and Social Research. This file contains all known executions in the U.S.A., and for this project the New York series proved invaluable. Table 5.8A shows a coefficient of 2.36 with a more confidence inspiring Chi 2 than those in the two previous tables. The coefficient gives strong indication of the increased probability of execution for blacks offenders versus non-blacks. Note that the negative coefficient for the Year variable shows that the probability of execution, for all, was declining.

TABLE 5.8A   Executions (N = 1182 chi2(2) = 32.06 Pseudo R2 = 0.1465)

Executed	Coefficient	Standard Error	t	P>|t|	[95% Confidence Interval]	
Killer Black	2.36	.4953	4.770	0.000	1.391	3.334
Year died	-.0387	.0088	-4.399	0.000	-.056	-.021
Constant	67.39	16.22	4.155	0.000	35.57	99.21

TABLE 5.8B   Executions Predicted by Offender's Race and Year, All Cases, Assumption that all Persons White Unless Otherwise Identified. (N = 1561 chi2(2) = 30.03 Pseudo R2 = 0.099)

Executed	Coefficient	Standard Error	t	P>|t|	[95% Confidence Interval]	
Killer Black	2.021	.461	4.377	0.000	1.11	2.9279
Year died	-.0334	.007	-4.372	0.000	-.0484	-.0184
Constant	57.74	14.10	4.096	0.000	30.09	85.40

TABLE 5.8C   Executions Predicted by Both Offender and Victim's Race and Year, All Cases, Assumption that all Persons White Unless Otherwise Identified. (N = 1561 chi2(3) = 30.11 Pseudo R2 = 0.0989)

Executed	Coefficient	Standard Error	t	P>|t|	[95% Confidence Interval]	
Killer Black	2.1336	.594	3.591	0.000	.9680	3.299
Victim Black	-.2160	.748	-0.289	0.773	-1.684	1.252
Year died	-.03357	.0076	-4.390	0.000	-.0485	-.0185
Constant	58.05	14.11	4.114	0.000	30.37	85.73

Table 5.8B relaxes the assumption that an offender's race cannot be inferred: instead, all persons not identified as black are assumed to be white. There are several instances where this is risky—those, for example, where a victim was found and there was never a hint of the murderer's identity. Note that the fit of this equation is not as good as that in Table 5.8A, but that the coefficients are very similar.

It seems that if the offender's race makes a difference in executions, then it is possible that the victim's race too would make a difference. Did the courts' get even harsher for black defendants when the victims were not black? Table 5.8C brings the victim's race into the equation, again with the assumption that black victims, being more unusual, would also be more likely to be identified. Here, victims without ethnic or racial identification are coded as white. The coefficient for victim's race turns out to be nonsignificant, meaning that it did not affect the outcome.

TABLE 5.8D Executions Predicted by Both Offender and Victim's Race and Year, All Cases, *No* Assumption that All Persons White Unless Otherwise Identified. (N = 675 chi2(3) = 23.12 Prob > Pseudo R2 = 0.1192)

Executed	*Coefficient*	*Stardard Error*	*t*	*P>|t|*	*[95% Confidence Interval]*	
Killer Black	1.888	.6537	2.889	0.004	.6048	3.172
Victim Black	-.242	.7946	-0.305	0.760	-1.802	1.317
Year died	.0302	.007	-3.856	0.000	-.0456	-.0148
Constant	52.31	14.4	3.620	0.000	23.94	80.68

In Table 5.8D, the assumption that nonidentified race means white is dropped, and the estimates are made only for that subset of cases (40 percent) where both persons have been identified. While the coefficient remains positive on the killer's race, that on the victim is nonsignificant, as in Table 5.8C.

Finally, there is another feature that may affect patterns of missingness in the data: known homicides that my research assistants and I have not yet uncovered. As made clear earlier in this chapter, this project depends on the work of many different people, searching less and less rich sources. One aspect of the work, for instance, is establishing that zero homicide years are really zero—not exciting research. In the intervening six months and approximately seven-hundred research hours since the original logit's were run, an additional homicide involving African-Americans has been found: on December 28, 1801, a man named Haisty murdered Lewis Smith, upping to 59 the number of black offenders. Because of the Espy data set, we know that Haisty was not executed, and the news item indicates an arrest, but we know no more. Table 5.8E reestimates Table 5.8D and Table 5.8F reestimates Table 5.8C. Table 5.8E makes a slight modification to the coefficients and fit of 5.8D, making the inferences from it slightly stronger. Table 5.8F has a similar resemblance to 5.8C, making the implications of its coefficients somewhat stronger.

TABLE 5.8E Executions Predicted by Both Offender and Victim's Race and Year, All Cases, *No* Assumption that All Persons White Unless Otherwise Identified. Test of Impact of Latest Observation. (N = 674 chi2(3) = 24.01 Pseudo R2 = 0.1239)

Executed	*Coefficient*	*Standard Error*	*t*	*P>|t|*	*[95% Confidence Interval]*	
Killer Black	1.904	.6528	2.918	0.004	.6228	3.186
Victim Black	-.1391	.7902	-.0176	0.860	-1.690	1.412
Year died	-.0312	.0079	-3.962	0.000	-.0468	-.015
Constant	54.18	14.53	3.729	0.000	25.65	82.72

TABLE 5.8F   Executions Predicted by Both Offender and Victim's Race and Year, All Cases, Assumption that all Persons White unless Otherwise Identified. Test of Impact of Latest Observation. (N = 1560 chi2(3) = 31.08 Pseudo R2 = 0.1021)

Executed	*Coefficient*	*Standard Error*	*t*	*P>|t|*	[95% Confidence *Interval]*	
Killer Black	2.15	.5905	3.645	0.000	.9943	3.310
Victim Black	-.1154	.7398	-0.156	0.876	-1.566	1.335
Year died	.0345	.0076	-4.510	0.000	-.0495	-.0195
Constant	59.8	14.13	4.235	0.000	32.14	87.60

NOTES

1. The research reported here has been supported by grants from the Academic Senate, University of California, Los Angeles. Many people have assisted in this project: graduate research assistants I wish to thank include Susan Meyer; Brian Griest; Sheila O'Hare; Tom Clark; Carol Winter; Rob Michaelson; and Matthew Lee. Elizabeth Stephenson and Martin Pawlicki of the Social Science Data Archives helped me with the Espy file. I wish to thank research assistants from the Student Research Program of the Honors College. These include Catharine Lamb; Sanjiv Rao; Gregg Doll; Cynthia Lum; Duyen Bui; Diane Kim; Sue Pak; Julie Jarboe; Serge Kogen; Tom Chung; Marcus Nenn; Colby Moldow; Mike Doyle; Cheryl Feiner; Robbyn Wilkins; Barry Dewalt; Paige Anderson; Christa Welch; Andy Bodeau; Mike Doyle; Kenneth So; and Christine Statler.

2. Historians have long noted the irony of the situation of African-Americans in northern cities prior to the ending of slavery: while free, and able to pursue their self-interests such as religion, northern blacks were systematically excluded from occupations open to them in the slave south. Frederick Douglass, for example, was unable to obtain work in northern shipyards as he had in Baltimore.

3. For the most recent work on the riots, see Bernstein (1990). His bibliographical essay, 341, summarizes the extensive literature on the riots.

4. I base this statement on the perusing of the *New York Times* and other materials. Only a handful of editorial comments on crime, with the exception of riots, ever appeared in print.

5. This discussion is built upon the extensive work by criminal justice historians that has focused on the kind and quality of information we have about the past. In particular the work of Roger Lane has helped us think about such frustrating problems.

6. Estimated by robust regression: black homicide slope = .033, nonblack homicide slope = 1.47. The latter changes to 1.81 for 1845 to 1874, a change visually apparent in the plotted actual numbers.

7. Note: I take the actual populations in 1865 here as Italians were not reported for 1855. These figures are not directly comparable to the mid-point estimates used above.

8. In all cases, these are for victims.

REFERENCES

Anderson, Margo J. 1988. *The American Census: A Social History.* New Haven: Yale University Press.

Bernstein, Iver. 1990. *The New York City Draft Riots: Their Significance for American Society and Politics in the Age of the Civil War.* New York: Oxford University Press.

Chudacoff, Howard P. 1989. *How Old Are You? Age Consciousness in American Culture.* Princeton: Princeton University Press.

Emerson, Haven, and Harriet E. Hughes. 1941. *Population, Births, Notifiable Diseases, and Deaths, Assembled for New York City, New York, 1866–1938, from Official Records.* New York, DeLamar Institute of Public Health, College of Physicians and Surgeons, Columbia University.

———. 1955. *Supplement 1936–1953 to Population, Births, Notifiable Diseases, and Deaths, Assembled for New York City, New York, 1866–1938, from Official Records.* New York: DeLamar Institute of Public Health, College of Physicians and Surgeons, Columbia University.

Espy, M. Watt. 1987. *Executions in the U.S., 1608–1987: [computer file, the Espy-file,* principal investigators, M. Watt, Espy and John]. 1st ICPSR ed. Tuscaloosa, Ala.: John Ortiz Smykla (producer). Ann Arbor, Mich.: Inter-university Consortium for Political and Social Research (distributor).

Gurr, Ted R. (ed.) 1989. *Violence in America.* Newbury Park, Calif.: Sage Publications.

Hodges, Graham R. 1986. *New York City Cartmen, 1667–1850.* New York: New York University Press.

Johnson, Julie. (Forthcoming.) "Coroners, Corruption, and the Politics of Death: Forensic Pathology in the United States," in Michael Clark and Catherine Crawford (ed.), *Legal Medicine in History.* New York: Cambridge University Press.

Lane, Roger. 1979. *Violent Death in the City: Accident, Suicide and Homicide in Philadelphia, 1850–1900.* Cambridge: Harvard University Press.

———. 1986. *Roots of Violence in Black Philadelphia, 1860–1900.* Cambridge, Mass.: Harvard University Press.

————. 1991. *William Dorsey's Philadelphia and Ours.* New York: Oxford University Press.

Parkerson, Donald (ed.). 1991. Special Issue on the Underenumeration of the US Census, 1850–1880. *Social Science History* (Winter) 15:4.

Rosenwaike, Ira. 1972. *Population History of New York City.* Syracuse: Syracuse University Press.

Scott, Kenneth. 1973. *Rivington's New York Newspaper: Excerpts from a Loyalist Press, 1773–1783.* New York Historical Society.

————. 1989. *Coroner's Reports New York City, 1823–1842.* New York: New York Geneological and Biographical Society.

————. 1991. *Coroner's Reports New York City, 1843–1849.* New York: New York Geneological and Biographical Society.

————. 1988–1989. "Early New York City Coroner's Reports," *The New York Genealogical and Biographical Record,* April 1988, 76–79, July 1988, 145–50, October 1988, 217–19, January 1989, 18–20, April 1989, 88–92.

Soman, Alfred, 1980. "Deviance and Criminal Justice in Western Europe, 1300–1800: An Essay in Structure." *Criminal Justice History* 1:1–28.

E.M. BECK
STEWART E. TOLNAY

6

Violence toward African Americans in the Era of the White Lynch Mob

The years between 1882 and 1930 witnessed an unprecedented wave of lethal violence toward African-Americans in the American south.[1] We estimate that at least three thousand black men, women, and children were murdered by white gangs during this era of the lynch mob, and this toll does not count other racially motivated murders or black deaths from race riots.[2] Yet the frequency of mob violence was not constant across time or space—the most significant swell of antiblack violence erupted in the decade of the 1890s, and then again in the early 1920s. Mississippi, Georgia, and Alabama accounted for the largest share of lethal violence, while lynching in bordering states such as Tennessee and Kentucky was noticeably less frequent, although certainly not unheard of. The *facts* of lynching and many of their details are now well-documented, but what were the underlying social forces molding these deadly patterns?

In this chapter we first sketch the bare bones of a theory of racial violence, and then empirically examine one component of that theory. The basic elements of the theory originated in research into the causes of mob violence in the American south during the lynching era. While there had been previous work on the psycho-dynamics of mob behavior and narrative histories of individual lynching events, we wanted to investigate racial violence at another level of analysis.[3] Our studies focused on the social, economic, and political conditions associated with lynch-prone regions of the south, and with conditions correlated with periods of frequent lynching activity during the five decades of the lynching era. After spending several years assembling and verifying an inventory of known lynching victims,[4] we launched into extensive investigations into the factors shaping the frequency and spatial distribution of mob violence.

Based on this empirical research, on historical narratives of lynchings, and on surveys of past research, we developed a framework for thinking about racial violence as the product of four synergistic (interactive) factors, each of which is a *necessary* ingredient in the overall formula for violence, yet none of which is sufficient to produce disorder itself:

$$\begin{matrix} \text{RACIAL} \\ \text{VIOLENCE} \end{matrix} = \left(\underbrace{\begin{bmatrix} \text{Racist} \\ \text{Ideology} \end{bmatrix} \times \begin{bmatrix} \text{Permissiveness} \\ \text{of the State} \end{bmatrix} \times \begin{bmatrix} \text{Competition} \\ \text{for Resources} \end{bmatrix}}_{\text{Violence Potential}} \right) \times \begin{pmatrix} \text{Threshold} \\ \text{Event} \end{pmatrix}$$

The first three factors cluster to form the *violence potential,* by which we mean the *strength* of the response after a threshold or triggering event. These three factors may be thought of heuristically as charging a social capacitor, which can violently discharge after stresses within the system build to some critical value, and are then tripped by a racial incident.[5]

The first critical element is the presence of a racist ideology, which defines the intellectual foundations for violence by rationalizing the inferior status of the target group and by justifying the superior position of the dominant group. The importance of this supremacist ideology is that it provides a credible story legitimating the dehumanization of those destined to be targets of violence—it provides a moral imperative for violence. To legitimate violence this ideology must not only be present but it must become part of the shared folklore of the dominant culture.

After the Civil War, there was a significant change in the way whites viewed blacks. The stereotype of the contented plantation *sambo* was pushed into the background, to be replaced by the image of the retrogressive black *brute* so viciously described by fashionable writers, editorialists, and cartoonists of the day. These new images portrayed southern blacks as threatening beasts requiring stern control to protect white society. From the fiction of Thomas Dixon (1902, 1907) to the scientific racism of the eugenicists (Hoffman, 1896), this more sinister image of blacks—especially males—was propagated and legitimized. There is no way of knowing precisely how widely these stereotypes were believed or how intense was the racism that they engendered. But based on the documented fame of racist writers, the success of race pandering politicians, and the frequency of racist images in popular culture, we can only conclude that virulent racism was solidly entrenched in the structure of southern society.[6] Once institutionalized, racism became the lens through which all perceptions and social interactions were channeled and shaped. Yet we believe that racism by itself would not have produced violence unless at least two other factors were present—a permissive legal system and interracial competition for scarce resources.

Second, we believe that the state—the formal system of social control—plays an essential role in either producing or inhibiting violence. The historical record is clear that when officials took decisive steps to defuse potentially volatile situations, racial violence was diminished. Likewise, when they either actively advocated mob behavior or turned a blind eye, violence was encouraged. A classic example of state complicity is the lynching of Willis Jackson in Anderson County, South Carolina, in October 1911. In this incident, one of the mob leaders was Joshua W. Ashley, a member of the South Carolina state legislature. After Willis Jackson's murder at the hands of white rabble, South Carolina Governor Cole Blease refused to bring the mob leaders to court, and even regretted that he had not lead the gang himself.[7] The actions of these two civil leaders left little doubt as to the legitimacy of mob violence against African-Americans.

From the local sheriff who presented only token resistance to a lynch mob, to grand juries who refused to indict known mob participants, to race-baiting politicians, to U.S. congressmen filibustering federal antilynch legislation, they all sent an unambiguous message that violence against African-Americans would be tolerated—if not commended—and the participants had little to fear from the white-controlled formal system of justice. Through their actions, or inactions, the state was often a willing partner to many black lynchings, and gave a clear stamp of approval of white mob violence against African-Americans.

The third component of the *violence potential* cluster involves interracial competition. The primary driving force behind racial violence is competition for the scarce resources of economic wealth, political power, and social status. During Reconstruction much racial violence centered on who would control the political machinery of the south. Although this issue became moot after redemption, and later black disenfranchisement, racial violence continued because of competition in the economic and social arenas. More will be said of this critical component in the following section.

The last factor that must be present is some threshold or triggering event, which provides the immediate justification for violent action directed toward the target group. Alleged black capital offenses against whites (murder or rape, typically) have been historically common triggering incidents, but in many instances, the threshold event involved a status offense such as being disrespectful of a white person or acting above one's station in society—serious breaches of racial etiquette in a racist society. In the absence of extenuating factors, such incidents might normally either receive nonlethal punishment—being publicly rebuffed, for example—or sanctioning would be administered through the formal system of justice. But when such incidents occurred against the backdrop of interracial competition and racism, the reaction of white society could be decidedly more deadly.[8]

COMPETITION AND THREAT

Slavery was an extremely effective institution for controlling the southern black population. Not only did it curtail black individual freedom and mobility, but it also restricted the black ability to compete openly with whites for the scarce resources in southern society. Denied the vote, lacking access to the marketplace, and assigned an unquestionably inferior position in the southern status hierarchy, slaves posed little threat to the average white.

Following the Civil War this situation changed dramatically. Virtually overnight, former slaves were granted the franchise and were forced to struggle for economic survival along with their white counterparts. Suddenly during Reconstruction, blacks were thrust into direct competition with whites for political power and threatened the economic security of many whites.[9] And to the extent that they were successful in these competitions, freed men also challenged the southern status hierarchy. For example, black successes in the political and economic arenas tended to erase the objective measures of white superiority, and thereby cast doubt on the traditional claims of racial superiority that had guaranteed virtually all southern whites at least some measure of exalted status. Lynching was one potential response by southern whites to political and economic competition from blacks.

Wright (1990) claims that Kentucky lynchings reached their peak during the Reconstruction era as whites sought to neutralize the black political threat. Others (Corzine et al., 1983; Olzak, 1990; and Reed, 1972) have also inferred an important link between political competition and southern lynchings. Indeed, one can point to specific lynching incidents that were clearly political in nature. The August 1882 lynching of Jack Turner in Choctaw County, Alabama, is a good example. After Turner's lynching the white press attempted to justify the murder by describing the victim as "a turbulent and dangerous character" who was masterminding a conspiracy to kill all white people in the county. In truth, Turner and his "co-conspirators" were simply Republicans trying to defeat Democratic candidates—all of them white.

Despite the occurrence of *political* lynchings like Turner's, there are compelling reasons to believe that political competition played a relatively minor role in the broader history of southern violence after Reconstruction. First, it did not take long for whites to *redeem* southern politics from the radical post–Civil War era. Through a combination of fraud, bribery, and restrictive legislation, the political power of southern blacks was severely compromised by the late nineteenth century (Kousser, 1974; Woodward, 1966). Although still able to influence elections in some locales, especially where their populations were relatively large, southern blacks represented a dwindling political threat as the century came to a close. Second, efforts to demonstrate a linkage between black political competition and lynching have been largely unsuccessful. Thus far, we have been unable to find clear evidence of an important political dimension to southern lynchings between 1882 and 1930. Elsewhere we have shown that the time trend in lynching appears to have been insensitive to the implementation of black disenfranchisement, and that lynchings actually appear to have been *less common* where the dominant Democratic party was threatened by Republicans or Populists (Tolnay and Beck, 1992).

Arthur Raper (1933) was among the first to argue that southern lynchings were the product (at least partially) of *economic competition* between southern blacks and whites. He claimed that whites resorted to racial violence in order to displace black workers, thereby making room for unemployed whites. Since Raper, others have pointed to economic motives for southern lynching (Beck and Tolnay, 1990; Hovland and Sears, 1940; Myers, 1991; Olzak, 1990). In fact, economic competition between southern blacks and whites did intensify during that latter part of the nineteenth century. Moreover, it was not possible to neutralize economic competition with relatively easy strategies, such as restrictive voting statutes, which were effective responses to political competition.

The economic status of many southern whites deteriorated steadily during the late nineteenth and early twentieth centuries. High fertility in the rural south fueled rapid population growth, which in turn created intense pressure on available land. While some families migrated toward the southwest in search of economic opportunity, most stayed put and tried to scratch a living from shrinking farms with exhausted soil. To make matters worse, the price of cotton plummeted during the 1890s, reducing profits from the dominant cash crop in the region. The end result of these events was increased suffering, and declining security, for many white farmers. Countless owners of small farms lost their land and were reduced to tenancy. New young whites faced increasingly bleak prospects for farm ownership and joined the growing ranks of landless tenants.

In isolation these trends would have been discouraging enough for struggling whites. However, in addition to a decline in their *absolute* levels of economic well-being and opportunity, the *relative* advantage of whites over blacks also narrowed significantly. Many white farmers found themselves in direct competition with blacks for the best tenant farms. And some white laborers competed for jobs with blacks who often worked for lower wages. To the increasingly marginalized whites, it must have seemed as though the two races were following divergent economic trajectories. Whereas the economic fortunes of whites were in decline, blacks were actually better off than they had been during slavery. By offending the racial sensibilities of southern whites, such perceptions might have let to *expressive* and *instrumental* lynchings by poor whites. That is, some lynchings may have been the result of frustrated economic aspirations, as argued by Hovland and Sears (1940), while others were intended to frighten and intimidate blacks, possibly causing them to leave the community, as suggested by Raper (1933).

The economic interests of well-to-do southern whites should not be ignored. Although somewhat less vulnerable to the vagaries of the cotton-driven economy, planters and employers may also have perceived certain benefits to heightened racial tensions—including violence (Bloom, 1987). As many southern whites sank to the same economic level of blacks, the white elite faced the threat of a possible coalition between these two dispossessed groups. In order to prevent such a coalition, and to preserve their privileged position in southern society, it was in their interest to maintain antagonistic relations between poorer whites and blacks. By fanning the flames of racial supremacy, and the fear of *negro domination,* influential whites used the *race card* to trump the threat of the *class card.* If an occasional lynching was one by-product of increased racial tension, it was an acceptable price to pay.

In combination with the prevailing racist ideology, and the state's tolerant attitude toward lynching, these competitive relations made racial violence an acceptable response to the deteriorating position of whites. It is not necessary to argue that every lynching was the result of a specific competitive encounter between blacks and whites. Rather, competitive relations threatened the dominant position that southern whites took for granted, and created a volatile atmosphere in which *threshold events,* real or fabricated, often led to mob violence with a black victim.

EFFECTS OF INTERRACIAL COMPETITION

In this section we will show that violence toward southern blacks was more common when there was increased racial competition over scarce resources. While we have no direct measure of racial competition, we can infer the level of competition based on economic conditions and the size of the black population. Given the relative positions of blacks and whites in southern society even during the best of times, we can assume that during hard economic downturns there would have been greater interracial competition as many whites found themselves slipping uncomfortably toward the status of blacks. Second, we can infer heightened interracial competition in the regions of the south where the black population was relatively large, and hence represented a *threat* to the white population.

In sum, we believe that antiblack mob violence will be more intense during economic slippages, and in places within the south where blacks constituted a relatively large share of the local population. To examine the first of these hypotheses, we turn to a time-series analysis of blacks lynched by white mobs in the south between 1882 and 1930, then we consider evidence from a cross-sectional analysis of mob violence in southern counties. In order to conduct this investigation into the relationship between racial competition and lynching, we must make some *simplifying assumptions* about the other components of the theory of racial violence outlined earlier in the chapter. Specifically, we will assume: (1) that a racist ideology was in place; (2) that the state maintained a permissive stance regarding lynching; (3) that threshold, or precipitating, events were readily available, or easily concocted; and (4) that these three components were invariant over time and across space during this era. Obviously, these are assumptions that might be challenged as naive for a 48-year period of southern history, and for a geographic region of the size and complexity of the south. Nonetheless, we do not believe that they seriously undermine our objective here—that is, to determine whether the historical evidence for the lynching era supports an inference of association between racial violence and racial competition.

Time series Evidence. We use time-series data on southern black lynching to investigate the relationship between mob violence and economic competition. In these analyses we formulate a model linking the annual number of black victims of white mob violence to economic conditions and a set of control variables:

$$\text{Log Victims}_t = \beta_0 + \beta_1(\text{Log Wholesale Deflated Price of Cotton}_t) +$$
$$+ \beta_2(\text{Log}[\text{CPI}_{t-1}/\text{CPI}_{t-2}]) + \beta_3(\text{Log Cotton Bales Produced}_t) +$$
$$+ \beta_4(\text{Log Size of Black Population}_t) +$$
$$+ \beta_5(\text{Log White Lynch Victims}_t) + u_t$$

where β_0 is a constant, β_ks are the effects of the predictor and control variables, and u_t is a disturbance term.[10] In this model we use two indicators of the health of the southern economy: the first is the deflated (constant dollar) wholesale price of cotton and the second is the rate of inflation (changes in the consumer price index). While it is true that many areas of the south were not highly dependent on cotton production, it is also true that cotton was the primary force driving much of the southern economy—when the real dollar price of cotton fell, the ill-effects would trickle down to adversely affect many southerners. The second indicator of economic conditions is the rate of

TABLE 6.1   Time-Series Regression of Number of Black Victims of White Mobs (Log) on Cotton Price and Related Variables for Cotton-Dominant Counties in the South, 1882–1930[a]

| Predictor Variable | Error and Model Specification | | | |
| | AR(1) | | MA(1) | |
	Model A	Model B	Model A	Model B
Log Wholesale Price of Cotton$_t$	−0.5902	−0.5124	−0.5770	−0.4676
	(−2.633)	(−2.035)	(−2.478)	(−1.824)
Log (CPI$_{t-1}$/CPI$_{t-2}$)	2.2091	2.3024	2.4841	2.7488
	(2.346)	(2.198)	(2.584)	(2.628)
Log Bales of Cotton Produced$_t$	—	0.0199	—	−0.0741
		(0.074)		(−0.266)
Log Size of Black Population$_t$	—	1.7496	—	1.3585
		(0.548)		(0.578)
Log White Lynch Victims$_t$	—	0.0733	—	0.0954
		(0.840)		(1.048)
AR(1) or MA(1) Coefficient	−0.4345	−0.4538	−0.4549	−0.4911
	(−2.773)	(−2.733)	(−3.353)	(−3.381)
R^2	0.7674	0.7728	0.7727	0.7799
Adjusted R^2	0.7566	0.7444	0.7623	0.7531
Standard Error of the Estimate	0.3248	0.3328	0.3186	0.3247
Q-Coefficient	16.179	15.603	13.160	13.673

[a]All variables differenced once. t-ratios in parentheses.

inflation, which reflects the stresses created when the purchasing value of the dollar declines. Independent of the price of cotton, the rate of inflation was an important factor shaping the economic security and well-being of all southerners.

In Table 6.1 we report the results of the time-series analysis of the frequency of white mobs killing southern blacks. We estimated baseline models composed of only the price of cotton and rate of inflation—lagged one year—as predictors (the Model As in Table 6.1), and then enhanced the models by including the size (log) of the black population, the size (log) of the cotton crop, and he number (log) of white lynch victims as control variables (the Model Bs in Table 6.1).[11]

The findings reported for the baseline Model As in Table 6.1 show that regardless of whether we assume a simple autoregressive disturbance or a first-order moving-average disturbance, the price of cotton and the rate of inflation have significant effects on the frequency of antiblack violence. In both specifications, a 1 percent increase in cotton price is associated with a 0.6 percent *reduction* in the number of black victims. The effect of the rate of inflation is stronger: a 1 percent growth in the rate of inflation will increase the toll of black victims by between 2.2 percent and 2.5 percent depending upon specification. Both of these findings are consistent with our expectations that favorable economic conditions, high real prices of cotton, and low rates of inflation were associated with periods of *reduced* lethal aggression toward southern blacks.

In the enhanced Model Bs we have included controls for changes over time in the size of the black population, the size of the cotton crop, and the general climate of mob violence. In these additional regressions, the effect of cotton price is slightly attenuated, but it is still an important factor in influencing antiblack violence. The effect of inflation is, however, marginally larger in these models as compared with the results of the model without control variables. The important conclusion is, however, that the introduction of the control variables does *not* alter the inference that the frequency of white mob violence toward blacks was affected by economic conditions in the south. When the southern economy soured, whites were more likely to invoke lethal mob violence against their African-American neighbors than in times when the economy was buoyant.

While the results in Table 6.1 are instructive, to gain a more refined understanding of the economic basis of white aggression, we want to entertain the idea that the relationship between violence and economic conditions was not constant across time, but allow for the possibility that the relationship varied during the lynching era. There are several different methodologies available for decomposing an aggregate time-series, but the one we have selected involves an anchored moving-regression framework.[12] The basic principle is straightforward. First we estimate a time-series model for a span of years shorter than the whole period, then we add a year to that abbreviated series and reestimate the model. By comparing the shift in the coefficients of the predictor variables between these two regressions, we can assess the influence of that additional year on the primary results. This basic process is then repeated until all the data have been exhausted. In our specific case, we anchored our first time-series at 1884, and estimated the effects of cotton price and inflation on black lynching victims for the years 1884–1898.[13] Next we added the data for 1899 to the series and reestimated the model for the years 1884–1899; in the next iteration, the data covered the period 1884–1900, and so forth, until the last estimation covered the entire span 1884–1930. In each of these thirty-three cycles, the model we used was comparable to Model A of the moving-average specification in Table 6.1.[14] This procedure yielded thirty-three time-ordered sets of nonindependent estimates of the effects of cotton price and inflation on antiblack violence.

By plotting these estimates against time, we are able to determine if the relationship between economic conditions and white aggression remained constant throughout the lynching era. In Figure 6.1 we have graphed the

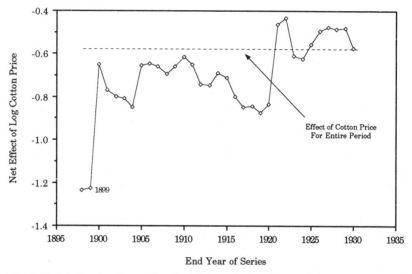

FIGURE 6.1 Moving-Regression Coefficients for Log Cotton Price

anchored moving-regression coefficients for the net effect of the price of cotton (log deflated wholesale price) on the yearly number of blacks murdered
by white mobs. This plot shows that the effect of cotton price on lynching
peaked in 1899, and then after the turn of the century, it declined markedly.
This can be readily verified by dividing the lynching era into two segments
(1884–1899 and 1900–1930) and then reestimating our moving-average
model for each period separately. Doing this we found that the estimated effect of cotton price was − 1.2272 for the earlier segment and −0.4748 for the
later period. This indicates that real dollar price of cotton had roughly three
times stronger an effect on black lynchings before 1900 than it did afterward.

In Figure 6.2 we have plotted the anchored moving-regression coefficients for the net effect of the rate of inflation—lagged one year—on the annual toll of blacks lynched by white mobs. This figure shows clearly that the
net effect of inflation was particularly strong in the period through 1907, but
in the subsequent years, the effect of inflation declined throughout the whole
period. Again, dividing the series into two segments (1882–1907 and 1908–
1930) we reestimated the moving-average model and computed that the net
effect of inflation was about four times greater in the early period as opposed
to the years after 1907: nets effects of 8.8812 versus 1.7983, respectively.

Taking Figure 6.1 and 6.2 together, the evidence suggests that economic conditions in general, and the fortunes of cotton in particular, were
more instrumental in affecting antiblack mob violence during the first half of
the lynching era than in the latter half, after about 1906 or 1907. But why

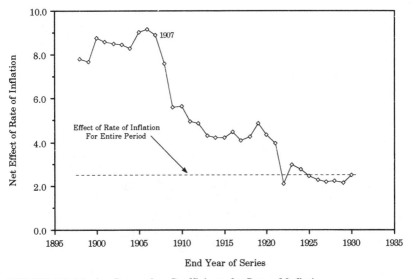

FIGURE 6.2 Moving-Regression Coefficients for Rate of Inflation

did that happen? We speculate that by roughly that time, Jim Crow legislation and political disenfranchisement were becoming effective and institutionalized policy instruments for controlling the south's black population, thus reducing the need for extralegal social control. Alternatively, it is possible that shifts in the other components of *Violence Potential* were operating. For example, either a less permissive attitude by the state, or a weakening of the racist ideology supporting racial violence, may have occurred near the turn of the century. If so, our simplifying assumptions mentioned above would be inaccurate and the inference of a weakening importance of economic conditions could be misleading. However, we are very doubtful that such transitions in either state permissiveness or racist ideology occurred so early in the century.

In sum, the time-series analysis provides empirical evidence that white mob violence toward African-Americans increased during economic downturns. The anchored regressions provided additional insight by showing that this association between economic conditions and violence was stronger in the earlier years of the lynching era than later in the twentieth century. These conclusions refer to the trend in the annual toll of southern blacks killed by white mobs, but the question of the factors explaining the spatial distribution of mob violence within the south remains open.

Not all regions of the south experienced equal amounts of antiblack violence, with lynching being commonplace in Georgia and Mississippi, but rather infrequent in North Carolina, for example. In the next section we use cross-sectional, as opposed to time-series, data to examine the hypothesis that the intensity of mob violence against blacks was stronger in regions of the south where the black population posed a greater threat to the white community.

Cross-Sectional Evidence. In this section we consider the relationship between the magnitude of the black threat and the likelihood of white mob violence. Missing a direct measure of *threat,* we employ the relative size of the local black population as a proxy. It is argued that as the percent population black rises, local whites fear heightened competition for limited economic resources and political power, hence the black population is increasingly viewed as menacing the status of whites. Blalock (1967) has argued that this relationship may not be linear. If the black threat is viewed as being primarily economic, Blalock predicts that after some critical tipping point is reached, further gains in the relative size of the black population will not produce more threat. If the threat is primarily political, however, threat should continue to rise—possibly disproportionately—with increased percent black.[15]

To investigate the relationship between the relative size of the black population and antiblack mob violence, we use counties in the south as our units of analysis. The basic data consist of the number of blacks lynched by white mobs in the county and the relative size of the country's black population during each of five time periods: 1882–1889, 1890–1899, 1900–1909, 1910–1919, and 1920–1929. Within each time period we examine the relationship between these two variables using a regression-type framework. Since the dependent variable is the count of the number of black victims in each county, some special attention must be given to developing a formal model linking violence to the size of the black threat. One statistical approach is to model the number of victims as outcomes of a poisson process. Specifically, if Y_i is the number of victims in the ith county during a particular period of t years, the probability that the ith county would experience exactly y victims is given by:

$$\text{Prob } (Y_i = y_i) = \exp^{-\lambda_i} \frac{\lambda_i^{y_i}}{y_i!}$$

which has a single distribution parameter λ_i that governs how many African-American victims of white violence the ith county would experience in t years. λ_i is interpreted as the intensity of antiblack violence within the ith county. Under this specification, variation in racial violence must be due to intercounty differences in the poisson parameter λ.

We argue that spatial variation in the λs—and hence variation in the intensity of racial violence—is the product of intercounty differences in the degree of the black *threat* to the white community, as discussed above. However, the size of the threat is not the only factor that might affect white violence, and in order to avoid spurious conclusions concerning threat effects, we want to control on other relevant factors. In particular, it is expected that a county's history of violence—or *proneness* to violence—toward blacks, and a county's tendency toward extralegal sanctioning in general, would have important effects on the intensity of racial violence.[16] We also include a statistical control for the absolute size of the county's black population.

Given these considerations, we specify that the poisson parameter λs are an additive function of the predictor variables and a disturbance term.[17] For the ith county,

$$\text{Log } \lambda_i = \beta_0 + \beta_1(\%\text{Black}_i) + \beta_2(\%\text{Black}_i{}^2) +$$
$$+ \beta_3(\text{Log Size of Black Population}_i) +$$
$$+ \beta_4(\text{Number of White Lynchings}_i) +$$
$$+ \beta_5(\text{Proneness to Antiblack Violence}_i) + \epsilon_i$$

where λ_i is the county's poisson parameter, β_0 is a constant across counties, β_ks are parameters indicating the effect of the predictor variables on the intensity of racial violence, and ϵ is a random disturbance with a gamma distribution. The racial composition variable enters the model with both linear and quadratic terms. As discussed above, Blalock's theory of minority competition—or *threat* in our terms—posits a nonlinear effect of racial composition. If the threat is primarily economic, we would expect β_1 to be positive and β_2 to be negative; if the threat is more political in nature, Blalock's theory suggests that β_1 will be either positive or insignificant, and β_2 will be positive.

In Table 6.2 we report for five time periods the results of the poisson-gamma regression of the number of black lynching victims on the county's racial composition, the size of the local black population, the number of white victims of lynchings, and the county's proneness to antiblack mob violence.[18] Of primary interest in Table 6.2 are the effects of racial composition.

In each time period, both the linear and quadratic effects of percent black are significant predictors of the intensity of antiblack violence. Consistent with the economic interpretation of the black threat potential, we find that the linear effect is positive and the quadratic effect is negative, indicating that up to some critical tipping point increases in the relative size of the county's black population are associated with greater racial conflict, but once beyond that critical tipping point, further increases in percent black are associated with reduced antiblack violence.

TABLE 6.2   Poisson-Gamma Regression of Number of Black Lynching Victims of White Mobs on Racial composition, and Related Variables for Counties in the South by Decade[a]

Predictor Variable[b]	Decade				
	1882–89	1890–99	1900–09	1910–19	1920–29
Constant	-2.393	-1.377	-2.139	-2.849	-3.739
	(-7.50)	(-6.82)	(-8.73)	(-10.41)	(-10.49)
Percent Population Black	0.047	0.036	0.052	0.055	0.088
	(2.49)	(2.78)	(3.37)	(3.44)	(4.20)
Percent Population Black^2	-0.0005	-0.0004	-0.0004	-0.0004	-0.0008
	(-2.79)	(-2.82)	(-2.77)	(-2.55)	(-3.95)
Log Size of Black Population (1000s)	0.478	0.298	0.180	0.196	0.154
	(3.71)	(3.34)	(1.72)	(1.82)	(1.25)
White Lynchings	0.418	0.153	0.591	0.864	0.396
	(3.30)	(2.42)	(2.20)	(2.28)	(0.98)
Proneness to Antiblack Violence	—	0.146	0.099	0.105	0.074
		(3.17)	(3.47)	(5.04)	(3.30)
ψ Parameter	2.349	1.452	1.957	1.352	1.451
Number of Observations	784	803	809	830	858

[a]Asymptotic t-ratios in parentheses
[b]Percent population black and the size of the black population measured in 1880, 1890, 1900, 1910, and 1920. White Lynchings refer to the total number in each period: 1882–89, 1890–99, 1900–09, 1910–19, 1920–29. Proneness is the cumulative number of black victims of white mobs from 1882 to be beginning of the time period.

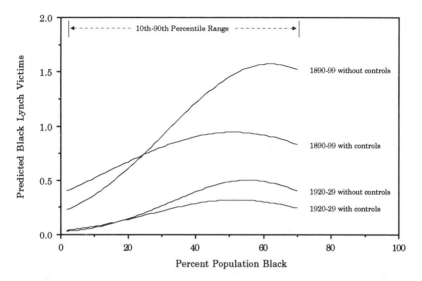

FIGURE 6.3 Relationship between Racial Composition of the Population and Antiblack Mob Violence, 1890–99 and 1920–29

We also note in Table 6.2 that in each period the historical proneness of a county to antiblack violence is a significant predictor of the county's present use of mob violence against its black citizenry. Complementary to this relationship is the finding that those counties with greater records of lynching whites tend to be the same counties where blacks were lynched with increased frequency.[19] These two results taken in concert indicate that a county's tendency to engage in extralegal sanctioning in general, as well as its *history* of antiblack violence in particular, are significant forces in explaining current behavior toward their African-American citizens.

The most important conclusion to be drawn from the results presented in Table 6.2 is that even after a county's history of violence is factored into the analysis, the racial composition of the county remains an important determinant of the level of white violence directed toward blacks, and this relationship holds for each time period from 1882 through 1929. It appears that the black *threat* had very real consequences.

To examine this threat-violence connection in more detail, we have plotted the relationship between the racial composition of the local population and the predicted number of black lynch victims in Figure 6.3. To avoid unnecessary complexity, we have chosen to focus on only two time periods: 1890–1899 and 1920–1929. The 1890–1899 span encompassed the peak of the antiblack mob violence in the south, and the 1920–1929 decade captures the end of the southern lynching era. For each period we estimated two models: (1) a model with the percent black and percent black squared variables alone (without controls for other factors), and (2) a model that augments this basic specification with the control variables listed in Table 6.2.[20]

Figure 6.3 clearly shows that increases in the black *threat*, as reflected in the racial composition of the population, were associated with greater numbers of African-Americans being lynched by white mobs until counties became about 55 percent black—after that point,[21] further increases in the relative size of the local black population were associated with *fewer* incidents of antiblack violence. In other words, in both time periods, where blacks significantly dominated—numerically—the local population, there was less white lynching behavior as compared to areas where blacks were in a demographic minority.

Two further comparisons in Figure 6.3 are worth note. First, within each time period, adding the control variables to the model flattens the effects of percent black; that is, the effects of racial composition on black lynching are reduced after the control variables are included in the basic model. This is not unexpected, because percent black is strongly correlated with the log of the absolute size of the black population.[22] Nevertheless, racial composition remains a significant predictor of antiblack violence in all time periods, as shown in Table 6.2. Second, although it is not completely obvious from Figure 6.3, it can be shown mathematically that changes in the percent black have a greater effect on black lynchings in the 1890 to 1899 period than in the 1920 to 1929 years, regardless of whether we consider the relationship with or without controls.[23] This means that in most counties of the south,[24] increases in the relative size of the black population were associated with more frequent antiblack violence, but this relationship was stronger in the early years of the lynching era than in the following years. These findings indicate that violence toward blacks became *less* sensitive to the *threat* later in this century—at least to the degree to which the *threat* is synonymous with the relative size of the black population. Interestingly, this trend is consistent with the findings from the time series analyses, which showed a weakening linkage between economic conditions and lynchings after the turn of the century.

The implications of the cross-sectional analyses are quite clear. The findings suggest that in some counties of the south, there was an acceptance of, or at least permissiveness toward, extralegal sanctioning of blacks and whites for violations of the normative order. Over and above this climate of violence, our analysis shows that in areas where blacks were in the numerical minority, the amount of antiblack violence was a function of the size of the black *threat*—the greater the threat, the more frequent blacks were killed by white mobs.[25] But the treat-violence relationship was not invariant across time. It was stronger before the turn of the century than after World War I.

CONCLUSIONS

In the broadest terms, we argued in the first part of this chapter that the degree of racial violence in the south during the lynching era was a function of four necessary factors: a climate of interracial competition for scarce resources where blacks represented a threat to the advantage enjoyed by many whites, a racist ideology rationalizing white dominance and black inferiority, a state sector with permissive attitudes toward white violence toward blacks, and some threshold incident triggering white mob violence. Of these essential ingredients, the empirical analysis focused on demonstrating the role of competition and threat in generating antiblack violence.[26]

Although we have had to rely on proxy measures of racial competition, the evidence from time-series and cross-sectional analyses is consistent. We believe that the amount of interracial competition is a critical factor in understanding why southern blacks became a target for white persecution during the lynching era, 1882 to 1930. The time-series findings demonstrated that antiblack violence was more frequent during periods when the real price of cotton was falling and during periods when the rate of inflation was high. The findings from the cross-sectional analyses indicated that racial violence was more frequent in southern counties where the relative size of the black population was larger—the greater the black threat, the more frequent the violence toward African-Americans. The exception to this principle were regions where blacks numerically dominated the white population—these counties had *lower* levels of interracial violence.

Both the time-series and cross-sectional analyses further indicated that the salience of racial competition and threat in generating racial violence declined in the twentieth century—mob violence increasingly became untied to competition and threat. The weakening of this association in the years after World War I may have been due, in part, to the exodus of blacks from the south during this period, and the declining significance of cotton (Tolnay and Beck, 1992). Simply put, the need for extralegal white control of the south's African-American population appears to have been greater in the 1890s than in the 1920s.

NOTES

1. In this paper we use the terms *African-Americans* and *blacks* interchangeably. For ease, we refer to European-Americans simply as *whites*. For our purposes the American south is defined as Alabama, Arkansas, Florida, Georgia, Kentucky, Louisiana, Mississippi, North Carolina, South Carolina, and Tennessee.

2. If the border states of Missouri, Oklahoma, Texas, Virginia, and West Virginia were included, the total would be significantly greater.

3. For classic descriptions of lynchings, see Jessie Ames (1942), *The Changing Character of Lynching. Review of Lynching, 1931–1941;* Arthur Raper (1933), *The Tragedy of Lynching;* Walter White (1929[1969]). *Rope and Faggot: A Biography of Judge Lynch;* Ida B. Wells (1892[1969]), *Southern Horrors. Lynch Law in All Its Phases;* and James Cutler (1905), *Lynch-Law: An Investigation Into the History of Lynching in the United States.* More contemporary work includes James McGovern (1982), *Anatomy of a Lynching: The Killing of Claude Neal;* Howard Smead (1986), *Blood Justice: The Lynching of Charles Mack Parker;* Leonard Dinnerstein (1987), *The Leo Frank Case;* Dennis Downey and Raymond Hyser (1991), *No Crooked Death: Coatesville. Pennsylvania and the Lynching of Zachariah Walker;* George Wright (1990), *Racial Violence in Kentucky, 1865–1940: Lynchings, Mob Rule, and "Legal Lynchings";* and W. Fitzhugh Brundage (1993), *Lynching in the New South: Georgia and Virginia, 1880–1930.*

4. See Beck and Tolnay (1990) and Tolnay and Beck (1994) for a detailed description of the new lynching inventory.

5. This does not imply that the role of competition, the state, and ideology are independent factors unrelated to each other. On the contrary, they are intertwined dimensions of the political economy that are interdependent and mutually reinforcing. One implication of this kind of model is that if any one of the elements is missing, or reduced in strength, the likelihood for violence declines proportionally.

6. This is not to imply that racism was a singularly southern phenomenon. On the contrary, racism was thoroughly American (Takaki, 1990; Roediger, 1991), and racial violence could be found all in sections of the country (Shapiro, 1988).

7. *Atlanta Constitution,* October 11, 1911, p.1; *Augusta Chronicle,* October 11, 1911, p.1; NAACP (1919[1969]): 18–19.

8. When the three factors (competition, racism, and legal permissiveness) were sufficiently strong and reached a critical mass, even superficially minor confrontations between whites and blacks could spark a violent response. Thus, we feel that it is not the apparent seriousness of an incident that triggers violence, but rather it is the *timing* of the incident in relation to the other factors in the model that is important. If the violence potential is high enough, a triggering incident can always be found *or created.*

9. It is clear that in some counties in the south, the numerical superiority of African-Americans posed a very real and tangible threat to white political hegemony. In regions where white landowners were dependent upon black labor, the control of this labor posed real problems, and the lack of control would be defined as a threat. In some instances, however, it could be argued that blacks represented no *real,* demonstrable threat to white interests, thus questioning salience of *threat* as an explanation of racial violence. But how does one determine what constitutes a *real,* as opposed to *fictional,* threat? It seems clear that if whites defined blacks as being threatening, regardless of the objectivity of the situation, then the perceived threat was real in its consequences for the African-American community.

10. We considered two specifications for the disturbance term in time-series model: first, we entertained a model where the disturbance term was assumed to follow a simple (AR1) autoregressive scheme, hence

$$u_t = \rho u_{t-1} + \epsilon_t$$
$$t = 1,2, \ldots n \; years$$

where ρ is the first-order autocorrelation coefficient and ϵ_t is a random error. The second specification assumed the disturbance term followed a first-order (MA1) moving-average process, hence

$$u_t = \epsilon_t + \phi \epsilon_{t-1}$$
$$t = 1,2, \ldots n \; years$$

where ϕ is the first-order moving-average coefficient and ϵ_t is a random error. For discussions of the differences between the autoregressive and moving-average specifications, see McCleary and Hay (1980), and Gottman(1981). We entertained both because we wanted to demonstrate that the empirical results were essentially the same regardless of which specification was used.

11. In all specifications in Table 6.1, the variables have been differenced once.

12. See Isaac and Griffin (1989) for an informative discussion of the limitations of traditional ahistorical time-series analyses.

13. While the original time series begin in 1882, two observations are lost through differencing and lagging. Thus the models are actually predicting black victims for the years 1884 through 1930.

14. We chose this simple model to save degrees of freedom. It should be noted that none of the other terms in the more complex models reported in Table 6.1 attain traditional statistical significance at conventional levels of Type I error.

15. See Tolnay, Beck, and Massey (1992).

16. Antiblack *proneness* effects are operationalized as the total number of blacks murdered by white mobs in the county in periods *prior* to the time period being studied; and our measure of the generalized tendency toward extralegal sanctioning is the number of white victims of white mobs during the time period under investigation.

17. In the simple poisson regression model, the λs are an exact function of the predictor variables, and $V(Y) = E(Y|X)$. This specification is of limited value, however, since count data are often *overdispersed* and do not fit the simple poisson regression model satisfactory; that is, typically $V(Y) > E(Y|X)$. To account for the overdispersion, the poisson regression model is modified by adding a random disturbance to the specification. When this disturbance follows a gamma distribution, the resulting compound poisson-gamma regression model is identical to a negative binomial specification for the count variable (Cameron and Trivedi, 1986; Hinde, 1982;

Lawless, 1987). The parameters of the poisson-gamma regression were estimated by Bennett's algorithm (Bennett, 1988) in GLIM (see Aitkin et al., 1990; McCullagh and Nelder, 1983).

18. Since our data cover the years 1882 through 1930, we have no information on the amount of antiblack violence prior to 1882, thus the proneness variable could not be included in the regression for the 1882–1889 period.

19. This does not apply, however, to the 1920–29 period, where the white lynching variable is an insignificant predictor of black lynchings. This is likely due to the extremely small number of white victims of mob violence during these years.

20. Percent black was plotted over the range between the 10th and 90th percentiles—2% to 70% black. In other words, only 10% of the counties had percent black less than 2% and only 10% of the counties had percent black greater than 70%. Furthermore, for the *with control* plots in Figure 6.3, the effects of the control variables were evaluated at their medians.

21. The exact point at which the relationship reverses depends upon which model and time period is being considered: for the 1890–98 period, the tipping point is 62.1% black for the model without controls and 51.1% black for the model with controls; for the 1920–29 period, the point is 55.4% black for the model without controls and 51.9% black for the specification with controls.

22. For the 1890–99 period, the zero-order correlation between percent black and the size (log) of the black population is 0.812, and for the 1920–29 period the correlation is 0.746.

23. The specification for the model without controls is:

$$\text{Log}\lambda = \beta_0 + \beta_1 P + \beta_2 P^2$$

which is equivalent to:

$$\lambda = \exp(\beta_0 + \beta_1 P + \beta_2 P^2) \qquad \text{Eq. 1}$$

where P is the percent black in the local population and the β_ks are parameters to be estimated. In this model, Eq. 1, the effect of percent black is:

$$d\lambda/dP = exp(\beta_0 + \beta_1 P + \beta_2 P^2) \qquad \text{Eq. 2}$$

Let us suppose that we estimate Eq. 1 for the 1890–99 period and obtain empirical estimates of the parameters, β_0, β_1, and β_2, and compute $d\lambda/dP$ for a specific value of P. Next we estimate the same model for the 1920–29 period and obtain those empirical estimates, β_0^*, β_1^*, and β_2^*, and compute $d\lambda/dP$ for this period at the same value of P, which we shall call $d\lambda^*/dP$. The ratio of $d\lambda/dP$ to $d\lambda^*/dP$ is a measure of the relative importance of percent black in the two periods for a given value of percent black (P). If percent black had the same effect in both periods, the ratio of $d\lambda/dP$ to $d\lambda^*/dP$ will be unity; if percent black had a stronger effect in the 1890–99 period, the ration of $d\lambda/dP$ to $d\lambda*/dP$ will be greater than unity; and if percent black had a weaker effect in the 1890–99 period, the ratio of $d\lambda/dP$ to $d\lambda*/dP$ will be less than unity. Now, it is easily shown that

$$(d\lambda/dP) / (d\lambda*/dP) = \exp[(\beta_0 - \beta_0*)$$
$$+ (\beta_1 - \beta_1*)(P) + (\beta_2 - \beta_2*)(P^2)] \qquad \text{Eq. 3}$$

When we plug in our actual estimates of the parameters in Eq. 3, we find that the ratio $d\lambda/dP$ to $d\lambda*/dP$ is greater than unity for all values of P, the percent black. When the comparable procedure is followed for the model with control variables, we also find that the ratio of net effects of percent black is greater than one for all values of percent black.

24. Namely, those counties where the population was less than about 55% black. See note 20.

25. In counties where African-Americans were numerically dominant, however, the size of the black threat was either unrelated or negatively related.

26. In personal communication, Darnell Hawkins offers a viable alternative interpretation of our findings. Hawkins suggests that factors such as inflation and failing cotton prices may not have been fundamental causative factors as we suggest, but may have been simple *threshold events,* similar in function to the kinds of *triggering incidents* we discuss. From this point of view, white violence was displaced aggression and African-Americans were scapegoats. To be sure, we can present no evidence that this interpretation is unreasonable. How much violence can be attributed to displaced aggression and scapegoating, as opposed to violence generated by competition for scarce resources, is a debatable question, and one that probably does not have an empirical answer.

REFERENCES

Aitkin, Murray, Dorothy Anderson, Brian Francis, and John Hinde. 1990. *Statistical Modelling in GLIM.* Oxford: Clarendon Press.

Ames, Jessie Daniel. 1942. *The Changing Character of Lynching. Review of Lynching, 1931–1941.* Atlanta: Commission on Interracial Cooperation.

Beck, E.M., and Stewart E. Tolnay. 1990. "The Killing Fields of the Deep South: The Market for Cotton and the Lynching of Blacks, 1882–1930." *American Sociological Review* 55:526–539.

Bennett, Steve. 1988. "An Extension of Williams' Method for Overdispersion Models." *GLIM Newsletter* 17:12–18

Blalock, Hubert M. 1967. *Toward a Theory of Minority-Group Relations.* New York: Wiley.

Bloom, Jack M. 1987. *Class, Race, and the Civil Rights Movement.* Bloomington: Indiana University Press.

Brundage, W. Fitzhugh. 1993. *Lynching in the New South: Georgia and Virginia, 1880–1930.* Urbana: University of Illinois Press.

Cameron, A. Colin., and P. Trivedi. 1986. "Econometric Models Based on Count Data: Comparisons and Applications of Some Estimators and Tests." *Journal of Applied Econometrics* 1:29–53.

Cutler, James E. 1905. *Lynch Law: An Investigation into the History of Lynching in the United States.* New York: Longmans-Green.

Corzine, Jay, James Creech, and Lin Corzine. 1983. "Black Concentration and Lynchings in the South: Testing Blalock's Power-Threat Hypothesis." *Social Forces* 61:774–96.

Dinnerstein, Leonard. 1987. *The Leo Frank Case.* Athens: University of Georgia Press.

Dixon, Thomas, Jr. 1902. *The Leopard's Spots. A Romance of the White Man's Burden—1865–1900.* New York: Doubleday, Page.

———. 1907. *The Clansman. An Historical Romance of the Ku Klux Klan.* New York: A. Wessels.

Downey, Dennis B., and Raymond H. Hyser. 1991. *No Crooked Death: Coatsville, Pennsylvania and the Lynching of Zachariah Walker.* Urbana: University of Illinois Press.

Gottman, John M. 1981. *Time-Series Analysis: A Comprehensive Introduction for Social Scientists.* Cambridge: Cambridge University Press.

Hinde, John. 1982. "Compound Poisson Models." Pp. 109–21 in Robert Gilchrist (ed.), *GLIM82: Proceedings of the International Conference on Generalised Linear Models.* New York: Springer-Verlag.

Hoffman, Frederick L. 1896. *Race Traits and Tendencies of the American Negro.* New York: Macmillan.

Hovland, Carl I., and Robert R. Sears. 1940. "Minor Studies of Aggression: Correlations of Economic Indices with Lynchings." *Journal of Psychology* 9:301–10.

Isaac, Larry W., and Larry J. Griffin. 1989. "Ahistoricism in Time-Series Analysis of Historical Process: Critique, Redirection, and Illustrations for U.S. Labor History." *American Sociological Review* 54:873–90.

Kousser, J. Morgan. 1974. *The Shaping of Southern Politics: Suffrage Restriction and the Establishment of the One-Party South.* New Haven: Yale University Press.

Lawless, Jerald F. 1987. "Negative Binomial and Mixed Poisson Regression." *Canadian Journal of Statistics* 15:209–25.

McCleary, Richard, and Richard A. Hay, Jr. 1980. *Applied Time Series Analysis for the Social Sciences.* Beverley Hills, Calif.: Sage Publications.

McCullagh, P., and J.A. Nelder. 1983. *Generalized Linear Models.* London: Chapman and Hall.

McGovern, James R. 1982. *Anatomy of a Lynching: The Killing of Claude Neal.* Baton Rouge: Louisiana State University Press.

Myers, Martha A. 1991. "Economic Conditions and Punishment in Postbellum Georgia." *Journal of Quantitative Criminology* 7:9–121.

National Association for the Advancement of Colored People. 1919 [1969]. *Thirty Years of Lynching in the United States.* Reprint. New York: Arno Press.

Olzak, Susan. 1990. "The Political Context of Competition: Lynching and Urban Racial Violence, 1882–1914." *Social Forces* 69:395–421.

Raper, Arthur F. 1933. *The Tragedy of Lynching.* Chapel Hill: University of North Carolina Press.

Reed, John Shelton. 1972. "Percent Black and Lynching: A Test of Blalock's Theory." *Social Forces* 50:356–60.

Roediger, David R. 1991. *The Wages of Whiteness: Race and the Making of the American Working Class.* London: Verso.

Shapiro, Herbert. 1988. *White Violence and Black Response: From Reconstruction to Montgomery.* Amherst: University of Massachusetts Press.

Smead, Howard. 1986. *Blood Justice: The Lynching of Mack Charles Parker.* New York: Oxford University Press.

Takaki, Ronald. 1990. *Iron Cages: Race and Culture in 19th-Century America.* New York: Oxford University Press.

Tolnay, Stewart E., and E.M. Beck. 1992. "Racial Violence and Black Migration in the South, 1910 to 1930." *American Sociological Review* 57:103–16.

———. 1994. *A Festival of Violence: An Analysis of the Lynching of African-Americans in the American South, 1882–1930.* Urbana: University of Illinois Press.

Tolnay, Stewart E., E.M. Beck, and James Massey. 1992. "Execution of Blacks as Social Control in the Cotton South." *Social Science Quarterly* 73:627–44.

Wells-Barnett, Ida B. 1892 [1969]. *On Lynchings: Southern Horrors: A Red Record: Mob Rule in New Orleans.* Reprint. New York: Arno Press.

White, Walter Francis. 1929 [1969]. *Rope and Faggot: A Biography of Judge Lynch.* Reprint. New York: Arno Press

Woodward, C. Vann. 1966. *The Strange Career of Jim Crow.* New York: Oxford University Press.

Wright, George C. 1990. *Racial Violence in Kentucky, 1865–1940: Lynchings, Mob Rule, and "Legal Lynchings."* Baton Rouge: Louisiana State University Press.

MARTHA A. MYERS

7

The New South's "New" Black Criminal: Rape and Punishment in Georgia, 1870–1940*

In the postbellum south, the image of blacks as a race was unambiguous. Inherently inferior, they possessed a dual nature: docile and loyal under white control, but savage and impulsive if left to their own devices (Friedman, 1970; Frederickson, 1972; Williamson, 1984). At the turn of the century, the "black image in the white mind" underwent a fundamental transformation, and the specter of young black men sexually assaulting white women loomed large (Williamson, 1984). Economic and political crises lay at the root of this image, which was the frontispiece of a virulent racist mentality that flourished between 1889 and 1914. This mentality justified numerous repressive measures directed against blacks. Some, such as segregation and disenfranchisement, were sanctioned by law; others, such as lynchings and race riots, were not. This paper focusses on black men convicted of sexual assault, and examines their treatment within the criminal justice system itself. It embeds their punishment in two related contexts: changing economic conditions that threatened white hegemony and the incidence of a particularly infamous form of informal social control—namely, lynchings on the pretext of assault.

THE "NEW NEGRO" CRIMINAL

As Cell (1982: 114) eloquently put it, the "ladder of Southern agrarian society had slippery rungs" in the late nineteenth and early twentieth centuries. Heavy dependence on cotton as a cash crop permitted the economy to prosper only when cotton prices were high. Declining prices precipitated depressions and accelerated the decline of independent white farmers into tenantry (Woodward, 1971; Hahn, 1983; Bloom, 1987). The economic gap that had so sharply divided whites and blacks narrowed considerably with time, and increasing numbers of whites faced the prospect of competing with blacks for land and jobs (Higgs, 1977). Volatile economic conditions and the resulting Populist movement generated a context of threat. Consistent with Blalock's (1967) theory, it stimulated the development of numerous mechanisms designed to reinforce blurring caste lines and deflect attention from class divisions among whites (Cell, 1982; Bloom, 1987). City ordinances and state statutes increasingly required segregated public accommodations and business establishments (Woodward, 1974; Cell, 1982). Literacy tests and poll taxes deprived blacks and most poor whites of the vote by 1909 (Kousser, 1974; Cell, 1982; Bloom, 1987).

Accompanying these economic and political upheavals was an increasingly popular *radical* racist mentality (Frederickson, 1971; Williamson, 1984). At its heart was a form of black criminality that bore little resemblance to traditional images. White perceptions of blacks had always included an assumption of criminality that involved petty thievery rather than serious crimes against person or property (Bruce, 1889; Smith, 1893). The rape of black women, for example, was reportedly uncommon (Bruce, 1889; Page, 1904), while the rape of white women by black men was simply unheard of (Smith, 1893; Hoffman, 1896; Page, 1904).

This image of black criminality altered radically between the late 1880s and World War I. Concern with theft receded and the sexual assault of white women moved to the forefront. This crime was considered a *new* phenomenon, which inflicted unspeakable damage on victims (Smith, 1893; King, 1900) and threatened white hegemony and purity (King, 1900; Cash, 1940). Its mere existence was seen as symptomatic of what whites perceived to be general and alarming changes in their relationships with blacks. Two of the most prominent "changes" were the movement toward social equality, which to the "ignorant" black man meant equal access to white women (Harvey, 1903; Page, 1904), and the cessation of contact with and restraint by whites, without which blacks would purportedly revert to the original African (that is, savage) type (Bruce, 1889). As further evidence of deleterious *changes,* critics noted that a "new race of Negroes" (King, 1900: 162), born after emancipation and "untrained" by slavery, perpetrated these assaults (Haygood, 1893; Smith, 1893; Tillinghast, 1902; Page, 1904). The crime and the criminal were thus seen as delayed and increasingly visible legacies of emancipation and Reconstruction.

To counter this threat, whether real or perceived, repressive measures were undertaken or proposed. Between 1882 and 1930, 436 blacks were lynched in Georgia alone, 38 percent on the pretext of an actual or potential assault of a white woman or girl.[1] While few contemporaries publicly condoned such actions, most agreed that the crime itself and inadequacies within the criminal justice system rendered them understandable (Page, 1893; Haygood, 1893; Hoffman, 1896; Page, 1904). To reduce both rape and lynching, critics urged swifter imposition of the death penalty and the use of sanctions that would strike terror in the hearts of black males contemplating rape (King, 1900: 163; Cockran, 1900: 203).

Public officials in Georgia appeared to pay little attention to these demands. Legal penalties for rape, as well as for most other offenses, remained unchanged during the late nineteenth and early twentieth centuries. As yet unknown, however, are whether and to what extent officials in the criminal justice system heeded public calls for punitiveness and altered their reactions to rape offenders accordingly. We do know that general rates of penitentiary incarceration increased during periods when cotton prices declined and economic conditions worsened (Myers, 1991). Since interracial sexual assault was at the heart of public perceptions of crime, a similar relationship may characterize penalties for sexual assault and periods of chronic economic distress (for example, 1889–1914).

As noted above, contemporaries believed that inadequate penalties for rape were one factor that accounted for lynching; presumably, more severe penalties would contribute to its demise. In essence, contemporaries saw the two responses to rape as substitutes for one another. Recent studies of lynching and executions question this commonsense understanding and provide evidence of a mutually reinforcing relationship grounded in white perceptions of black threat (Massey and Myers, 1989; Beck et al., 1989; Tolnay and Beck, 1992). What remains unspecified is the relationship between two forms of social control with the same target.

In addition to linking criminal punishment with its broader economic context, then, this paper examines the relationship between criminal penalties for sexual assault and lynchings on the pretext of sexual assault. Of central interest is whether increases in rape-related lynchings contributed to more punitive reactions within the criminal justice system, and whether increases in the severity of criminal penalties had the anticipated effect of rendering lynching superfluous.

METHODS

Sources and Measures of Punishment

Although felons convicted in Georgia during this period were sentenced to the state penitentiary, few served their time behind prison walls. Rather, all able-bodied felons convicted before 1909 were leased to private contractors for hard manual labor; after 1909, they built and maintained public access roads and other projects under county authorities. The state archives provided information about these offenders. The first source of data was the Principal Keeper of the Georgia Penitentiary. His reports, issued between 1874 and 1896, identified and described all inmates on hand at the end of the reporting period. The second source of data was a microfilmed series of manuscript inventories, which included descriptive information about offenders convicted between 1817 and 1942.[2] Table 7.1 describes the population of offenders convicted of sexual assault between 1870 and 1940. Over three-quarters were black, and the majority of both blacks and whites fit the stereotypic image of youthful offenders. In most respects, blacks faced more severe punishment than did whites. They were also less likely than whites to be released early, whether through conditional release, pardon, or commutation of their sentence.

This population of offenders provided the raw material for three aggregate measures of criminal punishment, computed by race on an annual basis. The first measure, depicted in Figure 7.1, is the admission rate, which is the number of males convicted of sexual assaults and sentenced to the penitentiary, per 10,000 males. Included for comparative purposes is the rate at which black males were lynched on the pretext of rape, available between 1882 and 1930. Note that black admission rates and lynchings both peaked in 1899, but thereafter the two trends diverge markedly. The latter declined at the turn of the century, while the black admission rate fluctuated widely.

The second punishment measure is the average sentence imposed on offenders, in years. Between 1870 and 1940, rape was punishable by death or, upon jury recommendations of mercy, by a term of one-to-twenty years. The only other rape-related offense, assault with intent to rape, carried a sentence of one-to-twenty years as well. Average sentence length is based, then, only on those offenders who received neither life nor the death penalty. The trend, depicted in Figure 7.2, provides no evidence that the prison sentences imposed on blacks became longer at the height of the radical racist mentality. The final punishment measure, also shown in Figure 7.2, is the average length of time served in the penitentiary, in years. It is based on those offenders (70 percent of blacks and 85 percent of whites) who left the system normally—that is, via discharge, commutation, pardon, or conditional release.

General inspection of these trends provides some evidence of enhanced punitiveness toward those blacks convicted of sexual assault during the height of public concern with interracial rape (1889–1914). Black admission rates peaked at the turn of the century, and black inmates served more time during the late 1880s. This harshness was nevertheless short-lived. Black admission rates had been trending upward long before 1890, and they even began to subside between 1903 and 1913. The length of time blacks served in the peni-

TABLE 7.1   Descriptive Frequencies by Race

	Black (n = 1,796)	White (n = 509)
Race	22.1	77.9
Median age	22	27
Offense type		
Rape	48.4	55.6
Rape and other offense	1.0	.4
Assault with intent to rape	49.7	43.8
Assault with intent to rape and other offense	.9	.2
Percent receiving life imprisonment	.5	1.0
Percent receiving death penalty	3.3	.8
Sentence length in years[a]		
Mean	9.4	5.6
(s.d.)	(7.8)	(6.5)
Disposition of inmate		
Discharged	41.2	18.1
Commuted/pardoned	6.3	20.1
Conditional release	25.5	46.4
Escaped	11.3	7.2
Died in penitentiary	11.4	4.7
Executed	3.6	.2
Served no time	.4	2.3
Other	.3	1.0
Years of sentence served[b]		
Mean	6.2	3.5
(s.d.)	(4.9)	(3.5)

[a]Sentence length is based on offenders who received neither a life nor a death sentence.
[b]Length of time actually served in the penitentiary is based on all inmates who were discharged, commuted, pardoned, or conditionally released.

tentiary had begun to decline by 1895. Perhaps most intriguing is the harsher punishment imposed on whites convicted of sexual assault between 1889 and 1914. During the period when harsher treatment of blacks was expected, white males often received longer sentences. They also served more time in the penitentiary than was the case before or after heightened awareness of interracial sexual assault.

Analytic Strategy

Of central interest in the analysis is the extent to which these shifts in punishment can be traced to unsettled economic conditions. To address this ques-

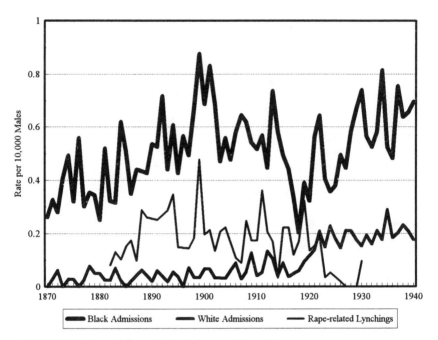

FIGURE 7.1 Sexual Assault Admissions and Lynchings

tion, the series are analyzed using ARIMA modeling procedures (Makridakis et al., 1983). Given its utility in previous work (Beck and Tolnay, 1990; Myers, 1991), the price of cotton in constant cents per pound (1900) indicates the condition of the agrarian economy (U.S. Bureau of the Census, 1975: 208–9). Blalock's (1967) economic competition argument suggests that declines in racial inequality, such as those experienced in post-Reconstruction Georgia, precipitate punitive reactions against blacks. Empirical work (Myers, 1991, 1993) indicates that under these conditions whites may have become more vulnerable to incarceration as well. To assess its relevance to punishments imposed on a single type of offender, racial inequality is included in the analysis and is indicated by the ratio of white to black per capita property values in constant dollars of 1900 (Comptroller-General Office, 1874–1936).

Since punishment during this period involved forced labor, analysis controls for indicators of labor market conditions. Earlier work (Myers, 1990b, 1991) provides grounds for expecting that declines in the cotton harvest generated a labor surplus, a portion of which the penitentiary could absorb and control. The size of the cotton harvest in 1,000s of acres is a rough indicator of the demand for agrarian labor (U.S. Department of Agriculture, 1951–52). The expected relationship is inverse: as harvests shrink and the

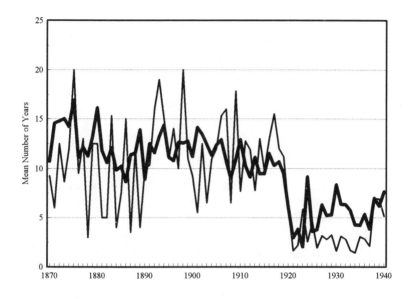

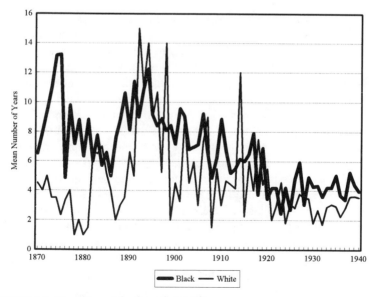

FIGURE 7.2 Time Served for Sexual Assault

surplus agrarian population increases, criminal punishment should become more severe. To indicate the available supply of black labor, percent black male in the total population is included. The expected relationship is also inverse: declines in supply should be compensated for by intensified levels of punishment (Myers, 1990a). The census provided population figures; intercensus figures were estimated by linear interpolation. Finally, in the absence of direct measures of crime, analysis includes percent young (20–29 years old) in the black and white male populations, also based on census data.

To produce the stationary mean needed for ARIMA modeling, each series was differenced. Given obvious fluctuations in variance over time, the white male sentence length and time served series were logged to produce the required stationarity. Cross-correlation functions were calculated to locate and identify relationships between input series and output series. Prior to calculating these functions, dependence among the input series was removed, as were autocorrelated errors within the input series.[3] To determine whether effects were stable over time, additional analysis used the "moving" time series strategy (Isaac and Griffin, 1989). Each punishment series was disaggregated into a set of shorter series fifteen years long. The first subseries, for example, includes the period 1874 to 1888, the second 1875 to 1889, and so on. When chronologically plotted, the resulting estimates reveal temporal changes in the direction and magnitude of the relationship.

RESULTS

Table 7.2 presents cross-correlation functions, by race, for each output series. Preliminary models included transfer functions for all input series whose cross-correlations were either statistically significant or exceeded .20. After deleting insignificant transfer functions, models were reestimated with the components necessary to produce residuals that were white noise. Table 7.3 presents these models. As expected, black admission rates increased as cotton prices declined. Figure 7.3 indicates that the link between cotton prices and black admission rates tightened between 1890 and 1914, a period that encompassed two major depressions and heightened concern with interracial sexual assault. In addition to cotton prices, the rate at which black males were admitted to the penitentiary for sexual assault declined as relative property values declined and increased as the relative size of the black male population declined. None of these factors influenced the rate at which whites were admitted to the penitentiary for sexual assault. Instead, whites' risk of incarceration increased as cotton harvests became smaller.

Table 7.3 indicates that the average sentence imposed on blacks lengthened as cotton prices declined. This relationship was particularly strong (see

TABLE 7.2   Cross-correlations between Punishment and Economic/Demographic Conditions

		Admission Rate		Sentence Length		Time Served	
	Lag	Black	White	Black	White	Black	White
Cotton price[a]	0	−.22	−.05	.10	.10	−.10	.22
	1	−.08	−.21	−.06	.06	−.01	−.06
	2	.09	.26*	.03	−.16	−.00	−.03
	3	.07	−.14	−.35*	.05	−.08	.11
	4	.16	.21	.04	−.19	.07	−.06
	5	−.08	−.08	−.02	.12	−.11	−.03
Relative	0	.03	−.02	−.12	−.10	−.19	−.15
property	1	−.16	.01	.25	.22	.02	−.05
value	2	.10	.14	−.02	−.15	.07	−.13
	3	−.02	−.07	−.07	−.02	−.06	.17
	4	−.13	.20	.06	.19	−.01	−.07
	5	.29*	−.05	.11	−.15	.09	.11
Cotton	0	.06	−.24*	.13	.06	.09	.11
harvest	1	−.07	−.08	−.09	.03	.07	−.08
	2	.02	−.09	.14	−.10	−.22	−.05
	3	.15	.12	−.08	.17	.18	.13
	4	.01	−.08	.13	−.15	.02	.09
	5	.17	−.08	−.07	.05	−.01	.04
Percent black	0	−.26*	−.04	−.01	.18	−.06	.04
male	1	.02	−.14	.05	−.15	.12	−.21
	2	.15	.14	−.17	−.10	.00	.10
	3	.14	−.06	−.18	.00	−.07	−.05
	4	−.13	.28*	.24	.12	.11	.17
	5	.09	−.06	−.01	.01	−.12	−.14
Percent young	0	−.07	.11	−.01	.15	.13	−.14
male	1	.25*	−.05	.08	−.05	−.02	−.03
	2	−.20	−.05	−.15	−.22	.04	−.12
	3	.13	.06	.37*	.23*	.11	.15
	4	−.08	.11	−.29*	−.22	−.16	−.12
	5	.09	−.18	.00	.13	−.05	.20

[a]Dependence among and autocorrelations within input series were removed before estimation.
*p < .05.

Figure 7.3) during the 1890s and after World War I. In addition to cotton prices, declines in the size of the young male population also increased the length of sentences imposed on blacks. Again, neither factor accounted for the sentences white males received. The final punishment measure—time served—responded to declines in cotton prices in an unexpected manner:

TABLE 7.3   Maximum Likelihood Estimates for Determinants of Punishments for Sexual Assault

	Function/Parameter		Blacks Estimate (SE)	Whites Estimate (SE)
Admission rate				
Cotton price[a]	ωX_t	ω	−2.32 (.81)	
Relative property value	ωX_{t-5}	ω	.06 (.02)	
Cotton harvest	ωX_t	ω		−.12 (.04)
Percent black male	ωX_t	ω	−1.31 (.48)	
Noise component(s)				
Incarceration	ϕY_{t-1}	ϕ	−.46 (.12)	−.73 (.12)
	ϕY_{t-2}	ϕ		−.52 (.12)
σ^2			.014	.0012
X^2 of residuals(p)			4.3 (.50)	2.0 (.70)
Sentence length				
Cotton price	ωX_{t-3}	ω	−45.80 (12.04)	
Percent young	ωX_{t-4}	ω	−10.76 (5.41)	
Noise				
Random noise	$-\theta e_{t-1}$	θ	−.52 (.12)	.66 (.09)
σ^2			3.01	.297
X^2 of residuals(p)			3.2 (.70)	2.4 (.80)
Time served				
Cotton price	ωX_t	ω		5.53 (3.64)
Noise				
Incarceration	ϕY_{t-1}	ϕ		−.59 (.10)
Random noise	$-\theta e_{t-1}$	θ	.65 (.10)	
σ^2			3.19	.340
X^2 of residuals(p)			2.8 (.70)	4.8 (.40)

[a]Input series are prewhitened and independent of each other. Estimates are 1.5 times their standard errors.

whites served *less* time in prison. Figure 7.4 suggests that this relationship was far from uniform: it shifted in the expected direction during the depression of 1893–1897 and remained so until the end of the depression of 1903–1907.

The second question of interest was whether the criminal penalties imposed on blacks became more punitive as a specific response to lynching. To address this question, the lynching rate was designated the input series and cross-correlations between lynching and each punishment series were calculated.[4] Presented in the top half of Table 7.4 are the relevant cross-correlations. Where cross-correlations were significant or exceeded .20, theeffect was modeled with other input series whose cross-correlations met the

Black Admission Rate

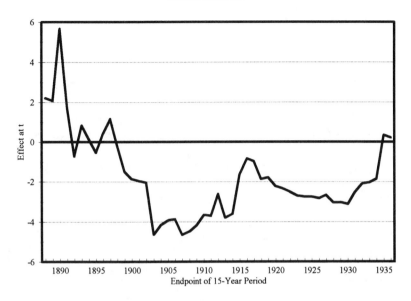

Black Sentence Length

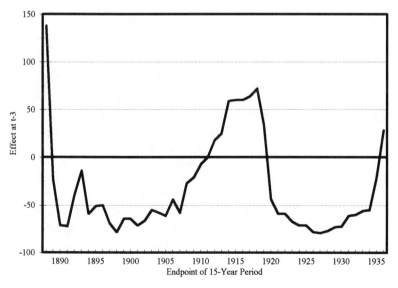

FIGURE 7.3 Effect of Cotton Price over Time

White Time Served

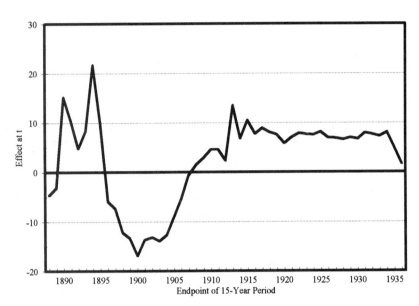

FIGURE 7.4 Effect of Cotton Price over Time

same criteria. The results (not presented) indicate that lynchings affected neither black admission rates nor the length of time black men served in the
penitentiary. As lynching rates increased, however, the sentences imposed on
blacks tended to become shorter. Figure 7.5 indicates that these decreases
occurred *after* the height of public concern with interracial sexual assault.
Throughout most of the period, lynching had little effect on the length of
prison sentences imposed on blacks. The remaining results were also unexpected. As lynching rates increased, so too did the rate at which white males
were admitted to the penitentiary and the length of time they served in the
penitentiary. For the admission rate, the impact of lynchings on the admission
rate was fairly consistent with time (results not presented). For time served,
lynching rates had a particularly pronounced effect during the height of public concern with sexual assaults by black men (see Figure 7.5).

The final question considered in the analysis is whether legal punishments for rape had any dampening effect on the incidence of illegal reactions—namely, lynching. These cross-correlations are presented in the
bottom half of Table 7.4.[5] Neither the length of sentence nor the time actually
served for rape affected lynching rates. However, as the rate at which both
black and white males were admitted to the penitentiary for rape increased,

TABLE 7.4 Cross-correlations between Punishments for Sexual Assault and Rape-related Lynchings

	Admission Rate		Sentence Length		Time Served	
Lag	Black	White	Black	White	Black	White
Rape-related lynchings as input series[a]						
0	−.13	.05	−.09	−.05	−.06	−.18
1	−.17	.21	.06	.18	.02	.27
2	.11	.04	.03	−.26	.02	−.06
3	.18	−.05	−.35*	.16	−.16	.11
4	−.08	.05	.08	−.16	.16	−.09
5	.18	.08	.12	−.08	.01	−.16
Estimates[b]						
ωX_{t-n}		.004	−.18			.06
		(.002)	(.08)			(.03)
σ^2		.00092	1.70			.28
Rape-related lynchings as output series						
0	−.22	−.06	−.22	.00	−.04	−.10
1	−.28*	−.23	.00	.06	−.01	.09
2	.02	.15	−.12	−.15	−.11	−.07
3	−.12	.12	−.23	−.05	−.19	−.00
4	.16	−.05	−.10	−.23	−.21	.02
5	.09	−.12	−.02	−.16	−.05	.08
Estimates[c]						
ωX_{t-1}	−6.93	−20.74				
	(3.65)	(12.23)				
σ^2	4.94	5.02				
σ^2(Noise)		5.40				

[a]Input series were prewhitened and rendered independent of one another before calculating cross-correlations and estimating transfer functions.
[b]Estimates are net of other determinants of punishment. Standard errors are in parentheses. For white admission rate and time served, n = 1. For black male sentence length, n = 3. Complete models are available on request.
[c]Estimates are net of other determinants of punishment, with standard errors in parentheses.
*

lynching rates declined, after a delay of one year. Figure 7.6 provides some indication of the nature of these effects over time. The impact of admission rates for black males on lynching was relatively small and became slightly stronger over time. In contrast, white admission rates had a more pronounced impact, one that grew stronger with time, at least until the end of World War I.

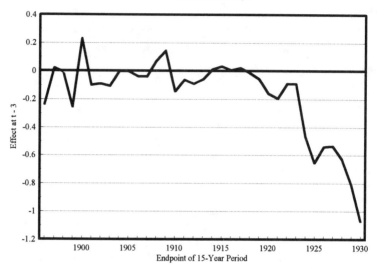

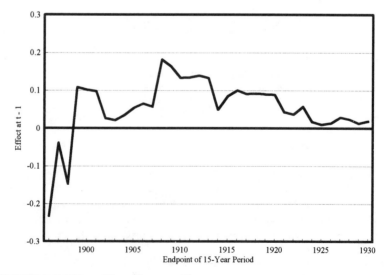

FIGURE 7.5 Effect of Lynching over Time

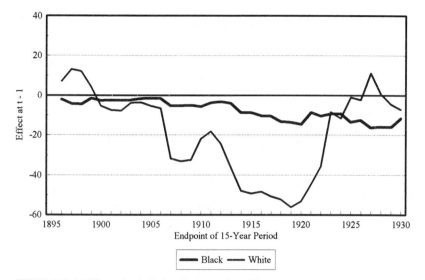

FIGURE 7.6 Effect of Admission Rates on Lynching

DISCUSSION

This paper sought to link the punishment of sexual assault offenders with two central features of post-Reconstruction society: fluctuating economic conditions and the presence of lynching as an alternative though illegitimate reaction to criminality. Initial inspection of trends in criminal punishment suggested short-lived increases in punitiveness during the period most closely associated with unsettled economic conditions and with the radical racist mentality that highlighted interracial sexual assault. This punitiveness was not only directed toward black males but toward their white counterparts as well. More systematic analysis, using ARIMA modeling, substantiated the expected link between economic conditions and punishment. Consistent with work on other social control mechanisms, declines in cotton prices increased the rate at which black males were admitted to the penitentiary and the length of their sentences. These impacts were particularly pronounced between 1889 and 1914, the height of the radical racist mentality documented by Williamson (1984).

Economic conditions played a more circumscribed role in the punishment of whites. Shifts in cotton prices had no significant impacts on either the rate at which whites were admitted to the penitentiary for rape or for the length of sentences judges imposed on them. Moreover, declining prices tended to produce the anticipated increase in the length of time whites served in the penitentiary only during the period anchored by the most intense economic difficulties, the depressions of 1893–1897 and 1903–1907.

In sum, the punishment of blacks and, to a much lesser degree, that of whites, became harsher as economic conditions deteriorated. Since the historical record gives no clear sense of the crime problem, we may never know the extent to which the effect of economic conditions is mediated by increases in criminality. As a result, it is impossible at this point to specify with any certainty the independent contribution to punishment of punitive ideologies or of perceived threats posed by blacks in other arenas (for example, economic, political).

Cotton prices were undoubtedly important influences on some dimensions of punishment, but other forces played key roles as well. Previous work led us to expect that the erosion of white economic resources would increase their vulnerability to punishment (Myers, 1991). While this may have been true of punishment in general, it was not the case for the punishment of whites convicted of sexual assault. The economic competition argument fared poorly as well. Analysis yielded no evidence that a narrowing of economic differences between the races increased repression against blacks. Instead, declines in racial economic inequality reduced black vulnerability to incarceration. Part of this decline can be traced to marginal increases in black prosperity. In 1874, for example, blacks owned only one of every 85 acres of improved land in Georgia. By 1903, they owned one in every 25 acres (Banks, 1905). At least until 1915, the per capita value of black-owned property rose steadily. It is possible that the enhanced economic position of blacks as a group, however slight, reduced their vulnerability to social control by white elites (Blalock, 1967: 139, 141). It did little, however, to improve their relations with lower-class whites, who were increasingly threatened by black prosperity.

As noted earlier, punishment was deeply implicated in the labor market conditions of an agrarian political economy. Earlier work led us to expect that declines in the cotton harvest would generate a labor surplus, a portion of which the penitentiary could control. Only for white males did the anticipated relationship obtain: as harvests became smaller, admission rates increased. Also supported by the analysis was the expected compensatory increase in punishment as a reaction to declines in the supply of agrarian labor. As the size of the black male population declined, due largely to out-migration, black males ran a greater risk of being admitted to the penitentiary.

Using the size of the young male population as a surrogate for criminality, the final expectation was that declines in the size of that population would reduce rates of criminality, which would ultimately be reflected in declining admission rates. This was not the case. As the population of young males became smaller, the sentences imposed on black males actually became longer. A similar relationship has surfaced elsewhere, in the tendency for black and white incarceration rates to rise between 1897 and 1936 in response to declines in the size of the population of young black and white males (Myers, 1993). It is possible that this particular demographic shift sheds more light on the supply of youthful laborers than it does on the magnitude of criminality. If so, then the finding suggests that declines in supply shaped not only the general risk of being incarcerated but also the actual length of time a convict's labor was expropriated.

Apart from embedding punishments for rape in the context of the political economy, this analysis sought to explore the link between punishment and lynchings, a lethal form of informal social control. The key issue was whether and to what extent the two mechanisms of social control substituted for or reinforced one another. The use of time series analysis uncovered no evidence that an increase in lynchings increased the rate at which blacks were admitted to the penitentiary. Nor was there evidence of a reluctance to release black males as a response to increased lynchings. At the height of public concern with sexual assault, lynchings did affect the length of sentences, but only weakly. Only after public concern with rape subsided and public impatience with lynching grew, were the two social control mechanisms linked. The nature of that link was unanticipated: lynchings tended to shorten the sentences imposed on blacks.

In short, then, there was no indication that the punishment of black males became increasingly severe as a specific reaction to increases in lynching. Instead, lynchings influenced the subsequent punishment of white males. Increases in lynchings fostered an increase in the rate at which white males were admitted to the penitentiary and in the length of time previously convicted white males served in the penitentiary. Heightened concern with interracial sexual assault apparently reinforced not only the moral boundary specifying the appropriate relationship between the races. A general context emphasizing threats to white women apparently decreased the tolerance level for white transgressions of the moral boundary that specified the appropriate relationship between the sexes. In addition, rapes involving white men may have become especially intolerable for an additional reason: the same class of white men who were raping white women may have been responsible for lynching blacks for the same offense.

Also considered in the analysis was whether increases in punishment helped render lynchings on the pretext of rape superfluous, whether by deterring interracial assaults or by imposing punishments of sufficient gravity to satisfy whites incensed by the crime. The findings support the conventional wisdom that the two mechanisms of social control were substitutes for one another. As blacks were admitted with greater frequency to the penitentiary for rape, the rate at which black males were lynched on the pretext of rape declined. Thus, lynchings did not appear to increase black admission rates, but as admission rates increased, the incidence of lynchings declined. More interesting, perhaps, was the tendency for increases in the rate at which white males were incarcerated for sexual assault to have a similar if not stronger dampening effect on lynchings.

IMPLICATIONS

In recent years, more research has taken as its central focus the nature of the relationship among various forms of social control (see Massey and Myers, 1989; Liska, 1992; Tolnay and Beck, 1992, 1994). From the work reported here, it becomes clear that an understanding of lynchings, which heretofore revolved around economic conditions and legitimate lethal alternatives, hinges on a consideration of the use of legitimate *nonlethal* mechanisms of social control. Similarly, formal social control mechanisms cannot be understood apart from informal and, in this case, patently illegal mechanisms. Though qualitatively distinct, formal and informal responses to black and white criminality, whether alleged or real, were nevertheless linked with one another. In particular, the formal social control of white men appeared to influence, and to be influenced by, the informal social control of black men.

As the analysis makes clear, to specify the relationships among forms of social control accurately is a complicated endeavor. It requires a strategy that traces the relationship through time, and careful attention to social and economic forces that may obscure or distort the relationship. Equally if not more important is greater sensitivity to the various forms each mechanism of social control takes. Admission rates, sentence lengths, and time served were three qualitatively distinct dimensions of post-Reconstruction formal social control. They were differentially embedded in broader social forces and differentially imposed on black and white males. Most notably, despite a pattern of findings linking lower cotton prices with increased levels of incarceration and lynching, the results here suggest that for some forms of punishment during some periods of time, the relationship is reversed. Also, one dimension of punishment, the length of time served, proved to be particularly insulated from external forces. Given the centrality of hard labor, this aspect of punishment may have been more responsive to internal forces such as shifts in the age composition of the felon labor pool.

Forms of informal social control may be qualitatively distinct as well. By design, this paper focused narrowly on one type of lynching. In contrast traditional research tends to conceptualize the phenomenon monolithically and to examine all lynchings together, regardless of the pretexts under which they were undertaken. Whether this strategy would yield the same relationships found here is an assumption that must be reconstituted as an empirical question meriting attention. In sum, then, research that attempts to link social control mechanisms must first *problematize* its conceptions of these mechanisms, in both their formal and informal manifestations.

NOTES

*Revision of a paper presented at the annual meeting of the American Society of Criminology, November 3–7, 1992, New Orleans.

1. I am grateful to E. M. Beck and Stewart E. Tolnay for permission to use their lynching inventory for the state of Georgia. Included here are lynchings on the pretexts of rape (44), attempted rape (59), assault to rape (50), rape and murder or robbery (13), and complicity in rape (1).

2. The Central Register of Convicts, volumes 1 through 13, was obtained from the Georgia Department of Archives and History, with the kind permission of the Department of Corrections.

3. For a description of the procedures used, see McCleary and Hay (1980). Specific information about interrelationships among input series is available on request.

4. Prior to calculating cross-correlations, preliminary analysis examined the possible influence on lynching of the remaining input series. The lynching rate series was modeled as a first-order moving average process, with zero-order transfer functions to represent the delayed effects of cotton price and cotton harvest. The residuals of this model, a white noise process, constituted the input series for calculating cross-correlations with the punishment series.

5. Before calculating cross-correlations, the punishment series were prewhitened and purged of any significant effects for the remaining input series including the lynching series. Details are available on request.

REFERENCES

Banks, Enoch Marvin. 1905. *The Economics of Land Tenure in Georgia.* New York: Columbia University Press.

Beck, E. M., and Stewart E. Tolnay. 1990. "The Killing Fields of the Deep South: The Market for Cotton and the Lynching of Blacks, 1882–1930." *American Sociological Review* 55: 526–39.

Beck, E. M., James L. Massey, and Stewart E. Tolnay. 1989. "The Gallows, The Mob, The Vote: Lethal Sanctioning of Blacks in North Carolina and Georgia, 1882 to 1930." *Law & Society Review* 23: 317–31.

Blalock, Hubert M. 1967. *Toward a Theory of Minority-Group Relations*. New York: John Wiley.

Bloom, Jack M. 1987. *Class, Race and the Civil Rights Movement*. Bloomington: Indiana University Press.

Bruce, Philip A. 1889. *The Plantation Negro as a Freeman*. New York: Putnam's Sons.

Cash, W. J. 1940. *The Mind of the South*. London: Thames and Hudson.

Cell, John W. 1982. *The Highest Stage of White Supremacy: The Origins of Segregation in South Africa and the American South*. Cambridge: Cambridge University Press.

Cockran, W. Bourke. 1900. "The Negro and the Social Order." Pp. 194–218 in *Race Problems of the South: Report of the Proceedings of the First Annual Conference of the Southern Society for the Promotion of the Study of Race Conditions and Problems in the South*. Richmond: B. F. Johnson Publishing Company.

Comptroller-General Office. *1874–1936. Annual Report*. Atlanta: Stein Printing.

Frederickson, George M. 1971. *The Black Image in the White Mind: The Debate on Afro-American Character and Destiny, 1817–1914*. Middletown, Conn.: Wesleyan University Press.

Friedman, Lawrence J. 1970. *The White Savage: Racial Fantasies in the Postbellum South*. Englewood Cliffs, N. J.: Prenctice-Hall.

Hahn, Steven. 1983. *The Roots of Southern Populism: Yeoman Farmers and the Transformation of the Georgia Upcountry 1850–1890*. New York: Oxford University Press.

Harvey, George. 1903. "The Negro Problem and the New Negro Crime." *Harpers Weekly* 47 (June 20): 1050–51.

Haygood, Atticus G. 1893. "The Black Shadow in the South." *The Forum* 16 (October): 167–75.

Higgs, Robert. 1977. *Competition and Coercion: Blacks in the American Economy 1865–1914*. New York: Cambridge University Press.

Hoffman, Frederick L. 1896. "Race Traits and Tendencies of the American Negro." *Publications of the American Economic Association* 12 (August): 1–329.

Isaac, Larry W., and Larry J. Griffin. 1989. "Ahistoricism in Time-Series Analyses of Historical Process: Critique, Redirection and Illustrations from U.S. Labor History." *American Sociological Review* 54: 873–90.

King, Alexander C. 1900. "The Punishment of Crimes Against Women: Existing Legal Remedies and their Sufficiency." Pp. 160–70 in *Race Problems of the*

South: Report of the Proceedings of the First Annual Conference of the Southern Society for the Promotion of the Study of Race Conditions and Problems in the South. Richmond: B. F. Johnson Publishing Company.

Kousser, J. Morgan. 1974. *The Shaping of Southern Politics: Suffrage Restrictions and the Establishment of the One-Party South 1880–1910.* New Haven: Yale University Press.

Liska, Allen E. 1992. Ed. *Social Threat and Social Control.* Albany: State University of New York Press.

Makridakis, Spyros, Steven C. Wheelwright, and Victor E. McGee. 1983. *Forecasting: Methods and Applications,* 2nd edition. New York: John Wiley.

Massey, James L., and Martha A. Myers. 1989. "Patterns of Repressive Social Control in post-Reconstruction Georgia, 1882–1935." *Social Forces* 68: 458–88.

McCleary, Richard, and Richard A. Hay, Jr. 1980. *Applied Time Series Analysis for the Social Sciences.* Beverly Hills, Calif.: Sage Publications.

Myers, Martha A. 1990a. "Black Threat and Incarceration in Postbellum Georgia." *Social Forces* 69: 373–93.

———. 1990b. "Economic Threat and Racial Disparities in Incarceration: The Case of Postbellum Georgia." *Criminology* 28: 627–56.

———. 1991. "Economic Conditions and Punishment in Postbellum Georgia." *Journal of Quantitative Criminology* 7: 99–121.

———. 1993. "Inequality and the Punishment of Minor Offenders in the Early 20th Century." *Law & Society Review* 27(2): 313–43.

Page, Thomas. 1904. *The Negro: The Southerner's Problem.* New York: Charles Scribner's Sons.

Page, Walter, 1893. "The Last Hold of the Southern Bully." *The Forum* 16 (November): 303–14.

Smith, Charles H. 1893. "Have American Negroes too much Liberty?" *The Forum* 16 (October): 176–83.

Tillinghast, Joseph Alexander. 1902. "The Negro in Africa and America." *Publications of the American Economic Association,* Third Series III (May): 1–228.

Tolnay, Stewart E., and E. M. Beck. 1994. "Lethal Social Control in the South: Lynchings and Executions Between 1880 and 1930." Pp. 176–194 in George S. Bridges and Martha A. Myers, eds., *Inequality, Crime and Social Control.* Boulder: Westview.

———. 1992. "Toward a Threat Model of Southern Black Lynchings." Pp. 33–52 in Allen E. Liska, ed., *Social Threat and Social Control.* Albany: State University of New York Press.

U.S. Bureau of the Census. 1975. *Historical Statistics of the U.S.: Colonial Times to 1970*. Washington, D.C.: Government Printing Office.

U.S. Department of Agriculture (1951–52). *Statistical Bulletin #99*. Bureau of Agricultural Economics. Washington, D.C.: Government Printing Office.

Williamson, Joel. 1984. *The Crucible of Race: Black-White Relations in the American South since Emancipation*. New York: Oxford University Press.

Woodward, C. Vann. 1971. *Origins of the New South 1877–1913*. Baton Rouge: Louisiana State University Press.

————. 1974. *The Strange Career of Jim Crow*. New York: Oxford University Press.

Part III

Contemporary Issues and Debates

GARY LaFREE

8

Race and Crime Trends in the United States, 1946–1990*

Although it is difficult to guess how history will remember it (or indeed if it will be remembered), the use of Willie Horton by George Bush's 1988 presidential campaign provides some important insights into current assumptions about race and crime in the United States. Horton was a black man serving a murder sentence in a Massachusetts state prison. He escaped while on a weekend furlough in 1986, raped a white Maryland woman, and stabbed her fiancé. The Bush campaign made the Massachusetts prison furlough program a central issue in its election contest against Democratic candidate and Massachusetts governor, Michael Dukakis. The Horton story was cited by Mr. Bush in campaign speeches, shown in television commercials, and featured in fliers distributed by Republican state committees. The *New York Times* (1988, p. 1) concluded that the Horton story was "highly effective in damaging Mr. Dukakis's image and left the Democrats scrambling for ways to respond."

Apart from the direct impact the Horton story had on the election, it is an important event in U.S. history for at least two reasons. First, it shows how critical crime has become in setting national policy. This influence is relatively recent. Caplan (1973, p. 583) argues that crime first emerged as a major national issue only in the 1964 presidential campaign when Senator Barry Goldwater and his Republican strategists made law and order their principal campaign issue. It was not until the mid-1960s that crime began to show up near the top of opinion polls as the most serious domestic problem facing the nation (Smith, 1980). When we examine the enormous size and scope of federal crime control bureaucracies today, it is easy to forget that these creations are relatively recent.

Second, the Horton incident also shows how easily crime and race stereotypes can be linked in the public mind. While Republican campaign officials denied that the selection of a black man accused of raping a white woman was intentional (*New York Times,* 1988, p. B5), the incident provoked responses that were obviously connected to race. Moreover, stereotypes about the link between race and crime are not the same for all minority groups. In fact, it is an interesting exercise to read the news stories about the incident and try to imagine their political effect if Horton had been Asian-American instead of African-American. The incident was politically effective precisely because Horton was a black man.

Despite the centrality of race issues to criminology research and policy for the past three decades, most criminologists have ignored race in explanations of crime. There are some compelling reasons for this. Wilson (1984) claims that many researchers have avoided race-related research on crime because of the earlier sharp criticisms aimed at scholars (Moynihan, 1965; Rainwater, 1966), who directly confronted these issues. Indeed, as labeling and conflict perspectives gained ground in criminology in the 1960s, researchers developed a new sensitivity to research that "blamed the victim" (Gibbons, 1979; Gibbs, 1985). More generally, the most popular theories of crime have emphasized characteristics of social structure (for example, poverty, inequality, social disorganization) or of social process (for example, differential association, social control) that should have identical effects across racial groups.

Nonetheless, there are also compelling reasons to carefully examine crime differences by race. First and most obviously, the criminal justice system, especially for African-Americans, has entered a period of unprecedented crisis. Although blacks represent only 12 percent of the U.S. population, they now account for 64 percent of robbery arrests, 55 percent of homicide arrests, and 32 present of burglary arrests (Federal Bureau of Investigation, 1989). Similarly, black incarceration rates have reached alarming proportions. Black males born in the U.S.A. today now face a one-in-five lifetime chance of serving a sentence in an adult state prison (U.S. Bureau of Justice Statistics, 1985, p. 5). For the age range 20–29, the U.S.A. now has substantially more black men in prison or on probation or parole (609,690) than in colleges and universities (436,000; Mauer, 1990; Langan, 1991). Clearly, our failure to study the connection between race and crime has not made race-related crime problems and stereotypes go away.

Second, given that most crime is intraracial, blacks are disproportionately affected by high crime rates. African-American men now face a one-in-21 lifetime chance of being murdered (U.S. Bureau of Justice Statistics, 1985, p. 8). In fact, homicide has become the leading cause of death among black men, aged 15–24 (U.S. Center for Disease Control, 1990).

Finally, the fact that most researchers have ignored race does not mean that it has become less important in everyday thinking about crime. On the contrary, the Willie Horton story illustrates how the basest kind of prejudice is free to flourish in the absence of more objective analysis. Wilson (1984, p. 90) notes that because there has been so little recent systematic research on blacks, racial stereotypes have not been sufficiently rebutted.

In this paper I consider some of the practical difficulties of examining the relationship between race and crime in the United States.[1] I begin with cross-sectional data on arrest rates for African-Americans, American Indians, Asian-Americans, and whites, and consider some of the issues raised by these data. For blacks and whites only, I next present arrest trend data from 1946 to 1990 and then consider the differing implications of several common social-structural theories for black and white crime trends.

MEASURING CRIME TRENDS BY RACE

In terms of crime trends by race, data options in the United States are limited. Neither self-report nor victimization surveys have been collected systematically for a long enough period to permit annual time-series analysis. Moreover, neither of these data sources include yearly estimates for the 1960s—a period when the largest crime increases in the postwar period began. This means that the only annual time-series data available for the United States in the postwar period are from the Federal Bureau of Investigation's Uniform Crime Report (UCR) system. In the next section, I briefly consider the development of the UCR and its suitability for measuring crime rates by race.

Arrest Rates

The development of national crime statistics in the United States has probably lagged behind other countries in part because its federal system gives states a good deal of control over their internal affairs, including their legal systems. This may make it more difficult to produce national crime statistics in the United States than in countries with more centralized administrations. The movement that eventually resulted in the first U.S. nationwide crime data system did not begin until 1927. In that year the International Association of Chiefs of Police formed a committee on Uniform Crime Records and gave it the task of developing a system of standardized police statistics. After studying state criminal codes and evaluating police record-keeping practices in various jurisdictions, in 1929 the committee completed a plan for standardized crime reporting, which it referred to as the Uniform Crime Reports (UCR).

In 1930 the Federal Bureau of Investigation compiled the first annual UCR report. Since its inception, the basic structure of the UCR system has remained remarkably consistent: crime definitions, classifications, and mode of data collection are virtually the same in 1990 as they were in 1930.[2] The most reliable UCR data have been collected on the seven crimes that make up the UCR crime *index:* murder, rape, robbery, aggravated assault, burglary, theft, and motor vehicle theft.[3]

The most unique aspect of the UCR is its reliance on the voluntary co-operation of thousands of individual police departments across the country to provide crime information. In general, UCR coverage has been most complete for major metropolitan areas in which about 98 percent of the population is represented and least complete for rural areas in which about 90 percent of the population is represented (U.S. Federal Bureau of Investigation, 1985).

The UCR has consistently collected two main types of crime information: total crimes *known to police* and total arrests. Crimes known to police are supposed to include all crimes reported to police, observed or discovered by police, or reported from other witnesses or complainants. Crimes are to be classified as cleared by arrest if a suspect is arrested, charged, and turned over to the courts for prosecution, or by *exceptional means.* The latter term applies to situations in which the police believe that they have solved the case but have nonetheless made no arrest. Most often cases are cleared by exceptional means when the police feel that further processing is impractical: for example, a suspect has already been arrested in another jurisdiction, a key witness refuses to press charges, or a suspect has fled the country.

Because the crimes known to police measure depends less on the decision-making of police than arrests do, researchers have generally preferred this measure. However, the UCR measure of crimes known to police does not report the suspect's race. Thus, the only U.S. crime measure that includes race and has been collected for the entire postwar period is the UCR measure of arrests.

The most common criticisms of UCR data point to its scope and validity. Many critics (Geis, 1972; Chambliss, 1988; Harris, 1991) have argued that the UCR emphasis on street crime focuses attention on crimes that are more common among minorities and the poor, and less common among non-minorities and the wealthy. However, the incompleteness of the UCR should not be seen as a fatal deficiency. While it is true that the seven index crimes for which the UCR includes the most complete data are only a subset of all crimes, it is also true that they are of substantial policy interest. Few would argue that we should reject data on murder, for example, just because we do not have equally valid data on embezzlement.

The validity of UCR statistics, especially arrest statistics, has been hotly debated for more than half a century (Warner, 1931; President's Commission, 1967; Gove, Hughes, and Geerken, 1985; Blumstein, Cohen, and Rosenfeld, 1991). Apart from the many technical issues, most of the criticisms reflect a concern with either citizen or police reporting. Both of these concerns have important implications for conclusions about crime trends by race. For example, if nonminorities are more likely than minorities to report crimes to police, then conclusions about crime rates by race will be erroneous. Similarly, if police arrest decisions are influenced by race, then conclusions about crime from different race groups will also be biased.

Fortunately, the National Crime Survey (NCS) victim surveys now provide a comparative data source independent of the criminal justice system that allows us to partially assess these concerns. In general, analysis of the NCS and other victim survey data shows little variation in reporting by race (Block, 1974; Hindelang, 1978). Typical of these studies is Skogan (1984, p. 125), who concludes that, ''surprisingly, race differences are small in crime reporting.''

The possibility that UCR arrest statistics by race are determined more by police decision-making than actual behavior has also been frequently examined (Hindelang, 1978; O'Brien, 1985). To the extent that racial correlates of arrest rates are the same as offending rates measured by the NCS, researchers can have greater confidence in the validity of UCR data. Indeed, systematic comparisons of UCR index arrest rates with offending rates for robbery and burglary estimated from the NCS show remarkable similarity. For example, Hindelang (1978, p. 100) found that 62 percent of the robbery offenders reported by victims were black, compared with an identical 62 percent of blacks arrested for robbery in UCR arrest data for the same year. In a detailed follow-up study, Hindelang (1981) found that even for burglaries— where the offender is seen in only 6 percent of the NCS cases—there was a very strong correspondence between UCR arrest statistics and the NCS survey on the offenders' race.

More generally, a large and reliable body of evidence shows that crime seriousness is consistently the strongest predictor of arrest (Black and Reiss, 1970; Gottfredson and Gottfredson, 1980). Thus, in their exhaustive analysis of the validity of UCR reports, Gove et al. (1985) conclude that ''the perceived seriousness of the crime . . . accounts for most of the variance in whether a crime is reported and officially recorded; personal characteristics of the offender and victim have only minor effects'' (p. 451). Hence, after providing the appropriate words of caution, the available evidence suggests that UCR arrest data, especially for serious crimes, provides information that is at least highly correlated with actual crime trends by race.

However, the measurement of race and ethnicity in UCR arrest statistics raises further limitations and difficulties. First, the UCR does not allow an analysis of Hispanic arrest rates over time. The UCR included the category *Mexican* in 1934, but dropped it in 1941. Besides Mexican-Americans, other Hispanic groups have never been separately distinguished. Second, because the UCR system is based on the voluntary compliance of police agencies, and because American Indians fall under the jurisdiction of a complex combination of native and nonnative legal entities, UCR trend data for American Indians are also problematic (Peak and Spencer, 1987; Zatz, et al., 1991). Third, before 1970, the UCR included categories for *Chinese, Japanese,* and *all others.* After 1970, it replaced Chinese and Japanese with *Asian* and dropped the *other* category. Because many Asians were included as *others* prior to 1970, a practical consequence of these changes is that there is no obvious way of constructing trend data for Asian-Americans in the postwar period based on UCR arrest statistics.

Finally, population statistics included in UCR annual reports are not broken down by race. Given that the UCR purports to be a national data set, we could nonetheless use total U.S. population by race to estimate arrest rates. However, recall that the proportion of the population included in UCR reports has also changed over time. This is not a trivial point, especially for early years of the UCR. In 1946, the UCR reports were based on an estimated reporting population of 62 million at a time when the total U.S. resident population was 141 million (44.0 percent). By 1990 the UCR report was based on an estimated reporting population of 205 million at a time when the total U.S. resident population was 248 million (82.7 percent). The biggest change in UCR coverage came in 1960, when the population included jumped from 56 to 109 million. In terms of the total proportion of U.S. citizens included in UCR reports, the most successful year was 1985, when 86.4 percent of the total U.S. population was included in jurisdictions that reported complete UCR data.[4]

To summarize, the UCR is currently the only U.S. data source that includes longitudinal crime data by race for the postwar period. However, the difficulties of using the UCR for this purpose are such that we should think of analysis as more similar to archeology than econometrics. However, I would argue that just as a serious archeologist would not throw out relevant information—no matter how imperfect—so too a responsible criminologist cannot afford to ignore the major source of longitudinal data on race and crime in North America. Even so, because of changes in the way the UCR collected arrest data over time, trend analysis for groups other than blacks and whites is probably not defensible. And even with the analysis of blacks and whites, we should proceed with the utmost caution. Before turning to an examination of crime trends, I consider first what cross-sectional data based on UCR arrest statistics tells us about crime differences by race.

CROSS-SECTIONAL ARREST RATES BY RACE, 1990

Table 8.1 shows total arrests by race for the seven UCR index crimes. To allow comparisons, I calculated race-specific UCR arrest rates as $R_t = [a_t/(u_t p_t)] *100,000$, where R is the rate, t is the year, a is the number of UCR arrests for whites or blacks, u is the proportion of reporting UCR jurisdictions, and p is the proportion of the total U.S. resident population by race. Consider again all the appropriate cautions about interpreting UCR data: if crimes are not reported to police, they generally do not come to police attention, the police decision to arrest may be biased, the UCR does not include all jurisdictions (in 1990, complete UCR data were obtained from 10,676 police agencies, representing 204,563,914 residents—82.7 percent of total U.S. residents). Having offered these warnings, can we nonetheless draw any useful interpretations from these data? First, note that crime rates for these racial and ethnic groups follow the same sequence for all seven crimes. For each, black rates are highest, followed by American Indians, whites, and Asians.[5] These are not trivial differences. Black robbery rates are more than eleven times higher than white rates. They are more than twenty-one times higher than Asian-American rates.

Second, differences by race vary by crime type. The largest discrepancy by race is for robbery, where blacks account for 62 percent of all arrests, followed by murder (55 percent), rape (44 percent), aggravated assault and motor vehicle theft (33 percent), and burglary and theft (31 percent). In general, the greatest discrepancies for blacks are for violent street crime (robbery, murder, rape) and the least, are for property crimes involving no direct contact between victim and offender (burglary, theft).

Even allowing for the fact that UCR crime data are imperfect, these data raise some serious issues for criminology. Given our worst fears about police racism, can we reasonably conclude that police discrimination accounts for a difference of the magnitude shown in Table 8.1? Moreover, if the results are mostly determined by police discrimination, would we not expect this discrimination to also affect arrest rates for American Indians and Asians? Is there any reason to believe that our legal system has taken a kinder orientation toward minorities other than blacks? Research on the varying quality of different types of UCR data raises further issues.

Both critics (O'Brien, 1985) and supporters (Gove et al., 1985; Devine, Sheley, and Smith, 1988; Harer and Steffensmeier, 1992) of UCR data agree that its quality is generally highest for more serious crimes, in which citizens are more likely to report crimes to police and police arrest is more likely. Following this reasoning, discriminatory behavior on the part of police might be expected to be most pronounced for those less serious crimes for which police have the greatest discretion. However, Table 8.1 shows that

TABLE 8.1 UCR Arrest Rates by Race, United States, 1990

Race	Murder		Rape		Robbery		Aggravated Assault		Burglary		Theft		Motor Vehicle Theft	
	N	R*	N	R	N	R	N	R	N	R	N	R	N	R
Asian	166	2.8	276	4.6	1039	17.4	2865	47.9	2961	49.5	15381	257.1	2321	38.8
Black	10645	43.2	14384	58.3	91164	369.6	154838	627.8	110181	446.7	402526	1632.1	71029	287.9
Indian	133	8.3	249	15.5	486	30.2	3588	222.7	3054	189.5	13460	835.4	1279	79.4
White	8312	5.1	18033	10.9	53755	32.7	235126	143.2	242508	147.7	866426	527.5	105018	63.9
Total	19256	9.4	32942	16.1	146444	71.6	396417	193.8	358704	175.4	1297793	634.4	179647	87.8

*R = [a/(up)] *100,000, where R is the rate, a is the number of UCR arrests by race, u is the population of reporting UCR jurisdictions, and p is the proportion of the total U.S. resident population by race.

the greatest differences by race are precisely for the most serious and presumably most reliably measured crimes (robbery, murder) and lowest for the least serious and, presumably, least reliably measured crimes (burglary, theft). In short, even accepting the limitations of UCR arrest data, the differences in Table 8.1 are so large and exhibit patterns that are so distinctive that the hypothesis of no difference by race seems unlikely. In the next section I turn to longitudinal comparisons for blacks and whites.

TRENDS IN AFRICAN-AMERICAN AND WHITE CRIME RATES, 1946–1990

Given that UCR arrest data are the only source that provides longitudinal trends for the entire postwar period disaggregated by race, the most basic issue is the extent to which these data may be usefully examined as proxies for black and white crime rates. A complete analysis of this issue is beyond the scope of the present paper. However, in addition to the arguments already presented in a longitudinal analysis of murder, robbery, and burglary rates, 1957–1988, my colleagues and I (LaFree and Drass, 1992; LaFree, Drass, and O'Day, 1992) tested the association by combining UCR arrest rates disaggregated by race and then comparing them to the more widely used UCR measure of crimes known to police. This analysis showed a strong correspondence between the disaggregated arrest rates and the measures of crimes known to police for the crimes we analyzed: robbery, $r = .98$; murder, $r = .97$; burglary, $r = .95$.

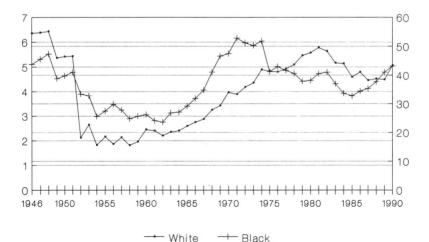

— White   — Black

FIGURE 8.1 Murder Arrests per 100,000, United States, 1946–1990

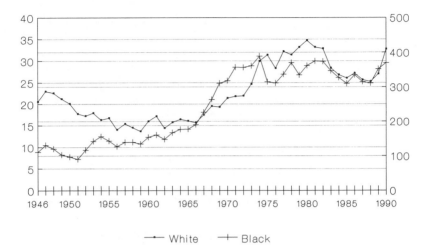

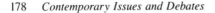

FIGURE 8.2 Robbery Arrests/100,000 United States, 1946–1990

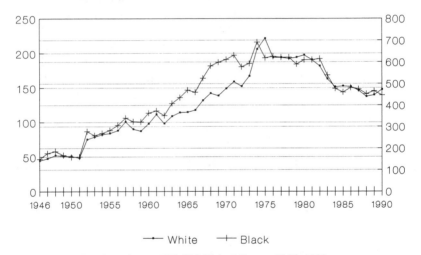

FIGURE 8.3 Burglary Arrests/100,000 United States, 1946–1990

Most likely, the disaggregated arrest data are a better proxy for more serious crimes that are widely reported to police (robbery, murder) than for less serious crimes (theft) or for crimes that are less frequently reported to police (rape, aggravated assault). Moreover, arrest data are probably a better proxy for actual crimes committed in more recent years; especially after 1960, when the FBI launched a major effort to improve the scope and quality of UCR data (Akiyama and Rosenthal, 1990).

With these caveats in mind, Figures 8.1 to 8.3 compare black and white arrest trends for murder, robbery and burglary. These figures permit at least two related conclusions. First, while the size of differences varies greatly by specific crime type and period, black arrest rates are substantially higher than white rates for all three crimes and from 1946 to 1990. Second, despite the fact that black arrest rates are generally much higher than white rates, both black and white trends show important similarities. Correlations between black and white rates for all three crimes are highly significant: burglary ($r = .95$), robbery ($r = .81$), and murder ($r = .70$).

These patterns suggest that some part of the postwar variation in crime rates for blacks and whites may have similar causes, other sources of variation may be distinct, and that the balance may depend on crime type. Thus, the correlation between black and white burglary rates is so high that we might suspect largely similar underlying dynamics. By contrast, correlations for murder and robbery allow the possibility of substantially different dynamics by race. It could be that a close examination of different crime trends might help us sort out some of the differences and similarities between black and white crime in the postwar period. For example, compared to other crimes, why are burglary trends similar for blacks and whites? By contrast, why are murder trends so different?

If we examine these three figures for general patterns, the most consistent similarity is a rapid increase in the 1960s and early 1970s for both blacks and whites. Similarly, arrest rates for all three crimes have leveled off or even declined since the 1970s. Detailed analysis of changes such as these could be important in advancing our understanding of crime in the United States.

Table 8.2 compares black to white arrest ratios, 1946–1990, for all seven UCR index crimes. For example, Table 8.2 shows that in 1990 blacks were arrested 8.53 times more often than whites for murder. Table 8.2 displays a clear ordering of offense types by race. Compared to white rates, black rates are generally highest for violent crimes (murder, robbery, assault, rape) and lowest for property crimes (burglary, theft, motor vehicle theft). If we limit comparisons to the period 1960–1990, the period for which UCR data are most valid, black to white arrest ratios are consistently highest for robbery and murder, and consistently lowest for burglary, theft, and motor vehicle theft.

These data raise important research issues. First, what explains variation in the rates? For example, why did the ratio of black to white murder arrests decline by more than 50 percent from 1971 to 1984? Second, what explains the long-term differences between black and white arrest rates? For example, although there is substantial variation over the postwar period, compared to whites, black arrest rates for robbery range from a low of 4.83 times greater (1950) to a high of 16.35 times greater (1971). That is, regardless of other considerations, black robbery arrest rates have been consistently much higher than white robbery arrest rates.

TABLE 8.2 Ratio of Black to White UCR Arrest Rates, 1946–1990

	Murder	Robbery	Aggravated Assault	Rape	Burglary	Theft	Motor Vehicle Theft
1946	6.89	5.43	6.34	3.35	3.35	3.97	1.51
1947	7.13	5.70	6.92	3.71	3.71	4.18	1.84
1948	7.36	5.33	7.40	3.86	3.55	4.03	1.96
1949	7.24	4.85	7.26	3.89	3.27	3.85	1.90
1950	7.33	4.83	7.56	3.59	3.11	3.95	2.04
1951	7.56	5.11	7.70	3.56	3.32	4.17	2.08
1952	15.78	6.75	14.95	5.25	3.69	4.04	1.99
1953	12.42	7.93	14.76	5.76	3.29	3.96	2.33
1954	14.07	9.56	13.68	5.66	3.27	3.80	2.18
1955	12.71	8.53	14.83	6.15	3.36	3.82	2.02
1956	16.01	9.04	17.06	6.68	3.48	3.74	2.31
1957	13.06	9.08	15.21	6.47	3.38	3.54	2.01
1958	13.69	9.60	14.53	7.94	3.59	3.67	2.08
1959	13.07	9.81	14.44	8.44	3.70	3.87	2.12
1960	10.70	9.60	11.91	7.20	3.70	3.83	2.29
1961	10.00	9.33	10.77	6.63	3.35	3.47	2.07
1962	10.72	10.25	10.63	6.90	3.58	3.59	2.52
1963	11.39	10.58	10.65	7.81	3.75	3.74	2.93
1964	11.30	10.75	9.35	7.75	3.82	3.75	3.17
1965	11.22	11.01	9.12	8.42	4.10	3.60	3.33
1966	11.59	12.14	8.42	7.54	3.91	3.59	3.31

1967	12.09	12.93	7.96	7.53	3.98	3.61	3.74
1968	12.63	13.53	8.01	7.15	4.09	3.74	4.44
1969	13.62	16.10	7.98	8.31	4.32	3.94	4.87
1970	11.96	14.86	6.89	7.63	4.10	3.70	4.63
1971	13.58	16.35	7.15	8.15	3.97	3.52	4.36
1972	12.25	16.26	6.67	7.10	3.79	3.52	4.20
1973	11.53	14.64	6.28	7.22	3.55	3.63	3.90
1974	10.57	12.97	5.56	7.07	3.35	3.41	3.27
1975	8.53	10.02	4.70	5.84	2.80	3.16	2.56
1976	8.95	10.99	5.04	7.12	3.23	3.81	2.95
1977	8.46	10.46	4.89	7.08	3.21	3.70	2.79
1978	7.97	11.78	5.13	7.53	3.23	3.69	3.04
1979	6.93	10.10	4.47	7.10	3.04	3.30	2.89
1980	6.85	10.42	4.25	6.94	3.09	3.36	3.29
1981	7.01	11.28	4.32	6.94	3.20	3.49	3.27
1982	7.28	11.38	4.63	7.29	3.38	3.69	3.35
1983	7.17	12.21	4.73	6.96	3.31	3.64	3.47
1984	6.56	12.21	4.78	6.61	3.15	3.61	3.53
1985	7.13	11.90	4.91	6.50	3.01	3.40	3.64
1986	7.20	12.31	4.87	6.63	3.17	3.35	4.23
1987	7.92	12.29	4.83	6.68	3.24	3.37	4.48
1988	8.35	12.32	4.94	6.16	3.29	3.43	4.84
1989	9.13	13.03	4.84	6.15	3.33	3.53	5.23
1990	8.53	11.28	4.39	5.31	3.03	3.09	4.50

To summarize, when we compare black and white arrest rates in the postwar years, we find intriguing similarities and differences. Both blacks and whites generally experienced rapid arrest increases in the 1960s and early 1970s. Black and white trends are most similar for theft and burglary. Regardless of crime type or year, black arrest rates are substantially higher than white rates. The differences are greatest for the violent crimes of robbery, murder, and rape.

EXPLANATIONS FOR CRIME DIFFERENCES BY RACE

While it is difficult enough to describe black and white crime trends in the postwar period, it is even more complex to understand and explain them. The most influential social-structural explanations of crime in the postwar years have emphasized deterrence (Wilson, 1975; Tittle, 1980), economic stress (Merton, 1938; Cohen, 1955; Cloward and Ohlin, 1960), or social disorganization (Shaw et al., 1929; Shaw and McKay, 1942). In the next section I briefly consider some of the implications of each of these perspectives for the estimation of black and white crime trends in the postwar period.

Deterrence Perspectives

For both laypersons and legal agents, the single most popular explanation for crime in the postwar period has probably been some form of the deterrence argument. Elaborated in the eighteenth century by social reformers like Bentham and Beccaria, and jurists like Blackstone, Romilly, and Feuerbach, deterrence theorists argue that crime can be reduced by increasing the costs of criminal behavior or increasing the awards of noncriminal behavior.

Deterrence perspectives among social researchers were not common in the early part of the postwar period, but gained momentum beginning in the 1970s (Wilson, 1975; Tittle, 1980; Murray, 1984). The implications of the theory are straightforward: criminal behavior will be deterred to the extent that punishment for it is more severe, certain, and swift.

Deterrence perspectives have generally assumed similar dynamics across race and ethnic groups (Tittle, 1980; Ross and LaFree, 1986). However, given the extraordinarily high rates of legal punishment African-Americans have experienced in recent years, they are an interesting test case of deterrence models. In fact, the limitations of deterrence perspectives are especially clear in the case of blacks. While aggregate incarceration rates for the United States are now among the highest in the world, rates become truly staggering when estimated separately for African-Americans (Langan, 1991). A study by Mauer (1990) shows that 23 percent of all black men, ages

20 to 29, are currently in prison or on probation or parole in the United States on any given day. Despite these unprecedented punishment levels, black crime rates remain at historically high levels. Even as a purely practical matter, it seems obvious to question the logic of a social policy that applies serious sanctions to nearly one-quarter of a major segment of the population.

Social Disorganization Perspectives

Social disorganization theory first gained popularity in the U.S.A. in the early part of the twentieth century (Shaw et al., 1929; Shaw and McKay, 1942) and can be traced in part to Durkheim's ([1893] 1947) assessment of the transition from traditional to modern industrial society. According to Shaw and McKay (1942), social disorganization increases in communities characterized by high rates of population turnover and heterogeneity. The disruption of established systems of role allocation and the emergence of new roles not yet fully institutionalized and integrated into society make normative guidelines ambiguous and may disrupt traditional support mechanisms. Bursik (1988, p. 521) argues that the strongest argument can be made by conceptualizing social disorganization as "a group-level analog of control theory." This approach emphasizes the negative impact social disorganization has on informal sources of social control, especially the ability of family and neighborhoods, to effectively socialize and integrate their members.

The idea that crime rates, especially black crime rates, are directly linked to increasing family disorganization has been popular throughout the postwar period (Frazier, 1950; Moynihan, 1965; Rainwater, 1970; Sampson, 1987; Jencks, 1992). Indeed, by the early 1980s, 48 percent of black families with children under 18 were headed by women (compared to 14 percent for white; Bureau of the Census, 1984), 68 percent of births to black women aged 15 to 24 were outside marriage (U.S. Bureau of the Census, 1983), and 69 percent of all black women had never been married (Bureau of the Census, 1981). Black women are more likely to head their own families, have more children outside marriage, and are less likely to marry and remarry; black children are less likely to live with both biological parents.

However, despite the popularity of the argument, empirical support from the extensive cross-sectional literature has been limited (Robins and Hill, 1966; Chilton and Markle, 1972; Ross and Sawhill, 1975; Rosen and Neilson, 1978; Montare and Boone, 1980; Harris, 1991). In our recent time-series analyses of black robbery, burglary, and homicide arrest rates in the postwar period (LaFree et al., 1992; LaFree and Drass, 1992), we found that increasing rates of female-headed households were generally associated with decreases rather than increases in black crime arrests. In fact, several considerations lead us to question the widely assumed link between female-headed households and crime—especially for blacks.

First, comparative and historical research do not consistently support the view. For example, many countries of western Europe have relatively high rates of divorce and female-headed households (Rogers and Norman, 1985; Popenoe, 1988) and yet, compared to the U.S.A., very low crime rates. Similarly, some of the largest increases in female-headed households in the U.S.A. came not in the 1960s, when crime was dramatically increasing, but rather in the mid-1970s and 1980s, when crime rates had already stabilized.

Second, although the linkage between female-headed households and declining income is well documented for both blacks and whites (Farley, 1984), the longitudinal connections between crime and poverty are inconsistent. Moreover, the assumption that women are always *pushed* into heading families by economic necessity is questionable. In fact, there is growing evidence that when given the economic opportunity, a large proportion of women—especially black women—choose something other than husband-wife families. Hill (1981, p. v) reports that between 1970 and 1979, female-headed families increased ten times faster among college educated (and presumably, more economically marketable; 308 percent) than grade-school educated (32 percent) black women. Similarly, using quasi-experimental data from New Jersey, Bishop (1980) found that marital dissolution rates were 66 percent *higher* for black families receiving guaranteed incomes compared with a control group that did not receive such economic guarantees. In contrast, Bishop found no difference between the experimental and control groups for white families.[6]

Third, the economic stress produced by heading a household for women is also dependent on the income of the spouse. Throughout the postwar period, this fact has had different implications for black and white women. Given that median income for African-American and white women is now identical, but that median income for black men continues to lag far behind that of white men (Farley, 1984, p. 79), the relative economic impact of female-headed households for black women may be less than it is for white women.

Finally, social disorganization theories link female-headed households to crime by emphasizing the role of the family in controlling the delinquent and criminal behavior of children. But this reasoning does not take into account a situation in which frequent contacts with the legal system have become nearly normative. For example, as we have seen, on any given day in the U.S.A., nearly a quarter of all black men, ages 20 to 29, are either in prison or on probation or parole (Mauer, 1990). Clearly, this calls into question assumptions about the role of husband-wife families in controlling the delinquency of children.

Economic Stress Perspectives

The idea that African-American and white crime rates in the postwar period are related to deteriorating economic conditions has probably produced the largest body of research to date (Long and Witte, 1981; Cantor and Land, 1985; Chiricos, 1987). Merton's (1938) well-known anomie theory applied economic stress arguments directly to the United States by linking crime to a social structure that bombards Americans with the goal of monetary success, but does not equally distribute legitimate economic opportunities for attaining this goal. This imbalance creates isolated, anomic individuals with new, unpredictable, and potentially unfillable desires. Building on Merton's work, Cloward and Ohlin (1960, p. 86) constructed an influential *opportunity and crime* theory that attributes high crime rates in the U.S.A. to "limitations on legitimate avenues of access to conventional goals." Economic stress arguments have led researchers to study either the absolute effect of economic well-being (especially unemployment and poverty, Cantor and Land, 1985; Sampson, 1987), or the relative effect of economic inequality (Blau and Blau, 1982; Stack, 1984) on crime.

Given that economic conditions for blacks have been (and remain) far worse than they are for whites, economic stress arguments would appear to be especially relevant for blacks. However, when we (LaFree, et al., 1992; LaFree and Drass, 1992) examined the effect of unemployment and income measures on black and white rates of robbery, burglary and homicide, 1957–1988, we found that none of these measures had expected effects for blacks, although many did for whites. Similarly, when we included relative deprivation measures in our longitudinal analyses (based on comparing black to white economic stress measures), we found no significant effect for black crime rates.

While researchers have most often measured black relative deprivation by comparing blacks to whites (but see Harer and Steffensmeier, 1992, p. 1036), relative deprivation theorists (Runciman, 1966; Merton, 1968; Clark, 1972) have long argued that comparisons that result in relative deprivation are most likely made to groups sharing important status attributes. Research showing that blacks generally do not use whites as referents for feelings about themselves (McCarthy and Yancey, 1971; Heiss and Owens, 1972) and research on the past (Molotch, 1972; Pearce, 1979) and continuing (Massey and Fong, 1990) racial segregation of the U.S.A., lends support to the hypothesis that lower-class blacks might more readily compare themselves to middle-class and upper-class blacks than to whites. Conceptualized in this way, relative deprivation is related to the concept of "polarization."

Farley (1984, p. 9) defines polarization as intraracial inequality. The concept can be traced back to the mid-1960s research of Moynihan (1965, pp. 5–6), who claimed that African-Americans were increasingly dividing into a relatively stable and steadily growing middle class and an increasingly disorganized and disadvantaged lower class. Similarly, Clarke (1965, p. 28) argued that "the masses of Negroes are now starkly aware of the fact that recent civil rights victories benefitted a very small percentage of middle-class Negroes while their predicament remained the same or worsened." More recently, Wilson (1987) has claimed that many seemingly anomalous findings for African-Americans may be explained by the widening gap between successful middle-class blacks and a growing black *underclass*. If lower-class blacks have experienced an increasing sense of injustice and frustration as they have witnessed the gains made by middle-class blacks, increasing intraracial inequality may be associated with higher black crime rates.

In our analyses of black and white robbery, murder, and burglary rates for the United States, 1957–1988 (LaFree and Drass, 1992), we found evidence for a polarization argument. Our measures of income polarization had significant effects on street crime rates for both blacks and whites. Our results strongly suggest that both black and white crime rates increased in the postwar period along with increases in intraracial inequality.

CONCLUSIONS

Based on our review, it seems fair to conclude that thus far efforts to explain black crime rates in the postwar years using deterrence, social disorganization, and economic stress perspectives have been only partially successful. The most promising of these to date looks at the impact of growing intraracial inequality on crime for the black lower class. However, much work remains to be done. The best evidence suggests that black crime rates—especially for violent street crimes—are much higher than white rates or rates for other minorities, and that while black crime rates have fluctuated a good deal during the postwar years, they have nonetheless been considerably higher than comparable rates for whites throughout the period.

My major assumption in preparing this paper is that it is time for social researchers in the United States to face issues of race squarely and forthrightly. While criminologists have largely ignored connections between race and crime during the past three decades, the involvement of African Americans in the legal system has reached crisis proportions. The story of Willie Horton clearly illustrates how racial stereotypes operate in the absence of more objective analysis. I am arguing that paradoxically, it is only by bringing race issues to the fore that we may be able, at long last, to develop an uneasy truce among ourselves and ultimately, lay race issues to rest.

NOTES

*This research was funded in part by a grant from the Harry Frank Guggenheim Foundation. I assume full responsibility for the results and interpretations presented here. I would like to thank Kriss Drass who has collaborated on much of this research and Jackie Bergdahl for her assistance with the graphics.

1. A full exploration of the complexities of measuring and conceptualizing race is well beyond the scope of this paper. However, it is worth at least noting some of these complexities, because they are so frequently disregarded in research that examines race. If race is defined in physical terms (Barrera, 1979; Davis, 1991, p. 18), racial membership is a matter of ancestry. But the issue of what proportion of one's ancestors must be of a particular race to qualify an individual for membership in a given racial group is handled inconsistently both by researchers and the public. Even assuming that individuals usually know their ancestry and will accurately report it, different criteria are often applied to different racial categories in the United States. Thus, Davis (1991) points out that individuals are generally classified as African-American if they have any known African black ancestry. This *one-drop rule* is not applied to any other racial group in the United States and is rarely applied to any group outside the U.S.A. Probably in response to the obvious problems raised by basing racial distinctions on ancestry, starting in 1980, the U.S. Census began asking household heads to indicate the race of household members. But this simply raises another set of measurement problems. For example, many blacks follow the *one-drop rule* and self-identify as African-Americans. However, many Spanish-speaking people with some black ancestry identify themselves as Hispanics or whites (Davis, 1991). Moreover, racial self-designations vary by region of the country and over time (Jaffe, Cullen, and Boswell, 1980). Given these considerations, it seems clear that racial distinctions in most official data are probably based on a combination of commonsense informed haphazardly and inconsistently by respondent self-identification.

2. However, the program has gone through modifications in the past sixty years, some of which are relatively important (Akiyama and Rosenthal, 1990: Chilton, 1991).

3. The term crime *index* refers to the FBI's long-term practice of reporting combined rates for these seven crimes per 100,000 population. The FBI added *arson* to the other index crimes in the mid-1980s (Akiyama and Rosenthal, 1990; Chilton, 1991).

4. Reporting rates are somewhat higher if jurisdictions that reported less than complete data are included.

5. After African-Americans, American Indians had the highest arrest rates in 1990 (with the exception of robbery, where white rates are higher than those of American Indians). In fact, some analyses of UCR arrest rates (Stewart, 1964; Reasons, 1972) have concluded that American Indian arrest rates for several crimes are higher than for any other racial or ethnic group, including blacks. However, the quality of

UCR data for American Indians and the relatively small size of the Indian population make comparisons like these—especially for less common crimes and earlier years—questionable. For example, in 1950, the UCR reported only 36 American Indian murder and 93 robbery arrests for the entire country (U.S. Federal Bureau of Investigation, 1951).

6. In a related study in Seattle and Denver, Groeneveld, Tuma, and Hannan (1980) found that two years after the beginning of the study, 23% of the black couples with a guaranteed income compared with 15% of those in the control group separated or divorced; among whites the proportions were 17% for those with a guaranteed income and 10% for those without it. In a reanalysis of the Groeneveld et al. data, Cain and Wissoker (1990, p. 1256) conclude that while negative income tax payments had no effect on the rate of marital dissolution for whites and Hispanics, its effect on marital instability for black couples was "positive (destabilizing) and large." Murray (1984, p. 153) argues that the differences in studies like these might have been even greater if the control groups had not included families who were receiving all the usual welfare benefits and if the participants had not known from the outset that the experiment would last for only three years.

REFERENCES

Akiyama, Yoshio, and Harvey M. Rosenthal. 1990. "The Future of the Uniform Crime Reporting Program: Its Scope and Promise," Pp. 49–74 in *Measuring Crime*, edited by D. L. MacKenzie, P. J. Baunach, and R. R. Roberg. Albany: State University of New York Press.

Barrera, Mario. 1979. *Race and Class in the Southwest: A Theory of Racial Inequality*. Notre Dame, Indiana: University of Notre Dame Press.

Bishop, John. 1980. "Jobs, Cash Transfers and Marital Instability: A Review and Synthesis of the Evidence." *Journal of Human Resources* 15:301–34.

Black, Donald, and Albert J. Reiss, Jr. 1970. "Police Control of Juveniles." *American Sociological Review* 35:63–77.

Blau, Judith R., and Peter M. Blau. 1982. "The Cost of Inequality: Metropolitan Structure and Violent Crime." *American Sociological Review* 47:114–29.

Block, Richard. 1974. "Why Notify the Police: The Victim's Decision to Notify the Police of an Assault." *Criminology* 11:555–69.

Blumstein, Alfred, Jacqueline Cohen, and Richard Rosenfeld. 1991. "Trend and Deviation in Crime Rates: A Comparison of UCR and NCS Data for Burglary and Robbery." *Criminology* 29:237–63.

Bursik, Robert J., Jr. 1988. "Social Disorganization and Theories of Crime and Delinquency: Problems and Prospects." *Criminology* 26:519–52.

Cain, Glen G., and Douglas A. Wissoker. 1990. "A Reanalysis of Marital Stability in the Seattle-Denver Income-Maintenance Experiment." *American Journal of Sociology* 95:1235–69.

Cantor, David I., and Kenneth C. Land. 1985. "Unemployment and Crime Rates in the Post–World War II United States: A Theoretical and Empirical Analysis." *American Sociological Review* 50:317–32.

Caplan, Gerald. 1973. "Reflections on the Nationalization of Crime, 1964–1968." *Law and the Social Order* 3:583–635.

Chambliss, William J. 1988. *Exploring Criminology.* New York: MacMillan.

Chilton, Roland J. 1991. "Images of Crime: Crime Statistics and Their Impact." Pp. 45–94 in *Criminology,* edited by Joseph Sheley. Belmont, Calif.: Wadsworth.

Chilton, Roland J., and G. E. Markle. 1972. "Family Disruption, Delinquent Conduct, and the Effect of Subclassification." *American Sociological Review* 37:93–99.

Chiricos, Theodore. 1987. "Rates of Crime and Unemployment: An Analysis of Aggregate Research Evidence." *Social Problems* 34:187–212.

Clark, Robert E. 1972. *Reference Group Theory and Delinquency.* New York: Human Sciences.

Clarke, Kenneth B. 1965. *Dark Ghetto: Dilemmas of Social Power.* New York: Harper & Row.

Cloward, Richard A., and Lloyd E. Ohlin. 1960. *Delinquency and Opportunity: A Theory of Delinquent Gangs.* New York: Free Press.

Cohen, Albert K. 1955. *Delinquent Boys.* Glencoe, Ill.: Free Press.

Davis, F. James. 1991. *Who is Black? One Nation's Definition.* University Park: Pennsylvania State University Press.

Devine, Joel A., Joseph F. Sheley, and M. Dwayne Smith. 1988. "Macroeconomic and Social-Control Policy Influences in Crime Rates, 1948–1985." *American Sociological Review* 53:407–21.

Durkheim, Emile. [1893] 1947. *The Division of Labor in Society.* Tr. by George Simpson. Glencoe, Ill.: Free Press.

Farley, Reynolds. 1984. *Blacks and Whites: Narrowing the Gap.* Cambridge, Mass.: Harvard University Press.

Federal Bureau of Investigation, 1946–1991. "Crime in the United States." *Uniform Crime Reports.* Washington, D.C.: Government Printing Office.

Frazier, E. Franklin. 1950. "Problems and Needs of Negro Children and Youth Resulting from Family Disorganization." *Journal of Negro Education* summer:269–77.

Geis, Gilbert. 1972. "Statistics Concerning Race and Crime." Pp. 61–69 in *Race, Crime and Justice,* edited by C. E. Reasons and J. C. Kuykendall. Pacific Palisades, Calif.: Goodyear.

Gibbons, Don C. 1979. *The Criminological Enterprise: Theories and Perspectives.* Englewood Cliffs, N.J.: Prentice-Hall.

Gibbs, Jack P. 1985. "Review of *Crime and Human Nature,* by James Q. Wilson and Richard J. Herrnstein." *Criminology* 23:381–88.

Gottfredson, Michael R., and Don Gottfredson. 1980. *Decision Making in Criminal Justice.* Cambridge, Mass.: Ballinger.

Gove, Walter R., Michael Hughes, and Michael Geerken. 1985. "Are Uniform Crime Reports a Valid Indicator of the Index Crimes? An Affirmative Answer with Minor Qualifications." *Criminology* 23:451–501.

Groeneveld, Lyle P., Nancy Brandon Tuma, and Michael T. Hannan. 1980. "The Effects of Negative Income Tax Programs on Marital Dissolution." *Journal of Human Resources* 15:654–74.

Harer, Miles, D., and Darrell Steffensmeier. 1992. "The Differing Effects of Economic Inequality on Black and White Rates of Violence." *Social Forces* 70:1035–54.

Harris, Anthony R. 1991. "Race, Class and Crime." Pp. 95–120 in *Criminology,* edited by Joseph F. Sheley. Belmont, Calif.: Wadsworth.

Heiss, Jerald, and Susan Owens. 1972. "Self-Evaluation of Blacks and Whites." *American Journal of Sociology* 78:360–70.

Hill, Robert. 1981. *Economic Policies and Black Progress: Myths and Realities.* Washington, D.C.: National Urban League.

Hindelang, Michael J. 1978. "Race and Involvement in Crime." *American Sociological Review* 43:93–109.

———. 1981. "Variation in Rates of Offending." *American Sociological Review* 46:461–74.

Jaffe, A. J., R. M. Cullen, and T. D. Boswell. 1980. *The Changing Demography of Spanish Americans.* New York: Academic.

Jencks, Christopher. 1992. *Rethinking Social Policy.* Cambridge: Harvard University Press.

LaFree, Gary, and Kriss A. Drass. 1992. "Race, Crime and Polarization in Postwar America, 1957–1987." Paper presented at the annual meetings of the American Society of Criminology, New Orleans.

LaFree, Gary, Kriss A. Drass, and Patrick O'Day. 1992. "Race and Crime in Postwar America: Determinants of African-American and White Rates, 1957–1988." *Criminology* 30:157–88.

Langan, Patrick A. 1991. *Race of Prisoners Admitted to State and Federal Institutions, 1926–1986.* U.S. Department of Justice. Washington, D.C.: Government Printing Office.

Long, Sharon K., and Anne D. Witte. 1981. "Current Economic Trends: Implications for Crime and Criminal Justice." Pp. 69–143 in *Crime and Criminal Justice in a Declining Economy,* edited by Kevin Wright. Cambridge, Mass.: Oelgeschlager, Gunn, and Hain.

Massey, Douglas S., and Eric Fong. 1990. "Neighborhood Quality: Blacks, Hispanics and Asians in the San Francisco Metropolitan Area." *Social Forces* 69:15–32.

Mauer, Marc. 1990. *Young Black Men and the Criminal Justice System.* Washington, D.C.: The Sentencing Project.

McCarthy, John, and William L. Yancey. 1971. "Uncle Tom and Mr. Charlie: Metaphysical Pathos in the Study of Racism and Personal Disorganization." *American Journal of Sociology* 76:648–72.

Merton, Robert K. 1938. "Social Structure and Anomie." *American Sociological Review* 3:672–82.

———. 1968. *Social Theory and Social Structure.* Glencoe, Ill: Free Press.

Molotch, Harvey. 1972. *Managed Integration: The Dilemmas of Doing Good in the City.* Berkeley: University of California Press.

Montare, A., and S. L. Boone. 1980. "Aggression and Paternal Absence: Racial-Ethnic Differences Among Inner-City Boys." *Journal of Genetic Psychology* 137:223–32.

Moynihan, Daniel P. 1965. *The Negro Family: The Case for National Action.* Office of Policy Planning and Research, Department of Labor, Washington, D.C.: Government Printing Office.

Murray, Charles. 1984. *Losing Ground: American Social Policy, 1950–1980.* New York: Basic Books.

New York Times. October 24, 1988. "Foes Accuse Bush Campaign of Influencing Racial Tensions." Section A, p. 1; Section B, p.5.

O'Brien, Robert. 1985. *Crime and Victimization.* Beverly Hills, Calif.: Sage.

Peak, K., and J. Spencer. 1987. "Crime in Indian Country: Another 'Trail of Tears.'" *Journal of Criminal Justice* 15:485–94.

Pearce, Diana M. 1979. "Gatekeepers and Homekeepers: Institutional Factors in Racial Steering." *Social Problems* 26:325–42.

Popenoe, David. 1988. *Disturbing the Nest: Family Change and Decline in Modern Societies.* New York: Aldine DeGruyter.

President's Commission on Law Enforcement and Administration of Justice. 1967. *Task Force Report: Crime and Its Impact—An Assessment.* Washington, D.C.: U.S. Government Printing Office.

Rainwater, Lee. 1966. "Crucible of Identity: The Negro Lower-Class Family." *Daedalus* 95:176–216.

———. 1970. *Behind Ghetto Walls: Black Families in a Federal Slum.* Chicago: Aldine.

Reasons, Charles E. 1972. "Crime and the Native American." Pp. 79–95 in *Race, Crime and Justice,* edited by C. E. Reasons and J. L. Kuykendall. Pacific Palisades, Calif.: Goodyear.

Robins, Lee N., and Shirley Y. Hill. 1966. "Assessing the Contribution of Family Structure, Class and Peer Groups to Juvenile Delinquency." *Journal of Criminal Law, Criminology, and Police Science* 57:325–34.

Rogers, John, and Hans Norman, eds. 1985. *The Nordic Family: Perspectives on Family Research.* Uppsala University.

Rosen, Lawrence, and Kathleen Nielson. 1978. "The Broken Home and Delinquency." Pp. 406–15 in *Crime in Society,* edited by Leonard D. Savitz and Norman Johnston. New York: Wiley.

Ross, H. Laurence, and Gary LaFree. 1986. "Deterrence in Criminology and Social Policy." Pp. 129–52 in *Behavioral and Social Science Knowledge: Discovery, Diffusion and Social Impact.* Washington, D.C.: National Research Council.

Ross, Heather, and Isabel Sawhill. 1975. *Time of Transition: The Growth of Families Headed by Women.* Washington, D.C.: Urban Institute.

Runciman, Walter G. 1966. *Relative Deprivation and Social Justice.* Berkeley: University of California Press.

Sampson, Robert J. 1987. "Urban Black Violence: The Effect of Male Joblessness and Family Disruption." *American Journal of Sociology* 93:348–82.

Shaw, Clifford R., and Henry McKay. 1942. *Juvenile Delinquency and Urban Areas.* Chicago: University of Chicago Press.

Shaw, Clifford R., Henry D. McKay, Frederick M. Zorbaugh, and Leonard S. Cottrell, Jr. 1929. *Delinquency Areas.* Chicago: University of Chicago Press.

Skogan, Wesley G. 1984. "Reporting Crimes to the Police: The Status of World Research." *Journal of Research in Crime and Delinquency* 21:113–37.

Smith, Tom W. 1980. "America's Most Important Problem—A Trend Analysis, 1946–76." *Public Opinion Quarterly* 44:164–80.

Stack, Steven. 1984. "Income Inequality and Property Crime: A Cross-National Analysis of Relative Deprivation Theory." *Criminology* 22:229–57.

Stewart, Omer. 1964. "Questions Regarding American Indian Criminality." *Human Organization.* 23:61–66.

Tittle, Charles. 1980. *Sanctions and Social Deviance.* New York: Praeger.

U.S. Bureau of the Census. 1981. "Marital Status and Living Arrangements, March 1980." *Current Population Reports.* Washington, D.C.: Government Printing Office.

———. 1983. "Fertility of American Women, June 1981." *Current Population Reports,* Series P-20. Washington, D.C.: Government Printing Office.

———. 1984. "Household and Family Characteristics, March 1983." *Current Population Reports,* Series P-20, no. 388. Washington, D.C.: Government Printing Office.

U.S. Bureau of Justice Statistics. 1985. *The Risk of Violent Crime: Department of Justice Special Report.* Washington, D.C.: Government Printing Office.

U.S. Center for Disease Control. 1990. "Homicide Among Young Black Males— United States, 1978–1987." *Morbidity and Mortality Weekly Report* 39:869–73.

Warner, S. B. 1931. "Crimes Known to the Police—An Index of Crime." *Harvard Law Review* 45:307–34.

Wilson, James Q. 1975. *Thinking About Crime.* New York: Basic.

Wilson, William Julius. 1984. "The Urban Underclass." In *Minority Report,* edited by Leslie W. Dunbar. New York: Pantheon.

———. 1987. *The Truly Disadvantaged: The Inner City, the Underclass and Public Policy.* Chicago: University of Chicago Press.

Zatz, Marjorie S., Carol Chiago Lujan, and Zoann K. Snyder-Joy. 1991. "American Indians and Criminal Justice: Some Conceptual and Methodological Considerations." Pp. 100–112 in *Race and Criminal Justice,* edited by M. J. Lynch and E. B. Patterson. New York: Harrow and Heston.

9

Ethnicity, Labor Markets, and Crime

While most people will acknowledge that there are important racial differences in criminal behavior, social scientists disagree about the sources of these differences. Fortunately, few among us continue to argue that observed differences are due to inborn tendencies toward criminality among some groups. Most contemporary explanations focus on either social structural forces or "subcultures" that differentially affect some minority groups. This chapter considers one particular set of structural forces, the effects of labor market experiences and labor market stratification, as contributing factors to racial and ethnic differences in criminal involvement.

The disadvantage experienced by racial and ethnic minorities in the United States has been frequently documented (Wilson, 1987; Freeman, 1991; Lieberson, 1980; Jaynes and Williams, 1989). The question here is: To what extent can observed racial patterns in criminality be accounted for by labor market disadvantages experienced by African and Latino Americans?[1]

While the correlations between race and crime and between race and employment disadvantage are well established, the association between crime and employment is not so clear. Most sociological discussions of the relationship between work and crime have been concerned with the effect of unemployment, and this research has not found a consistent relationship between the two (Gillespie, 1975; Box, 1987; Cantor and Land, 1985; Chiricos, 1987; Parker and Horwitz, 1986).

When consideration is broadened to examine not simply unemployment rates, but also patterns of occupational stratification and the kinds of jobs that potential criminals hold, the picture becomes quite complex. Crutchfield

(1989) argued that unemployment and unstable work affect both individuals and neighborhoods. There are consequences for communities when their members' employment is unstable and of low quality. McGahey (1986) reported that persistent unemployment among adults weakens informal social controls in neighborhoods, which in turn leads to increased delinquency among the young. Crutchfield (1989) found that census tract crime rates were higher where relatively large segments of the work force were marginally employed.

Recognition that the quality of employment affects both the quality or social integration of neighborhoods and the criminality of individuals inevitably leads to questions about the role of race in determining the quality of jobs that people have, and to the effects of low-quality employment on racial patterns in criminality. Duster (1987) and Auletta (1982) have both argued that employment discrimination reduces attachment to the labor market which theoretically can lead to higher crime rates. We should ask, then, to what extent can racial patterns of criminal involvement be traced to the reduced labor force participation of racial and ethnic minority peoples?

The perspective taken in this paper is that some jobs, those in what dual labor market theorists call secondary sector occupations, are less likely to bond young adults to the work place. Those less bonded are, to use Hirschi's word (1969) *freed* to commit delinquency (adult crime in this case). Crutchfield and Pitchford (1989) found that characteristics of employment do in fact affect the criminality of individuals. This is consistent with arguments advanced by other researchers that the quality of work can affect propensity toward crime through attachments to legitimate work and *stakes in conformity* (Votey and Phillips, 1974; Cook, 1975; Jeffery, 1977; Orsagh and Witte, 1981; Crutchfield, 1989).

The alternative explanations for higher levels of criminality among racial and ethnic minorities are of three types. The first, the *opportunity structure thesis,* traces the sources of higher crime rates to material deprivation (see Cloward and Ohlin, 1960). These explanations either explicitly or implicitly argue that many criminals pursue crime as a means to make up for financial deprivation.

The second explanation focuses on the existence of procrime subcultures in black and some Latino neighborhoods (Curtis, 1974; Banfield, 1970). These arguments center on persistent values that allegedly characterize particular segments of the population. These values are associated with poverty and, in particular, concentrations of people living in poverty.

The third set of explanations might be lumped together under the heading of *conflict explanations.* The defining characteristic of these perspectives is their focus on institutionalized inequality. Because the present analysis is anchored in dual labor market conceptions of occupational distribution and because I am not assuming that crime is necessarily a utilitarian response to deprivation, it should be placed in this latter category. The analysis is designed to asses the importance of labor stratification in explaining racial and ethnic differences in criminality, but it will be possible to make some inferences about the subculture and structure of opportunity theses too.

LABOR MARKET INSTABILITY AND CRIMINALITY

Unemployment and marginal employment are not seen here as necessarily directly criminogenic, but they, along with other employment characteristics, should be viewed as important determinants of context in which the effects of other social forces and situational factors may lead to crime. The nature of a person's work, or lack of work, is an important determinant of his or her lifestyle. Dual labor market theory posits a dichotomy of occupations into primary and secondary sectors (see, for example, Doeringer and Piore, 1971, for a complete description of this type of labor market segmentation). Primary sector jobs are characterized by relatively high pay, stable employment with possibilities for promotion and "building a future," good benefits, and a tendency by employees to develop attachments to professional/occupational organizations or co-workers. Occupations in this category range from the professions to skilled labor to unskilled workers in *good, solid, blue-collar jobs* (the auto and steel industries used to be classic examples).

Secondary sector work by contrast is low-paying, unstable, has limited benefits, and workers tend not to build strong ties with coworkers but rather maintain closer relationships to those in their home neighborhood. Typical of this category are unskilled nonunion positions, domestic workers, many waiters and waitresses, and generally the nonprofessional service jobs.

Crutchfield (1989) argued that marginal employment has an effect on individual propensity to engage in crime, because of its effects on individuals' lifestyles. Moreover, high levels of unemployment or secondary sector employment deleteriously affect neighborhoods, which further increases crime rates. When communities are characterized by a relatively high percentage of persons in secondary sector occupations, the community may experience the kind of destabalization that is criminogenic (Auletta, 1982; Duster, 1987; Crutchfield, 1989). Since secondary sector workers typically maintain close associations with people in their neighborhoods, when communities have large numbers of these workers, concentrations of people with weakened ties to the labor market spend time with each other, socialize with one another, and at times even victimize each other.

Crutchfield and Pitchford (1989) reported that three employment characteristics affected the criminal involvement of a sample of young adults:

(1) the length of time they expected to be employed at their current job; (2) the amount of time in the past year that they were out of the labor force; and (3) whether they were in a secondary sector job (low-quality work)[2] in a county with a relatively high percentage of its people employed in the service sector.[3] They also found, after statistically controlling for several important variables, that race was not significantly related to overall criminal involvement, and that contrary to popular stereotypes blacks were less likely than whites to commit property crimes. But the blacks in the sample were more likely to engage in violent crimes after other factors were taken into account.

In this chapter I will consider the extent to which employment differences account for racial differences in criminality. The analysis will examine black, Latino, and white differences in crime and the variable effects of work and labor market characteristics on each group's criminality.

THE DATA

The data used in this analysis are from the National Longitudinal Surveys of Youth (NLSY) Labor Market Experience. These data are taken from an annual longitudinal survey that has been following a sample of approximately twelve thousand males and females who were between the ages of 14 and 21 in 1979, the initial year of the survey.

Several features of the NLSY make it nearly ideal to test the proposed thesis. The NLSY data were collected to obtain detailed personal and work histories of those in the sample. This detail enables us to move beyond the simple dichotomy of primary and secondary sector jobs. The analysis will be able to consider specific characteristics of the respondents' employment and other personal characteristics.

The NLSY oversampled blacks and Latinos to ensure that there were sufficient numbers of them for analysis. The sample is weighted in this analysis to make it representative of the American population in this age group. In the initial year of data collection respondents were asked about their criminal behavior.

Another feature of the NLSY is that respondents are matched with *geocoded data* in the form of county level census information, which can be matched to cases as measures of the macrolevel, local labor market forces that may affect work or crime. These data are coded so that they can be treated as characteristics of the individuals in the sample.

THE ANALYSIS

This analysis is of a subsample of those responding in the first year of the NLSY. Persons over the age of eighteen who are not in the military and not students are included in this analysis (N = 4,146). This study has been limited to adults, because of evidence that employment among juveniles is positively related to delinquency (West and Farrington, 1977). The direct and indirect effects of work on juvenile delinquency are very important, but the important questions for school-aged and more than school-aged youth are sufficiently different to warrant separate treatment.

Military personnel have not been included in the analysis because they are subject to greater "regimentation," social control, and enhanced employment opportunities than their age compatriots in the general population. Also, the characteristics of their current employment are much like those associated with primary sector occupations. To include them would unreasonably bias the analysis in favor of the thesis. Students were excluded because they and their lifestyles, as well as the social control forces affecting them, are radically different from those affecting adults in the "real world."

The exclusion of these two groups makes this an extremely conservative analysis. The truncated occupation distribution that results will make it more difficult for employment variables to explain variation in the dependent variables. In fact, the majority of people in this sample are employed in secondary sector jobs, but there is sufficient variation on other employment variables to test the basic thesis that patterns of employment for whites, blacks, and Latinos will in part explain differences in their respective criminality.

This analysis consists of a series of ordinary least squares (OLS) regressions. First, I will present a model predicting involvement in crime for the full sample. I will then analyze two separate models, the first defining property crime as the dependent variable and the other using violent crime as the dependent variable. The separate models for property and violent crime show results for white, black, and Latino subsamples.

Two dummy variables were used in the analysis to measure race (black = 1) and ethnicity (Latino = 1) along with three additional types of variables: (1) personal characteristics of the respondents, (2) characteristics of the respondent's current job, and (3) characteristics of the local labor market where respondents live. Six personal characteristics are included in the models: age, sex (0 = female, 1 = male), marital status (0 = unmarried, 1 = married), family income, education (highest grade completed), and a variable that asks respondents if they were ever suspended from school. This latter variable was include for two reasons: first as an alternative measure of education (bonding to education more than educational attainment), and second, as a measure of prior rule-breaking behavior. To isolate the effects on crime of current lifestyle from the effects of the early development of deviant patterns, this variable was included as a control variable.

Three job characteristics have been included: whether the respondent's job was a primary sector or a secondary sector occupation (0 = primary, 1 = secondary), expected duration of current employment, and the amount of time that respondents were out of the labor force in the year preceding the interview (this variable was highly skewed so the natural log of it was used in the analysis).

Four characteristics of the local labor market are in the analysis. These variables are measured for the counties in which the respondents live as reported by the Bureau of the Census. The four variables are: the unemployment rate, the poverty rate, the percentage of the county that was *nonwhite*,[4] and the percentage of labor force employed in service sector occupations. For a detailed discussion of the logic of selecting these variables for the analysis, see Crutchfield (1989).[5] In the initial regression the dummy variables for race and ethnicity are included, but obviously they are not in the race-specific analyses. These variables can be included together because they do not covary. Only four persons in the sample were coded as black-Latinos.

As is customary when linking microlevel and macrolevel data, a number of interaction terms that are theoretically important were included in the analysis.[6] These terms were calculated by multiplying macro variables and the equivalent micro variables. The only interaction term that was significant in any of the analyses is a combination of the individual's occupation (primary or secondary) and the percent of the work force in that persons's county of residence employed in service sector industries. This interaction term has been kept in the analysis, but the others have been excluded. Several of these excluded interaction terms will be discussed below, because their insignificance has substantive import.

As mentioned above, the NLSY included crime questions during the first year of administration. Ten questions ask if respondents had committed a specific crime in the past year. The crimes range from the very serious to quite mild.[7] For this analysis I have used summary measures, which include all crimes, property crimes and violent crimes. These variables measure whether the respondent committed a crime one, two, three, or more times in the year prior to the interview. Because of the skewed distribution for all three crime variables, the natural log of each was taken and used as the dependent variables in the analysis.

RESULTS

In this sample blacks are more likely to have committed a crime than nonblacks (Chi-Square significant at .01) and, specifically, to have been involved in violent acts (Chi-Square significant at .001), but there was no sig-

TABLE 9.1 Standardized Regression Coefficients with Total Criminal Involvement, Property Crime Involvement, and Violent Crime Involvement As Dependent Variables

Independent Variables	Total Crime	Property Crime	Violent Crime
Race (1 = Black)	−.040[a]	−.079[c]	.014
Ethnicity (1 = Hispanic)	−.120[c]	−.085[c]	−.096[c]
Employment Variables			
Secondary Sector Employment	.003	.016	−.021
Expected Duration	−.036[a]	−.035[a]	−.025
Out of Labor Force	.048[a]	.058[b]	.044[a]
Interaction Term -			
Percent In Service Sector			
* Secondary Sector Employment	.049[c]	.014	.055[c]
Aggregate Variables			
Unemployment Rate	.012	−.018	−.010
Families in Poverty	.010	−.007	.034
Percent in Service Sector	−.010	−.005	.003
Percent Non-White	−.000	0.021	−.017
Individual Variables			
Age	−.041[c]	−.066[c]	−.036[a]
Sex	.208[c]	.140[c]	.262[c]
Marital Status	−.112[c]	−.112[c]	−.066[c]
Family Income	.028	.054[b]	.009
Education	.025	.006	−.023
School Suspension	.177[c]	.157[c]	.184[c]
Adjusted R^2	.130	.092	.145

[a] significance < .05
[b] significance < .01
[c] significance <.001

nificant difference in the probability that blacks and nonblacks would have committed a property crime. The Latinos in this sample were significantly less likely to have been involved in crime (Chi-Squares for each crime variable as the dependent variable are significant at .001) than non-Latinos. Some of these results are consistent with popularly held beliefs, while others are at variance with *conventional wisdom*. Nevertheless, these patterns constitute the starting point for this analysis of racial and ethnic distributions of criminality and the effect of employment on these distributions.

Table 9.1 presents the results of an OLS regression for the full sample. Both race and ethnicity are included as independent variables, as well as three employment variables, four aggregate variables, the six individual variables, and an interaction term.

Three patterns are noteworthy. First, contrary to popular belief and much criminological research, after other factors are taken into account, blacks in this sample are not more likely than nonblacks to have been involved in criminal activity. In fact, nonblacks are more likely than blacks to commit property violations. The lowered criminal involvement for Latinos that was observed in the Chi Square analysis holds after the other factors are taken into account. Second, employment variables are important predictors of criminality and, in particular, the time that individuals spend out of the labor force and the employment interaction term are good predictors of criminal involvement. The significance of the interaction term is evidence of the criminogenic effect of having a secondary sector worker living among concentrations of other secondary sector workers.[8] Third, none of the aggregate variables significantly predicts individual criminality. In other analyses (data not shown), interaction terms for individual characteristics and the equivalent aggregate variable were included, but none of these terms (with the exception of the employment interaction term) was statistically significant. The lack of significance for the percent nonwhite, the unemployment rate, and the percentage of families in poverty is not consistent with subcultural explanations of crime. The implications of these results will be discussed below.

Finally, in this table, as in the others to follow, one can see that for the most part the individual variables are associated with crime as one would expect. There are two notable exceptions. First, family income is positively related to property crime involvement; and second, education does not appear to affect criminality. I doubt that this latter finding actually means that education is unrelated to criminality, because the subsample used here, which leaves out young adult students and those in the military, has a truncated education distribution. Also, in other analyses (Crutchfield and Pitchford, 1989) we found that education does have an indirect effect through the quality of employment variables.

For our purposes, it is important to focus on the effect that jobs have on the criminality of members of racial and ethnic groups. Before turning to the analysis of subsamples, though, we should more closely examine the attenuation of the bivariate correlation between race and crime, particularly that association when violent crime is the dependent variable. To do this, I ran a regression that only included the age, sex, race, and ethnicity variables as predictors. Race was a strong predictor of involvement in violent crime (Beta = .053, p < .001).

In the second regression, education and school suspension were added. Education, as we have seen, had no direct effect, but it was school suspension that really attenuated the relationship between race and violent crime. With these data we cannot know whether this variable is simply measuring "bad actors" who continue their "evil ways" or the extent to which racial disproportionality in school suspensions may be leading to or exacerbating behavioral problems. If black children are unreasonably sanctioned at school, these results suggest that the consequences for them and their communities may be enormous.

Table 9.2 presents the results of separate OLS regressions on property crime for whites, blacks, and Latinos. Table 9.3 presents results when violent crime is the dependent variable. The individual variables work as predicted, with one notable exception: the criminality of blacks in the sample is not affected by marriage.

It appears that characteristics of employment are more important in explaining black criminality than either that of whites[9] or Latinos. The most consistent predictor is the interaction term, which is associated with higher levels of violence among all three groups, and also of property crime for the Latino subsample. It is important to note that this effect is considerably stronger for blacks (three to four times stronger) and Latinos (nearly nine times stronger) than the effect for whites.

Except for the negative relationship between employment sector and property crime for Latinos, the only other significant associations beside the noted interaction term are in the black subsample. *The more frequently that African-Americans have been out of the labor force, the more likely it is that they have been involved in property and violent crime. Jobs with longer expected duration have a dampening effect on black criminality too.* The relationship for duration is significant in the property crime equation and nearly so when predicting violent crime.[10]

Unlike the findings for the full sample, property crime involvement is predicted by some of the aggregate variables. Whites are less likely to commit property violations when they live in counties with higher levels of poverty, but blacks are more likely. And, to confound the interpretation more, blacks are less likely to engage in property crimes where the unemployment rate is relatively high. Each of these variables was analyzed in other equations with the appropriate interaction terms (interaction terms for the aggregate variable and an appropriate individual level variable), but these interaction terms were unrelated to criminality. That is, it is not whether the person is impoverished or unemployed in the midst of people who are also in poverty or out of work, but rather simply living where poverty is high appears to increase property crime among blacks but decrease it among whites, no matter what their individual economic circumstance.

This pattern is all the more interesting because there is at least the suggestion in these data that it is among whites that there is a positive association between income and property crime at the individual level (see note 8).

For blacks the negative relationship between the unemployment rate and property crime and the positive association between the poverty rate and

TABLE 9.2   Regression Coefficients for Whites, Blacks, and Latinos with Property Crime*

Race or Ethnicity	Whites	Blacks	Latinos
Employment Variables			
Secondary Sector Employment	−.016	−.097	−.174[a]
	(.032)	(.068)	(.085)
Expected Duration	−.015	−.034[a]	−.007
	(.010)	(.017)	(.019)
Out of Labor Force	.015	.040[b]	.025
	(.010)	(.013)	(.018)
Percent in Service Sector			
* Secondary Sector Employment	−.580	1.774	7.620[a]
	(.710)	(1.797)	(3.097)
Aggregate Variables			
Unemployment Rate	.005	−.057[a]	−.028
	(.015)	(.024)	(.029)
Families in Poverty	−.775[b]	.995[a]	.741
	(.293)	(.473)	(.502)
Percent Service Sector	−.005	−.276	.745
	(.269)	(.560)	(1.052)
Percent Nonwhite	.199	−.346	−.316
	(.131)	(.181)	(.317)
Control Variables			
Age	−.033[c]	−.047[c]	.003
	(.010)	(.014)	(.018)
Sex	.161[c]	.197	.127[b]
	(.026)	(.036)	(.048)
Marital Status	−.143[c]	−.005	−.181[c]
	(.026)	(.049)	(.046)
Family Income	.000	.000	.000
	(.000)	(.000)	(.000)
Education	.000	.010	−.006
	(.006)	(.009)	(.011)
School Suspension	.192[c]	.148	.287[c]
	(.026)	(.035)	(.052)
Adjusted R^2	.083	.096	.120

* Standard Errors are in brackets beneath coefficients
[a] significance < .05
[b] significance < .01
[c] significance < .001

TABLE 9.3 Regression Coefficients for Whites, Blacks, and Latinos with Violent Crime*

Race or Ethnicity	Whites	Blacks	Latinos
Employment Variables			
Secondary Sector Employment	−.043	−.006	−.115
	(.031)	(.071)	(.082)
Expected Duration	−.015	−.031	0.002
	(.010)	(.017)	(.019)
Out of Labor Force	.012	.039[b]	.004
	(.009)	(.014)	(.017)
Percent in Service Sector			
* Secondary Sector Employment	1.397[a]	4.905[b]	9.771[b]
	(.690)	(1.870)	(3.017)
Aggregate Variables			
Unemployment Rate	.018	−.045	−.041
	(.014)	(.025)	(.028)
Families in Poverty	.354	.860	.446
	(.285)	(.493)	(.489)
Percent Service Sector	−.199	.389	.302
	(.261)	(.583)	(1.025)
Percent Nonwhite	.016	−.301	0.077
	(.127)	(.188)	(.309)
Control Variables			
Age	−.012	−.017[c]	.029
	(.009)	(.014)	(.017)
Sex	.335[c]	.281[c]	.241[c]
	(.025)	(.038)	(.047)
Marital Status	−.081[b]	−.044	0.130[b]
	(.025)	(.051)	(.045)
Family Income	.000	.000	.000
	(.000)	(.000)	(.000)
Education	.000	−.008	−.012
	(.007)	(.009)	(.010)
School Suspension	.229[c]	.124[c]	.364[c]
	(.025)	(.037)	(.050)
Adjusted R^2	.140	.095	.171

* Standard Errors are in brackets beneath coefficients
[a] significance < .05
[b] significance < .01
[c] significance < .001

property crime should be considered in the context of the individuals' employment characteristics. Individuals' stability of employment lessens criminal involvement for blacks more than for whites, yet these same individuals, even when taking into account their own circumstances, are less likely to engage in crime when unemployment rates are high, but more likely when poverty is high. I will consider alternative explanations for this seeming anomalous set of findings below.

We can clearly conclude from this analysis that the nature of work, but perhaps most importantly the context of the labor market in which people live and labor, affects criminality, and that the effect appears to be most dramatic for blacks. The effect of job stability in the form of expected job duration and time out of the labor force predicts black criminality, but not that of either whites or Latinos. Finally, blacks in this sample appear to be importantly affected by other social context characteristics: the percent in poverty and the unemployment rate have independent and direct affects on black property crime involvement. Whites are less likely to engage in property crime when they live in counties where poverty is higher.

DISCUSSION

Secondary sector jobs are less bonding because they are less stable than primary sector jobs and they are less likely to cause workers to believe that keeping their job is a means of building for the future. Thus, they have little at risk if they lose these jobs, since they are probably going to end soon anyway. In the vernacular of control theory, secondary sector jobs do not build stakes in conformity (Hirschi, 1969).

Furthermore, I have suggested here and elsewhere (Crutchfield, 1989; Crutchfield and Pitchford, 1989) that not only the nature of employment of the individual, but the character of the local labor market, will affect that individual's likelihood of criminal involvement. A large number of secondary sector workers in a community destabalizes that community, and when a person is in an unbonded work situation in these unstable communities, he or she is more likely to engage in crime. Unbonded people are freer to spend time "hanging out," because they are less restrained by *having to be at work in the morning,* or if they must go, they can be less concerned about the state they will be in when they get there. When they spend substantial amounts of time with other marginally employed people in bars, on corners, or in pools halls, they are more likely to become involved in crime.

This analysis supports this perspective for young African-Americans. It is less clear that employment factors have the same consistent effect on whites and Latinos, although there are some observable effects for these groups as well. This may be because blacks not only are frequently employed in the service sector, but they are also more likely to be on the margins of this marginal sector of the labor market. Thus when industrial shifts and economic downturns occur, blacks are less likely to be bumped from the primary sector to the secondary sector, but rather from the secondary sector out of the work force to unemployment.

We are left to speculate about the social mechanics that produce these observations. I prefer what I believe to be the more parsimonious of the possibilities, that known as "the routine activities perspective" (Cohen and Felson, 1979). This perspective simply argues that crime occurs when motivated actors (in this case unbonded people) come together with potential victims, who may be other unbonded people, those in unstable work situations on the same street corner, or other unfortunate people passing by, in the absence of guardians.

We no not know the extent to which these particulars occurred in the specific criminal events committed by the people in this sample, but the significant association between the interaction term for individual secondary sector employment and the size of the local service sector suggest that as concentrations of service sector workers increases, the criminality of those on the labor market margins also increases. This is consistent with the routine activities perspective.

We can draw two things from this analysis. First, marginally employed people, no matter what their race or ethnicity, are more likely to be involved in crime, and in particular violent crime, when they reside in areas with concentrations of similarly employed people. This effect is substantially more important as an explanation of criminality among people of color. Second, black crime is additionally responsive to employment instabilities, such as increased time out of the labor force and jobs of short duration.

Alternative explanations to the occupational stratification argument are the opportunity structure and the subcultural theses. The opportunity structure thesis cannot be adequately tested with the data included in this analysis, but the lack of association between income and crime, to say nothing of the positive relationships to property crime that I have observed, suggests that this theory does not contribute to our understanding of crime in general or ethnic differences in criminality. In particular the positive relationship between income and property crime for whites is counter to the predictions of this theory.

A true test of the subculture thesis must include not just characteristics of the areas in which people live, but some measure of the values of these people. We know nothing about the values internalized by the people in this sample unless we wish to engage in the hopelessly tautological exercise of concluding that "they broke the law, so they must not hold conventional values." Without independent measures of what they believe, we must draw our conclusions based on observable factors. Here the aggregate measures might be thought of as approaching operationalization of key subculture concepts. In particular the poverty rate and the percent nonwhite are consistent with some subculture of poverty arguments. Yet the results are either clearly at variance with the subculture thesis (no relationship between percent nonwhite and crime) or they are inconsistent. The subculture of poverty thesis, when measured by the poverty rate, is not supported for the white subsample. But this theory has either been explicitly (Curtis, 1974) or implicitly (Murray, 1984) linked to blacks. There is a positive relationship between poverty rate and individual property crime involvement among blacks, but it is offset by lower violation rates where there is high unemployment. These findings seem to contradict each other.

Perhaps the best explanation for these patterns is similar to that offered by LaFee, Drass, and O'Day (1990) in order to explain why economic expansion seems to depress white criminality but increase that among blacks. They argue that the black underclass is left out of these economic good times leading to increased frustration and crime. The results of the current analysis may be indicative of a similar phenomenon. In those counties with low unemployment and high poverty the general level of frustration may be increased among some segments of the black population leading to more criminal involvement. Also, in the case of violence, these macro level variables have no direct effect. Perhaps a regional pattern (a finer distinction than the typical south-nonsouth categorization) exists that future analyses may be successful in uncovering.

The dual labor market thesis was initially developed to explain the continued economic disadvantage of some segments of the population, in particular racial and ethnic minorities. This analysis suggests that not only are these groups economically disadvantaged by labor market segmentation, but their heightened probability of engaging in crime is in part due to this disadvantage. Remember, this analysis excluded students, and few college graduates are included so the racial and ethnic patterns observed here would probably be more dramatic if the general population were considered.

Early on I noted the importance of *suspension from school* as a predictor of criminality. This variable was included in part to control for prior established patterns of rule-breaking. Minority children in many school districts are substantially more likely than white children to have been suspended. No doubt most school districts would argue that this is a consequence of behavior problems among African-American and Latino-American students. Just as certainly there are those in minority communities who argue that these patterns are produced by overt or covert forms of discrimination. In this sample, people from both minority groups were significantly more likely to have been suspended from school (Chi-square significant at .001 for both racial—black, nonblack, and ethnic—Latino, non-Latino differences).

We must be concerned about this pattern and seriously consider the extent to which the isolation and disadvantage that we later see in the labor market begins with school suspensions and the overall alienation from school that accompanies these sanctions. Researchers and school officials should consider the importance of suspension as a predictor of crime, and also the reasons for the racial and ethnic differences in suspension rates. They must seriously evaluate why students are being sanctioned and whether this particular form of sanction hurts more than it helps.

Finally, much is periodically made of the demise of urban America. Some have had the wisdom to focus on jobs, in particular good, primary sector, bule-collar jobs (Wilson, 1987), as opposed to moral or value inferiority arguments (Banfield, 1970; Murray, 1984). This analysis suggests that a complete understanding of race and crime in the United States should include the distribution of jobs, and labor market inequalities. Both crime and *urban unrest* can be seen as consequences of disadvantaging people in the labor market, and of the increasing residential concentration and economic isolation of these marginalized people.

At the outset I did not expect, and I would assume that most social observers would not expect, that all racial differences in criminality could be accounted for by taking work experience into account. And they do not. What we learn from this analysis is nevertheless important. Crime in the black community in particular seems to be sensitive to the impact of employment dislocation. The continuing labor market marginalization of African-Americans disadvantages this group economically and appears to differentially lead to crime by its members. Since we know that crime by blacks is most often visited upon other blacks, we must recognize that the African-American community is victimized first in the work place, again when victimization leads to increases in crime, and yet again when that resulting crime ravages their communities.

NOTES

1. The research reported in this paper was partially supported by a grant from the Graduate Research Fund, University of Washington. I would like to thank Susan Pitchford, Charles Hirschman, Rob Sampson, Ross Matsueda, and Darnell Hawkins for commenting on drafts of this paper or for helpful suggestions.

2. See Crutchfield (1989) for a discussion of labor market segmentation and crime, and see Piore (1975), Doeringer and Piore (1971), for a more detailed discussion of the dual labor market thesis.

3. Service sector jobs are not the same as secondary sector jobs, but among them are the prototypical secondary sector positions.

4. The percent nonwhite was used in the analysis after initial regressions were run with percent black and percent Latino included as variables in their respective equations. Neither variable was significant. So, in order to have comparable equations, and to keep some type of macro measure of racial/ethnic composition in the analysis, the percent nonwhite variable was used in all the final regressions.

5. In a number of instances when there was too much case attrition because of pair-wise deletion, the missing cases were recoded to either the lowest value for that variable or the mean of that variable, depending on why the respondent was missing. Very often data were missing because of "valid skips" of questions that depended on earlier questions, so it was possible to make a judgment of whether a case should be forced into the analysis. In selecting the value to assign, I *always* make the most conservative choice, so that bias introduced would work against and not for the thesis.

6. Interaction terms were calculated by subtracting the mean for each variable before multiplying them to avoid collinearity problems when they were included in the regressions.

7. NLSY respondents were asked if they had engaged in any of the following behaviors in the past year: intentionally damaged property, fought at school or work, shoplifted, stolen someone else's belongings of value under $50, stolen belongings of value over $50, used force to obtain things, seriously threatened to hit or hit someone, attacked someone with intent to injure or kill, taken an auto without the owner's permission, broken into a building, or knowingly sold or held stolen goods.

8. Remember that the percent in service sector variable that is used to create this interaction term *is not* actually a measure of secondary sector workers but rather of the percentage of workers in service industries. But the proportion of persons in these industries who are secondary sector workers is high. Obviously it would have been better to use a variable that more clearly measured "proportion secondary sector workers" for the aggregate measure, but that was not available.

9. Some coefficients and standard errors appear as zeros because of the coding that was used. When rounding takes place, they show up as zero. The association between income and property crime for whites is nearly significant at the .05 level (B = .0000048, Standard Error = .0000028).

10. The coefficient for expected duration predicting violent crime just misses statistical significance at the .05 level. This subsample is comparatively small, just under 1,000; so it would have been reasonable to use the more liberal .10 standard, in which case the coefficient would have achieved significance.

REFERENCES

Auletta, Ken. 1982. *The Underclass.* New York: Random House.

Banfield, Edward C. 1970. *The Unheavenly City: The Nature and the Future of Our Urban Crisis.* 2d ed. Boston: Little, Brown.

Box, Steven. 1987. *Recession, Crime and Punishment.* Totowa, N.J.: Barnes and Noble.

Cantor, David, and Kenneth C. Land. 1985 "Employment and Crime Rates in the Post–World War II United States: A Theoretical and Empirical Analysis." *American Sociological Review* 50:317–32.

Chiricos, Theodore G. 1987. "Rates of Crime and Unemployment: An Analysis of Aggregate Research Evidence." *Social Problems* 34:187–212.

Cloward, Richard A., and Lloyd E. Ohlin. 1960. *Delinquency and Opportunity: A theory of Delinquent Gangs.* New York: Free Press.

Cohen, Lawrence, and Marcus Felson. 1979. "Social Changes and Crime Rate Trends: A Routine Activity Approach." *American Sociological Review* 44:588–608.

Cook, Philip J. 1975. "The Correctional Carrot: Better Jobs for Parolees," *Policy Analysis* 1:11–54.

Crutchfield, Robert D. 1989 "Labor Stratification and Violent Crime," *Social Forces* 68:489–512.

Crutchfield, Robert D., and Susan R Pitchford. 1989. "Occupation, Lifestyle, and Criminal Behavior." Annual Meetings of the American Society of Criminology, Reno, Nevada.

Curtis, Lynn. 1974. *Criminal Violence: National Patterns and Behavior.* Lexington, Mass.: D.C. Heath.

Doeringer, Peter B., and Michael J. Piore. 1971. *Internal Labor Markets and Manpower Analysis.* Lexington, Mass.: D.C. Heath.

Duster, Troy. 1987. "Crime, Youth Unemployment, and the Black Underclass," *Crime and Delinquency* 33:300–316.

Freeman, Richard B. 1991. "Employment and Earnings of Disadvantaged Young Men in a Labor Shortage Economy," in *The Urban Underclass,* edited by Christopher Jencks and Paul E. Peterson. Washington, D.C.: Brookings Institution.

Gillespie, Robert W. 1975. *Economic Factors in Crime and Delinquency: A Critical Review of the Empirical Evidence.* Washington, D.C,: National Institute of Law Enforcement and Criminal Justice, Department of Justice.

Hirschi, Travis. 1969. *Causes of Delinquency.* Berkeley: University of California Press.

Jaynes, Gerald David, and Robin M. Williams, Jr. 1989. *A Common Destiny: Blacks and American Society.* Washington, D.C.: National Academy Press.

Jeffery, C. R. 1977. *Crime Prevention through Environmental Design,* rev. ed. Beverly Hills, Calif: Sage Publications.

LaFree, Gary, Kriss Drass, and Patrick O'Day. 1990. "Race and Crime in Postwar America: Determinants of African-American and White Rates, 1958–1988." Paper presented at the American Society of Criminology, Baltimore.

Lieberson, Stanley. 1980. *A Piece of the Pie: Blacks and White Immigrants Since 1880.* Berkeley: University of California Press.

McGahey, Richard M. 1986. "Economic Conditions, Neighborhood Organization, and Urban Crime," in Albert J. Reiss, Jr., and Michael Tonry, eds., *Communities and Crime.* Chicago: University of Chicago Press.

Murray, Charles. 1984. *Losing Ground: American Social Policy, 1950–1989.* New York: Basic Books.

Orsagh, Thomas, and Ann Dryden Witte. 1981. "Economic Status and Crime: Implications for Offender Rehabilitation." *Journal of Criminal Law and Criminology* 72:1055–71.

Parker, Robert Nash, and Allan V. Horwitz. 1986. "Unemployment, Crime, and Imprisonment: A Panel Approach." *Criminology* 24:751–73.

Piore, Michael J. 1975. "Notes for a Theory of Labor Market Stratification," in *Labor Market Segmentation,* edited by Richard C. Edwards, Michael Reich, and David M. Gordon. Lexington, Mass.: Heath.

Votey, Harold L., Jr., and Llad Phillips. 1974. "The Control of Criminal Activity: An Economic Analysis," in Daniel Glaser, ed., *Handbook of Criminology.* Chicago: Rand McNally.

West, Donald, and David Farrington. 1977. *The Delinquent Way of Life.* London: Heinemann.

Wilson, William Julius. 1987. *The Truly Disadvantaged: The Inner City, the Underclass, and Public Policy.* Chicago: University of Chicago Press.

DOROTHY LOCKWOOD
ANNE E. POTTIEGER
JAMES A. INCIARDI

10

Crack Use, Crime by Crack Users, and Ethnicity

In their many analyses of the crack epidemic, journalists have portrayed crack use and crack-related crime as essentially problems of blacks in inner-city neighborhoods. Magazine photographs show young black American men and women smoking crack in abandoned buildings, minority youth with guns in their jeans and handfuls of crack, and even Marion Barry, former Washington, D.C. mayor, smoking crack. Headlines proclaim "A Tide of Drug Killings: The Crack Plague Spurs More Inner-City Murders" and "Prisoners of Crack: Eight Years of Reagan Politics Corrupted a Generation of Urban Black Americans and Devastated their Communities." Feature articles highlight "Drugs and the Black Community" and "The New Criminal Recruits of the Inner City, the Children who Deal Crack." Altogether, journalists have presented a crack/crime/black interconnection that would appear to be a simple, well-established fact of American life.[1]

The problem with this picture is that the only part clearly documented by media reports is that crack has had a destructive impact on black inner-city communities. The evidence presented for more specific crack/crime/black connections is far more tenuous, leaving a series of unanswered logical questions. Is the crack/crime association mere sensationalism, or are crack users commonly involved in criminal behavior? Is any crack/crime relationship really a more general cocaine/crime association, or are crack users more crime-involved than other cocaine users? Is it really so that most crack users are black, as portrayed in media reports? Are users of any and all forms of cocaine predominantly black, or are black cocaine users more likely than white or Hispanic users to use cocaine in the specific form of crack? Has not crack spread well beyond inner-city neighborhoods into working class suburbs, and if so, is there not a white crack/crime problem? Is any such white crack/crime association different in degree or type from that for blacks? Are any such ethnic differences anything more than socioeconomic differences?

These questions, even without answers, suggest a considerably more complex relationship between crack use, crime by crack users, and ethnicity than that implied by mass media reports. Much of the complexity is due to the fact that multiple considerations other than ethnicity correlate with or cross-cut ethnicity, and therefore confound apparent ethnic differences. These factors cannot be disentangled with urban war zone reporting techniques, but instead require scientific methods of sample selection and data analysis. At the same time, traditional scientific methods require random samples drawn from a known total population—a procedure that in practice is simply not possible when studying such highly deviant behaviors as crack use and street crime. Furthermore, separating ethnicity from its correlates requires sample types and sizes that are especially difficult for researchers to obtain. These methodological problems, combined with the relative recency of widespread crack use, have resulted in a published social science literature on the topic that is still very limited.

Prior research relevant to the crack/crime/ethnicity issue is briefly reviewed in the next section; the two basic questions that *have* been answered are noted, as well as the complications other researchers have encountered in studying more complex aspects of the subject. Following this, data from a new study are described, in which crack use and criminal activity were studied among a sample of white Anglo, African-American, and Hispanic cocaine users in Miami, Florida.

PRIOR RESEARCH

The relationship between crack use and crime has been a major focus of social science research on crack to date. This work has not identified ethnic differences, but at least the crack/crime results are rather clear cut. A variety of studies document the existence of an association between crack use and criminal behavior, particularly drug dealing and violence (Goldstein et al., 1991; Hamid, 1990; Inciardi, Lockwood, and Pottieger, 1993, pp. 116–31; Inciardi and Pottieger, 1991; Klein and Maxson, 1985; McBride and Swartz, 1990). The media reports appear to be correct in implying that crack users are commonly involved in criminal behavior.

Prior research is also fairly consistent in its answer to a second basic question about the crack/crime/black connection: that of whether crack users are predominantly black. Disproportionate crack use among blacks is indicated in official statistics from the National Institute on Drug Abuse (NIDA) Household Survey. In 1991, 4.3 percent of blacks surveyed had used crack, compared to only 1.5 percent of whites and 2.1 percent of Hispanics. Ethnic differences in lifetime crack use were especially large among persons aged 26 to 34 years old: the 9.2 percent of blacks reporting use is some three times that of the 2.8 percent for whites or 3.7 percent for Hispanics (National Institute on Drug Abuse, 1991). However, because whites represent the majority of the U.S. population, these percentage estimates still imply that most crack users are *not* black. The NIDA estimates of current crack use—defined as use in the past month—are 0.7 percent for blacks, 0.4 percent for Hispanics, and 0.2 percent for whites. This translates to population estimates of 172,000 black crack users, 68,000 Hispanic crack users, and 238,000 white crack users. That is, of the 479,000 crack users estimated for the 1991 U.S. household population, 49.9 percent were white, 14.2 percent Hispanic, and only 35.9 percent were black.

While the NIDA Household Survey provides the *best available* evidence on ethnic distributions of crack users, it should also be noted that this does not mean it is necessarily a *good* estimate. Very low percentage estimates in this type of study—such as those given for current crack use—mean less reliable estimates. Further, as a survey of the household population, the NIDA study does not include populations critical to examining ethnic differences in crack use, such as runaways and other homeless people, addicts in residential treatment, incarcerated populations, and those in the street drug subcultures that are generally inaccessible through standard survey methods. Other official statistics do include some of these populations—notably the National Institute of Justice's Drug Use Forecasting (DUF) program and the NIDA Drug Abuse Warning Network (DAWN)—but they cannot separate crack use from other cocaine use and they do not report statistics in a way that permits extrapolation to population estimates. For example, the 1991 DAWN data indicate twice as many cocaine-related emergency room (ER) *mentions* for blacks as for whites (National Institute on Drug Abuse, 1992). However, this is a count of ER *visits* in which one drug mentioned was cocaine; it is *not* a count of *persons* who used cocaine. Further, the *reason* for cocaine-related ER visits in at least 46 percent of all cases is related to *cocaine dependence*—involving persons seeking detoxification (25.3 percent) or experiencing debilitating effects seen only in chronic users (20.6 percent). For such problems, one chronic user may make multiple cocaine-related ER visits and this is presumably more common among those who cannot afford to go anywhere but an emergency room for treatment. Thus, more black cocaine-related ER visits may simply mean more multiple visits by black than white cocaine users.

Beyond these two points—a strong crack/crime relationship and no more than a weak crack/black association—very little published research exists on ethnic differences specifically among *crack* users, let alone ethnic differences in crimes among crack users. In fact, there is surprisingly little research on ethnic differences concerning any type of illegal drug use or its correlates. Moreover, the work that has been done is suspect for purposes of understanding ethnicity/drug-use relationships, because it is almost all based on samples of either students or drug treatment patients, and ethnic minorities have both higher rates of school dropout and lower rates of treatment seeking than whites (Collins, 1992; Rebach, 1992).

The greatest research attention has been devoted to adolescents, primarily students. The findings generally show that ethnic differences in drug use are explained by background variables, particularly income and availability (Adlaf, Smart, and Tan, 1989; Kandel, Single, and Kessler, 1976; Maddehian, Newcomb, and Bentler, 1986; Wallace and Bachman, 1991). More importantly, studies indicate that most drug use rates—including those of alcohol, cocaine, pills of all types, cigarettes, hallucinogens, and inhalants—are *lowest* among black adolescents (Bachman et al., 1991; Kandel, Single, and Kessler, 1976; National Institute on Drug Abuse, 1991; Rebach, 1992; Segal, 1989). Hispanic males, however, are generally found more likely to have used cocaine than either whites or blacks (Bachman et al., 1991; Marin, 1990; National Institute on Drug Abuse, 1991; Wallace and Bachman, 1990).

Among adult drug users, most research on ethnic differences comes from studies of heroin addicts in treatment in which, usually, only two ethnic categories are compared: black and white, or Hispanic and white Anglo. These studies suggest that minorities, including African-Americans, Puerto Ricans, and Mexican-Americans, are overrepresented among heroin users (Anglin et al., 1988; Ball and Chambers, 1970; Kleinman and Lukoff, 1978). Studies of cocaine and crack users also indicate disproportionate use among minorities (Carroll and Rounsaville, 1992; Johnson, Elmoghazy, and Dunlap, 1990). As in the studies of students, however, ethnicity generally is found to interact with other variables. In particular, an interaction effect between gender and ethnicity has been documented in several studies (Austin and Gilbert, 1989; Prendergast et al., 1989), and other researchers have presented their results separately for males and females to clarify the ethnic differences within gender categories and to avoid the complexity of this interaction (Anglin et al., 1988; Wallace and Bachman, 1991). More recently, treatment status also has been recognized as an important confounding factor in the study of ethnic differences in drug use. One recent study, for example, found that 55 percent of 298 cocaine users in treatment were white, whereas among 101 cocaine users *not* in treatment, only 14 percent were white (Carroll and

Rounsaville, 1992). Treatment status of cocaine users also appears to be entangle with gender and other differences (Boyd and Mieczkowski, 1990; Brunswick, Messeri, and Aidala, 1990; Chitwood and Morningstar, 1985; Griffin et al., 1989; Rounsaville and Kleber, 1985).

Altogether, social science research pertinent to the alleged crack/crime/ black linkage can be summarized as follows. First, it is limited, particularly on the specific topic of crack. Second, it has documented a *crack/crime* association. Third, it suggests that any *black/crack* association is a limited one—higher rates of crack use for blacks than for whites and Hispanics, but fewer black crack users than nonblack crack users. Fourth and most importantly, it repeatedly documents the complexity of drug use/ethnicity relationships and the consequent requirement for a large, demographically diverse sample in order to study this subject adequately. Drug users who differ in ethnicity invariably also differ in ways that have nothing to do with ethnicity, such as gender, and in additional ways that are correlated with ethnicity, such as income levels and residence patterns, and in still other ways such as treatment status for which relationships to ethnicity are still not well understood. These other differences tend to either explain the drug/ethnicity differences or to make the sample size too small for the kind of analysis that would even permit study of this possibility. For the specific problem of the crack/crime/ black association alleged in media reports, many of these methodological difficulties are overcome in a recent study of a large, demographically diverse sample of cocaine users.

METHODS

Drug use patterns and criminal behavior were the major concerns of a study conducted between September 1987 and August 1991 in the Miami, Florida, metropolitan area. A total of 699 cocaine users were interviewed, 349 of them in residential treatment at the time and 350 on the street. Other than demographic subsample targets, discussed below, the only sample eligibility criterion was use of any kind of cocaine during "the last ninety days on the street." For the street sample, this was the ninety days prior to interview. For the treatment sample, it was the most recent continuous ninety days on the street prior to termination of a typical usage pattern due to treatment entry (including a treatment-preceding event such as arrest or dosage reduction in anticipation of treatment entry). This ninety-day period was required to be within the two years prior to interview. The total time period referenced by all respondents' "last ninety days on the street" was November 1986 through December 1989.

The interviewers were highly experienced in talking to persons involved in drug use and street crime, and they were intensively trained in administering the study's interview schedule. Questions about drug use and criminal behavior were asked during an interview lasting thirty to sixty minutes, and respondents were paid $10 for their time. Legal protection for subjects was assured by anonymity and a certificate of confidentiality from the National Institute on Drug Abuse. This guaranteed that project employees could not be compelled by any court or law enforcement agency to reveal information sources or questionnaire data. Treatment program clients were assured that neither participation nor nonparticipation would effect their program status and that their answers would not be seen by counsellors or other program personnel.

Selection of both street and treatment respondents was guided by subsample targets for gender, age, and ethnicity in order to ensure a demographically diverse sample. In the treatment programs, this generally meant returning repeatedly to interview every new client in the hard-to-fill subsamples (younger and white or Hispanic) and, in the end, significant departures from the planned subsample goals because respondents in given age/ethnicity categories were simply not available. Specifically, no treatment subsample for adolescent females was possible, and in the last two months of interviewing, only the gender target specifications were kept for treatment interviews. On the street, subsample targets meant pushing the interview process into a variety of neighborhoods to get the required ethnic diversity, but age ranges were not a problem and all targeted subsample Ns were met. Street respondents were located through standard multiple-starting-point *snowball sampling* techniques in neighborhoods with high rates of cocaine use by a street interviewer familiar with and well known in the target areas. The details of how this kind of street data collection is done are described elsewhere (Inciardi, Horowitz, and Pottieger, 1993, pp. 64–67; Inciardi, Lockwood, and Pottieger, 1993, pp. 147–51).

The final sample was 66 percent male and 34 percent female. The 285 black respondents comprised 34 percent of the males and 54 percent of the females; the 273 white respondents were 36 percent of the males and 46 percent of the females; and the 141 Hispanics (108 of them Cuban) were the remaining 30 percent of the male respondents. Modal age was 20 to 29 (46 percent of the respondents), while 28 percent were ages 13 to 19, and 26 percent were 30 to 49 years old.

Questions about cocaine use in the last ninety days on the street were asked separately for six types of cocaine use: snorting, intravenous (IV) use, crack smoking, other (pure, ether-based) freebasing, coca paste smoking, and any other (new) form of cocaine. For each type and for each of two time periods—the last thirty days and then the sixty days prior to that—respondents were asked how many days cocaine was used and, on a day used, how many doses were *usually* used. "Amount of cocaine use" was then calculated by multiplying "number of usual doses per day" by "number of days that dosage was used," and adding the results to arrive at an estimated total quantity for each cocaine type used in the respondent's last ninety days on the street. These figures permitted calculation of each cocaine user's *primary cocaine type*—the one cocaine form, if any, which accounted for 75 percent or more of all cocaine used by each respondent in the last ninety days on the street. For analysis of cocaine quantity used, however, the estimated totals were based on too many assumptions to be treated as true interval measures; thus, they were recoded into simple seven-category ordinal level variables coded from $0 =$ none to $6 = 1350+$ doses.

Measures for illegal activities were constructed similarly. For each of 23 crime types, for the last thirty days and then for the sixty days prior to that, respondents were asked on how many days the offense was committed and the usual number of offenses per day. Total crimes for the ninety days were then computed for each specific offense type. These totals were combined into totals for six general crime types—violence-related, major property crime, petty property crime, prostitution and procuring, drug trafficking or manufacture, and street-level drug sales. These totals in turn were reduced to ordinal-level scores, using a coding system that gave higher scores for a given number of offenses as the general offense type was more serious. For example, the highest score for violence-related crimes (7) was assigned for $40+$ offenses; the equivalent score for petty property crimes required $90+$ offenses. Finally, scores for each of the six specific types were added to form an overall crime score that would indicate the relative seriousness of respondents' criminal activity regardless of specific crime types. Details for the scoring system and resulting totals are shown in Tables 10.2 and 10.3 later in this paper for a subsample of the respondents (*young street crack users*, defined in the context of discussing those tables).

FINDINGS

This analysis focuses on the primary type of cocaine used, and the crack/crime connection, in general and by ethnicity, and specifically among African-Americans.

The Crack/Black Connection

The first question addressed is that of whether black cocaine users were more likely than their white and Hispanic counterparts to have crack as their *primary cocaine type*. A breakdown by ethnicity alone suggests no black/crack association: the only apparent differences by ethnicity are (1) for Hispanics, more preference for snorting (31.9 percent, compared to 12.3–13.2 percent of blacks and whites) and thus *less* preference for crack (58.2 percent, compared to 74.5 percent for both blacks and whites), and (2) more IV use for blacks (8.4 percent, compared to 1.4–1.8 percent for Hispanics and whites).

Because prior research suggests that gender, age, and treatment status might all be interrelated with ethnic differences, these other three factors were used as controls for a more detailed examination of ethnicity and primary cocaine type. The results, as shown in Table 10.1, indicate that among users ages 13 to 29 years who were interviewed on the street, there were extremely few differences in cocaine use by either ethnicity or gender. Crack was the primary cocaine type for every single street respondent under age 20, and for over 90 percent of street respondents ages 20 to 29 with the sole exception of Hispanic males.

For the older cocaine users interviewed on the street, in contrast, both ethnic and gender differences appear. Among whites ages 30 to 49 years, all of the women and most of the men had crack as their primary cocaine type; the Hispanic men this age were split exactly 50–50 between crack and snorting; and black cocaine users this age were clearly *least* likely to be primary crack users. In fact, among cocaine users ages 30–49 interviewed on the street, it was not crack but IV cocaine that was the primary cocaine type much more likely among blacks than among whites and Hispanics.

The treatment groups present an even more complicated picture. Over 40 percent of the adolescent respondents used cocaine primarily by snorting, as did 20 percent or more of all women and all Hispanics. Further, a significant minority of respondents in an apparently random selection of gender, age, and ethnicity subgroups used such a variety of cocaine forms that no one type accounted for 75 percent of their total use. This pattern of *no primary cocaine type* was not seen for even one street respondent. Thus, crack use was clearly less common among the cocaine users in treatment than among their counterparts interviewed on the street, with a particularly strong contrast among users under age 30.

In a followup analysis, correlates of having crack as a primary cocaine type were computed using the Spearman (rank order) Correlation Coefficient (*rho*). The results indicate that in this sample of 699 cocaine users, the only crack/ethnicity correlation significant at the .05 level is a weak negative one ($-.15$) with being a Hispanic male. That is, being black (or white, for that matter) was unrelated to having crack as a primary cocaine type. Being younger, on the other hand, was related (rho with age = $-.10$, $p < .003$), as was being female (rho = $.19$, $p < .0005$). Being on the street as opposed to in treatment was even more strongly related (rho = $.30$, $p < .0005$).

For still another way of looking at the crack/black connection, correlates were computed for amount of crack used in the last ninety days by only

TABLE 10.1   Primary Cocaine Type: Percentage of Group

Group		(N)	Crack	Snort	IV	None
Total Sample		(699)	71.4	16.6	4.4	7.6
St M 13–19	Black	(25)	100.0	0.0	0.0	0.0
	White	(23)	100.0	0.0	0.0	0.0
	Hispanic	(27)	92.6	7.4	0.0	0.0
St M 20–29	Black	(28)	92.9	0.0	7.1	0.0
	White	(33)	90.9	3.0	6.1	0.0
	Hispanic	(25)	64.0	36.0	0.0	0.0
ST M 30–49	Black	(17)	47.1	5.9	47.1	0.0
	White	(16)	75.0	12.5	12.5	0.0
	Hispanic	(18)	50.0	50.0	0.0	0.0
St F 13–19	Black	(26)	100.0	0.0	0.0	0.0
	White	(26)	100.0	0.0	0.0	0.0
ST F 20–29	Black	(29)	93.1	0.0	6.9	0.0
	White	(34)	97.1	2.9	0.0	0.0
St F 30–49	Black	(14)	21.4	14.3	64.3	0.0
	White	(9)	100.0	0.0	0.0	0.0
Tr M 13–19	Black	(25)	12.0	84.0	0.0	4.0
	White	(21)	33.3	52.4	0.0	14.3
	Hispanic	(22)	36.4	40.9	0.0	22.7
Tr M 20–29	Black	(36)	69.4	8.3	0.0	22.2
	White	(50)	58.0	16.0	2.0	24.0
	Hispanic	(28)	39.3	28.6	7.1	25.0
Tr M 30–49	Black	(25)	84.0	8.0	4.0	4.0
	White	(22)	50.0	22.7	0.0	27.3
	Hispanic	(21)	61.9	38.1	0.0	0.0
Tr F 18–19	Black	(2)	50.0	50.0	0.0	0.0
Tr F 20–29	Black	(36)	83.3	8.3	0.0	8.3
	White	(20)	75.0	20.0	0.0	5.0
Tr F 30–49	Black	(22)	81.8	9.1	9.1	0.0
	White	(19)	47.4	21.1	0.0	31.6

the 499 primary crack users. The prior analyses suggest that *among cocaine users,* being black is *not* associated with being a crack user. This analysis asked whether *among crack users,* blacks use *more* crack than whites and Hispanics. Again, Spearman coefficients were calculated and ethnicity was treated as three dichotomous variables. The results showed no relationship between amount of crack used and being black—or white or Hispanic, or of one gender rather than the other. Amount of crack used by primary crack users was significantly although weakly correlated, however, with being in treatment (rho = .14, p < .001), and it was clearly related to being older (rho with age = .33, p < .0005).

The Crack/Crime Connection

The second question of interest is that of whether the crack/crime relationship documented in prior studies is really a more general cocaine/crime association, or, instead, crack users are actually more crime-involved than other cocaine users. Correlational analysis suggests that primary cocaine type is less important than amount of cocaine used. For all 699 cocaine users in the sample, total crime score was clearly related to total amount of cocaine used—rho = .34, p < .0005—but it was not related to having crack as a primary cocaine type. The probable reason is that primary crack users tended to use less total cocaine than other cocaine users—rho = −.26, p < .0005. However, computations for only the 499 primary crack users indicated that the crack/crime correlation for them—rho = .43, p < .0005—is even stronger than the general cocaine/crime correlation for all 699 cocaine users. These results suggest that the crack/crime association reported by other researchers is more than just a part of some general correlation between cocaine use and crime.

Crack/Crime Differences by Ethnicity

Given a definite crack/crime connection but only a very weak crack/black connection, the question for analysis necessarily shifts to that of whether there are differences in the crack/crime relationship for crack users of different ethnicities. Too many crack users are *not* black for the crack/crime association to be a black phenomenon. Thus, is the white or Hispanic crack/crime connection different in degree or type from that for blacks?

This more detailed analysis of the crack/crime relationship was done for only the 257 primary crack users ages 13 to 29 years who were interviewed on the street—the *young street crack user* subsample. As previously seen in Table 10.1, young respondents on the street—regardless of gender or ethnicity—were much more consistent than any other subgroup of cocaine users in preferring crack as their primary cocaine type. Confining further analysis to this subsample thus permits the clearest view of the crack/crime/ ethnicity relationship—that is, complications of treatment status and older age groups can be ignored. Further, youth and young adult crack users who are not in treatment are also the crack users who present the most obvious problem to policy makers and the criminal justice system, as well as to their families and neighborhoods. Thus, the *young street crack user* subsample is arguably also the most appropriate and important one in which to more closely examine the crack/crime relationship.

The criminal involvement of this subsample is extensive, as shown in table 10.2. Over 96 percent of each gender/ethnic category is involved in dealing drugs, most respondents did petty property crimes, and some also committed major property crimes (burglary or motor vehicle theft) or violent offenses (robbery, assault, or weapons use). However, gender and ethnic differences also appear—more prostitution and procuring for women, and especially black women; more major property crimes for men, and especially Hispanic men; more petty property crimes among women; more violent offenses among blacks; and more drug dealing by men, especially black men.

These cross-cutting variations could conceivably cancel each other out and total up to only differences in crime *types*, not overall criminal involvement. Thus, the total crime scores were computed as previously described to look at degree of criminal involvement regardless of crime type. When the results are displayed for gender/age/ethnic categories, as shown in table 10.3, all three demographic variables appear to define differences in level of criminal involvement. For instance, among teenage males, blacks appear to be more heavily involved in crime than either whites or Hispanics, and the criminal involvement of the latter two groups is almost identical. However, among males ages 20 to 29, a much higher percentage of Hispanics than blacks or whites are in the *high typical* category, and Hispanics have the highest median crime score. For both males and females, the teenage respondents are less crime-involved than those ages 20 to 29. Gender differences appear minimal for black teenagers, whereas black women ages 20 to 29 appear to be more involved in crime than black men in the same age group. Similarly, white women ages 20 to 29 are more crime-involved than white men of the same age. For both age groups, more black than white women are in the highest crime categories.

The extent to which these variations in level of criminal involvement are related to amount of crack used varies greatly by crime type. As indicated in Table 10.4, the correlation in most subgroups is most likely to be strong—.50 or more—for drug sales. Violence-related offenses are also correlated with amount of crack used for five of the ten subgroups. Petty property crime, in contrast, is correlated with amount of crack used only among Hispanic males aged 13 to 19, and that is a negative relationship. Major property crimes, prostitution, and drug trafficking are not significantly related to amount of crack used for any of the subgroups.

These results display no clear pattern of differences by ethnicity, gender, or age in the relationships between type of crimes committed and amount of crack used. This is partially due to the overall level and diversity of criminal involvement of this group—all respondents were criminally active and most were committing a variety of crimes during the ninety days prior to interview. In addition, for all the lack of criminal specialization in this subsample, respondents in every ethnic and gender group were *most* likely to be involved in street-level drug dealing—and for all subgroups, this was the offense most likely to be highly correlated with total crack used.

TABLE 10.2 Crimes Done in the Last 90 Days Types by 257 Primary Crack Users Ages 13–29 Interviewed on the Street: Percentage of Sex/Ethnicity Group and Total Subsample

Crime Type, (Score, and Number Committed)	Male			Female		Total Subsample
	Black (N=51)	White (N=53)	Hispanic (N=41)	Black (N=53)	White (N=59)	(N=257)
Violence-Related						
0 None	74.5	81.1	80.5	60.4	83.1	75.9
1 1–2	0.0	5.7	9.8	17.0	10.2	8.6
2 3–11	7.8	1.9	4.9	17.0	6.8	7.8
4 12–36	13.7	7.5	4.9	5.7	0.0	6.2
7 40+	3.9	3.8	0.0	0.0	0.0	1.6
Major Property						
0 None	86.3	84.9	73.2	96.2	100.0	89.1
1 1–2	3.9	5.7	12.2	0.0	0.0	3.9
2 3–11	9.8	7.5	14.6	3.8	0.0	6.6
4 12–33	0.0	1.9	0.0	0.0	0.0	0.4
Petty Property						
0 None	35.3	37.7	22.0	11.3	20.3	25.3
1 1–11	33.3	30.2	29.3	20.8	40.7	31.1
2 12–39	25.5	24.5	34.1	54.7	32.2	34.2
4 40–89	5.9	7.5	14.6	11.3	5.1	8.6
7 90+	0.0	0.0	0.0	1.9	1.7	0.8
Prostitution/Etc.						
0 None	98.0	100.0	100.0	32.1	62.7	77.0
1 1–30	2.0	0.0	0.0	22.6	10.2	7.4
2 34–85	0.0	0.0	0.0	30.2	18.6	10.5
4 90–285	0.0	0.0	0.0	13.2	5.1	3.9
8 300+	0.0	0.0	0.0	1.9	3.4	1.2
Drug Traffick						
0 None	100.0	98.1	100.0	98.1	100.0	99.2
1 1–30	0.0	1.9	0.0	1.9	0.0	0.8
Dealing						
0 None	0.0	0.0	0.0	3.8	3.4	1.6
1 1–80	2.0	0.0	0.0	1.9	5.1	1.9
2 90–364	0.0	7.5	7.3	3.8	10.2	5.8
4 420–1800	7.8	45.3	41.5	26.4	39.0	31.9
6 1950–4380	27.5	30.2	29.3	32.1	20.3	27.6
8 4500+	62.7	17.0	22.0	32.1	22.0	31.1

TABLE 10.3   Crime Level and Crime Score among 257 Youth and Young Adult Primary Crack Users Interviewed on the Street: Row Percentages and Median Score

Group	(N)	Low Score 1–3	Low Typical 4–8	High Typical 9–14	Very High 15+	Crime Score Median
Total Subsample	(257)	4.3	54.1	37.7	3.9	8.0
M 13–19 Black	(25)	0.0	60.0	40.0	0.0	8.0
White	(23)	4.3	87.0	8.7	0.0	5.0
Hispanic	(25)	8.0	84.0	8.0	0.0	6.0
M 20–29 Black	(26)	0.0	46.2	42.3	11.5	10.0
White	(30)	3.3	50.0	43.3	3.3	8.0
Hispanic	(16)	0.0	25.0	75.0	0.0	11.0
F 13–19 Black	(26)	0.0	57.7	38.5	3.8	8.0
White	(26)	19.2	69.2	11.5	0.0	5.0
F 20–29 Black	(27)	3.7	18.5	59.3	18.5	12.0
White	(33)	3.0	42.4	54.5	0.0	9.0

"Crime Score" is the sum of the scores on the six crime types shown in Table 100.2. Note: More scores are represented in the total sample of 699; for this youth/young-adult subsample, no respondent did major property crimes at the score 7 level or drug trafficking/manufacture at the score 2, 3, or 4 level. Overall "Crime Score" range for the total sample of 699 is 0 to 30 points. "Crime Level" is a simple recode of "Crime Score" into five categories—the four reported on this table plus the category of "None (Score 0)," which did not apply to any respondent in this subsample.

To explore the crack/crime relationship further, analyses were done on an additional set of questions about methods of obtaining the crack used in the last ninety days. These questions specified crack obtained for personal use (that is, excluding crack obtained for resale), and asked "Out of every twenty times, about how many of the twenty did you get crack by . . . ?" These number-per-twenty responses were then translated to percentages. For this analysis, as shown in Table 10.5, ethnic differences do appear to follow a pattern. Blacks were less likely than whites and Hispanics to obtain crack by paying for it in cash or getting it for free (for example, sharing with friends or having it provided by a dealer friend or spouse). Instead, they were more likely than whites and Hispanics to obtain crack by earning it as pay (most often for drug sales) and slightly more likely to have traded for it (mainly trading stolen goods), or to have stolen it. These differences suggest a general lifestyle difference in which blacks are *less likely* to operate on a cash basis, or to depend on someone else to obtain crack for them, or to get crack without committing a crime other than buying crack, and are instead *more likely* to be involved in a barter system that includes both criminal activity and drug access—that is, a system that uses both crack and crime like money.

TABLE 10.4 Total Crack Used in Relation to Crime-Type Scores among 257 Youth and Young Adult Primary Crack Users Interviewed on the Street: Spearman Correlation Coefficients

Group (N)	Violent Crime	Major Prop	Petty Prop	Prostitute Procure	Drug Traffic	Drug Sales	Total Crime
Male 13–19							
Black (25)	.10	−.24	.16	.—	.—	.63**	.46*
White (23)	.35	.14	.24	.—	.35	.65**	.57*
Hispanic (25)	.35*	−.15	−.36*	.—	.—	.63**	.10
Male 20–29							
Black (26)	.11	.16	.23	.19	.—	.22	.34*
White (30)	.40*	.10	.00	.—	.—	.72**	.54**
Hispanic (16)	.46*	.02	−.11	.—	.—	.50*	.39
Female 13–19							
Black (26)	.25	.28	.23	.22	.06	.61**	.70**
White (26)	.35*	.—	.12	.16	.—	.01	.31
Female 20–29							
Black (27)	−.11	.05	.11	.06	.—	.56**	.27
White (330	.31*	.—	−.08	.21	.—	.58**	53**

Significance: ** p ≤ .001, * p < .05 "—" = correlation N/A See Table 100.2 for frequency distributions and full labels for crime types.

Correlations were computed between percentage of times crack was obtained in these various ways and the three ethnic dichotomies (0 = no, 1 = yes for black, white, and Hispanic). The results confirmed the apparent differences displayed in Table 10.5, showing small but significant correlations:

- Paying cash was negatively related to being black (rho = −.27) but had a positive relation to being white (.17) or Hispanic (.12).
- Earning crack as pay had a positive relation to being black (.27) but was negatively related to being white (−.23).
- Getting crack free was negatively related to being black (−.13) but had a positive relation to being white (.15).
- Stealing crack and trading for it were related to being black (rho of .13 and .15 respectively) but not to being white or Hispanic (no rho significant at p < .05).

The Crack/Crime/Black Connection

The final question is why this apparent pattern of differences in the crack/crime relationship exists. The similarity between white and Hispanic crack/crime patterns and their contrast to that for blacks is what would be expected

TABLE 10.5   How Crack Used in the Last 90 Days Was Obtained by 257 Youth and Young Adult Primary Crack Users Interviewed on the Street: Percentage of Gender/Ethnicity Group and of Total Subsample

| | Male | | | Female | | Total |
How Got Crack	*Black* $(N=51)$	*White* $(N=53)$	*Hispanic* $(N=41)$	*Black* $(N=53)$	*White* $(N=59)$	*Subsample* $(N=257)$
Paid cash						
90% +	13.7	28.3	22.0	5.7	18.6	17.5
50–85%	43.1	54.7	63.4	73.6	66.1	60.3
< Half	43.1	17.0	14.6	20.8	15.3	22.2
Earned as pay						
25% +	68.6	34.0	36.6	39.6	30.5	41.6
5–20%	13.7	37.7	48.8	52.8	40.7	38.5
None	17.6	28.3	14.6	7.5	28.8	19.8
Got it free						
25% +	0.0	0.0	0.0	5.7	13.6	4.3
5–20%	29.4	58.5	73.2	79.2	71.2	62.3
None	70.6	41.5	26.8	15.1	15.3	33.5
Stole it						
15% +	2.0	0.0	0.0	0.0	1.7	0.8
5–10%	7.8	5.7	2.4	9.4	0.0	5.1
None	90.2	94.3	97.6	90.6	98.3	94.2
Traded for it						
25% +	2.0	0.0	0.0	1.9	0.0	0.8
5–20%	7.8	9.4	0.0	9.4	0.0	5.4
None	90.2	90.6	100.0	88.7	100.0	93.8
Made from powder						
5–20%	3.9	0.0	2.4	1.9	0.0	1.6
None	96.1	100.0	97.6	98.1	100.0	98.4

in a Miami sample if the difference were primarily one of differing socio-economic status. In Miami—as is *not* the case in many other cities—general socioeconomic indicators for whites and Hispanics, especially Cubans, are highly similar, whereas such indicators as income, education, and residential patterns show markedly greater poverty among blacks.

One aspect of ethnic socioeconomic differences is available economic resources. When respondents in this study were asked about sources of legal income or support, results indicated that job income was highly unusual. In the young street crack user subsample, job income was reported by none of the teenagers and only four (3.0 percent) of the respondents ages 20 to 29. Welfare, disability, or other assistance were also rare; such income was reported by three of the sixty women ages twenty to twenty-nine (5.0 percent of this subgroup) and none of the other young street crack user subsample. Unexpectedly, some kind of investment income was actually more common—bank account interest or income from stocks or rental property was reported by eighteen respondents in this subsample. Unlike job income or government assistance, furthermore, reports of this income type were very imbalanced by ethnicity—one of 104 blacks (1.0 percent), one of 41 Hispanics (2.4 percent), and 16 of 112 whites (14.3 percent). Thus, having investment income was significantly and positively correlated with being white (rho = .24, $p \leq .001$) and significantly and negatively correlated with being black (rho = −.20, $p \leq .001$). No estimates were obtained for how much income came from these various sources, so that it seems probable that actual amounts were relatively small. Nonetheless, total numbers of respondents with employment, assistance, and investment income indicate that whites were three times more likely to have such conventional economic resources than were blacks and Hispanics.

Most respondents, however, did have some legal source of support—most commonly, parents, spouse, or other people. Thus, only one in six of the young street crack user subsample reported obtaining all or nearly all of their living expenses from crime. This question asked respondents to estimate how much of such expenses were paid for out of crime, specifying crime the respondent did personally—not crime done by someone else in the household—and asking a totally separate question for drug expenses as opposed to living expenses. Response categories for both items were none, a little (5–20 percent), some (25–45 percent), half or more (50–75 percent), and all or nearly all (90 percent +). Results for the *young street crack user* subsample, as shown in Table 10.6, indicate ethnic, gender, and age differences. Teenagers were usually living at home and thus only rarely had to rely on crime for significant amounts of their living expenses, while most adults—and men more than women—paid for at least some living expenses through crime. However, amount of living expenses paid for by crime is positively correlated with being black (rho = .19, $p \leq .001$) and negatively correlated with being white (rho = −.17, $p < .05$); the relationship to being Hispanic is not significant. Again, the implication for black/white differences is that white crack users have more access to legal economic resources.

Economic support from parents, spouse, or other people also has a very different kind of crack/crime relevance—some persons who help pay for a crack user's living expenses may also help support a crack/crime lifestyle. Three relevant questions were asked about living circumstances—(1) persons lived with last week—coded as yes/no for (a) parents (with or without siblings), (b) spouse/opposite-sex partner, and (c) other people; (2) Do any of these people use crack or other cocaine?; and (3) Do any deal it? All co-residents reported as dealers were also reported as users. Results in the young street crack user subsample indicated that *every* respondent living with a

TABLE 10.6   How Much of Living Expenses Were Paid for by Crime among 257 Youth and Young Adult Primary Crack Users Interviewed on the Street: Cumulative Row Percentages

Group		(N)	90% +	50% +	25% +	Any
Total Subsample		(257)	16.3	29.6	39.3	54.1
Black		(104)	21.2	36.5	46.2	67.3
White		(112)	10.7	22.3	33.0	44.6
Hispanic		(41)	19.5	31.7	39.0	46.3
M 13–19	Black	(25)	12.0	24.0	36.0	56.0
	White	(23)	0.0	0.0	4.3	13.0
	Hispanic	(25)	4.0	4.0	8.0	16.0
M 20–29	Black	(26)	50.0	73.1	76.9	96.2
	White	(30)	26.7	50.0	63.3	76.7
	Hispanic	(16)	43.8	75.0	87.5	93.8
F 13–19	Black	(26)	0.0	3.8	7.7	26.9
	White	(26)	3.8	3.8	3.8	15.4
F 20–29	Black	(27)	22.2	44.4	63.0	88.9
	White	(33)	9.1	27.3	48.5	60.6

spouse (including unmarried live-in situations) reported living with another cocaine user, as did 90.9 percent of respondents living with persons other than spouse or parents but only 30.4 percent of those living with their parents. Presumably, although no data were collected on the subject, many of the user co-residents for this last group were siblings rather than parents.

The user/dealer co-resident data were used to construct a four-category ordinal indicator for the degree of co-residents' cocaine involvement: (4) dealer, (3) user who does not deal, (2) no co-resident (lives alone, with or without children—who would be very young in this subsample), and (1) non-user co-resident/s. For the total 257 young street crack users, this indicator was significantly related to gender, age, and ethnicity. The relationship was strongest for age: the correlation between being age 20+ and amount of co-resident cocaine involvement is .48; this is doubtless a result of the negative correlation between being age 20+ and living with parents (rho = −.54). More co-resident cocaine involvement was also related to being female (rho = .34); over half of both black and white women ages 20 to 29 lived with dealers, as did a third of the younger black women. The correlation was also positive with being black (.35) and negative with being white (−.20) or Hispanic (−.21). Ethnic differences were especially apparent for teenagers— 100.0 percent of white males, 96.0 percent of Hispanic males, and 88.5 percent of white females lived with nonusers, compared to 60.0 percent of black males and only 11.5 percent of black females. The relevance of greater cocaine involvement of co-residents is indicated by its marked correlations with other crack/crime indicators—more crack use (rho = .46), more living expenses from crime (rho = .48), and more overall crime (rho = .60).

The preceding discussion may seem to imply that the crack/crime relationship differs by ethnicity because young black crack users are more likely to be in a living situation supportive of crack use. However, an additional importance of co-resident cocaine use appears in correlation between it and the respondent's total crime score. With controls for ethnicity, age, and gender, the results indicate that the four correlations for blacks are not significant, while for whites and Hispanics, most of the six are significant: .35 for teenage Hispanic males .36 for teenage white females, .55 for women ages 20 to 29, and .69 for men ages 20 to 29. (For white teenage males, there was no variation—all were living at home, with nonusers; for Hispanic males ages 20–29, the smallest subgroup analyzed, at N = 16, the correlation of .32 was positive and almost as large as for Hispanic teenage males but not quite significant—p = .11.) Thus, the young black crack users in this subsample were more likely than their white and Hispanic counterparts to be living with cocaine-involved people. However, the effects of such co-residence were more strongly related to crime involvement for the white and Hispanic crack users than for the black crack users.

The general crack/crime intercorrelations found in the subsample of youth and young adults interviewed on the street, and the relationship of these crack and crime variables to ethnicity, are summarized in Table 10.7. These results indicate unusually high correlations for social science research between level of criminal activity, amount of crack used, amount of living expenses paid for by crime, and the degree of cocaine involvement of people living with the respondent. Although no causal inferences can be made from this analysis, it does suggest that crime and crack use are part of a more general lifestyle that includes such everyday elements as persons with whom one lives and ways of meeting living expenses.

The correlations with ethnicity shown in the table suggest, however, that ethnic differences—particularly black/white differences—exist in both elements of that lifestyle and, probably, influences on it. Being white is significantly correlated with less crime, but also with less apparent need for crime to pay for living expenses, plus less cocaine involvement among people respondents lived with. Correlations with being black show the opposite pattern—more crime, more living expenses paid for by crime, and more cocaine involvement among people respondents lived with. The difference suggests that the basic meaning of *black* and *white* in these analyses is socioeconomic: degree of access to income sources other than crime, and likelihood of living in a high drug/crime-rate environment.

A third and final way in which Table 10.7 summarizes this analysis is the contrast between the drug/crime correlations and those for ethnicity. Crack use, cocaine involvement of people lived with, criminal activity, and crime just to support living expenses are all moderately to strongly related to each other, with the coefficients ranging from .46 to .63. The relationship

TABLE 10.7 Crack/Crime Intercorrelations and Relationships to Ethnicity among 257 Youth and Young Adult Primary Crack Users Interviewed on the Street: Spearman Correlation Coefficients

	Crime Score (0 = None 30 = Max)	Crack Doses (1 = <180 6 = 1350+)	Living Expenses from Crime (0 = None 4 = 90%+)	Co-Residence Cocaine (1 = Nonuser 4 = Dealer)
Crime score	1.00	.60**	.63**	.60**
Crack doses	.60**	1.00	.68**	.46**
Living Expenses from Crime	.63**	.68**	1.00	.48**
Co-Resident Cocaine Use	.60**	.46**	.48**	1.00
Ethnicity (0 = No, 1 = Yes)				
Black	.32**	.12*	.19**	.35**
White	−.27**	−.07	−.17*	−.20**
Hispanic	−.07	−.06	−.03	−.21**

Significance: ** p ≤ .001, *p < .05

between any of these elements and ethnicity, in contrast, is markedly weaker: of twelve correlations, four are not significant, five are no higher than .21, and the strongest three are only .27 to .35. This difference is what one would expect if the major role of ethnicity in crack/crime patterns were *primarily* historical—differential modes of entry and initial patterns of drug access for different ethnic groups. Once a crack/crime lifestyle has begun, however, the same kinds of factors are important in understanding levels of crack use and criminal activity regardless of ethnicity or gender.

CONCLUSIONS

The preceding analysis suggests that the relationships among crime, crack use, and ethnicity are complex. The primary dynamic appears to involve participation in a crime-and-cocaine street lifestyle, in which the particulars—cocaine preferences, ways of obtaining crack, type and level of criminal involvement—will vary by age, gender, and treatment status as well as ethnicity. The more entrenched crack users are in street life, the greater their crack use and criminal activity. Involvement in this lifestyle is partially the result of and is exacerbated by other aspects of street life and poverty, such as poor employment history, residence in high drug/crime-rate neighborhoods, and limited economic resources even to obtain food and housing.

The primary implication of this analysis for evaluating the crack/crime/black connection repeatedly portrayed in the popular media is that this portrait is an overstatement. To say that the economic resources and residence patterns associated with poverty help lead to and then exacerbate participation in a crack/crime lifestyle is, anywhere in this country today, to say that African-American youth are at greater risk of being swallowed up by street life than are white Anglos or, in some cases, Hispanics. But at the same time, the cocaine type preferences of the total Miami sample of 699 cocaine users would make a better argument on behalf of a white/crack affinity than for some clear black/crack connection. Further, although the preceding analysis does demonstrate black/white differences in the degree and type of association between crack use and crime, it also suggests that those differences are less important than media reports imply.

NOTE

1. See Daniel Lazare, "Crack and AIDS: The Next Wave?" *Voice*, May 8, 1990, pp. 29–32; "The Men Who Created Crack," *U.S. News and World Report*, August 19, 1990, p. 3; "Busting the Mayor: Caught in a Web of Drugs, Lies and Videotape Marion Barry is Arrested on Cocaine Charges," *Newsweek*, January 29,

1990, p. 24; "A Tide of Drug Killings: The Crack Plague Spurs More Inner City Murders," *Newsweek*, January 16, 1989, p. 44; "Prisoners of Crack: Eight Years of Reagan Politics Corrupted a Generation of Urban Black Americans and Devastated Their Communities," *Rolling Stone*, February 9, 1989, p. 61; "Drugs and the Black Community: The Other Side of the Picture," *USA Today*, July 19, 1990, p. 35; "Kids Who Deal Crack," *Time*, May 9, 1988, p. 20.

REFERENCES

Adlaf, Edward. M., Reginald. G. Smart, and S. H. Tan. 1989. "Ethnicity and Drug Use: A Critical Look." *International Journal of the Addictions* 24:1–18.

Anglin, M. Douglas, Mary W. Booth, Timothy M. Ryan, and Yih-Ing Hser. 1988. "Ethnic Differences in Narcotics Addiction. II. Chicano and Anglo Addiction Career Patterns." *International Journal of the Addictions* 23:1011–27.

Austin, Gregory A., and M. Jean Gilbert. 1989. "Substance Abuse Among Latino Youth." *Prevention Update* 3:1–26.

Bachman, Jerald G., John M. Wallace, Jr., Patrick M. O'Malley, Lloyd D. Johnston, Candace L. Kurth, and Harold W. Neighbors. 1991. "Racial/ethnic Differences in Smoking, Drinking, and Illicit Drug Use Among American High School Seniors, 1976–89. *American Journal of Public Health* 81:372–77.

Ball, John C., and Carl D. Chambers. 1970 "Overview of the Problem." Pp. 5–21 in John C. Ball and Carl D. Chambers (eds.) *The Epidemiology of Opiate Addiction in the United States*. Springfield, Ill.: Charles C. Thomas.

Boyd, Carol J., and Thomas Mieczkowski. 1990 "Drug Use, Health, Family and Social Support in 'Crack' Cocaine Users." *Addictive Behaviors* 15:481–85.

Brunswick, Ann, Peter A. Messeri, and Angela A. Aidala. 1990. "Changing Drug Use Patterns and Treatment Behavior: A Longitudinal Study of Urban Black Youth." Pp. 263–311 in R. R. Watson (ed.), *Drug and Alcohol Abuse Prevention*. Clifton, N.J.: Humana Press.

Carroll, Kathleen, and Bruce J. Rounsaville. 1992. "Contrast of Treatment-Seeking and Untreated Cocaine Abusers." *Archives of General Psychiatry* 49:646–71.

Chitwood, Dale D., and Patricia C. Morningstar. 1985. "Factors Which Differentiate Cocaine Users in Treatment from Nontreatment Users." *International Journal of the Addictions* 20:449–59.

Collins, R. Lorraine. 1992. "Methodological Issues in Conducting Substance Abuse Research in Ethnic Minority Populations." *Drugs and Society* 6:59–77.

Goldstein, Paul J., Patricia A. Belluci, Barry J. Spunt, and Thomas Miller. 1991. "Volume of Cocaine Use and Violence: A Comparison Between Men and Women." *Journal of Drug Issues* 21:345–67.

Griffin, Margaret L., Roger D. Weiss, Steven M. Mirin, and Ulrike Lange. 1989. "A Comparison of Male and Female Cocaine Abusers." *Archives of General Psychiatry* 46:122–26.

Hamid, Ansley. 1990. "The Political Economy of Crack Related Violence." *Contemporary Drug Problems* 17:31–78.

Inciardi, James A., Ruth Horowitz, and Anne E. Pottieger. 1993. *Street Kids, Street Drugs, Street Crime*. Belmont, Calif.: Wadsworth.

Inciardi, James A., Dorothy Lockwood, and Anne E. Pottieger. 1993. *Women and Crack-Cocaine*. New York: Macmillian.

Inciardi, James A., and Anne E. Pottieger. 1991. "Kids, Crack and Crime." *Journal of Drug Issues* 21:257–70.

Johnson, Bruce D., Elsayed Elmoghazy, and Eloise Dunlap. 1990. "Crack Abusers and Noncrack Drug Abusers: A Comparison of Drug Use, Drug Sales, and Nondrug Criminality." Paper presented at the American Society of Criminology Annual Meetings, Baltimore, November 8, 1990.

Kandel, Denise B., Eric Single, and Ronald Kessler. 1976. "The Epidemiology of Drug Use among New York State High School Student: Distribution, Trends and Changes in Use." *American Journal of Public Health* 66:43–53.

Klein, Malcolm W., and Cheryl Maxson. 1985. " 'Rock' Sales in South Los Angeles." *Sociology and Social Research* 69:561–65.

Kleinman, Paula Holzman, and Irving Faber Lukoff. 1978. "Ethnic Differences in Factors Related to Drug Use." *Journal of Health and Social Behavior* 19:190–99.

Maddehian, Ebrahim, Michael D. Newcomb, and Peter M. Bentler. 1986. "Adolescents' Substance Use: Impact of Ethnicity, Income and Availability." *Advances in Alcohol and Substance Abuse* 5 (3):63–78.

Marin, Barbara V. 1990. "Hispanic Drug Abuse: Culturally Appropriate Prevention and Treatment." Pp. 151–65 in R. R. Watson (ed.), *Drug and Alcohol Abuse Prevention*. Clifton, N.J.: Humana Press.

Mcbride, Duane C., and James A. Swartz. 1990. "Drugs and Violence in the Age of Crack Cocaine." Pp. 141–69 in Ralph Weisheit (ed.), *Drugs, Crime and the Criminal Justice System*. Cincinnati: Anderson.

National Institute on Drug Abuse. 1991. *National Household Survey on Drug Abuse: Population Estimates*. Rockville, Md.: National Institute on Drug Abuse (U.S. Department of Health and Human Services publication no. [ADM] 92–1887).

National Institute on Drug Abuse. 1992. *Annual Emergency Room Data 1991: Data from the Drug Abuse Warning Network (DAWN)*. Rockville, Md.: National Institute on Drug Abuse (U.S. Department of Health and Human Services publication no. [ADM] 92–1955).

Prendergast, Michael L., Gregory A. Austin, Kenneth I. Maton, and Ralph Baker. 1989. "Substance Abuse Among Black Youth." *Prevention Research Update* 4:1–27.

Rebach, Howard. 1992. "Alcohol and Drug Use Among American Minorities." *Drugs and Society* 6:23–57.

Rounsaville, Bruce J., and H. D. Kleber. 1985. "Untreated Opiate Addicts: How Do They Differ from Those Seeking Treatment?" *Archives of General Psychiatry* 42:1072–77.

Segal, Bernard. 1989. "Drug-Taking Behavior Among School Aged Youth: The Alaska Experience and Comparisons with Lower 48 States." *Drugs and Society* 4:1–17.

Wallace, John M., Jr., and Jerald G. Bachman. 1991. "Explaining Racial/Ethnic Differences in Adolescent Drug Use: The Impact of Background and Lifestyle." *Social Problems* 38:333–57.

11

Crime Control and Ethnic Minorities: Legitimizing Racial Oppression by Creating Moral Panics

On November 19, 1993, the U.S. Senate overwhelmingly passed a $23 billion crime bill, which authorizes $8.9 billion to hire 100,000 new police officers, $3 billion for high-security prisons, another $3 billion for boot camps for young offenders, $1.8 billion to combat violence against women, and $100 million for metal detectors for schools. In addition the bill makes being a member of certain types of gangs a federal offense, expands the death penalty to cover fifty-two additional offenses, and it permits the deportation of foreigners who are *suspected terrorists* without trial. Street crimes involving firearms would become a federal offense: continuing a long-time trend of expanding federal responsibilities for crime control. And the bill contains the infamous *three strikes and you're out* provision, providing mandatory sentences for persons convicted of three felonies. This provision, as it stands, would force judges to sentence a person convicted of three assaults to a mandatory life in prison.

The bill has created a furor in the press and has divided the law enforcement community. Philip Heymann, formerly the second highest person in the Justice Department, said simply that the bill "sounds terrific but doesn't make any sense" (*Washington Post*, Feb. 16, 1994: A1). He added, "It's become too easy to pretend we're going to solve this [the crime] problem with a set of remedies that look good for the first 15 seconds you look at them and very bad when you get to half a minute." Despite the divided opinion in the media and among judges, prosecutors and police, the bill has been hailed almost universally by politicians.

This bill, like a spate of anticrime bills dating back to the late 1960s, is the culmination of the politicization of crime, a process that began when the Republican Party under the leadership of Barry Goldwater's presidential campaign in 1964 first raised *crime in the streets* as a major political issue (Chambliss and Sbarbaro, 1993). The end result of this process has many dire consequences, including that (1) the United States incarcerates more of its citizens than any other country in the world (Figure 11–1), (2) federal and state budgets have shifted public expenditures from other, more important, social services to crime control, and (3) racism and the systematic oppression of minority groups, especially young African American men, has been legitimized and institutionalized in the criminal justice system. ·

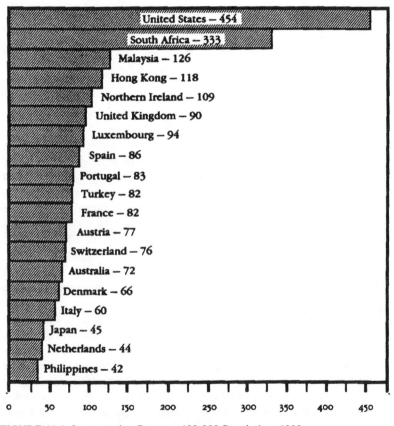

FIGURE 11.1 Incarceration Rate per 100,000 Population: 1990

CRIME CONTROL: THE NATION'S GROWTH INDUSTRY

Even before the Senate passed the 1993 crime bill, expenditures on criminal justice had increased more than fivefold between 1972 and 1988 (Table 11.1). The number of police officers in the U.S.A. doubled, and the number of people incarcerated increased by 150 percent (Maguire, Pastore, and Flanagan, 1992). Between 1969 and 1989 per capita spending on criminal justice in America's cities (municipal expenditures) rose from $34 to $120. County expenditures as a percentage of total budget rose from 10 to 15 percent between 1973 and 1989 (Figures 11.2; 11.3). State expenditures showed even greater increases, rising tenfold from per capita expenditures on police and corrections of $8 in 1969 to $80 in 1989. State spending on prisons increased most dramatically, rising by a factor of twelve in this twenty-year period from $5 per capita to over $60 (Table 11.1). State government expenditure for building prisons increased 593% in actual dollars. Spending on corrections—prison building, maintenance, and parole—has more than doubled in the last ten years (Maguire and Flanagan, 1990; Maguire, Pastore, and Flanagan, 1992).

The target group most affected by increased incarceration are African Americans who account for almost fifty percent of the people in prison, even though they represent less than thirteen percent of the population (Table 11.2).

In times of budget deficits, public expenditures in one area mean a reduction of expenditures in others. The most significant shift in public expenditures is from expenditures on education to expenditures on crime control. The federal government halved its contribution to education between 1980 and 1990. County expenditures as a percent of the total budget devoted to education declined from 16 percent in 1974 to 14 percent in 1989. As a result, criminal justice expenditures have, for the first time in U.S. history, received

TABLE 11.1   Federal and State Expenditures on Criminal Justice Selected Years: 1972–1988

Year	State Expenditures	Federal Expenditures
1972	$ 3,026,000,000	$1,475,000,000
1976	5,194,000,000	2,356,000,000
1979	6,831,000,000	3,229,000,000
1985	15,697,000,000	5,546,000,000
1988	21,597,000,000	7,185,000,000

Source: Sourcebook of Criminal Justice Statistics, Washington, D.C., Bureau of Justice Statistics, 1984, 1988, 1992.

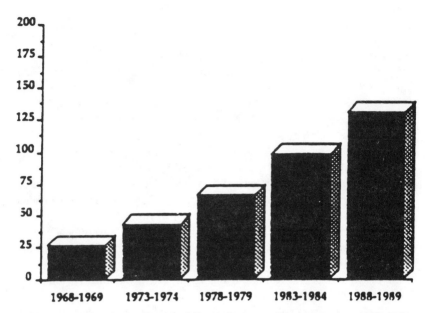

FIGURE 11.2 Per Capita Municipal Expenditures on Criminal Justice, 1972–1988
Source: U.S. Department of Commerce, Bureau of Census, *State Government Finance,* 1968–1969, 1973–1974, 1978–1979, 1983–1984, 1988–1989.

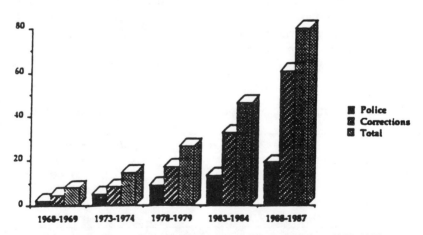

FIGURE 11.3 Per Capita State Expenditures on Criminal Justice, 1968–1989
Source: U.S. Department of Commerce, Bureau of Census, *City Government Finance,* 1968–1969, 1973–1974, 1978–1979, 1983–1984, 1988–1989.

TABLE 11.2   Prisoners under Jurisdiction of State and Federal Correctional Authorities, by Race, 1991

Total	White	Black	Other
824,133	365,347	395,245	63,541

Source: Sourcebook of Criminal Justice Statistics, 1992.

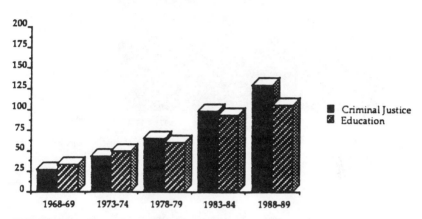

FIGURE 11.4   Comparison of per Capita Municipal; Expenditures on Criminal Justice and Education, 1968–1989
Source: U.S. Department of Commerce: Bureau of Census, *City Government Finances:* 1968–69, 1973–74, 1978–79, 1983–84, and 1988–89.

more public funds from state, county, and municipal governments than has education (Figures 11.4 and 11.5).

The same trend is indicated by percentage increases in state expenditures on education and corrections between 1989 and 1990 (Tables 11.3 and 11.4).

Where state government's priorities are most clearly revealed is in the decision of where to allocate funds for facilities. Table 11.4 indicates that education is falling far behind corrections in the competition for these scarce resources despite widespread agreement that schools are generally in abominable physical condition.

The federal government increased its allocation of resources for criminal justice without a pause. The war on drugs, with a budget of $1 billion in 1981, received $13.4 billion in 1993. The government added seven hundred FBI agents in 1990, an increase of 25 percent. In Illinois in 1990 nearly two thousand teachers were laid off. Welfare for the poor was also severely cut. In real dollars the Aid to Dependent Children program's cash contribution to a mother with two children and no outside employment dropped from $7,836

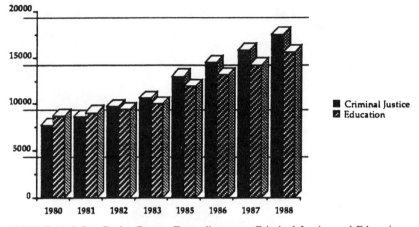

FIGURE 11.5 Per Capita County Expenditures on Criminal Justice and Education, 1980–1988
Source: U.S. Department Bureau of Census, *County Government Finances:* 1983–84 and 1988–89.

TABLE 11.3   Percent Increase in Elementary and Secondary Education Compared to Percent Increase in Expenditures for Corrections 1989–1990

Percent Increase in Elementary and Secondary Education	*Percent Increase in Corrections*
7.3%	29%

Percent Increase in State Capital Expenditures for Higher Education and Corrections 1989–1990

Percent Increase for Higher Education	Percent Increase for Corrections
46%	150.6%

Source: The National Association of State Budget Offices

in 1982 to $4,801 in 1991. The criminal justice system, by contrast, is virtually immune from the cuts experienced by other public services. On those rare occasions when a mayor or governor suggests cutting justice expenditures or even holding steady the number of police officers, politicking and arm-twisting by the police unions quickly reverse the decision. In Prince George's County, a suburb of Washington, D.C., for example, there was talk of layoffs and pay cuts for police. The police officer's union hired a public relations firm and ran television commercials citing increasing crime rates and accusing the county executive of hand-cuffing police officers with proposed budget cuts. The union spent over $10,000 in one week on television

TABLE 11.4   Capital Expenditures by Selected States (in $ millions)

Eight states spent more money for capital expenditures on correctional facilities than for higher education facilities from 1988 through 1990, fiscal years. Leading this trend is Texas, which spent $0 on higher education facilities while spending $500 million on correctional facilities.

	Corrections	vs.	Higher Education	=	Difference
Texas	500		0		500
New York	612		314		298
Massachusetts	396		137		259
Connecticut	139		72		67
Ohio	30		0		30
New Jersey	199		166		30
New Hampshire	36		16		20
Maine	17		7		10
Total Difference					*1187*

In these eight states almost $1.2 billion more was spent for construction of prisons than on construction for higher education.

The state which spent the greatest amounts on capital expenditures for correctional construction was California. California spent $1.2 billion between 1988 and 1990, fiscal years. Its higher education capital expenditures for this period were $1.4 billion.

Source: The National Association of State Budget Officers.

and newspaper advertisements. The correctional officers association of California is the second largest lobby in the state as measured by dollars spent in support of favored candidates for political office. The message is clear: you can increase the number of students in already overcrowded classrooms, fire teachers, cut head start and summer programs, but you dare not touch the police or prisons. One predictable result of the increase in expenditures and police officers is a doubling of the number of people in prison (Figure 11.6 and Table 11.5).

All these expenditures, arrests, and law enforcement policies are justified by an alleged increase in crime. The statistics and public statements generated and manipulated by the police and the FBI (particularly the Uniform Crime Reports) almost always paint the picture of an "alarming" increase in crime. These data are political, not factual, statements (Chambliss, 1993). The fact is that, law enforcement, media, and political propaganda notwithstanding, the crime rate has not changed significantly since at least 1973 (Figure 11.7).

As Bogess and Bound have shown after systematically analyzing data provided by the FBI in the Uniform Crime Reports and data from the National Crime Victim Survey, "the large increase in the incarceration rate is

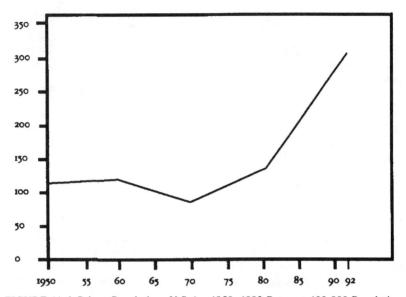

FIGURE 11.6 Prison Population, U.S.A., 1950–1992 Rate per 100,000 Population
Source: K. Maguire, A. Pastore, and T. Flanigan, *Sourcebook of Criminal Justice Statistics,* Washington, D.C., U.S. Dept. of Justice. Bureau of Justice Statistics, 1980, 1988, 1992.

attributable primarily to an increase in the likelihood of incarceration given arrest,'' not to an increase in the crime rate (Bogess and Bound, 1993). Bogess and Bound go on to point out that most of the increase in crime reported by the FBI in its annual Uniform Crime Reports (UCR) is attributable to *an increase in the reporting of crime by citizens,* not to an actual increase in crime. The FBI practice of manipulating the reports to justify increased expenditures on criminal justice by the use of misleading gimmicks, such as a *crime clock* that purports to depict how frequently different types of crime are committed, makes these data suspect. The UCR selects data as well to emphasize any increase in crime while ignoring decreases. In 1992, for example, the UCR reported an increase in the murder rate from 1988 to 1992 without noting that between 1980 and 1988 the murder rate had actually declined (Table 11.8).

That the murder rate has shown no appreciable increase since the 1980s is particularly noteworthy, given the fact that the weapons in use today are more efficient than ever before. Pistols have been replaced with rapid-firing automatic weapons that leave a victim little chance of escaping with a wound. It follows that the victim survey findings of a decline in overall violence rates is reflected in a murder rate that is stable over a ten-year period, given that

TABLE 11.5 Change in the State and Federal prison populations, 1980–92

Year	Number of inmates	Annual percent change	Total percent change since 1980
1980	329,821	—	—
1981	369,930	12.2%	12.2%
1982	413,806	11.9	25.5
1983	436,855	5.6	32.5
1984	462,002	5.8	40.1
1985	502,752	8.8	52.4
1986	545,378	8.5	65.4
1987	585,292	7.3	77.5
1988	631,990	8.0	91.6
1989	712,967	12.8	116.2
1990	773,124	8.4	134.4
1991	824,133	6.6	149.9
1992	883,593	7.2	167.9

Note: All counts are for December 31 of each year and may reflect revisions of previously reported numbers.
—Not applicable.
Source: Bureau of Justice Statistics Bulletin, May 1993.

Victimization trends, 1973-92
Number of victimizations

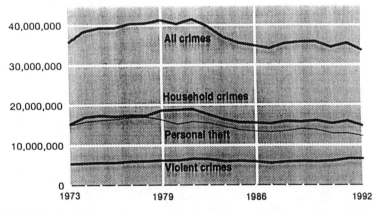

FIGURE 11.7 Respondents Reporting Being the Victim of Crime by Type of Crime
Source: Bureau of Justice Statistics Bulletin, Criminal Victimization, 1992, Washington, D.C., U.S. Department of Justice, 1992.

the likelihood of death from gun violence may actually have increased even though the number of violent acts has decreased.

It is important also to put in perspective the seriousness of the crimes reported by victims. For every type of crime reported, the least serious crime

US Murder Rates by Race, 1976–92

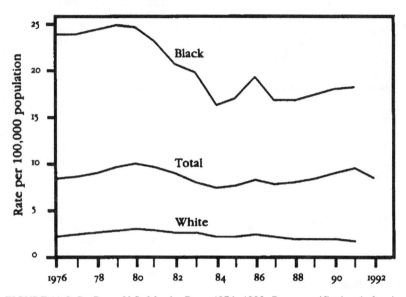

FIGURE 11.8 By Race: U.S. Murder Rate, 1976–1992. Race-specific data is for single victim/single offender murders.
Source: Current Population Reports, P25–1095; Crime in the U.S. and Statistical Abstract of the U.S., various years.

TABLE 11.6 Estimated Number of Personal Victimization Rates per 1,000 Persons over Age 12, 1989: Completed and Attempted

Crimes against the Person	Completed	Attempted
Aggravated Assault	2.9	5.4
Simple Assault	4.1	10.7
Larceny with Contact	.6	.2

is the most common. Attempted crimes are reported twice as often as completed crimes. Larceny without contact occurs more than 20 times as often as larceny with contact. (Tables 11.6 and 11.7).

Furthermore, the fact that for every type of crime there is less than a fifty-fifty chance the victim will report the crime to the police is an indication of the crimes seriousness. When asked why they do not report the crime, over half the victims say that the crime was "not important enough" or that "nothing could be done about it" (Bureau of Justice Statistics, 1993).

Finally, victim surveys show that it is very unlikely that anyone will be the victim of a crime in any given year. Over 90 percent of respondents report

TABLE 11.7   Estimated Rate of Victimization per 100,000 Population by Seriousness of Offense, 1982

More Serious Offenses	Less Serious Offenses
Larceny with Contact	Larceny without Contact
306	7,945
Aggravated Assault	Simple Assault 1,708
931	1,700
Robbery with Injury	Robbery without Injury
220	310
Attempted Robbery	Attempted Robbery
with Injury	without Injury
708	2,638

From: Sourcebook of Criminal Justice Statistics. 1984. Washington, D.C.: U.S. Department of Justice, Bureau of Justice Statistics.

that neither they nor any member of their household was the victim of a criminal offense. Indeed, over a lifetime it is unlikely that most people will be the victim of a serious offense. Langan and Innes show that the risk of being a victim of a violent crime in any given year is less than 3 percent. Furthermore, 2.5 percent of this is accounted for by being a victim of an assault (Langan and Innes, 1984:185).

CREATING MORAL PANIC

If actual crime rates have not been increasing, how did crime control come to take priority over almost every other social program? A review of the history of anticrime legislation from the 1960s suggests that it was a coalition of political, law enforcement, and mass media interests that, after thirty years of propaganda, created a moral panic about crime. That this moral panic derived from the manipulation of public opinion is revealed by an analysis of criminal law legislation and political campaigns in the 1960s when *street crime* first was raised as a major political issue in America (Chambliss and Sbarbaro, 1993).

Crime became a national political issue for the first time in fifty years with the presidential campaign of 1964 when the Republican candidate, Barry Goldwater, sounded the alarm (Cronin et al., 1981:18):

Our wives, all women, feel unsafe on our streets. And in encouragement of even more abuse of the law, we have the appalling spectacle of this country's Ambassador to the United Nations [Adlai Stevenson] actually telling an audience—this year, at Colby College—that, "in the great struggle to advance human civil rights, even a jail sentence is no longer a dishonor but a proud achievement.'' Perhaps we are destined to see in this law-loving land people running for office not on their stainless records but on their prison record. (*New York Times*, September 4, 1964:13)

Goldwater's hue and cry did not strike a resonant chord in the American public. As *Newsweek* magazine editors observed: ''Remarkably late in the campaign, Barry Goldwater was still a candidate in search of an issue that could score a voting breakthrough. . . . [He] did all he could to press the issue of law and order'' (*Newsweek*, October, 19, 1964:27–34). Public opinion polls taken at the time confirmed the *Newsweek* analysis.

In the months preceding the election, the Gallup poll asked a sample of Americans what they thought were ''the most important problems facing the nation.'' In spite of Goldwater's attempt to create moral panic, crime was not among them (Gallup, 1968).

The Gallup polls describe a public more concerned about war, civil rights, poverty, and unemployment than crime. Nonetheless, conservative Democrats, Republicans, and what Nils Christie aptly labels ''the crime control industry'' lobbied assiduously for harsher penalties and laws that gave more power to the police and fewer rights to the accused (Christie, 1993). Conservative legislators directed their attention primarily at Supreme Court decisions such as Miranda, Gideon, and Escobeda, which gave the accused the right to legal counsel, protection against coerced confessions, and the right to remain silent unless a lawyer was present.

Congressmen Ford and Senators McClellan, Stennis, Ervin, Hruska, Thurmond, Bible, and Lausche (a formidable conservative block of five Democrats and three Republicans) sponsored the Omnibus Crime Control and Safe Streets Act, which legalized wiretapping and ''bugging'' by federal agents and local police *without requiring a court order.* It authorized trial judges to admit confessions as voluntary after considering ''all factors,'' thus emasculating the Miranda decision. The bill exempted law enforcement agencies from having to meet the requirements of the 1964 Civil Rights Act, which did not allow federal grants to agencies or organizations that discriminate.

In the 1968 presidential campaign (Nixon v. Humphrey), Richard Nixon and his running mate, Spiro Agnew (both later to be accused of serious crimes themselves), hammered away at the issue of ''law and order.'' Nixon attacked the Johnson administration's focus on social conditions as the cause of crime:

By way of excuse, the present Administration places the blame on poverty. But poverty is just one contributing factor. During the Depression the crime rate was at an all-time low. The truth is that we will reduce crime and violence when we enforce our laws—when we make it less profitable, and a lot more risky to break them. (*New York Times*, October 25, 1968:34)

Nixon held the Supreme Court responsible for the crime problem. He assailed some of the court's decisions as having "tipped the balance against the peace forces and strengthened the criminal forces" (*New York Times*, September 30, 1968:1). Nixon further stated:

The Supreme Court is not infallible. It is sometimes wrong. Many of the decisions break down 5 to 4, and I think that often in recent years the five-man majority has been wrong and the four-man minority right. We need more strict constructionists on the highest court of the United States. (*New York Times*, October 23, 1968:1)

Hubert Humphrey placed the blame for crime elsewhere:

Crime rates were highest among the poor and disadvantaged—who commit more crime but who also suffer more crime. In the long run we can only cut crime by getting at its cause; slums, unemployment, run-down schools and houses. This is where crime begins and that is where it must end. (*New York Times*, September 12, 1968:1)

In November, 1968 Richard Nixon was elected president. And in August 1968 a public opinion poll showed for the first time in twenty years that "crime, lawlessness, looting and rioting" was perceived by 29 percent of those asked as one of "the most important problems facing the nation." Fifty-two percent of those surveyed mentioned the Vietnam war as the most important problem facing the United States, and 20 percent still mentioned race relations as the most pressing issue facing the nation (Gallup Poll, 1972:2107).

The campaign of conservative politicians supported by media coverage of crime and the law enforcement establishment's nonstop propaganda campaign succeeded in raising crime as a major issue for the American people. It must be noted, however, that this was at a time when riots in the cities and violent demonstrations were taking place throughout the country and "crime" was only mentioned by a significant number of respondents when it was collected together with lawlessness, riots, and looting. The public's concern also was short-lived, for crime is not mentioned again until 1980 when "drugs" is seen as one of the nations' most important problems (Table 11.8)

On January 15, 1969, Senator John McClellan, along with Senators Ervin and Hruska, the ranking members of the Senate judiciary subcommit-

TABLE 11.8   The Most Important Problem Mentioned in Gallup Polls from 1935 to 1990

1935	Unemployment	1963	Keeping peace, race relations
1936	Unemployment	1964	Vietnam, race relations
1937	Unemployment	1965	Vietnam, race relations
1938	Keeping out of war	1966	Vietnam
1939	Keeping out of war	1967	Vietnam, high cost of living
1940	Keeping out of war	1968	Vietnam
1941	Keeping out of war, winning war	1969	Vietnam
1942	Winning war	1970	Vietnam
1943	Winning war	1971	Vietnam, high cost of living
1944	Winning war	1972	Vietnam
1945	Winning war	1973	High cost of living, Watergate
1946	High cost of living	1974	High cost of living, Watergate, energy crisis
1947	High cost of living, labor unrest	1975	High cost of living, unemployment
1948	Keeping peace	1976	High cost of living, unemployment
1949	Labor unrest	1977	High cost of living, unemployment
1950	Labor unrest	1978	High cost of living, energy problem
1951	Korean War	1979	High cost of living, energy problem
1952	Korean war	1980	High cost of living, unemployment
1953	Keeping peace	1981	High cost of living, unemployment
1954	Keeping peace	1982	Unemployment, high cost of living
1955	Keeping peace	1983	Unemployment, high cost of living
1956	Keeping peace	1984	Unemployment, fear of war
1957	Race relations, keeping peace	1985	Fear of war, unemployment
1958	Unemployment, keeping peace	1986	Unemployment, fear of war
1959	Keeping peace	1987	Fear of war, unemployment
1960	Keeping peace	1988	Budget deficit, drug abuse
1961	Keeping peace	1989	Drugs, poverty, homelessness
1962	Keeping peace	1990	Budget deficit, drugs

tee on criminal law and procedures, introduced the Organized Crime Control Act (OCCA) in the Senate. McClellan took the opportunity to comment on his vision of future law enforcement under Nixon and to reprimand the Supreme Court: his speech made clear the fact that the concern was not only with organized crime but with overturning ''liberal'' Supreme Court decisions (Senate Hearings, 1969:512). Despite the fact that the bill was severely criticized as being unconstitutional by the ACLU, some members of congress and the New York Lawyers Association, the bill was passed into law. It contained measures that substantially increased police powers especially vis-à-vis poor defendants, thus reducing the civil liberties protections of earlier Supreme Court decisions such as Miranda, Escobeda, and Gideon.

On October 15, 1970, President Nixon signed the OCCA into law at the Justice Department. The bill contained some revolutionary changes in the administration of criminal law: it changed the evidence-gathering process, created new federal sanctions and punishments, created a powerful investigative grand jury, established the special grand jury with increased powers, including the ability to write reports, and for the first time, compelled witnesses to testify if they were granted limited immunity. The bill allowed district courts to incarcerate uncooperative witnesses for as long as the grand jury was in session, and, finally, it expanded the conditions under which witnesses could be charged with perjury.

The years following the Nixon presidency have witnessed a continued assault on civil liberties and an expansion of federal authority in crime control. The Reagan and Bush administrations hammered away at the issue of crime and created the "war on drugs," complete with a "drug czar" and the expenditure of billions of dollars for crime control. Although the public was slow to respond to the barrage, it gradually came around.

CRIME AND PUBLIC OPINION

Politicians, law enforcement officials, and the media made crime a national issue in the 1960s, 70s, and 80s, and thereby *legitimized* the passage of laws and the allocation of major resources to the problem. They claimed to be responding to "public opinion." The political scientist James Q. Wilson, citing the Gallup polls, supported the conservative assault:

In May 1965 the Gallup Poll reported that for the first time "crime" (along with education) was viewed by Americans as the most important problem facing the nation. In the months leading up to the Democratic National Convention in 1968—specifically in February, May and August—Gallup continued to report crime as the most important issue. (Wilson, 1985: 65–66)

There is no evidence to support these claims. Indeed, Wilson's statements are pure fiction, made up, apparently, to support his and conservative politicians' ideological bias. Crime was *not* reported in the Gallup poll of May 1965, as Wilson claims. In May 1965 the Gallup poll did not even ask what respondents thought was the most important problem facing the nation. But in June 1965 the question was asked and the responses were as follows: Vietnam: 23 percent; civil rights: 23 percent; threat of war: 16 percent; prestige abroad: 9 percent spread of world communism: 9 percent; juvenile delinquency: 2 percent (Gallup Poll, 1965).

It is a gross distortion of fact to say, as Wilson does, that the 1968 polls "in February, May and August Gallup continued to report crime as the most important issue." Gallup did not ask the question in February. In May 1968 the question was asked and only 15 percent of the respondents named crime including riots, looting, and juvenile delinquency as the most important problem, but 42 percent named Vietnam and 25 percent race relations. In August crime is mentioned by 29 percent as the most important problem, but the Vietnam was is seen as the most important problem by 52 percent (Gallup Poll, 1968).

These findings suggest the possibility that rather than responding to public concerns about crime, the crime issue was used by politicians as a smoke screen behind which they could carry out unpopular public policies, such as the Vietnam war, and pass laws that could be used to suppress public opposition and political dissent. But the long-term consequences have been even more sinister. For the end result of the law and order campaign begun in 1964 has been to criminalize an entire population of young black males and to fuel racism in America.

YOUNG BLACK MEN AND CRIME CONTROL

Although laws are in theory applied to all violators, they are in fact applied in a discriminatory fashion against minorities. While constituting less than 13 percent of the population, African Americans make up almost 50 percent of the inmates in prison and an even higher proportion of those in jail (Table 11.2). So ubiquitous is the pattern of discriminatory law enforcement that the effect has been to criminalize an entire population. Studies in Washington, D.C., and Baltimore, Maryland, have revealed that nearly 50 percent of the African American male population between the ages of 18 and 35 is at any given time either in prison, on probation, parole, or a warrant is out for their arrest (Miller, 1992).

Observations of the routine practices of police departments and prosecutorial practices expose the institutionalized racism resulting from the expansion of the crime control industry (Skolnick and Fyfe, 1993). Police departments across the nation police the urban underclass ghetto with a vigilance that would create political revolution were the same tactics and policies implemented in white middle-class communities. In Washington, D.C., for example, the police have established a rapid deployment unit (RDU: originally designed for riot control), which routinely patrols the black ghetto in search of law violators (Chambliss, 1993). Members of the RDU drive in patrol cars through the ghetto on nightly vigils looking for suspects. "Suspects" include all young black males between the ages of twelve and thirty who are visible: driving in cars, standing on street corners, or in a group observed through a window in an apartment.

To do their job, which members of the RDU see as "getting the shit off the streets," RDU officers express disdain for the constitutional rights of suspects or the department's guidelines for proper search, arrest, or use of force. The operational procedures followed in moving from seeing young black males to actually confronting them consists mainly of finding an excuse rather than a legal reason for stopping a suspect. For young black males driving in a car, the best excuse is some minor infraction: a broken taillight, an ornament hanging from the mirror, a license plate light that is not working. On occasion if the RDU officer has a "strong feeling" or a "solid hunch" that someone he sees driving around may be in possession of drugs or weapons, the officer may have to stop the car and create the broken taillight with a quick slap of his pistol butt.

Once the excuse to stop is found or created, the RDU officer calls in other cruising officers in the area. Each RDU cruiser has two officers. The call will usually bring two more cars, always at least one more car: four to six officers in all. In the case of stopping a car (which is how RDU does most of its business), the RDU cruiser siren is blasted like a bombshell through the night, the two or three police cars screech to a halt around the suspects' car, and the officers exit their cruisers with guns drawn. Keep in mind that this is because, except for the officers "hunch" based on the age and skin color of the occupants of the car, the only "crime" being committed here is that the car being stopped had a broken taillight or some ornament hanging from the mirror. The occupants of the car are instructed at gun point to get out of their car with their hands up. Racial slurs usually accompany the commands: "Get out of the car motherfucker and don't reach for nothing' or you'll be eating this gun for dinner."

Next comes the officers' superficial adherence to legality: "We're gonna search your car, OK?" An affirmative answer is assumed by either silence or any bodily gesture such as a shrug or a nod. Failing to get either a shrug a nod or if the suspect says no, which in my observation happened only once, the officers look for some reason to enter the car: a piece of paper in the back seat that could appear to be a marijuana paper in poor light, something white on the floor mat that might be cocaine. While two or three officers search the car, the other two or three have instructed the suspects to empty their pockets—slowly—all the while at gunpoint.

By these measures and other quasi-legal or undeniably illegal ones, the police in Washington arrest and incarcerate a higher proportion of the city's population than any other city in the world. For what? The majority of the arrests are for the possession of small amounts of crack, cocaine, or marijuana. A defendant's sentence, which in 90 percent of the cases, follows from

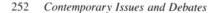

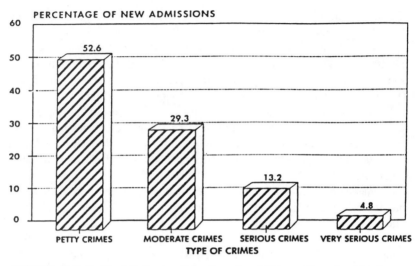

FIGURE 11.9 National Estimate of the Severity of Crimes Committed by Persons Admitted to State and Federal Prisons
Source: James Austin and John Irwin, *Who Goes To Prison?*, San Francisco: National Council on Crime and Delinquency, 1991.

a negotiated guilty plea is effected by *priors:* previous arrests for, usually, the same kind of offense.

Through such measures the prisons of America are overflowing with minor offenders. A study by the Department of Justice found that over 35 percent of all federal prisoners are "low-level drug offenders with no current or prior violent offenses on their records, no involvement in sophisticated criminal activity and no previous prison time (Bureau of Justice Statistics, 1994). Austin and Irwin in a study of inmates in federal and state prisons found that the majority of inmates were sentenced to prison for crimes which respondents to public opinion surveys described as "not serious" (Austin and Irwin, 1991). The authors conclude: "The vast majority of inmates are sentenced for petty crimes that pose little danger to public safety or significant economic loss to victims." (Figure 11.9.)

A 1989 survey of the arrest reports of a sample of inmates held in a jail housing over two-thousand prisoners found that trespassing and possession of small amounts of cocaine accounted for the majority of arrests. Trespassing was typically a crime committed by homeless black men seeking food in fast-food restaurants and possession narcotics consisted of the possession of small amounts (under $ forty worth) of marijuana, crack, cocaine, or "drug paraphernalia" (a pipe or even cigarette paper) (Holman and Chambliss, 1991).

Only a few miles from where the RDU and the narcs are active, lies "Foggy Bottom," home of George Washington University. On any night of the week one finds students at George Washington University enjoying leisurely evenings in their dormitory, fraternity, or sorority, underage students drink, use false ID's to go to bars and nightclubs, and in the presence of a "cool" professor they roll their marijuana cigarettes or stuff white powder up their noses. Not infrequently at fraternity parties or while out on a date these students commit rape and various other sexual assaults. Not all of them; but if the RDU paid half as much attention to the crimes of students at the universities as they do to young black males, the arrest and incarceration rate for young white males would certainly approach that of young black males. And if procedures that are followed routinely in the ghetto were followed here, the students would be violently shoved against a wall, called names, threatened with death, hand cuffed, banged around, shoved into a police car, and taken off to jail for booking. This does not happen at George Washington University or at any of the other Washington, D.C., campuses; not even at the predominantly black universities: Howard and the University of the District of Columbia. On those rare occasions when a student is found with drugs, is accused of "date rape," or of the crime of purposely getting a woman drunk in order to have sex with her, they are given counseling, not a jail sentence (Schreiber, 1993).

As a result of the treatment of young black males by the criminal justice system from arrest to incarceration, the poor black community is a community of ex-convicts. Men hardened by the experience of jail and prison; women with husbands, lovers, their children's father, brothers, uncles, and nephews with criminal records; men stigmatized and unable to break the stigma; men used to being brutalized by police, prosecutors, jailers, and other inmates. Men return with experiences of being raped, threatened, and assaulted by police and inmates. Some return to the community with AIDS and other diseases contracted while in jail or prison.

Most of the men arrested have children. The children know where their daddy is. For many children in the ghetto a visit to prison is more common than a visit to the zoo. In this way the children share the experience of prison. Prison becomes a normal part of the life of young people in the black ghetto. Virtually everyone has a close relative and over 50 percent have a parent in prison, on probation, parole, in jail, or in hiding because there is a warrant out for their arrest (Miller, 1992).

In prison African Americans are vastly overrepresented in the most severe conditions of incarceration. They comprise a disproportionate number of people in maximum security compared to their numbers in the prison population. In Maryland, for example, there are over eighteen-thousand prison inmates; 288 of these inmates are in "supermax": the Maryland Correctional

Adjustment Center. These inmates are confined to their cells from twenty-two to twenty-four hours a day. Their cell is an 8 by 12, cement block room with a cement bed on which is a thin mattress. There is an aluminum toilet (with no toilet seat), a washbowl, and two bookshelves. There are two windows about four inches in width and twelve inches long. The windows are covered by a thick steel mesh. The door to the cell is solid, except for a small window three inches by six inches. When these men leave their cells they must first strip down and hand their clothes to a guard through a small slot in the wall, which the guards can open but the inmates cannot. While the guard examines the clothing the inmate stands naked and must make a 360 degree circle so that the guard can see that he has no weapon on his body. After inspecting the clothing, the guard returns it and watches the inmate dress. The inmate then stands with his back to the slot in the wall; he places his arms through the slot, and the guard attaches handcuffs.

Inmates are sent to this prison from other prisons where they have been defined as dangerous to either other inmates or to prison guards. They are given a minimum thirteen-month sentence from which there is no possible reduction. Their sentence to this prison may be increased, but it cannot be reduced. For the first four months they are confined to their cell *twenty-three hours a day*. If they do not act up, or in the words of the prison wardens, if they "get with the program," they are then moved to the next level where they are confined for twenty-two and a half-hours a day. After three months at this level, assuming they have not been written up by a guard or prison official, they are confined to their cell for twenty-two hours a day. In each instance they are permitted recreation and a shower during the one to two hours they are out of their cell. Recreation consists of being allowed to play basketball or run around in an enclosed cage approximately twenty by twenty feet.

If an inmate is found guilty of committing an infraction of any of the rules—speaking to guards in unapproved ways, throwing feces or urine at the guards, being disruptive—he begins his thirteen-month confinement again. At the end of thirteen months, a board of three prison officials determines whether the inmate is ready to be returned to the prison population.

Of the 288 inmates in this "supermax" prison, *five* are white. That is, year in and year out, over 95 percent of the inmates confined to "supermax" are African Americans, whereas only 75 percent of the general prison population is African Americans.

The violence, anger, and message of revolt articulated so dramatically in the rap music of the current generation of young African Americans speaks volumes about the impact of the present criminal justice system on the attitudes of young black men. The songs encourage striking out at the police and the courts, not as symbols of white power but tools of the white man's oppression. When Rodney King was tried in a white suburban court by four white men, six white women, one Hispanic and one Filipino woman, but no black jurors, the consequences were apparent to everyone as angry black citizens rioted in the most costly and deadliest riot in American history. The riots left 54 people dead, over two-thousand injured, and five-thousand buildings destroyed or damaged. There were seventeen-thousand arrests, and property destroyed of more than $1 billion. Forty thousand jobs were lost as a consequence of the destruction. Although poorly publicized by the media reluctant to be accused of contributing to the spread of riots, there were outbreaks in Atlanta, Seattle, Washington, and Madison, Wisconsin, as well.

REDUCING CRIME

The official justification for the unprecedented expansion of the crime control industry is, of course, that it will reduce crime. Increased police surveillance, mandatory prison sentences, and more severe penalties have never effectively reduced crime. The criminal justice system is demonstrably the least effective and arguably the most counterproductive of all social policies designed to reduce crime. People whose lifestyle incorporates criminality into it, professional thieves, drug addicts, and drug dealers, accept the possibility of jail or prison as "the cost of doing business." As David Dragna, a heroin addict remarked after being sentenced to prison for the tenth time, "It's just getting easier. It doesn't bother me." As Harry King, a professional safecracker (at the other extreme of the criminal type from David Dragna) put it: "I don't like to go to prison any more than an office worker likes to punch the clock. It's just one of the bad parts of my profession. I live with it" (King and Chambliss, 1984).

The recidivism rate of ex-prisoners should be adequate evidence against the efficacy of imprisonment as a solution to crime. According to a study of recidivism conducted by the National Institute of Justice, "of the 108,580 persons released from prisons in 11 states in 1983, . . . an estimated 62.5% were rearrested for a felony or serious misdemeanor within 3 years." These findings are consistent with research dating back to the nineteenth century.

The criminal justice system as a means of coping with the problem of crime is an utter failure. It is the one institution that receives more public funding the more it fails. It is as though a university managed to take literate students in as freshman and graduated illiterates four years later, but was able to convince a gullible public that this was because it did not have enough money.

To be sure, we do not possess sufficient knowledge to confidently advocate alternative social policies that would be effective. Research on the impact of education suggests that early childhood education may effectively reduce the likelihood of being arrested as a teenager (Geiger, 1992). Prison education programs have been shown to substantially reduce recidivism (New York Department of Correctional Services, 1991; Littlefield, 1989; Holloway and Moke, 1986). And sociological theories of crime causation all suggest the importance of education. At the very least it is safe to conclude on the basis of extant knowledge that the massive expenditures on crime control would be more effective in reducing crime were they allocated instead to repairing the dismal condition of our public schools, especially those that serve the poor and minorities. But current policies have little to do with what works, but everything to do with politics, the creation of moral panics, racism, and the mobilization of bias (Chambliss and Zatz, 1994).

SUMMARY AND CONCLUSION

Between 1964 and 1990 a coalition of interests including conservative legislators, the crime control industry, and the media created a moral panic about crime in the United States. As a result, public expenditures at every level of government have been transferred from other social programs into crime control. Police powers have been substantially increased both by increases in numbers of police officers and laws giving the police a virtual carte blanche in dealing with suspects. The nature of policing in a class-society inevitably leads to policing the poor and minorities rather than those in social classes capable of creating problems if they are heavily policed. As a consequence, we have seen a dramatic increase in the number of arrests, convictions, and prison sentences meted out to the poor and especially the minority poor.

For the young black male population overpoliced and overincarcerated whose lives are a torment of poverty and policing, current policies have created a hostile and divided society. Racism is justified by the self-fulfilling prophesy of policing the ghetto and pointing the finger at ghetto crime rates as a justification for institutionalizing racism.

REFERENCES

Austin, James, and John Irwin. 1991. *Who Goes to Prison?* San Francisco: National Council on Crime and Delinquency.

Bogess, Scott, and John Bound. "Did Criminal Activities Increase During the 1980's? Comparisons Across Data Sources." 1993. *Research Report No. 93–280*, Ann Arbor, Mich. Population Studies Center.

Broderick, Vincent. 1969. "The Proposed Organized Crime Control Act of 1969." House Hearings, 1969:291.

Bureau of Justice Statistics. 1993. *Highlights from 20 Years of Surveying Crime Victims.* Washington, D.C. U.S. Department of Justice.

Bureau of Justice Statistics. 1994. "Drug Offenders in Federal Prison." U.S. Department of Justice, Washington, D.C. (February).

Chambliss, William J. 1991. *Trading Textbooks for Prison Cells.* Alexandria, Va.: National Center on Institutions and Alternatives.

Chambliss, William J., and Edward Sbarbaro. 1993 "Moral Panics, Repression, and Racism: The Drug War in America." *Socio-Legal Bulletin.* Summer: 4–11.

Chambliss, William J., and Marjorie Zatz. 1994. *Making Law: The Law, State and Structural Contradictions.* Bloomington: Indiana University Press.

Chambliss, William J., 1994 "Policing the Ghetto Underclass." *Social Problems,* May. (In Press)

Christie, Nils. 1993. *Crime Control as Industry.* London: Routledge.

Congressional Quarterly. 1965–1972.

Congressional Quarterly Almanac. 1965.

Cronin, Thomas E., Tania Z. Cronin, and Michael E. Milakovich. 1981. *United States Crime in the Streets.* Bloomington: Indiana University Press.

Gallup Polls. 1951–1992.

Geiger, Kent, 1992. "Education and Delinquency." Washington, D.C. National Education Association.

House Reports. U.S. House of Representatives. 1965–1975.

Holloway, Jerry, and Paul Moke. "Post Secondary Correctional Education: An Evaluation of Parolee Performance." 1986. Unpublished MS, Wilmington, Ohio.

Holman, Barry, and William J. Chambliss. 1991. "Residents in the Crossbar Jail." Paper delivered at the American Society of Criminology, San Francisco.

King, Harry, and William J. Chambliss. 1984. *Harry King: A Professional Thief's Journey.* New York: John Wiley.

Langan and Innes, eds. 1984. *Sourcebook of Criminal Justice Statistics.* U.S. Department of Justice. Bureau of Justice Statistics. Washington, D.C.: U.S. Government Printing Office.

Littlefield, John F. 1989. "Characteristics of the Ohio Inmate Intake Population and the Implications for Correctional Education Programming." Paper presented at International Conference of Prison Education, Milton Keynes, U.K.

Maguire, Kathleen, and Timothy J. Flanagan, eds. 1990; 1991. *Sourcebook of Criminal Justice Statistics 1990.* Washington, D.C.: Bureau of Justice Statistics.

Maguire, Kathleen, Anne L. Pastore, and Timothy J. Flanagan. 1992. *Sourcebook of Criminal Justice Statistics.* Washington, D.C. Bureau of Justice Statistics.

Miller, Jerome M. 1992. *Search and Destroy: The Plight of African American Males in the Criminal Justice System.* Alexandria, Va: National Center on Institutions and Alternatives.

Newsweek. 10/19/1964. "The Curious Campaign—Point by Point."

New York Department of Correctional Services. 1991 "Analysis of Return Rates of the Inmate College Program Participants." Albany. Division of Program Planning, Research, and Evaluation.

New York Times. January 6, 1991; Sept, 4, 1964; Sept. 12, 1968; Sept 30, 1968; Oct. 23, 1968; Oct. 25, 1968.

New York Times Magazine. 1964–1970.

Schreiber, Leslie. 1993. "Alcohol and Rape on College Campuses." PhD. dissertation. Washington, D.C. George Washington University.

Senate Hearings. U.S. Senate. 1965–1975.

Skolnick, Jerome H., and James J. Fyfe. 1993. *Above the Law.* New York: Free Press.

Uniform Crime Reports. 1980; 1984; 1988; 1992. "Crime in the United States." Washington, D.C.: U.S. Department of Justice.

Washington Post. Feb. 16, 1994.

Wilson, James Q. 1985. *Thinking about Crime.* New York: Vintage.

Wolfe, Alan. 1977. *The Limits of Legitimacy.* New York: Free Press.

CORAMAE RICHEY MANN

12

The Contribution of Institutionalized Racism to Minority Crime

This chapter explores the role that institutionalized racism plays in minority crime and justice in the United States. The racism found in each of the nation's established institutions is enormous, pervasive, and debilitating. At every level of contemporary human existence—education, housing, politics, health, law, welfare, economics, religion, and the family—racism and racial discrimination in American institutions have contributed to and continue to perpetuate the minority status and the current condition of African-Americans, Native Americans, Hispanic Americans, and Asian-Americans. I argue that criminal activity, as defined by those in power, may be one of the adaptive responses of racial minorities to institutionalized racism.

In this chapter the reader will learn of the predictable and disproportionate contribution to the nation's crime rate by peoples of color who are unemployed, underemployed, or only marginally employed, and have few opportunities to acquire the education and vocational skills necessary to become gainfully employed. When the dignity, pride, and responsibilities of working to support one's family and enjoy some of the perquisites associated with a middle-class income level are denied, while simultaneously the media and the world around you continually portray the "good life" you cannot have, anger, frustration, and concomitant criminal behavior often become one's only options. If a person is forced to rely on a punitive welfare system, which, in the process of becoming "eligible," destroys one's family unit, all too frequently that person ends up idle on inner-city street corners. The dangers and temptations of the "streets" can be quite alluring when there is little hope and no place to go. Every word can become a taunt; every glance a projected sneer; every move in your direction a threat. In such a milieu, when you respond to the words, glances, and moves, you go to jail and you collect a criminal record. Since you have no political power to change your destiny, much less change any of those institutions that have failed you and your loved ones, the cycle is constantly repeated.

DEFINITIONS OF TERMS AND CAVEATS

Minority here refers to historically disadvantaged peoples of color in the United States—Native, African, Hispanic, and Asian-Americans. Although females and juveniles are additional oppressed groups who face most of the same problems, the situation is especially acute for racial minorities, particularly African-Americans—a group that has been researched and reported on more than any other people of color in the United States. Takaki (1987:29) argues convincingly that a "racial and exclusionist pattern" has historically operated for all persons of color in America.

Inherent in *racism* is an assumption that race determines one's traits and abilities, and that a particular race is inherently superior to another race on the basis of those characteristics. More importantly, the group that defines itself as superior controls all institutional power. *Institutional racism* is present when "the social, political, economic, religious, and educational structures, or the major institutions in a society benefit a particular race—the 'white' race in the United States—at the expense of other races" (Mann, 1993). As Georges-Abeyie (1990:28) refines the term,

> The key issue is *result, not intent.* Institutional racism is often the legacy of overt racism, of *de facto* practices that often get codified, and thus sanctioned by *de jure* mechanisms. Examples of institutional racism include: the hiring of white guards and law enforcement officers; the election of white court officials; the implementation of "objective," Eurocentric testing procedures that select the most Eurocentric non-white available; and the subsequent institutionalization of seniority procedures that penalize the historically excluded.

The *white power structure* includes the primary beneficiaries of institutionalized racism or those persons who maintain power and control over persons of color due to their established positions of authority. White males predominate in this structure.

As used here, *crime* is circumscribed by *official statistics* such as those found in the Uniform Crime Reports (UCR) compiled by the Federal Bureau of Investigation. Hence, minority crime is primarily *crime in the streets*. It is exceedingly rare to find a person of color who embezzles millions of dollars, imports tons of cocaine, commits a million-dollar computer crime, pollutes the air and water, damages the atmosphere, invades neutral countries, sells arms to foreign countries holding hostages, and manufactures and distributes dangerous automobiles, pharmaceutical and other products. These criminals are primarily white n.ales.

The predominantly *street* criminal activity defined and ultimately punished harshly by the white power structure is one of the adaptive responses of minorities to institutionalized racism. Vastly different treatment is accorded the crimes for which minorities become enmeshed in the criminal justice system compared to the more leniently treated capitalistic (white-collar) crimes more commonly found among whites.

"OFFICIAL" MINORITY CRIME

Criminologists and other social scientists rely almost exclusively on the reported arrests noted in the UCR.[1] After 1986 the UCR no longer included Hispanic Americans as a separate minority group. Therefore 1986 arrest statistics are used below to provide a description of the possible deviant adaptive responses to the institutionalized racism faced by United States minorities.[2]

According to the 1980 U.S. census, minorities comprised about one-fifth (20.5 percent) of the total United States population yet accounted for 28.7 percent of the total persons arrested in 1986. On the other hand, whites represented 79.5 percent of the 1980 U.S. population, but were only 71.3 percent of the arrest total. For the most serious index crimes, or those most feared by the populace—murder and nonnegligent manslaughter, forcible rape, robbery, aggravated assault, larceny, burglary, motor vehicle theft, and arson—35.5 percent of the arrestees were minorities and 64.5 percent were white. The most disproportionate index crime representations by minority status in 1986 were the 62 percent of robbery arrests of African-Americans who were estimated at 12 percent of the U.S. population, and the 16.3 percent of arrests represented by Hispanics who were 6.5 percent of Americans at that time (U.S. Department of Justice, 1987:182, 185). Relative to their proportions in the general population, African- and Hispanic Americans were overrepresented in every category of index crime arrests and Native Americans were overrepresented in all categories but robbery and arson. In contrast, whites (79.5 percent of the population) and Asian-Americans (1.4 percent) were underrepresented in all index crime categories in relation to their percentage of the U.S. population.

As will be shown, the low crime rate of *some* Asian-Americans—that is, Japanese-Americans—is closely related to their overrepresentation at higher educational levels and the employment opportunities conjoined with those statuses. However, despite the recording of arrests that views Asian-Americans as a monolithic group, other Asian-American subgroups, for example, Chinese and Vietnamese, also have higher crime rates than whites.

INSTITUTIONALIZED RACISM IN AMERICAN INSTITUTIONS

Housing

In *And We Are Not Saved* (1987), Derrick Bell demonstrates the pervasiveness of racism in every aspect of African-American life and how it functions to benefit the white majority. Bell describes the genesis of this condition, and its persistence for over three centuries. In the area of housing, the proliferation of black ghettos, Latino barrios, and Chinatowns reflect the imposed racial segregation in urban areas, which even African-American conservative Shelby Steele (1991:79) states is "more entrenched in American cities today than ever imagined" and has "stagnated or regressed since the early seventies."

Discussing housing developments, Bell (1987:152) reports that "courts have tailored tenant racial balance to levels consistent with the refusal of whites to live in predominantly black residential districts" mainly to avoid *white flight* and the loss of white power structure control of the cities. African-American geographer Daniel Georges-Abeyie (1990:27) finds the problem is even more extensive: "increased residential segregation by census tract and census block is now a national phenomenon, a pattern which is not restricted to the large, northern inner-city."

Education

Education and training are essential requirements for entry into the more fruitful and lucrative jobs. Yet there are fewer African-American youths in college today than there were a decade ago. In fact (Steele, 1991:124) there are more African-American males under correctional control than there are in college:

> *The number of young* Black men under the control of the criminal justice system—609,690—is greater than the *total* number of Black men of *all ages* enrolled in college—436,000 as of 1986. For white males, the comparable figures are 4,600,000 total in higher education and 1,054,508 ages 20–29 in the criminal justice system. (Mauer, 1990:3)

Between 1960 and 1981, the difference in median level of schooling (above 12 years) between white and African-Americans was only six months—a level that peaked in 1976 and eroded thereafter. Whereas African-American students were 10.3 percent in 1976 of those enrolled in four-year institutions in 1972, by 1982 they had declined to 9.6 percent (Herbers, 1983).

Such educational erosion can be attributed to segregated inner-city schools that are "more crowded and employ fewer topnotch teachers than a white suburban public school" (Steele, 1991:132), thus putting students who are "poor, minority, and of limited English proficiency" at risk (Cole, 1991:25). In his treatise on the *truly disadvantaged,* Wilson (1987:136) accurately defines the etiology of the problem of deteriorated minority schools:

> The flight of the more affluent families to the suburbs has meant that the central cities are becoming increasingly the domain of the poor and the stable working class. Thus, in major cities, such as New York, Chicago, Atlanta, Washington, D.C., Philadelphia, St. Louis, and Detroit, not only have public schools become overwhelmingly populated with minority students, but the background of both minority and white students is primarily working or lower class. And in certain underclass neighborhoods in the inner city, neither children from middle-class families nor those from working-class families are represented in the public schools.

The median number of school years completed by Mexican-Americans is 9.8, but this figure drops when one considers older persons: for example, Mexican-Americans over age 25 have only a median of 8.8 years of school completed. Three percent of non-Hispanics have less than five years of school compared to 23.1 percent of Mexican-Americans. While 67.1 percent of non-Hispanics have more than twelve years of school, only 34.3 percent of Mexican Americans have achieved that education level. Two reasons may account for this lack of educational achievement. First, over half of foreign-born Mexican-Americans between the ages of 14 and 30 are not enrolled in school and therefore do not graduate from high school. Second, since over 80 percent of Mexican-American children have non-English-speaking backgrounds, the problems of educating such children are compounded (Heckler, 1985:53).

There are vast differences in educational level achievement within the Hispanic American group that are difficult to explain. Whereas Cubans have almost reached the educational level of the general U.S. population, Puerto Ricans lag far behind. One reason for this differential is that Puerto Ricans are such a young population; for example, 75 percent of Puerto Rican families have children under age 18, compared to about 50 percent of American families (Mizio, 1979:5). Since so few Puerto Ricans have reached adult status, the statistical average of their educational level has yet to be accurately determined. The high school dropout rate among Puerto Ricans, estimated at 50 percent, compounds the problem (Fitzpatrick and Parker, 1981:102). Recent U.S. Census figures (U.S. Department of Commerce, 1990:150) show that Puerto Ricans are slightly more likely to finish high school than Cubans (28.1 vs. 17.3 percent), but Cubans are almost twice as likely (17.2 percent) as Puerto Ricans (9.6 percent) to complete four years of college.

The Indian educational system is a federal system believed to be the worst in America. Since there are very few schools on the reservations, Native American children are educated in either schools operated by the Bureau of Indian Affairs or in public schools in the political subdivision where they reside. Compared to whites, Native Americans have always been at the bottom of the educational barrel in almost every measure of achievement. While the number of years of school completion varies from tribe to tribe, the average performance levels of Indian children attending public schools is two or three years below those of white children. One early national survey ranked American Indian school performances behind whites and Asian Americans, but ahead of Mexican-American, Puerto Rican, and African-American children. The national dropout rate of Indian students was found to be higher than for students in general (30.6 percent versus 27.7 percent), with regional dropout differences as high as 39 percent in, for example, the southwest (U.S. Commission on Civil Rights, 1975). By 1980, only 31 percent of American Indians had graduated from high school and just seven percent had college degrees (Heckler, 1985:58).

It is difficult to estimate the number of Native Americans in college. The Bureau of Indian Affairs suggests that about twenty-thousand Indians are attending college, but ''their statistics fail to include people on state, tribal, and private scholarships and often overlook students enrolled under general federal educational assistance programs'' (Deloria, 1981:145).

Asian-Americans consistently demonstrate excellence in the American educational system and today comprise the only nonwhite group to be overrepresented in higher education. In 1990, 40 percent of the adult Asian-American population (25 or older) had at least four years of college and 80 percent in this age group had completed high school (O'Hare and Felt, 1991:8). A higher proportion of Chinese Americans have Ph.D.s, particularly from higher ranked universities, and are significantly more qualified than either white or African-Americans in their occupations as academics, scientists, and engineers (Sowell, 1981:153).

Similar to the Chinese, Japanese have used education as a means for upward mobility in American society. As early as 1940, Japanese Americans had more education than white Americans and they have continued to widen the gap such that 88 percent of the third generation (Sansei) have attended college. By 1976, Japanese boys and girls had higher high school and college completion rates than the white majority group or any minority group, particularly in applied areas such as engineering, business administration, and optometry (Kitano, 1981; Sowell, 1981).

Despite the academic excellence of Asian-Americans, they are not exempt from the institutionalized racism faced by other peoples of color in this nation and the white backlash that is an integral part of it:

> In the face of rising applications from Asian-American students who are proud of their high grades and test scores, critics charge that Ivy League schools are imposing unwritten quotas making it more difficult for Asians to get into selective schools. For example, at Yale, the "admit" rate for Asian-Americans fell from 39 percent to 17 percent in the last decade. (Bell, 1987:268)

Many of the *reforms* in education initiated by state legislatures as a result of the shocking 1984 report on our educational system, *A Nation at Risk* (U.S. National Commission on Excellence in Education, 1984), have actually harmed minorities. African-American college enrollment declined precipitously when standards for college admission were raised without sufficient preparatory or support services for minority students (Cole, 1991:23–24). Minority teachers are being severely reduced in numbers or summarily eliminated through differential (less) merit pay, requirements of a five-year teaching degree, biased teacher competency testing, and other methods assured to guarantee that minority teachers will make up less than 5 percent of teachers in the year 2000. Yet, minority students are projected to comprise over 30 percent of the student population by the turn of the century (ibid.).

Family

The nexus between family structure and higher crime rates among minorities, especially African-Americans, has been in the forefront of criminological research and theoretical attention for decades. Most frequently, the empirical link was forged between the broken home and delinquency and crime (Glueck and Glueck, 1950; McCord, McCord, and Thurber, 1962; Chilton and Markle, 1972). More recently, Sampson (1987) attributed persistent high African-American crime rates to structural connections between family disruption, economic deprivation, and unemployment. Specifically, Sampson (1987:377) finds

> While male joblessness has little or no direct effect upon crime, it has the strongest overall effect on family disruption, which in turn is the strongest predictor of black violence.

The unique structures of minority families have frequently been linked to crime and anti-social conduct. For example, Moynihan (1965) suggested that the African-American family was disorganized and seriously harmed because of a matriarchal structure that resulted in the *psychological castration* of adolescent males. Some African-American social scientists vigorously challenged this position (Hill, 1972; Staples, 1973) by stressing the importance of the quality, not quantity (number of parents), of family life and the frequently overlooked positive influence of the extended family (Billingsley, 1968). More recently, Taylor (1993) confronts the myth of dysfunctional African-American families headed by welfare mothers by finding substantial bonding within these families that deters maladaptive behavior and delinquency in their children.

Similar criticisms of the Hispanic family may stem from misinterpretation of its balanced system of masculine and feminine roles and neglect of its strengths (Williams and Holmes, 1979). The connection between Hispanic crime and the stress initiated by culture shock emphasizes the transitional structure provided by Hispanic culture:

> Deviance and criminality are identified as an outcome of the breakup of traditional cultural forms, especially those associated with the family and its relations between the generations and between the sexes. It is within this context that explanations of juvenile delinquency among Hispanics in the United States are being developed. (Sissons, 1979:6)

Puerto Ricans are more capable of coping with the transition than other Hispanic newcomers, but previous strong family systems break down when one is labeled criminal and imprisoned, since such stigmatization elicits negative responses from Hispanic family members (ibid.).

Although little is known about Native American families, according to Deloria (1981:149), "urban Indians tend to be older than reservation Indians . . . to have smaller families, and to fit into the profile of second- and third-generation immigrant behavior patterns." These urban dwellers frequently return home to the reservations on long weekends and it is predicted that "the majority will eventually return to the reservations and live" (ibid).

Asian-American families appear to have characteristics of both other minority families and white families. The extended family arrangement is seen in the fact that Asian families double up in households twice as frequently as white families: "the probability of a parent and a grown child living together is five times higher in the Asian-American population than in the total population" (O'Hare and Felt, 1991:9). Most Asian-American homes contain two-parent families (84 percent) that stay intact, and Asian-Americans are half as likely to be divorced or separated as whites (ibid.).

Undoubtedly such a strong family system has tended to deter crime and delinquency among Asian Americans. Thus, much of the contemporary crime in Asian-American communities involves newly arrived immigrants who have few family ties and serious problems of assimilation into American culture.

Economics

Each of the previously described social institutions is intimately and drastically affected by economics. When these institutions fail, minority crime is enhanced. In smaller cities and rural areas, minority-occupied housing having a preponderance of inadequate or no utilities, a shortage or absence of plumbing, open sewage areas, and too frequent location near toxic waste dumps, contribute to disease, despair, and hopelessness. Such conditions often drive hapless African, Hispanic, and Native Americans from the hinterlands and reservations to the segregated ghettos of inner cities. Once relocated into segregated housing systems, peoples of color are contained in substandard, overcrowded, dilapidated housing in crime-ridden areas. As a result of these circumstances, physical and mental health deteriorate, and other institutions such as the family and religion are strained to the point of collapse. This depressing state of being for peoples of color—a sustained condition of poverty grounded in inequality—is fundamentally based on economics.

Only 56.3 percent of African-Americans over the age of 16 were employed in 1988, compared to 74 percent in 1960 (U.S. Department of Commerce, 1990:38). As a consequence of their depressed economic status, the median household income of African-American families in 1990 ($18,676) was 59.7 percent of the white median income of $31,231, while that of Hispanic Americans at $22,330 was 71.5 percent of whites (*Herald-Times*, September 27, 1991:1). There has been little change in the black-white income differential in over two decades. Since these are median income figures, they fail to reflect the extensive poverty experienced by many African-American families. The economic growth of the 1980s left millions of African-Americans behind. By 1988, 33.1 percent of African-Americans were at or below the poverty level compared to only 10.5 percent of white Americans (U.S. Department of Commerce, 1990:38).

The child poverty rates are much worse. In 1989, 11.2 million children (18 percent) lived in families below the federal poverty line of $9,885 for a family of three. Included were 39.8 percent of all African-American children, 38.8 percent of Native American children, 32.2 percent of Hispanic children, 17.1 percent of Asian-American children, and 12.5 percent of white children (*Herald-Times*, July 8, 1992:A4).

Although the Mexican-American unemployment rate tends to be about 50 percent higher than the national rate and is currently at 6.3 percent (U.S. Department of Commerce, 1990:40), Mexican-Americans have done fairly well considering their agricultural past and a tradition of having little exposure to formal education. Today, the median income for Mexican-Americans is $19,968, which, when compared to $15,185 for Puerto Ricans, reveals the income disparity within the Hispanic American population (U.S. Department of Commerce, 1990:40). Tremendous unemployment in Puerto Rico is a significant factor in Puerto Rican migration to the mainland. Whereas official statistics indicate that in 1988, 40.3 percent of Puerto Rican families in the United States were below the poverty level (U.S. Department of Commerce, 1990:40), according to López-Rivera, 62 to 64 percent of Puerto Ricans live under the poverty line, 65 percent depend on public assistance, and 100,000 are homeless (1989:164).

Their lack of skills and education makes Native Americans the most unemployed and poorest of all American subgroups. Some authors believe that extensive Indian poverty is a result of government policy and that Indians have had a much harder time in this country than the other minorities (Cummings and Harrison, 1972). The most recent data available show that in 1980 the Native American median income was only $13,678 and 23.7 percent of Indians were living at or below the poverty level (U.S. Department of Commerce, 1990:39). Although exploited in the past, a few reservation tribes are now earning royalties for the rich minerals, oil, and other natural resources found on their tribal lands. Ranching, farming, fishing, recreation, and timber production are other traditional sources of income found on these lands (Deloria, 1981:145–46).

Takaki (1989) considers the celebrated view of Asian-Americans as a *model minority* a myth. He disclaims the exaggerated Asian-American *success* in comparisons between Asian and white Americans as based on a flawed and misleading reliance on family incomes. In reality, the alleged higher family incomes of Asian-Americans represent "the presence of more workers in each family." For example, workers per California family in 1980 were 1.6 for white nuclear families, 2.1 for Japanese, 2.0 for immigrant Chinese, 2.2 for immigrant Filipino, and 1.8 for immigrant Korean family workers (Takaki, 1989:475). Further, reports of higher incomes among Asian-Americans compared to whites fail to reflect the regional location of the 59 percent of Asian-Americans who are highly concentrated in states with higher incomes—California, Hawaii, and New York (ibid.). Takaki finds that Asian-Americans have not reached equality in terms of personal income and in fact lag behind whites. When years of education and number of hours worked are considered, Japanese men still trail white men. Korean men earned only 82 percent of the income earned by white men; Chinese men earned only 68 percent; and Filipino men only 62 percent. Further, Takaki reports that 51 percent of the employed Chinese immigrants worked in menial jobs and low-skilled, blue-collar work (p. 425).

While not discounting race, recent publications suggest that the problem of economic disparity between whites and blacks is more a matter of class than of race (Steele, 1991; Wilson, 1978). In rebuttal, Pettigrew (1980:21) concludes that the significance of race is not declining but is *changing:*

> The black poor are far worse off than the white poor, and the black middleclass still has a long way to catch up with the white middleclass in wealth and economic security. Black median family income is not closing the gap with white family median income even within the growing disparity within black America.

Marrett (1980:18) suggested that the condition of the black middle class is tenuous and speculated that cut-backs in governmental spending would adversely affect both the black underclass and the black middle class—an indication that "the progress of the middle class may be shorter-lived and less sweeping."

When examined in combination with data released by the census bureau, the research findings of Oliver and Glick (1982) indicate that middle-class African-Americans have made little progress in terms of occupational upward mobility. In fact, "given present trends in mobility, another 200 years of striving with the same commitment and determination that blacks showed in the 1960s will be necessary to achieve occupational equality between the races" (ibid.). (*Herald-Times,* September 20, 1991:A6). According to the census report, in 1989 African-American men over 25 years of age with four or more years of college earned 23.6 percent less than white men with equal education. Within the same age group, who had four years of high school but no college, the gap between the salaries of African-American and white males was 23.5 percent. Thus, despite educational level, African-American men on average, earned 76 percent of the wages earned by white men. In fact, an African-American man with a college education only earned about 15 percent more than a white man with a high school education.

Numerous studies of African-American crime, especially violent crime, have emphasized its connection to some form of economic inequality as measured by rates of underemployment, unemployment, relative or absolute poverty, female-headed welfare households, and urbanism (Jacobs, 1981; Blau and Blau, 1982; Carroll and Jackson, 1983; Messner, 1983; Sampson, 1985; Messner and Tardiff, 1986; Krahn, Hartnagel, and Gartrell, 1986; Chiricos, 1987; Duster, 1987). Equally impressive is the abundant research on the influence of lower-class level and crime (Green, 1970; Tittle, Villemez, and Smith, 1978; Platt, 1978; Braithwaite, 1981).[3]

In light of these investigations and reported income disparities between whites and both Hispanic and Native Americans,[4] it seems that racial criteria are more instrumental in crime generation than is the class discrimination found in the labor market. The historic subjugation of peoples of color into subordinate economic roles (slavery, "coolie" and "stoop" labor) makes it difficult to separate race from class. Whether minority crime is associated with race or class is of little consequence because, in any event, most peoples of color are located in the lower economic strata. The white dominant group that makes the laws that define crime also controls law enforcement, legal punishing, and social-control institutions that apprehend and contain peoples of color. Braithwaite (1992) argues that in an unequal society both the poverty of the poor and the wealth of the rich contribute to crime: the crime motivation of the poor is based on need, whereas crimes of the wealthy are motivated by greed.

Political Power

Any person of color viewing the first day of the 41st Democratic National Convention in 1992 from the opening to closing ceremonies no doubt experienced intense feelings of exhilaration and hope after seeing the rainbow of peoples of color and representation from all segments of our nation—the young, the elderly, men and women, those with alternative lifestyles, the physically challenged. Political reality returned when one of the television commentators reported that only 16 percent of the delegates were African-American compared to the 22 percent they comprised at the 1988 convention. Although this proportion is still above the estimated 13 percent African-American population, it is doubtful that African-Americans and other peoples of color are fully represented in the political process.

The significance of the political institution for American minorities is related to the improvement of existing social programs, the institution of new social programs, and the requisite alterations in laws and the juvenile and criminal justice systems necessary to provide equal justice. None of these institutional changes can be accomplished without political power. Peoples of color comprise 20 percent of the U.S. population but, prior to the 1992 elections, were only 8.7 percent of national lawmakers among the 435 members of Congress (Barrow, 1992; Martinez, 1992).[5] Modest improvements in national representation are indicated by the recent elections. In the House there are now 39 African-Americans (including 11 women), 19 Hispanic Americans, and 7 Asian-Americans. For many decades prior to the 1992 election there were no African or Hispanic American U.S. senators. Joining the two Asian-American U.S. senators from Hawaii are the first African-American woman senator, Carol Mosely-Braun (Illinois) and the first Native American senator, Ben Campbell (Arizona).[6]

The 415 African-American state legislators in 1990 represented only 5.6 percent of the 7,466 members, but in some states there are much larger proportions (Joint Center, 1991:20). The south is particularly representative: African-Americans are 60 percent of the population in the south and 68 percent of all African-American elected officials in state legislatures are located in the south. The west region, which has only 4 percent of the African-American population, also contains 4 percent of the nation's African-American state legislators. Comparable figures in the midwest are 17 percent African-Americans and 18 percent African-American legislators, respectively. There is regional underrepresentation only in the northeast region, where 15 percent of the nation's African-American population reside, but only 10 percent of African-American state legislators are located (ibid). In 1987, the mean percent representation of Hispanics in lower state legislative chambers was 2.0 percent nationally with 1.9 percent in the north and 2.3 percent in the south (Nelson, 1991:25).

The Congressional Black Caucus (CBC), an organization of the African-American members in the U.S. House of Representatives, was formed in 1970 to conceive a plan that "black Americans could follow as we attempt to achieve the final, total liberation of our people in these United States of America" (Barrow, 1992:48). The alternative platforms and annual budgets for social programs proposed by the CBC represent the political needs of peoples of color, and the poor, in this nation. Unfortunately, the CBC goals are hampered by a small budget, lack of meaningful support from other congressional members, and harassment of African-American elected officials (Hatchett, 1992). The persecution of Dr. Martin Luther King, Jr., by the FBI, and the blatant targeted entrapment of former Washington, D.C., Mayor Marion Berry, are among the more notorious examples of governmental intensive scrutiny and interference in the activities and lives of African-America's leadership (wire tapping, camcording, corruption probes, newspaper *leaks*). At one time it was intimated by then FBI director William Webster that the FBI was investigating 40 percent of African-American elected officials (ibid., p. 50). Although scandals such as Watergate and the Iran-Contra conspiracy have resulted in a proliferation of investigations of elected officials, it appears that African-American politicians have been singled out especially for such law enforcement probes:

> To a number of authorities, there is little doubt that racism is at the core of the issue, much of which involves reporters and editors at white-owned newspapers working in a de facto alliance with FBI officials. (ibid.)

As a result of these and other racist practices impinging on the political process, African-American and other peoples of color are denied effective representation as lawmakers. Consequently, existing and proposed laws are made by persons who are not the people directly affected by those laws. The significance of this disenfranchisement is especially harmful to minorities, because:

> State legislatures have always played a central role in the criminal justice system. Traditionally this role focused on defining the scope of the criminal law and setting limits for criminal sentencing. State legislatures also establish budgets for many criminal justice agencies, and therefore shape the priorities of statewide criminal justice policy. (McGarrell and Flanagan, 1987:102)

One outcome of such an unjust condition is the legal persecution of U.S. minorities. In New York City, for example, crack cocaine cases were treated more harshly by the courts than cases involving powdered cocaine (Belenko and Fagan, 1987). Defendants on crack charges, who are typically peoples of color, were detained, tried as felons, and more frequently received jail or prison sentences than the predominantly white defendants who used powdered cocaine. This severe treatment was accorded after controlling for seriousness of the charges and prior criminal records. The increase in new state and federal laws that adversely affect peoples of color through the discriminatory enforcement of the law buttresses the fact that "the greater the number of laws, the greater the resulting discretion, and the more lawless the official part of the state becomes" (Reich, 1973:450).

MINIMIZING THE CONTRIBUTION OF INSTITUTIONALIZED RACISM TO MINORITY CRIME

A great deal of what we are told about social institutions, crime, the criminal justice system, and the concomitant programs and policies that emerge from government-funded research and elitist think tanks are molded by the white power structure in this nation. In a discussion of sociological research, Joan Moore, one of the country's most published experts on Mexican-Americans, observed that "the field in *some* way reflects the biases and limitations of the 98 percent Anglo white composition of the profession," which led her to ask, "What have we omitted by the *de facto* exclusion and haphazard inclusion of minorities from sociological research?" (1973:66). While she answered, "we do not know,"

> Several scholars have asserted the need for prominent involvement by black social scientists at all levels of research on social deviance among

black populations. Such involvement is needed to counteract the ethnocentric bias—racial, cultural, and class-perpetuated in research on social deviance. (Mann and LaPoint, 1987:227)

Further, as Takagi (1981:50) observes, "The etiology of crime in minority communities cannot be understood by a science that does not take into account thoughts and experiences of the people in the community." The earlier discussion of institutional racism in education, family, economics, and political power and the consequence of minority crime inherent in the failure of these institutions commands a response to Takagi's concern about the need for minority researchers of minority crime.

In 1980, the National Minority Advisory Council on Criminal Justice (NMACCJ) (1980:267) reported:

Not one black, Hispanic or Asian or Indian person has ever received a dollar to do research from the Juvenile Justice Institute to frame issues upon which other initiatives are raised so that they can commission a white person to advise them [LEAA] as to whether the Indian program ought to continue or not. They follow the advice of these people . . . 98% of those funds are going into white research hands.

Since the NMACCJ made that observation, with the exception of a few *token* or *wired* federal grants, little has changed in either the funding of social or criminological research undertaken by scholars of color. Even when the targeted subject of study is minorities, the white power structure is reluctant to allocate substantial funds to minority researchers if that money can be awarded to whites. The reasons for this denial are obvious—"minority researchers may view criminal behavior in terms of the *structures and institutions that shape minority life.* Consequently, research topics of interest to minorities may challenge existing paradigms and institutions. This would suggest that research sponsors may not have favorable regard for minority researchers" (ibid., p. 280; emphasis added).

Closely related to this argument is the fallacious notion that minority researchers are not as competent as white researchers. This institutionalized racist stereotype has led to either the systematic exclusion of minority researchers from funding or, on rare occasions, to the condescending, paternalistic practice of funding projects that include minority researchers as co-principal investigators in selected studies focused on minority issues.

As previously noted, annual proposals aimed at responding to racial disparities in crime and justice recommended by the congressional Black Caucus are ignored. Periodic meetings of African-American leaders representing hundreds of organizations and millions of constituents across the country who work diligently to present "national, political, social, economic and international" agendas find their deliberations and conclusions overlooked.[7] Little weight was given to the findings reported on the four major historically disadvantaged minority groups by the National Minority Advisory Council on Criminal Justice (1980) despite having been generated from an intensive review of criminal justice literature, minority citizens accounts in public hearings throughout the country, field and commissioned studies on particular issues, and critical analysis and review of national criminal justice policies and programs. If the recommendations of these comprehensive reports on peoples of color in 1980 had been implemented over the past twelve years, there would have been little need for this essay.

Although it has not been *proven* that discrimination by criminal justice agencies increases minority crime (Walker, 1985:207), there is an abundance of sources demonstrating that the failure of social and economic institutions for peoples of color contributes to minority crime. The public, and even some social scientists, do not understand why the most expansive Civil Rights legislation in history, the War On Poverty, the economic prosperity of the 1960s, and other programs instituted during the decades of the 1960s and 1970s, did not eliminate the devastating plight of those in the ghettos, barrios, reservations, and Chinatowns of today. Walker answers best when he states that "social tinkering will not reduce the level of serious crime" (ibid., p. 212). The programs and policies of the 1960s "did not represent a fundamental change and, as a consequence, had little impact on crime" (ibid.). Institutionalized racism in all basic institutions, or what Wilson (1987: 141) euphemistically refers to as *historic discrimination*—that is, discrimination before the mid-twentieth century—has become so systemic that a massive, intensive program of economic and social reform is necessary to assimilate peoples of color into American society.

For centuries the brunt of the institutional racism was borne most heavily by African-Americans, primarily because, among minorities, their skin is the darkest.

> Black skin has more dehumanizing stereotypes associated with it than any other skin color in America, if not the world (Steele, 1991: 43). . . . There are not only more stereotypes of blacks than of other groups, but these stereotypes are also more dehumanizing, more focused on the most despised human traits: stupidity, laziness, sexual immorality, dirtiness, and so on. In America's racial and ethnic hierarchy, blacks have clearly been relegated to the lowest level—have been burdened with an ambiguous, animalistic humanity. (ibid., p. 134)

These are no longer just the problems and condition of African-Americans. All racial minorities in this nation "have suffered historically from a more arbitrary and legally sanctioned exclusion and discrimination in America than have white immigrants" (Ringer and Lawless, 1989:30). The threat to the white power structure has been exacerbated by increased numbers of blacks. As the populations of other minority groups proliferate, they will pose a similar peril to white economic hegemony. These groups are expanding now—Asian-Americans have been described as America's fastest growing minority group (O'Hare and Felt, 1991), while the "growing Hispanic population presents challenges to U.S. policymakers in nearly every area, but most urgently in education, job training, and welfare" (Valdivieso and Davis, 1988:1). This minority growth and visibility has provoked a national white backlash of hate-motivated violence against peoples of color (*Washington Post,* January 14, 1988:A28). Such violence is based in fear and the deep-rooted and institutionalized racism is deeply entrenched in our nation. As Bernard Headley (1990:93) states:

> There is something incredulously insidious about arguing the absence of racism in any of the dominant institutions that comprise American society. All of the basic ingredients that structure one's life chances in this country—what kind of education you receive, how far you get in school, whether you get to write books about race, where you live, where you work, how much money you make, what kind of health and medical care you receive, whether in fact you *live* or *die*—are, like it or not, determined by race.

There is little doubt that it will be generations before minorities are no longer seen as peoples of color, and white people as white. When all people, regardless of skin color, have equal opportunities to achieve a meaningful education, to hold gainful and rewarding employment, to receive caring, professional medical care, and to live in secure and comfortable housing, those color barriers will collapse.

NOTES

1. For a detailed discussion of how these "official" statistics are replete with inaccuracies, limitations, and biases, see Mann (1993).

2. A comparison of *within-group* arrests reveals little variation in patterns of offending for the five racial/ethnic subgroups. For a detailed explanation of these patterns, see Mann, 1993.

3. For an in-depth discussion of these perspectives, see Mann, *Unequal Justice: A Question of Color* (1993).

4. Asian-Americans earn more than whites. In 1990, for example, the Asian-American median household income was $38,450 compared to $31,231 earned by whites.

5. There were 26 African-American (5.9 percent), 11 Hispanic Americans (2.5 percent), and one Asian-American from Hawaii. Four of the Hispanics were from Texas, three represented California, and there was one each from Florida, New Mexico, New York, and the lone woman legislator was from Arizona.

6. Sincere thanks are extended to Professor Leroy Rieselbach, Department of political science, Indiana University, for these data.

7. See, for example, *The National Black Agenda for the '80s*, Washington, D.C.: Joint Center for Political Studies, 1980.

REFERENCES

Barrow, L. C. 1992. "Helping Us or Just Helping Themselves." *Crisis 100 (5):26–28, 48, 69–70*.

Belenko, S., and J. Fagan. 1987. *Crack and the Criminal Justice System*. New York: New York City Criminal Justice Agency.

Bell, D. 1987. *And We Are Not Saved*. New York: Basic Books.

Billingsley, A. 1968. *Black Families in White America*. New York: Prentice-Hall.

Blau, P. M., and J. R. Blau. 1982. "The Cost of Inequality: Metropolitan Structure and Violent Crime." *American Sociological Review* 47 (1):114–29.

Braithwaite, J. 1981. "The Myth of Social Class and Criminality Reconsidered." *American Sociological Review* 46 (1):36–57.

Braithwaite, J. 1992. "Poverty, Power and White-Collar Crime: Sutherland and the Paradoxes of Criminological Theory." In K. Schlegel, *Edwin Sutherland Conference on White-Collar Crime: 50 Years of Research and Beyond*. Bloomington: Indiana University Press.

Carroll, L., and P. I. Jackson. 1983. "Inequality, Opportunity, and Crime Rates in Central Cities." *Criminology* 21 (2):178–94.

Chilton, R. J., and G. E. Markle. 1972. "Family Disruption, Delinquent Conduct and the Effect of Subclassification," *American Sociological Review* 37 (February): 93–99.

Chiricos, T. G. 1987. "Rates of Crime and Unemployment; An Analysis of Aggregate Research Evidence." *Social Problems* 34:187–212.

Cole, Beverly. 1991. "The School Reform of the Eighties and Its Implications for the Restructuring of the Nineties." *The Crisis* 98 (8):23–26, 47.

Cummings, H., and M. Harrison. 1972. "The American Indian: The Poverty of Assimilation." *Antipode* 4 (2):77–87.

Deloria, V. 1981. "Native American: The American Indian Today." *The Annals* 454 (March): 139–49.

Duster, T. 1987. "Crime, Youth Unemployment, and the Black Urban Underclass." *Crime and Delinquency* 33 (2):300–316.

Fitzpatrick, J. P., and L. T. Parker. 1981. "Hispanic-Americans in the Eastern U.S." *The Annals* 454 (March):98–110

Georges-Abeyie, D. E. 1990. "Criminal Justice Processing of Non-White Minorities." In B. D. MacLean and D. Milovanovic (eds.), *Racism, Empiricism and Criminal Justice*. Vancouver, Canada: Collective Press.

Glueck, S., and E. T. Glueck. 1950. *Unraveling Juvenile Delinquency*. New York: Commonwealth Fund.

Green, E. 1970. "Race, Social Status and Criminal Arrest." *American Sociological Review* 35:476–90.

Hatchett, D. 1992. "Harassment of Black Politicians." *Crisis* 100 (5):49–50, 54–56.

Headley, B. D. 1990. "What Really Lies Behind the Myth of 'No Discrimination' in the Criminal Justice System." In B. D. MacLean and D. Milovanovic (eds.), *Racism, Empiricism and Criminal Justice*. Vancouver, Canada: Collective Press.

Heckler, M. M. 1985. *Black and Minority Health*. Washington, D.C.: U.S. Government Printing Office.

Herald-Times [Bloomington, Indiana]. 1991. "Earnings disparity divides whites, blacks, report says." September 20:A6.

Herald-Times [Bloomington, Indiana]. 1991. "One of seven Americans in poverty." September 27:1.

Herald-Times [Bloomington, Indiana]. 1992. "Number of children in poverty increased in '80s." July 8:A4

Herbers J. 1983. "Economic Equality Eludes Blacks." *Tallahassee (Florida) Democrat*. July 24:1.

Hill, R. 1972. *The Strengths of Black Families*. New York: Emerson-Hall.

Jacobs, D. 1981. "Inequality and Economic Crime." *Sociology and Social Research* 66 (October):12–28.

Joint Center for Political and Economic Studies. 1991. *Black Elected Officials: A National Roster.* Washington, D.C.: Joint Center for Political and Economic Studies.

Kitano, H. L. 1981. "Asian-Americans; the Chinese, Japanese, Koreans, Filipinos, and Southeast Asians." *The Annals* 454 (March):125–38.

Krahn, H., T. F. Hartnagel, and J. W. Gartrell. 1986. "Income Inequality and Homicide Rates: Cross-National Data and Criminological Theories." *Criminology* 24 (2):495–504.

López-Rivera, O. 1989. "Who is the Terrorist? The Making of a Puerto Rican Freedom Fighter." *Social Justice* 16 (4):162–74.

Mann, C. R. 1993. *Unequal Justice: A Question of Color.* Bloomington: Indiana University Press.

Mann, C. R., and V. LaPoint, 1987. "Research Issues Relating to the Causes of Social Deviance and Violence Among Black Populations." In R. L. Hampton (ed.), *Violence in the Black Family.* Lexington, Mass.: Lexington Books.

Marrett, C. B. 1980. "The Precariousness of Social Class in America." *Contemporary Sociology* 9 (January): 16–19.

Martinez, A. D. 1992. *Who's Who: Chicano Office Holders 1992–94.* Silver City, N. Mex.: A. D. Martinez.

Mauer, M. 1990. *Young Black Men and the Criminal Justice System: A Growing National Problem.* Washington, D.C.: Sentencing Project.

McCord, J., McCord, W., and E. Thurber. 1962. "Some Effects of Paternal Absence on Male Children." *Journal of Abnormal and Social Psychology* 64 (May):361–69.

McGarrell, E. F., and T. J. Flanagan. 1987. "Measuring and Explaining Legislator Crime Control Ideology." *Journal of Research in Crime and Delinquency* 24 (2):102–18.

Messner, S. 1983. "Regional Differences in the Economic Correlates of the Urban Homicide Rate: Some Evidence on the Importance of Cultural Context." *Criminology* 21 (4):477–88.

Messner, S., and K. Tardiff. 1986. "Economic Inequality and Levels of Homicide: An Analysis of Urban Neighborhoods." *Criminology* 24 (2):297–317.

Mizio, E. 1979. *Puerto Rican Task Force Report.* New York: Family Service Association of America.

Moore, J. W. 1973. "Social Constraints on Sociological Knowledge: Academics and Research Concerning Minorities." *Social Problems* 21 (summer).

Moynihan, D. 1965. *The Negro Family: The Case for National Action.* Washington, D.C.: U.S. Department of Labor.

National Minority Advisory Council on Criminal Justice. 1980. *The Inequality of Justice.* Washington, D.C.: U.S. Department of Justice.

Nelson, A. J. 1991. *Emerging Influentials in State Legislatures: Women, Blacks, and Hispanics.* New York: Praeger.

O'Hare, W. P., and J. C. Felt. 1991. *Asian Americans: America's Fastest Growing Minority Group.* Washington, D.C.: Population Reference Bureau, Inc.

Oliver, M. L., and M. A. Glick. 1982. "An Analysis of the New Orthodoxy on Black Mobility." *Social Problems* 29 (5):511–23.

Pettigrew, T. F. 1980. "The Changing-Not Declining-Significance of Race." *Contemporary Sociology* 9 (January): 19–21.

Platt, T. 1978. "Street Crime—A View From the Left." *Crime and Social Justice* 9 (spring/summer):26–34.

Reich, C. 1973. "The Law and the Corporate State." In W. J. Chambliss (ed.), *Sociological Readings in the Conflict Perspective.* Reading, Mass.; Addison-Wesley.

Ringer, B. B., and E. R. Lawless. 1989. *Race-Ethnicity and Society.* New York: Routledge.

Sampson, R. J. 1985. "Race and Criminal Violence: A Demographically Disaggregated Analysis of Urban Homicide." *Crime and Delinquency* 31 (1):47–82.

———. 1987. "Urban Black Violence: The Effect of Male Joblessness and Family Disruption." *American Journal of Sociology* 93 (2):348–82.

Sissons, P. L. 1979. *The Hispanic Experience of Criminal Justice.* Bronx, New York: Hispanic Research Center, Fordham University.

Sowell, T. 1981. *Ethnic America: A History.* New York: Basic Books.

Staples, R. 1973. "The Myth of the Black Matriarchy." In H. L. Kitano (ed.), *Race Relations.* Cambridge: Winthrop Publishing.

Steele, S. 1991. *The Content of Our Character.* New York: HarperCollins.

Takagi, P. 1981. "Race, Crime, and Social Policy: A Minority Perspective." *Crime and Delinquency* 27 (1):48–63.

Takaki, R. 1987. *From Different Shores: Perspectives on Race and Ethnicity in America.* New York: Oxford University Press.

———. (1989). *Strangers From a Different Shore: A History of Asian Americans.* Boston: Little, Brown.

Taylor, D. L. (1993). *The Positive Influence of Bonding in Female-Headed African American Families.* New York: Garland Publishing.

Tittle, C. R., Villemez, W. J., and D. A. Smith. 1978. "The Myth of Social Class and Criminality: An Empirical Assessment of the Empirical Evidence." *American Sociological Review* 43 (5):643–56.

U.S. Census. 1980. *Statistical Abstracts of the United States, 1980.* Washington, D.C.: U.S. Government Printing Office.

U.S. Commission on Civil Rights. 1975. *The Southwest Indian Report.* Washington, D.C.: U.S. Government Printing Office.

U.S. Department of Commerce. 1990. *Statistical Abstract of the United States, 1990.* Washington, D.C.: U.S. Government Printing Office.

U.S. Department of Justice. 1987. *Crime in the United States, 1986.* Washington, D.C.: U.S. Government Printing Office.

U.S. National Commission on Excellence in Education. 1984. *A Nation at Risk: The Full Account.* Cambridge, Mass.: USA Research.

Valdivieso, R., and C. Davis. 1988. *U.S. Hispanics: Challenging Issues for the 1990s.* Washington, D.C.: Population Reference Bureau.

Walker, S. 1985. *Sense and Nonsense about Crime: A Policy Guide.* Monterey, Calif.: Brooks/Cole.

Washington Post. 1988. January 14:A28.

Williams, J. E., and K. A. Holmes. 1979. *Rape: The Public View—The Personal Experience.* Washington, D.C.: U.S. Government Printing Office.

Wilson, W. J. 1978. *The Declining Significance of Race: Blacks and Changing American Institutions.* Chicago: University of Chicago Press.

———. 1987. *The Truly Disadvantaged: The Inner City, the Underclass, and Public Policy.* Chicago: University of Chicago Press.

THEODORE G. CHIRICOS
CHARLES CRAWFORD

13

Race and Imprisonment: A Contextual Assessment of the Evidence

African-American men comprise less than 6 percent of the American population and almost one-half of its criminal prisoners (Miller, 1992:6).[1] Black men in this country are incarcerated at a rate—3,109 per 100,000—that is seven times higher than the rate for the United States as a whole, and four times higher than comparable rates in South Africa (Mauer, 1991:4). In some American cities, approximately half of all young (18–35) black men are either in prison or jail, on probation, parole, or bail, or sought in a search warrant (Miller, 1992).

Why are African-American men so disproportionately incarcerated? Three answers—not always mutually exclusive—have most often been given. Black men, it is argued, are either (1) more likely to commit crimes that lead to incarceration (Hindelang, 1978; Cohen and Kluegel, 1978); or (2) more likely arrested and involved in the process that may lead to incarceration (Blumstein, 1982); or (3) more often sentenced to prison upon conviction.

This chapter addresses the last of these possibilities. We provide a systematic review of thirty-eight empirical studies published since 1975 that report evidence of the direct effect of race on sentencing outcomes in noncapital cases. Unlike previous reviews, we make a careful distinction between the decision to incarcerate and decisions of sentence length. More important, we systematically[2] identify several *structural contexts* that may specify the race and imprisonment relationship. In this regard, we follow the strategy suggested by Hagan and Bumiller to study "those structural and con-

textual conditions that are most likely to result in racial discrimination''
(1983:21).

Specifically, we examine the possibility that the impact of race will be
stronger in southern jurisdictions, in places where there is a higher percentage of Blacks in the population or a higher concentration of Blacks in urban
areas, and in places with a higher rate of unemployment.

PREVIOUS REVIEWS OF RACE AND SENTENCING

John Hagan (1974) reviewed the findings of nineteen studies published
between 1928 and 1969. For each, he computed a common measure of association (tau-b) and statistical significance (chi-square). Hagan distinguished
between capital and noncapital cases, and between studies that did and did
not control for prior record. He did not, however, distinguish between incarceration and sentence length as an outcome for noncapital crimes. Hagan
summarized his findings:

> Evidence of differential sentencing was found in interracial *capital
> cases* in the southern United States. In samples of *non-capital cases*,
> however, when offense type was held constant among offenders with no
> prior record, the relationship between race and disposition was dimin-
> ished below statistical significance. (1974:378)

While Hagan included race among several *extralegal* factors potentially
related to sentencing, Gary Kleck's (1981) review was the first to focus exclusively on the impact of race. He examined the results of nineteen studies
of the death penalty published between 1940 and 1975, and forty studies of
noncapital sentencing published between 1935 and 1979. Like Hagan, Kleck
distinguished between studies that did and did not control for prior record.
Also like Hagan, he did not systematically distinguish in/out from sentence
length results for noncapital outcomes.

Concerning capital punishment, Kleck concluded that ''the death penalty has not been imposed in a discriminatory fashion toward Blacks except
in the south'' (1981:798). For noncapital sentencing he concluded that when
prior record was taken into account ''the evidence is largely contrary to a
hypothesis of general or widespread discrimination against Black defendants'' (1981:799).[3]

Under the auspices of the National Academy of Sciences, Hagan and
Bumiller (1983) compared race and sentencing research that used data prior
to and after 1969. Their findings showed that later studies were more likely

to control for crime (seriousness or type) and prior record. In addition, these later studies were almost twice as likely as earlier studies (50 percent versus 27 percent) to find evidence of a nonspurious and statistically significant racial disparity in sentencing.[4]

While Hagan and Bumiller did not distinguish between incarceration (in/out) and sentence length decisions, they did carefully describe the characteristics of research that reported evidence of racial differences. They concluded that each of these studies employed methodologies specifying "structural contexts in which discrimination by race is most likely to occur."[5] They noted "the emergence of what we have called a structural-contextual approach in sentencing research" (1983:31). It is this approach that we have systematically taken in the assessment of research evidence reported below.

Marjorie Zatz (1987) undertook a review of "racial/ethnic biases in sentencing" that effectively used *historical* context as a basis for distinguishing research approaches and findings. She described four *waves* of research that were characterized first by increasing methodological sophistication, and in addition by social and political conditions that provided a context for the research.

With respect to the latter, Zatz noted that wave I (1930s to mid-1960s) "preceded the major gains of the civil rights movements" (1987:71). Waves II and III (1960s to 1970s data) followed "in the wake of the civil rights movement" and were characterized by "increased fears of urban street crime and high rates of unemployment" (1987:73). Wave IV (late 1970s to 1980s) followed "the initiation of a policy change to determinate sentencing" (1987:78).

The discussion of research findings did not systematically distinguish between in/out and sentence length, and is briefly summarized as follows:

> Research conducted through the mid-1960s (Wave I) indicated some overt discrimination against minority defendants. Reanalyses of these studies during the late 1960's and 1970's (Wave II) concluded that with the exception of the use of the death penalty in the South, findings of discrimination were an artifact of poor research designs and analyses. . . . A third wave of research . . . published in the late 1970's and 1980's using data from the late 1960's and 1970's . . . benefited from advances in research design and analytic techniques and indicated that both overt and more subtle forms of bias . . . *did* occur, at least in some social contexts. . . . The fourth wave of studies begun in the early 1980's and relying on data from states following determinate sentencing guidelines . . . show subtle, if no longer overt bias against minority defendants. (1987:70)

The Myth of a Racist Criminal Justice System is the title of William Wilbank's (1987) assessment of the role of race in everything from police deployment and arrest through sentencing and parole. His conclusion is effectively summarized by his title. In the chapter on sentencing, Wilbanks distinguished seven "models of analysis and interpretation" within sentencing research literature, and provided exemplars and assessments of each. His objective in describing these varied models was to illustrate "how different research methods and interpretations lead to difficult conclusions" (1987:119).

Despite these differences, Wilbanks determined that several findings are "generally valid across the literature" (1987:119). Important among these are that "extralegal variables (for example, race . . .) are not as predictive of sentence as legal variables" (1987:120) and "the Black/White variation in sentences is generally reduced to near zero" with legal controls (1987:120).

Wilbanks did not distinguish in/out from sentence-length findings, and unlike Hagan and Bumiller (1983) and Zatz (1987) he did not conclude that race had a contextual impact. However, context was not altogether absent from his review, as in his assertion that the meaning given to research findings is "largely a function of the model of analysis and interpretation chosen" (1987:119). Similarly, Wilbanks's conclusion that race "does not have a consistent impact across crimes and jurisdictions" (1987:119) and that "discrimination in sentencing has declined over time" (1987:119) are both clearly contextual.[6] However, the absence of *consistent* evidence of a race effect was used to support "the myth of a racist criminal justice system" rather than as an indicator of a potentially contextual relationship.

In sum, previous reviews of the link between race and imprisonment have not established a clear and convincing pattern within available evidence. Some have concluded that race does not impact incarceration once legal variables have been effectively controlled for. Others have asserted that the inconsistency in findings offers clues to the contextual character of possible race effects (Hagan and Bumiller, 1983; Zatz, 1987). While several reviewers have distinguished between capital and noncapital punishments, none have distinguished between in/out and length of sentence findings.

RACE AND IMPRISONMENT: SPECIFYING CONTEXTUAL ISSUES

The present review not only extends the time frame for the assessment of research findings into the 1990s, but it distinguishes results involving in/out decisions from those involving length of sentence. In addition, we follow the lead of Hagan and Bumiller (1983) and *systematically* consider whether the impact of race is effected by several structural contexts that characterize the time and place of the various studies reviewed. Specifically, we examine whether results are different in southern as opposed to nonsouthern venues, in places with different racial and racial/urban compositions, and in places with different levels of unemployment.

Several other contextual factors have been discussed in the race/punishment literature, but are *not* examined here for varying reasons. For example, Blumstein (1982) demonstrated that *type of crime* was substantially relevant to the amount of racial disproportionality in imprisonment that could be accounted for by racial differences at arrest.[7] The importance of crime-type was also discussed at length by Hawkins (1987:728–31). Unfortunately, too few of the studies reviewed here afford sufficient information about crime type to be included in the kind of contextual disaggregation we describe below.

Victim's race is another contextual factor that has been shown to bear upon the race/incarceration relationship (Kleck, 1981; LaFree, 1980; Peterson and Hagan, 1984). As Hawkins (1987:726) notes, "offenses against whites are said to be more severely punished than those against Blacks regardless of the race of the offender." Much of the evidence for this issue has been generated by studies of capital offenses, which are not the subject of the current review. Moreover, the 38 studies reviewed here provide insufficient detail concerning victims to allow a contextual assessment.

The *urban/rural* context of sentencing is another contextual factor that has received notable attention in the race/punishment literature. A number of researchers have found racial differences more pronounced in rural courts (Austin, 1981; Hagan, 1977; Pope, 1976). But Myers and Talarico (1986b) report that for their data, risks of incarceration are increased for blacks in an urban context. Because much of the research reviewed here is reported for cities or states that are dominated by urban areas (California, Florida, Maryland, Pennsylvania) urban/rural variation was inadequate for our purposes.

Of the three contextual factors that *are* examined in this review, one (south/nonsouth) has been widely discussed in relation to race and sentencing; another (racial composition) has received some attention, and the third (unemployment) has been generally overlooked.

The contextual importance of *region* (south versus nonsouth) has been variously described. On the one hand, Hagan (1974) and Kleck (1981) have indicated that the only evidence of discrimination in the death penalty has been confined to the south. At the same time, it is increasingly clear that rates of incarceration for blacks are higher in northern as opposed to southern states (Bridges and Crutchfield, 1988; Hawkins and Hardy, 1989; Sabol, 1989).

Thus, Hawkins describes the general expectation "that the overall level for punishment will be higher in the South" while at the same time noting "it is also said that leniency (the underpunishment of Blacks . . .) occurs mainly in the more paternalistic South'' (1987:732). The former expectation is attributed by some to "northern tolerance" or "southern bigotry," while the latter is linked to "southern paternalism" or "northern racial egalitarianism" (Hawkins, 1987:731).

Racial composition, or more specifically, the relative size and distribution of minority populations, is another context that has been assumed relevant for the exercise of social control (Blauner, 1972; Turk, 1969). Several researchers (Michalowski and Pearson, 1990; Nagel, 1982) have shown that state rates of incarceration are associated with higher percentages of African-Americans in the states. Others have used Blalock's (1967) power-threat thesis to link *percent black in city populations* to police expenditures (Jackson, 1989) and overall rates of arrest (Liska 1992).[8]

However, direct application of this issue to the matter of postarrest processing has been limited. Bridges and Crutchfield (1988) have shown that states with *higher* percentages of black population have *lower* racial disparities in imprisonment. Similarly, Hawkins and Hardy (1989) found that states with relatively *smaller* black populations had *more* racial disproportionality at incarceration that could not be accounted for by differences in arrest (1989:86–87).

The latter have suggested that *percent black* may be an inadequate operationalization of the power-threat thesis in state-level studies of imprisonment. They note the considerable disparity in *distributions* of black populations in the various states, with some (northern) having large urban concentrations and others (southern) having greater geographical dispersion. They speculate that the *percent of blacks who are urban* in a state may be a better index of the power-threat issue.[9]

Almost half (18/38) of the studies reviewed here have operationalized the issue of race and incarceration at the city or county level. It is not clear which index of racial composition would be more appropriate for our purposes, so we make use of both *percent black* and *percent of black population that is urban* in our assessment of research findings. The former is measured for the specific geographic aggregation of each study and the latter is measured for *states* in each instance.

The relevance of *unemployment* as a possible contextual factor in relation to race and punishment is underscored by several considerations. The first is a growing awareness that unemployment and race are connected in ways that have literally come to define what Wilson (1987) terms an American *underclass.* Indeed, with unemployment rates of 30 and 40 percent in some cities, young black men may have become what Melossi (1989:317) calls a "privileged target group for imprisonment" in this country.

In this regard, Chiricos and Bales (1991) have shown that the *interaction* of race and unemployment significantly increased the chances of incarceration for both black and unemployed defendants, especially if they were young and male. Myers and Talarico found that in communities "where unemployment is pronounced . . . young Blacks are the most likely to be incarcerated" (1987:64).

The rationale for unemployment amplifying the impact of race on punishment has two possible bases. First, high levels of unemployment likely increase economic competition, which can foster perceptions of interracial threat and become a source of prejudice and discrimination (Blalock, 1967). In addition, high levels of unemployment may promote a diffuse anxiety or concern for order that several have suggested will amplify punitive rhetoric and popular demands for *getting tough* on criminals and *dangerous* people (Box and Hale, 1982, 1985; Melossi, 1989).

RACE AND INCARCERATION: ASSESSING THE EVIDENCE

Thirty-eight studies published since 1975 with empirical evidence on the race and imprisonment relationship are reviewed here.[10] We have included every available study using individual level data except those involving federal or military courts. The latter were excluded because our analysis disaggregates the research findings by region, unemployment rate, percent black and percent black/urban in the *place* where the research was done.

The studies were identified in a systematic search of criminology and sociology journals, abstracts, and indexes, and from the bibliographies of recent works on race and punishment. Only studies that report a measure of association between race and incarceration are included. Some of the studies are not primarily concerned with the question of race, but include measures of the relationship between race and incarceration.

Table 13.1 describes the methodology and principle findings of the studies reviewed here. The studies are listed in reverse chronological order, starting with the most recent. For each study, the first eleven columns of Table 13.1 describe: (1) author(s); (2) data year(s); (3) place studied; (4) sample characteristics; (5) controls for prior record; (6) controls for crime seriousness; (7) percent black in the place studied; (8) percent of blacks who are urban in the state studied, (9) unemployment rate in the place studied; (10) number of independent variables including race involved in the equation for which the results are reported and (11) the estimation technique used.[11]

The last two columns report on the net relationship between race and (12) incarceration (in/out) and between race and (13) length of incarceration. For each specific estimate we indicate whether that relationship is positive ($+$) or negative ($-$), and whether the relationship is statistically significant (a) after the effects of other variables are controlled.[12]

TABLE 13.1 Methodologies and Findings: Individual Studies of Race and Imprisonment

| | Data | | | Prior | Crime Serious- | Percent | Percent Black | Unemploy- | Number Independent | Estimating | Depend Variable | Depend Variable |
| 1 | 2 | 3 | 4 | 5 | 6 | 7 | 8 | 9 | 10 | 11 | 12 | 13 |
Study/Year	Year	Place	Sample	Record	ness	Black	Urban	ment Level	Variables	Technique	In/Out	SL
Chiricos & Bales 1991	1982	Florida	1431 Fel, Mis	Yes	Yes	13.8	89	8.2	10	Logit	(+)	
			233 Pub Ord	Yes	Yes				10	Logit	(−)	
			169 Drug	Yes	Yes				10	Logit	(+)	
			691 Prop	Yes	Yes				10	Logit	(+)	
			348 Violent	Yes	Yes				10	Logit	(+)	
			1219 Males	Yes	Yes				10	Logit	(+)[a]	
			628 Y Males	Yes	Yes				10	Logit	(+)[a]	
Unnever & Hembroff 1988	1971	Miami	313 Males, D	Yes	Yes	22.8	83	6.9	8	Logit	(+)[a]	
				No	No				1	PMr	(+)[a]	
Humphrey & Fogarty 1987	1978	6 Munic. Areas	3149 Males, Burg	Yes	No				6	Logit	(+)[a]	
				Yes	No				6	Logit	(+)	
Myers & Talarico 1987	1976–83	Ga. Counties	27702 Fel	No	Yes	26.7	73	6.7	16	OLS	(+)[a]	
			5039 Fel	Yes	Yes				21	OLS	(+)	
			4287 Fel	Yes	Yes				21	OLS	(−)	
			27613 Fel	Yes	Yes				27	OLS	(+)[a]	
			4271 Fel	Yes	Yes				32	OLS		(+)
			5022 Fel	Yes	Yes				32	OLS		(+)[a]
Myers 1987	1976–82	Georgia	15270 Fel	No	Yes	26.7	73	6.6	19	OLS	(+)[a]	
	1976–82	Georgia	3792 Inmates	Yes	Yes				23	OLS		(−)[a]

Study	Years	Jurisdiction	Sample						N	Method		
Miethe & Moore 1986	1977–78	Minnes	1659 Fel	Yes	Yes	1.0	98.0	4.5	14	OLS	(−)	
				Yes	Yes				15	OLS	(+)	
Myers & Talarico 1986a	1982	Georgia	16798 Fel	Yes	Yes				19	WLS		(−)[a]
Myers & Talarico 1986b	1976–82	Georgia	18404 Fel	No	Yes	26.7	73	6.6	12	WLS	(+)[a]	
			18007 Fel	No	Yes				19	WLS	(+)[a]	
			3407 Fel	Yes	Yes				19	WLS		(−)[a]
			3398 Fel	Yes	Yes				26	WLS		(−)[a]
Moore & Miethe 1986	1980–81	Minnes	1523 Fel	Yes	Yes	1.0	99.0	3.8	20	OLS	(+)	
			732 Fel	Yes	Yes				21	OLS		(−)
Kempf & Austin 1986	1977	Penn.	2907	No	No	8.7	98	7.7	1	PMr	(+)	
			2907	No	No				1	PMr	(+)	(+)
			2907	Yes	Yes				9	MR	(+)[a]	(−)
			1179 Rur	Yes	Yes				9	Logit	(+)	(−)
			257 Sub	Yes	Yes				9	Logit		(−)
			1142 Urban	Yes	Yes				9	Logit		(−)
Zatz & Hagan 1985	1977–79	California	460 NoPr/Pri	Yes	Yes				21	MLR	(+)	(+)
			6138 NoPr/Co	Yes	Yes				21	MLR	(−)	(−)
			9678 NoPr/Pro	Yes	Yes				21	MLR	(−)	(−)
			664 Pr/Pri	Yes	Yes				20	MLR	(+)	(+)
			3444 Pr/Co	Yes	Yes				21	MLR	(+)	(+)
			6544 Pr/Pro	Yes	Yes				22	MLR	(+)	(+)

(continued)

TABLE 13.1 continued

1	2	3	4	5	6	7	8	9	10	11	12	13
Study/Year	Data Year	Place	Sample	Prior Record	Crime Seriousness	Percent Black	Percent Black Urban	Unemployment Level	Number Independent Variables	Estimating Technique	Depend Variable In/Out	Depend Variable SL
Welch et al. 1985	1975–77	El Paso		Yes	Yes	3		7.6	9	OLS	(+)[a]	(+)
		Tucson		Yes	Yes	3.7		6.3	9	OLS	(+)	(−)
		New Orl.		Yes	Yes	54.7		6.8	9	OLS	(+)[a]	(+)
		Norfolk Va		Yes	Yes	34.9		7.5	9	OLS	(+)[a]	(+)
		Del Cty, Pa		Yes	Yes	9		5.7	9	OLS	(+)	(−)
		Seattle		Yes	Yes	9.4		5.7	9	OLS	(+)	(−)
Miethe & Moore 1985	1978	Minnes	1226 Fel1	Yes	Yes	1.0	98.0	3.8	16	OLS	(+)[a]	(−)
			1280 Fel2	Yes	Yes				16	OLS	(−)	(−)
Zatz 1984	1978	California	4729 Fel	Yes	Yes				24	OLS		(−)
Jendrek 1984	1978	Maryland	412 Fel	Yes	Yes				1	PMr	(+)	(+)
			412 Fel	Yes	Yes				6	MR	(−)	(−)
			412 Fel	Yes	Yes				10	MR	(+)[a]	(+)[a]
Peterson & Hagan 1984	1963–76	N.Y. City				18.4	98					
	63–68		Unsp Drug Con	Yes	Yes			4.3	15	Probit	(−)[a]	
	67–73		Unsp Drug Con	Yes	Yes			4.4	22	Probit	(−)	
	74–76		Unsp Drug Con	Yes	Yes			8.9	21	Probit	(−)[a]	
	63–68		Unsp Drug Con	Yes	Yes				16	OLS		(−)[a]
	67–73		Unsp Drug Con	Yes	Yes				23	OLS		(−)[a]

Study	Location	Period	Sample						N	Method		
		74–76	Unsp Drug Con	Yes	Yes				22	OLS		(−)[a]
			53 NW Big Del	No	Yes				6	OLS		(+)
			2052 Nw	No	Yes				6	OLS		(−)[a]
			Ord D									
Zimmerman Frederick 1984	NY	1980										
			6078 N.Y.C.	Yes	Yes	25.3	98	8.0	15	Logit	(+)	(+)[a]
			3285 Upstate	Yes	Yes				14	Logit	(+)[a]	(+)[a]
			1735 Suburban	Yes	Yes				14	Logit	(+)[a]	(+)
Petersillia 1983	Los Angel	1980	2198 Rob	Yes	Yes	17.0	98.0	10.4	18	MR	(+)[a]	
	California	1978	342 Inmates	Yes	Yes				16	MR		(+)
	Michigan	1978	346 Inmates	Yes	Yes				15	MR		(+)[a]
	Texas	1978	526 Inmates	Yes	Yes				15	MR		(+)
Pruitt & Wilson 1983	Milwaukee	1967–76				15.4	97					
		67–68	502 Rob/Bur	Yes	Yes			2.8	11	Probit	(+)[a]	
		71–72	524 Rob/Bur	Yes	Yes			4.8	12	Probit	(−)	
		76–77	486 Rob/Bur	Yes	Yes			4.9	12	Probit	(−)	
		67–68	502 Rob	Yes	Yes				12	OLS		(+)[a]
		71–72	524 Rob	Yes	Yes				13	OLS		(−)
		76–77	486 Rob	Yes	Yes				13	OLS		(−)
		67–68	502 Bur	Yes	Yes				12	OLS		(+)[a]
		71–72	524 Bur	Yes	Yes				13	OLS		(−)
		76–77	486 Bur	Yes	Yes				13	OLS		(+)
Unnever 1982	Miami	1971	313 Males, Drug	No	No	22.7	83	6.9	1	PMr	(+)[a]	
				Yes	Yes				11	Logit	(+)[a]	

(continued)

TABLE 13.1 continued

1 Study/Year	2 Data Year	3 Place	4 Sample	5 Prior Record	6 Crime Serious-ness	7 Percent Black	8 Percent Black Urban	9 Unemploy-ment Level	10 Number Independent Variables	11 Estimating Technique	12 Depend Variable In/Out	13 Depend Variable SL
Frazier & Bock 1982	1972–73	Florida	309 Fel	No	No	14.8	84	4.7	1	r	(+)[a]	
			245 Fel	Yes	Yes				10	OLS	(+)	
Thompson & Zingraff 1981	1969	Southeast		Yes	Yes				3	CHI		(−)
	1973	State		Yes	Yes				3	CHI		(+)
	1977			Yes	Yes				3	CHI		(+)[a]
Austin 1981	1975–76	Iowa	234 Rur Fel	I Yes	Yes	1.3	98	3.9	5	MR	(+)[a]	
			437 Sub Fel	I Yes	Yes				5	MR	(+)[a]	
			991 Urb Fel	I Yes	Yes				5	MR	(+)	
Spohn et al. 1982	1968–79	Metro city	2366 Fel Male	No	No	33.5	98	11.1	1	PMr	(+)[a]	(+)[a]
				Yes	Yes				3	PA	(+)[a]	(+)
				Yes	Yes				8	PA	(+)[a]	(+)
Unnever et al. 1980	1972–73	Florida	229 Fel	Yes	Yes	14.8		4.7	9	Logit	(+)[a]	
Lafree 1980	1970–75	Metro City	30 B/W Rape	No	Yes	18.9	97	5.3	1	Pmr	(+)[a]	(+)[a]
			30 B/W Rape	Yes	Yes				3	Step MR	(+)	(+)[a]
			37 B/B Rape	No	Yes				1	Pmr	(−)	(−)
			37 B/B Rape	Yes	Yes				3	Step MR	(NS)	(NS)

Study	Years	Location	Sample						n	Method		
Kruttischnitt 1980	1972–76	California	87 Fel Pub Ord	Yes	Yes				11	MR		(+)[a]
			111 Fel Assault	Yes	Yes				11	MR		(+)
			271 Fel Theft	Yes	Yes				12	MR		(−)
			205 Fel Forgery	Yes	Yes				11	MR		(+)[a]
			301 Fel Drug	Yes	Yes				12	MR		(+)[a]
Myers 1979	1974–76	Marion City, IN	205 Fel	Yes	Yes	19.9		5.7	21	Reg	(NS)	
Farrell & Swigert 1978	1955–73	Northeast City	444 Murder	No	No				1	PMr		(+)[a]
Lizotte 1978	1971	Chicago	431 Fel	Yes	Yes				1	PMr		(+)
			192	Yes	Yes				6	OLS		(+)
Uhlman 1977	1968–74	Northeast City	32,731 Fel, Male	No	No				1	PMr		(+)[a]
			32,731 Fel, Male	No	Yes				7	MR		(+)[a]
Hagan 1977	1973	Alberta Canada	265 Rural	No	No	1.4		5.6	1	r	(+)[a]	
			241 Urban	No	No				1	r	(+)[a]	
Bernstein et al. 1977	1974–75	City in NY	1,213	No	No				1	PMr		(−)
				Yes	Yes				8	MR		(−)
Rhodes 1977	1970	Minneapo	332 Drug	No	Yes	4.3	97	3.8	3	OLS	(+)	
			196 Bur	No	Yes				3	OLS	(+)[a]	
			154 Lar	No	Yes				3	OLS	(+)	

(continued)

TABLE 13.1 *continued*

	2	3	4	5	6	7	8	9	10	11	12	13
1	*Data*			*Prior*	*Crime Serious-*	*Percent*	*Percent Black*	*Unemploy-*	*Number Independent*	*Estimating*	*Depend Variable*	*Variable*
Study/Year	*Year*	*Place*	*Sample*	*Record*	*ness*	*Black*	*Urban*	*ment Level*	*Variables*	*Technique*	*In/Out*	*SL*
		St. Paul	89 Drug	No	Yes				3	OLS	(+)[a]	
			125 Bur	No	Yes	3.5		3.6	3	OLS	(+)	
			154 Lar	No	Yes				3	OLS	(+)[a]	
Kelly 1976	1974	Oklahoma	385 Bur	Yes	Yes				6	MR		(+)[a]
			356 Murder	No	Yes				6	MR		(NS)
Clarke & Koch 1976	1971	Meclenber Cnty, N.C.	748 Bur, Lar	No	No	30.3	49	5.2	1	PMr	(+)[a]	
Burke & Turk 1975	1964	Indianapol	3,941 Fel, Males	Yes	Yes				9	MR		(+)
Chiricos & Waldo 1975	1969–70	Florida	68 Mur	Yes	Yes				7	MR		(−)
			98 Msl	Yes	Yes				7	MR		(+)
			77 Rape	Yes	Yes				7	MR		(+)
			199 Asslt	Yes	Yes				7	MR		(+)
			437 Rob	Yes	Yes				7	MR		(+)
			606 Bur	Yes	Yes				7	MR		(−)
			235 Lar	Yes	Yes				7	MR		(−)
			67 Rsp	Yes	Yes				7	MR		(−)
			111 Auto	Yes	Yes				7	MR		(+)
			239 Forg	Yes	Yes				7	MR		(+)
			253 Drug	Yes	Yes				7	MR		(−)
			96 Esc	Yes	Yes				7	MR		(−)

In/Out	In/Out Decision
SL	Sentence Length
Fel	Felony
Mis	Misdemeanor
Pub Ord.	Public Order Offenders
Drug	Drug Offenders
Prop	Property Offenders
Violent	Violent Offenders
Assault	Aggravated Assault
Rob	Robbery
Bur.	Burglary
Rape	Rape
Lar.	Larceny
Theft	Theft
Forgery	Forgery
Males	Males
Y	Young
Pri	Prison
Con	Convict
Inm	Inmates
Msl	Manslaughter
Rsp	Receiving Stolen Property
Auto	Auto Theft
Esc	Escape

1	Pre Guideline
2	Post Guideline
B/W	Black & White
OD	Ordinary
NW	Non-white
Con	Convictions
Est.	Estimation
Tech	Technique
Ols	Ordinary Least Squares
Wis	Weighted Least Squares
PMr	Product Moment Correlation
CHI	Chi square analysis
MR	Multiple regression
Step MR	Stepwise Regression
PA	Path Analysis

a-$p < .05$ and all higher levels

TABLE 13.2   Summary of Direction and Statistical Significance of Race and Imprisonment Findings—Thirty Eight Studies: 1975–91

	(N)	Percent Positive	Percent Positive and Significant	Percent Negative and Significant
All relationships	(145)	.68	.33	.07
In/out	(66)	.85	.52	.03
Sentence length	(79)	.54	.20	.10
Controlling for Crime				
In/out	(51)	.82	.47	.04
Sentence length	(73)	.52	.15	.11
Controlling for Priors				
In/out	(46)	.80	.41	.04
Sentence length	(66)	.53	.15	.10
Controlling Crime and Priors				
In/out	(46)	.80	.41	.04
Sentence length	(66)	.53	.15	.10

Multiple results are reported for studies involving more than one time period, more than one sample, or more than one estimation technique. For studies otherwise reporting multiple results for a particular punishment measure, only the result is reported that the author indicates is derived from the *best fitting* equation or if not so identified, from the equation with the largest number of independent variables.

As Table 13.2 shows, the 38 studies have generated 145 estimates of the race/incarceration relationship. Overall, more than two-thirds (68 percent) of those estimates are positive (disadvantageous to blacks)[14] and one-third (33 percent) are both positive and statistically significant. Because "leniency" toward black defendants has been discussed as an empirical issue of some importance (Hawkins, 1987; Kleck, 1981)[15] significant *negative* relationships—reflecting leniency toward blacks—are highly relevant. For all estimates, they occur barely more often (7 percent) than would be anticipated by chance alone, and about one-fifth as often as significant positive relationships.

More important are the distinctions between in/out decisions and those involving length of sentence. As Table 13.2 shows, blacks are disadvantaged in 85 percent of the in/out estimates, and significantly so more than half of the time. However, for sentence-length decisions it is clear that race makes much less of a difference—even though significant positive relationships (disadvantage) occur twice as often as significant negative (leniency).[16]

The most compelling finding of Table 13.2 is the consistent difference that exists between in/out results and those involving sentence length in estimates that control for crime seriousness and prior record. In each instance, the frequency of positive findings for the in/out decision is more than half again as high as for length of sentence. Whereas minority status appears almost irrelevant for sentence length, it is a disadvantage for in/out decisions 80 percent of the time, even when crime seriousness and prior record are controlled for.

When only *significant* positive findings are considered, the difference between sentence length and in/out decisions are even greater. In each comparison, the frequency of significant racial disadvantage is approximately three times greater for in/out relationships as for those involving sentence length. Moreover, significant positive findings for in/out estimates occur at least eight times more often than expected by chance and ten times as often as significant negative estimates.[17]

In short, the evidence from Table 13.2 suggests that even when prior record and crime seriousness are controlled for, race is a consistent and frequently significant disadvantage for blacks when in/out decisions are considered. At the same time, it appears that race is much less of a disadvantage when it comes to sentence length. For this reason, the remainder of our analysis, which explores the contextual nature of the race and incarceration relationship, deals only with in/out findings.

Table 13.3 displays in/out results in several structural contexts. For each context, all in/out findings are considered as well as those controlling for prior record and crime seriousness.

South versus Nonsouth

The impact of race is clearly more consistent in the south than in nonsouthern states. For all relationships, black defendants are more likely incarcerated in the south 90 percent of the time, and this disadvantage is significant 70 percent of the time. Even when legally relevant factors are controlled, in/out relationships in the south are positive 88 percent of the time and significant more than ten times as often (53 percent) as chance would predict. By contrast, nonsouth relationships are positive (76 percent) and significant positive (34 percent) appreciably less often.[18]

Put another way, after controlling for the effects of prior record and crime seriousness in the south, incarceration of black defendants is significantly more likely 53 percent of the time. However, in no instance is the incarceration of white defendants significantly more likely in the south. This suggests that the *leniency* hypothesis—which would be supported by significant negative results—is not applicable in this context.

TABLE 13.3   Imprisonment (In/Out) Findings Controlling for Characteristics of Place Being Studied

	(N)	Percent Positive	Percent Positive and Significant	Percent Negative and Significant
All Relationships				
South	(24)	.92	.70	.00
Nonsouth	(42)	.81	.43	.05
Controlling Crime and Priors				
South	(17)	.88	.53	.00
Nonsouth	(29)	.76	.34	.07
All Relationships				
High percent Black	(38)	.79	.58	.05
Low percent Black	(22)	.91	.32	.00
Controlling Crime and Priors				
High percent Black	(24)	.75	.50	.08
Low percent Black	(15)	.87	.27	.00
All Relationships				
High percent Black urban	(38)	.79	.33	.06
Low percent Black urban	(24)	.92	.67	.00
Controlling Crime and Priors				
High percent Black urban	(27)	.74	.33	.08
Low percent Black urban	(14)	.88	.50	.00
All Relationships				
Unemployment > national	(17)	.94	.59	.06
Unemployment < national	(44)	.79	.43	.03
Controlling Crime and Priors				
Unemployment > national	(12)	.92	.58	.08
Unemployment < national	(26)	.88	.38	.00

Percent Black in the Population

When places with higher and lower percentages of African-Americans in the population are compared, the results are apparently mixed.[19] If only the frequency of positive findings is considered, there is little difference between places on the basis of percent black in the population. With and without controls for prior record and crime seriousness, blacks appear slightly more disadvantaged in places where they are in the minority. But this is probably misleading, as the distribution of significant results shows.

For the more meaningful index of *significant* positive findings, the picture is reversed. For these results, it is clear that black defendants are disadvantaged much more often when the black population exceeds the national average than when it does not. The frequency of significant positive findings is approximately twice as great for places with a higher percentage of blacks in the population, even after legal factors are controlled.[20]

Indeed, results from places with a high percentage of blacks in the population show a significant disadvantage for black defendants 50 percent of the time, after legal controls are introduced. This compares to 8 percent for white defendants. These data suggest that the *power-threat* hypothesis that has been applied to police expenditures (Jackson and Carroll, 1981) and rates of arrest (Liska, 1992) might also be applicable to the decision to incarcerate.

Percent of Blacks Who Are Urban

Because approximately half of the in/out studies were conducted in places where the percentage of blacks who were urban exceeded 90 percent, that was taken as the cutting point for designating *high* versus *low* percent urban.[21] It should be noted that the highest urban concentrations of African-Americans (97–99 percent) were consistently in *nonsouthern* places, such as Minnesota, Pennsylvania, New York, Wisconsin, Iowa. Indeed, all the places classified as *low* in urban concentration of blacks were *southern*.

Thus, it is little surprise that the results for urban black context closely parallel those for the south/nonsouth comparison. Specifically, the disadvantage to black defendants, as measured by significant positive results, is approximately twice as great in places where they are *less* concentrated in urban areas than in places where they are *more* concentrated.[22] This disadvantage is ten times greater than would be expected by chance when controls are present for crime and prior record. At the same time, there are no studies with a significant indication of leniency in places where blacks are less urbanized.

This finding may indirectly support the contention that at least outside the south, *urban* context may reduce the disadvantages and inequities of race. It appears from this review that where blacks are more concentrated in urban areas, at least outside the south, race is much less often a significant predictor of incarceration after other factors are controlled.

Unemployment Rate

The relevance of unemployment is explored in the context of places that are above and below the national average (mean) of unemployment for the time period studied.[23] For studies involving state-level data, this measure is particularly crude, because both labor markets and punishment policies are probably more local than state aggregations can capture. Nevertheless, the present assessment of research findings may be considered suggestive.

Table 13.3 indicates that the disadvantage of black defendants is more consistently demonstrated for places with higher levels of unemployment. With and without controls for prior record and crime seriousness, blacks are more likely incarcerated in 90 percent of the estimates from places with high unemployment. That increased likelihood is significant almost 60 percent of the time. Evidence of leniency, as indicated by significant negative findings, occurs one-eighth to one-tenth as often in the same context.

CONCLUSIONS

This review provides a fresh look at an issue that some may have considered all but closed. Two-thirds of the studies examined here were published since Kleck's (1981) review and more than half since Hagan and Bumiller's (1983).[24] Every one of the studies published since those earlier reviews have employed controls for prior record and crime seriousness. A number have made use of Probit and Logit for estimating in/out relationships, and a number have been sensitive to the problem of *selection bias* noted by Berk (1983) and others. In short, recent research may have fewer of the limitations attributed to earlier studies of this question.

Our findings show that at the final stage of the criminal punishment process—even after all prior and *indirect* effects of race have been realized—there remains frequently significant evidence of a *direct* impact of race on imprisonment. This evidence is found *only* for in/out decisions and *not* for those involving sentence length. Moreover, the relative significance of race for the decision to incarcerate endures even after the effects of prior record and crime seriousness are controlled.[25]

Just as important, perhaps, is the lack of evidence for *leniency* toward black defendants that has been noted in earlier reviews (Kleck, 1981; Wilbanks, 1987). While not the only indicator of *leniency,* the comparative disadvantage of whites in relation to blacks is certainly central to the issue (Kleck, 1981:799).[26] In this review, for in/out decisions, whites are significantly more likely incarcerated than blacks about as often as chance would predict, and about one-tenth as often as blacks are disadvantaged by the same outcome.

In addition, this review underscores the importance of specifying *structural contexts* (Hagan and Bumiller, 1983) that may condition the effect of race on punishment. Notwithstanding the limits of our contextual indicators, and the small N's that resulted in some of the contextual categories, the differences that were found are not unexpected and make sense theoretically. We claim nothing more in this regard than the *plausibility* of the differences described and the potentially fruitful lines of inquiry that they may encourage.

We have shown that black defendants are significantly more disadvantaged than whites at the point of incarceration in the south, in places where blacks comprise a larger percentage of the population and where unemployment is relatively high. Black defendants are less disadvantaged in places where they are more concentrated in urban areas (which are also nonsouthern). There is no context in which the hypothesis of leniency toward black defendants is supported.

These specific structural contexts lend support to the premise that criminal punishment not only responds to crime, but responds as well to specific community conditions. Racial composition and unemployment are separate indicators of conditions that may be regarded as socially and politically threatening. Either alone may constitute an important ideological environment for sentencing. Together, large numbers of unemployed blacks may well compound the threat in a way that could occasion what Box (1987) and others (Cohen, 1972; Jenkins, 1992) have termed *moral panic*.

It is interesting that all the research reviewed here was conducted *prior* to the explosion of media attention given to crack cocaine in the mid-1980s. This attention has seemingly fueled a *moral panic* around the issues of unemployed young black men, drugs, and crime in urban America (Reinerman and Levine, 1989). This *panic* and the attendant fear of young black men have likely played a significant if not determining role in the greatly expanded use of prison to control drug offenders and the rapidly expanding ratio of black to white prisoners (Miller, 1992). It is not unreasonable to expect that research using data from the 1980s may be able to capture and reflect the contextual importance of crack cocaine, if not a *moral panic* about it, for the race/ imprisonment relationship.

Notwithstanding the *conclusive* assessments of reviewers such as Wilbanks (1987), there is much yet to be learned about the issue of race and imprisonment. We are past the point of simply asking whether race makes a difference. The contexts in which race may be important for incarceration are only beginning to be understood. Unfortunately, the rapid expansion of prison populations and their increasing racial imbalance, afford ample opportunity for that understanding to be advanced.

NOTES

1. Black women are also vastly overrepresented among those incarcerated, comprising 48% of females in state and federal prison at year end in 1990 (U.S. Dept. of Justice, 1992).

2. Hagan and Bumiller (1983) and Zatz (1987) raised the issue of structural contexts in their reviews and selectively applied it to studies for illustrative purposes. In the present review, specific structural contexts are applied to all eligible studies.

3. In fact, of the 23 studies that did control for prior record, only 2 were characterized as *favorable* to the discrimination thesis and 8 were *mixed*.

4. Hagan and Bumiller calculated bivariate measures of correlation between race and sentencing outcome for 31 studies and concluded that the relationship is *generally weak* (1983:32–33).

5. Among the structural contexts they describe are rural as opposed to urban settings; crimes that are more often interracial; highly politicized crimes like drug felonies; the interaction of race and class and so forth.

6. To support the conclusion about declining race effects over time, Wilbanks cited earlier reviews (Hindelang, 1969; Kleck, 1981) but not the later and explicitly contradictory conclusions of Hagan and Bumiller (1983).

7. Blumstein (1982:1274) found that almost one-half of the disproportionality for drugs, larceny, and auto theft, and one-third for burglary could *not* be accounted for by arrest patterns.

8. It is interesting to note that Jackson and Carroll (1981) report a curvilinear relationship between percent black and per capita police expenditures for 90 cities, with expenditures dropping when blacks achieved majority status.

9. The rationale is that the power-threat thesis presumes "some level of interracial interaction as a basis for the differential effects of minority population size across areas" and the relevance of state distributions of racial groups may be attenuated for "local" incarceration decisions (Hawkins and Hardy, 1989:86).

10. We chose 1975 as the starting point to encompass all research published since Hagan's (1974) seminal review.

11. Because unemployment, percent black, and percent urban black are used only for the in/out findings, they are not reported for studies that are limited to sentence length as the dependent variable.

12. In Table 13.1, a positive (+) relationship means that minority defendants were *disadvantaged* in the punishment outcome. Because of coding differences among the studies, the original research may show such a relationship with a different sign.

13. The choice of estimates with the largest number of independent variables was intended to reduce the chances that the net effect of race would be statistically significant.

14. The term *disadvantage* is meant only to convey that blacks are more likely incarcerated than whites.

15. The discovery of studies indicating "more lenient treatment of black defendants than whites" was considered by Kleck (1981:799) to be "one of the more important subsidiary findings" of his review of the race/punishment literature.

16. It can be argued that only significant relationships matter and in that case, even for the in/out estimates a significant race effect is about as unlikely as it is likely. However, because *leniency* toward blacks has been seriously considered as a possible

justice outcome in some settings and circumstances, the relative frequency of positive significant as opposed to negative significant relationships seem germane to the issue.

17. The differences in Table 13.2 between in/out and sentence length in the percentage of significant and positive findings are all statistically significant (p < .01) using Chi-square with Yates correction.

18. The difference between south and nonsouth is marginally significant for all relationships (p < .10) but not with controls.

19. In Table 13.3, places are classified as "high % black" if the percentage is higher than the mean percent black for the nation in the time period involved. Because "percent black" is consistently available only for census years, the appropriate percentages were interpolated using the census years that bracket the year(s) for a given study.

20. This difference is marginally significant (p < .10) for all relationships, but not with controls.

21. Actually every place where the percentage exceeded 90 percent was between 97 percent and 99 percent. There were only two places with an urban concentration lower than 70 percent; these were Norfolk, Virginia, at 65 percent (Welch et al., 1985) and Mecklenberg County, North Carolina, at 49 percent (Clarke and Koch, 1976). As with percent black, the percentages of urban blacks were interpolated from decennial census estimates.

22. This difference is statistically significant (p < .10) for all relationships, but not for those with controls.

23. When a study involved data for more than one year, we took the mean level of unemployment for the years involved.

24. More specifically, the studies were published subsequent to the time periods included in the earlier reviews.

25. This is all the more impressive, considering the possible influence of *selection bias* in structuring the sample of defendants who get to the stage of sentencing. As Klepper, Nagin, and Tierney have shown, if blacks are disadvantaged relative to whites at earlier stages of the criminal process, and if unobservable factors playing a role at the sentencing stage also played a role at an earlier screening stage, then "selection bias would generally contribute to an underestimate of discrimination at the sentencing stage" (1983:91).

26. It could be argued that significant negative results, which reflect clear disadvantage to whites, are not the only possible indicator of *leniency* toward blacks. The latter could occur regardless of whether whites are punished *more* harshly, if because of their race, blacks receive more lenient treatment than "they would otherwise receive." This is difficult to know with certainty and we can only assume that control-

ling for crime and prior record substantially accounts for what defendants "would otherwise receive" in punishment outcomes.

REFERENCES

Austin, James, and Robert Tillman. 1988. *Ranking the Nation's Most Punitive States.* San Francisco: National Council on Crime and Delinquency.

Austin, Thomas L. 1981. "The influence of court location on type of criminal sentence: The rural-urban factor." *Journal of Criminal Justice* 9:305–16.

Berk, Richard A. 1983. "An introduction to sample selection bias in sociological data." *American Sociological Review* 48:386–98.

Bernstein, Ilene Nagel, William R. Kelly, and Patricia A. Doyle. 1977. "Societal reaction to deviants: The case of criminal defendants." *American Sociological Review* 42:743–55.

Blalock, Hubert M. 1967. *Toward a Theory of Minority-Group Relations.* New York: John Wiley.

Blauner, Robert. 1972. *Racial Oppression in America.* New York: Harper & Row.

Blumstein, Alfred. 1982. "On the racial disproportionality of United States' prison populations." *Journal of Criminal Law and Criminology* 73:1259–81.

Box, Steven. 1987. *Recession, Crime and Punishment.* Totowa, N.J.: Barnes and Noble.

Box, Steven, and Chris Hale. 1982. "Economic crisis and the rising prisoner population in England and Wales." *Crime and Social Justice* 17:20–35.

———. 1985. "Unemployment, imprisonment and prison overcrowding." *Contemporary Crises* 9:209–28.

Bridges, George S., Robert D. Crutchfield, and Edith E. Simpson. 1987. "Crime, social structure and criminal punishment: White and non-white rates of imprisonment." *Social Problems* 34:345–59.

Bridges, George S., and Robert D. Crutchfield. 1988. "Law, social standing and racial disparities in imprisonment." *Social Forces* 66:699–724.

Burke, Peter, and Austin T. Turk. 1975. "Factors affecting postarrest disposition: A model for analysis." *Social Problems* 22:313–32.

Chiricos, Theodore G. 1987. "Rates of crime and unemployment: An analysis of aggregate research evidence." *Social Problems* 34:187–212.

Chiricos, Theodore, G., and William D. Bales. 1991. "Unemployment and punishment: An empirical assessment." *Criminology* 29:701–24.

Chiricos, Theodore G., and Gordon P. Waldo. 1975. "Socioeconomic status and criminal sentencing: An empirical assessment of a conflict proposition." *American Sociological Review* 40:753–72.

Clark, Stevens H., and Gary G. Koch. 1976. "The influence of income and other factors on whether criminal defendants go to prison." *Law and Society Review* 11:57–92.

Cohen, Stan. 1972. *Folk Devils and Moral Panics: The Creation of the Mods and Rockers.* Oxford: Blackwell.

Cohen, Larry, and J. R. Kluegel. 1978. "Determinants of juvenile court dispositions: Ascriptive and achieved factors in two metropolitan courts." *American Sociological Review* 43:162–76.

Frazier, Charles E., and E. Wilbur Bock. 1982. "Effects of court officials on sentence severity." *Criminology* 20:257–72.

Gibson, James L. 1978. "Race as a determinant of criminal sentences: A methodological critique and case study. *Law and Society Review* 12:455–78.

Greenberg, David F., Ronald C. Kessler, and Colin Loftin. 1985. "Social inequality and crime control." *Journal of Criminal Law and Criminology* 76:684–704.

Hagan, John. 1974. "Extra-legal attributes and criminal sentencing: An assessment of a sociological viewpoint." *Law and Society Review* 8:357–83.

———. 1977. "Criminal justice in rural and urban communities: A study of the bureaucratization of justice." *Social Forces* 55:597–612.

Hagan, John, and Kristin Bumiller. 1983. "Making sense of sentencing: a review and critique of sentencing research." Pp. 1–53 in Alfred Blumstein, Jacqueline Cohen, Susan E. Martin, and Michael H. Tonry, (eds.), *Research on Sentencing: The Search for Reform.* Washington, D.C.: National Academy Press.

Hawkins, Darnell F. 1987. "Beyond anomalies: Rethinking the conflict perspective on race and criminal punishment." *Social Forces* 65:719–45.

Hawkins, Darnell F., and Kenneth A. Hardy. 1989. "Black-white imprisonment rates: A state-by-state analysis." *Social Justice* 16:75–94.

Hindelang, Michael J. 1969. "Equality under the law." *Journal of Criminal Law, Criminology and Police Science* 60:306–13.

———. 1978. "Race and involvement in common law personal crimes." *American Sociological Review* 43:93–109.

Humphrey, John, and Timothy Fogarty. 1987. "Race and plea bargained outcomes: A research note." *Social Forces* 66:176–82.

Jackson, Pamela I. 1986. "Black visibility, city size and social control." *Sociological Quarterly* 27:185–203.

————. 1989. *Minority Group Threat, Crime and Policing: Social Context and Social Control*. New York: Praeger.

Jacobs, David. 1979. "Inequality and police strength: Conflict theory and coercive control in metropolitan areas." *American Sociological Review* 44:913–24.

Jendrek, Margaret Platt. 1984. "Sentence length: Interactions with race and court." *Journal of Criminal Justice* 12:567–78.

Jenkins, Philip. 1992. *Intimate Enemies: Moral Panics in Contemporary Great Britain*. New York: Aldine De Gruyter.

Kempf, Kimberly L., and Roy L. Austin. 1986. "Older and more recent evidence on racial discrimination in sentencing." *Journal of Quantitative Criminology* 2:29–48.

Kleck, Gary. 1981. "Racial discrimination in criminal sentencing: A critical evaluation of the evidence with additional evidence on the death penalty." *American Sociological Review* 46:783–805.

Klepper, Steven, Daniel Nagin, and Luke-Jon Tierney. 1983. "Discrimination in the criminal justice system: A critical appraisal of the literature." Pp 55–128 in Alfred Blumstein, Jacqueline Cohen, Susan E. Martin, and Michael H. Tonry, (eds.), *Research on Sentencing: The Search for Reform*, vol 2. Washington: National Academy Press.

Kruttschnitt, Candace. 1980. "Social status and sentences of female offenders." *Law and Society Review* 15:247–65.

LaFree, Gary. 1980. "The effect of sexual stratification by race on official reactions to rape." *American Sociological Review* 45:842–54.

Liska, Allen, 1992. Social Threat and Social Control. Albany, N.Y.: SUNY Press.

Lizotte, Alan J. 1978. "Extra-legal factors in Chicago's criminal courts: Testing the conflict model of criminal justice." *Social Problems* 25:564–80.

Lotz, Roy, and John D. Hewitt. 1977. "The influence of legally irrelevant factors on felony sentencing." *Sociological Inquiry* 47:39–48.

Mauer, Marc. 1991. *Americans Behind Bars: A Comparison of International Rates of Incarceration*. Washington, D.C.: Sentencing Project.

Melossi, Dario. 1989. "An introduction: Fifty years later, *Punishment and Social Structure* in comparative analysis." *Contemporary Crises* 13:311–26.

Michalowski, Raymond J., and Michael A. Pearson. 1990. "Punishment and social structure at the state level: A cross-sectional comparison of 1970 and 1980." *Journal of Research in Crime and Delinquency* 27:52–78.

Miethe, Terance D., and Charles A. Moore. 1985. ''Socioeconomic disparities under determinate sentencing systems: A comparison of preguideline and postguideline practices in Minnesota.'' *Criminology* 23:337–63.

———. 1986. ''Racial differences in criminal processing: The consequences of model selection on conclusions about differential treatment.'' *Sociological Quarterly* 27:217–37.

Miller, Jerome G. 1992. *Search and Destroy: The Plight of African American Males in the Criminal Justice System.* Alexandria, Virginia: National Center on Institutions and Alternatives.

Moeller, Gertrude L. 1989. ''Fear of criminal victimization: The effect of neighborhood racial composition.'' *Sociological Inquiry* 59:208–21.

Moore, Charles A., and Terance D. Miethe. 1986. ''Regulated and unregulated sentencing decisions: An analysis of first-year practices under Minnesota's felony sentencing guidelines.'' *Law and Society Review* 20:253–77.

Myers, Martha A. 1979. ''Offended parties and official reactions: Victims and the sentencing of criminal defendants.'' *Sociological Quarterly* 20:529–40.

———. 1987. ''Economic inequality and discrimination in sentencing.'' *Social Forces* 65:746–66.

———. 1990a. ''Economic threat and racial disparities in incarceration: The case of postbellum Georgia.'' *Criminology* 28:627–56.

———. 1990b. ''Black threat and incarceration in post-bellum Georgia.'' *Social Forces* 69:373–93.

Myers, Martha A., and Susette Talarico. 1986a. ''The social contexts of racial discrimination in sentencing.'' *Social Problems* 33:236–51.

———. 1986b. ''Urban justice, rural injustice? Urbanization and its effect on sentencing.'' *Criminology* 24:367–90.

———. 1987. *The Social Contexts of Criminal Sentencing.* New York: Springer-Verlag.

Nagel, Jack. 1982. ''The relationship between crime and incarceration among the American states.'' *Policy Studies Review* 2:193–202.

Petersilia, Joan. 1983. *Racial disparities in the Criminal Justice System.* Santa Monica: Rand Corporation.

Peterson, Ruth, and John Hagan. 1984. ''Changing conceptions of race: Towards an account of anomalous findings of sentencing research. *American Sociological Review* 49:56–70.

Pope, Carl E. 1976. "The influence of social and legal factors on sentencing disposition: A preliminary analysis of offender based transaction statistics." *Journal of Criminal Justice* 4:203–21.

Pruitt, Charles R., and James Q. Wilson. 1983. "A longitudinal study of the effect of race on sentencing." *Law and Society Review* 17:613–35.

Rhodes, William M. 1977. "A study of sentencing in the Hennepin County and Ramsey County district courts." *Journal of Legal Studies* 6:333–53.

Sabol, William J. 1989. "Racially disproportionate prison populations in the United States." *Contemporary Crises* 13:405–32.

Spohn, Cassia, John Gruhl, and Susan Welch. 1982. "The effect of race on sentencing: A re-examination of an unsettled question." *Law and Society Review* 16:71–88.

Thompson, Randall, and Matthew Zingraff. 1981. "Detecting sentencing disparity: Some problems and evidence." *American Journal of Sociology* 86:869–80.

Turk, Austin. 1969. *Criminality and Legal Order.* Chicago: Rand McNally.

Unnever, James D. 1982. "Direct and organizational discrimination in the sentencing of drug offenders." *Social Problems* 30:212–25.

Unnever, James D., Charles Frazier, and John C. Henretta. 1980. "Race differences in criminal sentencing." *Sociological Quarterly* 21:197–207.

Unnever, James D., and Larry Hembroff. 1988. "The prediction of racial/ethnic sentencing disparities: An expectation states approach." *Journal of Research in Crime and Delinquency* 25:53–82.

U.S. Department of Justice, 1992. *Correctional Populations in the United States, 1990.* Washington: Bureau of Justice Statistics.

Welch, Susan, Cassia Spohn, and John Gruhl. 1985. "Convicting and sentencing differences among Black, Hispanic and White males in six localities." *Justice Quarterly* 2:67–77.

Willbanks, William. 1987. *The Myth of a Racist Criminal Justice System.* Monterey, Calif.: Brooks/Cole.

Wilson, William J. 1987. *The Truly Disadvantaged: The Inner-City, the Underclass and Public Policy.* Chicago: University of Chicago Press.

Zimmerman, Sherwood, and Bruce Frederick. 1984. "Discrimination and the decision to incarcerate." Pp. 315–34 in Daniel Georges-Abeyie (ed.), *The Criminal Justice System and Blacks.* New York: Clark Boardman.

Zatz, Marjorie S. 1984. "Race, ethnicity and determinate sentencing: A new dimension to an old controversy." *Criminology* 22:147–71.

———. 1987. "The changing forms of racial/ethnic bias in sentencing." *Journal of Research in Crime and Delinquency* 24:69–92.

Zatz, Marjorie, S., and John Hagan. 1985. "Crime, time and punishment: An exploration of selection bias in sentencing research." *Journal of Quantitative Criminology* 1:103–26.

ZOANN K. SNYDER-JOY

14

Self-Determination and American Indian Justice: Tribal versus Federal Jurisdiction on Indian Lands

The intervention of the United States government into American Indian tribal justice systems has resulted in a substantial loss of sovereignty for the Indian nations.[1] In particular, the federal government has substantially narrowed the authority of Indian tribes to maintain jurisdiction over many criminal activities in their communities. Which government maintains jurisdiction is not always clear. Deloria and Lytle (1983: 178) liken the contemporary American Indian justice system to a *jurisdictional maze* wherein the federal government, the state governments, or the tribal governments retain authority over certain criminal acts.[2]

Given the complex nature of American Indian criminal justice, questions must be raised regarding the impact this arrangement has had on the American Indian people. Current research indicates that one of the possible outcomes of the alterations of American Indian criminal justice systems is the disproportionate overrepresentation of American Indian defendants reported in the non-Indian criminal justice process.

This chapter addresses some of the statutes and case laws that the federal government has used to alter American Indian legal systems and structure American Indian law in the United States. American Indian criminality and its representation in crime statistics are also discussed. This chapter also proposes future research considerations as a means of arriving at more equitable American Indian justice processes both on and off reservations.

AMERICAN INDIAN LAW

The historical relationships between the federal government and American Indians were founded on the government's trust responsibility for American Indians. Hall (1980) provides a comprehensive definition of the federal trust responsibility. He defines the relationship as "the unique legal and moral duty of the United States to assist Indian tribes in the protection of their property and rights." He notes that the trust responsibility is based on treaties, court decisions, and laws.

Criminal laws and jurisdiction over crimes on Indian lands, while not part of the initial trust responsibility, have been defined and redefined over the course of the last two hundred years. Both laws and court decisions have greatly narrowed tribes' criminal jurisdictions over offenses committed on reservations. I review several of these decisions and laws as a means of depicting the encroachment of the federal government into the sovereignty of American Indian tribes, especially their inherent rights to maintain social control on their own lands. For a more comprehensive overview of Indian law, see Canby (1988), Cohen (1982), Shattuck and Norgren (1991), and Strickland (1975).

Sovereignty and the Cherokee Nation Cases

During the first third of the nineteenth century, a series of Supreme Court decisions were made regarding federal/Indian relations. These cases have had a profound impact on Indian legal systems and continue to influence decisions regarding tribal sovereignty and self-determination (Canby 1988). These rulings, often referred to as the Cherokee Nation cases (see Deloria and Lytle, 1983), are Cherokee Nation v. Georgia, 30 U.S. (5 Pet.) 1 (1831); and Worcester v. Georgia, 31 U.S. (6 Pet.) 575 (1832). In delivering its opinions, the Supreme Court recognized Indian tribes as distinct political entities with some rights to sovereignty.

In Worcester v. Georgia (1832), the Supreme Court decided that state laws were not enforceable in Indian country. The court, in recognizing the Cherokee nation as a state, noted:

> The Cherokee nation, then, is a distinct community, occupying its own territory, with boundaries accurately described, in which the laws of Georgia can have no force, and which the citizens of Georgia have no right to enter, but with the acts of Congress. The whole intercourse between the United States and this nation, is, but our Constitution and laws, vested in the government of the United States. (31 U.S. [6 Pet.] 515 [1832], 561)

Although the Supreme Court decided in support of American Indian sovereignty and self-government to the exclusion of state laws, this decision did not set a precedent for the federal Indian policies that followed. The expansion of white settlers into the territories west of the Mississippi River resulted in renewed efforts to dislocate American Indian claims to their lands. The intrusion of white settlers on Indian land was accompanied by federal encroachment into Indian land ways (Deloria and Lytle, 1983; Shattuck and Norgren, 1991). An incident in 1881 was used by the federal government to establish greater federal control over American Indian legal systems.

The Crow Dog Case and the Major Crimes Act

On August 5, 1881, Crow Dog shot and killed Chief Spotted Tail. Both the victim and assailant were Brule Sioux and Brule law required that Crow Dog make reparations to Spotted Tail's family, thus providing justice for the victim's family (Shattuck and Norgren, 1991). While justice was served under Brule law, non-Indian society was not satisfied with the outcome. Crow Dog was arrested and brought forward for a new trial, supposedly at the instigation of local whites who were not satisfied with the tribal resolution of the matter (Shattuck and Norgren, 1991). In his second trial, Crow Dog was found guilty of murder and sentenced to hang. An appeal was filed and the Supreme Court upheld the Sioux's treaty rights. The court maintained that the Sioux justice system was sovereign and exempt from outside interference (Shattuck and Norgren, 1991). However, the opportunity for federal intervention into Indian justice systems was also established in the Supreme Court's decision:

> Justice Matthew's opinion in Ex Parte Crow Dog (109 U.S. 556 [1883]) rejected the government's reading of the disputed Sioux treaties, arguing instead that Indian sovereignty, as described by Marshall in the 1830s Cherokee cases and as recognized by the United States when it entered into these treaties was binding. There should be no repeal of a treaty right by implication, and any new criminal jurisdiction policy on the part of the United States government would require *"a clear expression of the intention of Congress."* (Shattuck and Norgren, 1991: 93; emphasis added)

Soon after the Crow Dog decision, the Major Crimes Act (18 U.S.C.A. 1153) was passed in 1885, providing "federal jurisdiction over seven crimes committed by Indians in Indian country" (Canby, 1988: 105). The crimes covered by the Major Crimes Act were murder, manslaughter, rape, assault with intent to kill, arson, burglary, and larceny. Subsequent additions to the Major Crimes Act read:

Any Indian who commits against the person or property of another Indian or other person any of the following offenses, namely, murder, manslaughter, kidnaping, rape, carnal knowledge of any female, not his wife, who has not attained the age of sixteen years, assault with intent to commit rape, incest, assault with intent to commit murder, assault with a dangerous weapon, assault resulting in serious bodily injury, arson, burglary, robbery, and larceny within Indian country, shall be subject to the same laws and penalties as all other persons committing any of the above offenses, within the exclusive jurisdiction of the United States. (18 U.S.C.A. 1153)

The Major Crimes Act made substantial inroads into American Indian sovereignty to define and enforce criminal law on their own lands. The imposition of federal jurisdiction over Indian country was further expanded to include state authority in some areas.

Public Law 280 (67 Stat. 588), passed in 1953, granted some states criminal and civil jurisdiction over Indian lands. The states affected by the legislation were California, Minnesota (except the Red Lake Reservation), Nebraska, Oregon (except the Warm Springs Reservation), and Wisconsin (except the Menominee Reservation). Public Law 280 also provided that any states that wished to gain jurisdiction over tribes could do so by state law or by amending the state constitution. This latter activity could be done *without* the consent of the affected tribes. The passage of the Indian Civil Rights Act of 1968 modified state jurisdiction on Indian lands.

Indian Civil Rights Act of 1968 (82 Stat. 77)

The Indian Civil Rights Act of 1968 (ICRA) amended Public Law 280 such that Indians must vote to approve the extension of state civil and criminal jurisdiction over Indian land. The change in Public Law 280 is reported to have been widely approved by American Indians (Canby, 1988; Shattuck and Norgren, 1991).

The ICRA also extended most of the provisions of the Bill of Rights to the tribes. While some people criticized it as a further encroachment on tribal rights by the federal government (Shattuck and Norgren, 1991), others (Canby, 1988) praised this action as a means of upholding Indians' individual rights.

Shattuck and Norgren (1991: 169) assert:

From a tribal perspective, the imposition of constitutional rights and liberties standards on tribes was in direct conflict with principles of Indian sovereignty and tribal self-determination. Meaningful self-determination must preclude appeal to external authorities by reference to rules not congruent with traditional tribal concepts of authority and justice.

Canby (1988) suggests that while further federal intrusion into Indian internal matters does lessen the sovereignty of tribes, it could also be indicative of further support for tribal governments. He notes:

On the other hand, congressional action to require constitutional procedures by tribal governments seemed to contemplate the continued existence of those governments, rather than their withering away. (Canby, 1988: 29)

The impact of external authority on tribal self-determination and sovereignty was put to the test a few years later. The Oliphant decision brought about further restrictions for tribal sovereignty.

Oliphant v. Suquamish Indian Tribe (435 U.S. 191 [1978])

Mark Oliphant, a non-Indian living on the Port Madison Reservation (Washington), was arrested by tribal police and brought to trial for resisting arrest and assault of a police officer. In his appeal, Oliphant claimed that he could not be subject to Indian jurisdiction, because he was not an Indian.

The Supreme Court upheld Oliphant's claim and ruled that the tribe, due to its domestic, dependent status, does not have jurisdiction over non-Indians unless such power is granted by Congress.[3] In a subsequent decision, the Supreme Court further defined the power of tribes as that which "is necessary to protect tribal self-government or to control internal relations" (Montana v. United States, 450 U.S. 544 [1981]). The move to further restrict tribal criminal jurisdiction culminated with the Duro decision in 1990.

Duro v. Reina (110 S.Ct. 2053 [1990])

Perhaps one of the most debilitating decisions with respect to tribal sovereignty was passed down by the Supreme Court in Duro v. Reina. Albert Duro, an enrolled member of the Torres-Martinez Band of the Cahuilla Mission Indians (California), was living and working in the Salt River Pima-Maricopa Indian Community in Arizona. On June 15, 1984, Duro allegedly shot and killed a 14-year-old boy from the Gila River Indian Tribe while both parties were in the Salt River Pima-Maricopa Indian Community.

Duro was arrested by Salt River tribal police and held for trial in the Salt River Community. The tribe was to prosecute for discharging a firearm on the reservation. (The Indian Civil Rights Act of 1968 limited the criminal jurisdiction of tribes to misdemeanors, while the murder was under federal jurisdiction.) Duro filed a petition for habeas corpus in the United States district court. The writ was granted, for the district court maintained that the Indian Civil Rights Act of 1968 prohibits tribes from prosecuting non-Indians. The district court noted that "to subject a nonmember Indian to tribal jurisdiction where non-Indians are exempt would constitute discrimination based on race" (110 S.Ct. 2053 [1990], 2058).

The court of appeals reversed the decision and did not uphold the equal protection clause of the Indian Civil Rights Act of 1968. The court responded:

> It justified tribal jurisdiction over petitioner by his significant contacts with the Pima-Maricopa Community, such as residing with a member of the Tribe on the reservation and his employment with the Tribe's construction company. A need for effective law enforcement on the reservation provided a rational basis for the classification. (110 S.Ct. 2053 [1990], 2058)

The Supreme Court reviewed the case and determined that the Salt River community did not have jurisdiction over nonmember Indians. The majority decision was based on the fact that there was diversity among tribal social and cultural structures, and that the assumption should not be made that all tribes are alike. A second point presented in the court's decision maintained that enrolled membership in a tribal community constitutes consent to the authority of the tribe.

The dissenting opinion issued by Justices William Brennan and Thurgood Marshall criticized the logic of the court's decision. They noted:

> That the Court finds irrelevant the fact that we have long held that the term "Indian" in these statutes does not differentiate between members and nonmembers of a tribe. . . . Rather, the Court concludes that the federal definition of "Indian" is relevant only to *federal jurisdiction and is "not dispositive of a question of tribal* power". . . . But this conclusion is at odds with the analysis in Oliphant in which the congressional enactments served as evidence of a "commonly shared presumption" that tribes had ceded their power over non-Indians. Similarly, these enactments reflect the congressional presumption that tribes had power over all disputes between Indians regardless of tribal membership.
>
> By refusing to draw this inference from repeated congressional actions, the Court today creates a jurisdictional void in which neither federal nor tribal jurisdiction exists over nonmember Indians who commit minor crimes against another Indian. (110 S.Ct. 2053 [1990], 2069–70)

Brennan and Marshall's conclusion substantiates the concerns expressed by American Indians that the federal government had been employing contradictory approaches to Indian issues for some time and ignoring the mandates of Congress.

In response to the Duro v. Reina decision, Congress established a one-year reinstatement of the power of tribes to exercise criminal jurisdiction over Indians. On October 28, 1991, Congress passed Public Law 102–137 (105 Stat. 616, 1), "to make permanent the legislative reinstatement, following the decision of Duro against Reina, of the power of Indian tribes to exercise criminal jurisdiction over Indians." Given the conflicting actions taken by Congress and the Supreme Court, future actions regarding federal Indian law are anticipated with both hope and trepidation.

From the brief historical overview presented, it is clear that the federal government has greatly restricted the authority of American Indians to formally address crime in their on-reservation communities. What is not as clear is what impact this loss of power has had on American Indian criminality. The extant literature addresses the effects of the loss of sovereignty for American Indians and their tribal cultures (Deloria and Lytle, 1983, 1984; Green, 1991; Prucha, 1984, 1985; Snipp, 1986; Szasz, 1977, 1990).

I suggest that the American Indians' lack of representation in the legislation and enforcement of the law may result in the overrepresentation of American Indian defendants in the non-Indian criminal justice process. If American Indian cultures are not recognized in the policy-making process, it is possible that their norms and values may be viewed as deviant and subject to greater scrutiny by the dominant society's agents of social control. Because this may also be true of other ethnic and racial groups, African-Americans and persons of Hispanic origin, as well as American Indians, are compared with whites in arrest and correctional statistics.[4]

RACE, ETHNICITY, AND CRIME

The incidence and nature of criminality among racial and ethnic minorities has long been a topic of concern and inquiry in the United States. Questions have been raised as to whether or not nonwhites are more predisposed to criminal behavior than whites. The treatment of racial and ethnic minorities in the criminal justice system has also been the topic of a variety of discussions and debates in the literature (LaFree, 1985; Lynch and Patterson, 1991; MacLean and Milovanovic, 1990; Spohn, Gruhl, and Welch, 1987; Wilbanks, 1987; Zatz, 1987). While most of the work deals with African-Americans, several studies (Bachman, 1992; Bynum and Paternoster, 1984; French, 1982; Green, 1991; Hall and Simkus, 1975; Peak, 1989;

Peak and Spencer, 1987; Pommersheim and Wise, 1989; Swift and Bickel, 1974; Zatz, Lujan, and Snyder-Joy, 1991) have focused on American Indians, crime, and the criminal justice system.

American Indian representation in arrest figures, as is the case for other racial and ethnic minorities, is disproportionate to their numbers in the overall U.S. population. According to the 1990 census, there are 1,793,773 American Indians, Eskimos, and Aleuts, comprising approximately .7 percent of the total U.S. population. The 1991 Uniform Crime Report (UCR), however, notes that American Indians and Alaska Natives constitute 1.1 percent of all arrests. In comparison, African-Americans, who comprise about 12 percent of the total population, account for 29 percent of the arrest population. Whites, who are approximately 76 percent of the overall population, make up 69 percent of all arrests. Persons of Hispanic origin constitute 9 percent of the total population, but no arrest data is available from the UCR.[5]

Other criminal justice data also reveal racial disparities. American Indians represent .8 percent of the offenders sentenced to probation, while whites represent 68.4 percent and African-Americans 30.5 percent of the probation population (Bureau of Justice Statistics [BJS], 1992). Persons of Hispanic origin comprise 18 percent of the probation count.[6] Among those incarcerated in state or federal correctional facilities, we find .9 percent American Indian, 38.5 percent white, 46.3 percent African-American, and 13.3 percent Hispanic (Bureau of Justice Statistics, 1992). BJS (1992) reports that the parole population is .5 percent American Indian, 45 percent white, 40.3 percent African-American, and 14 percent Hispanic.

From these numbers alone, one cannot determine whether systematic discrimination, higher criminality among racial and ethnic minority people, or other influences account for the differences. Studies focusing on the experiences of American Indians in the criminal justice process have found that Indians have a disproportionately high arrest rate (Peak and Spencer, 1987), and are more likely to receive a prison sentence than non-Indians (Hall and Simkus, 1974; Pommersheim and Wise, 1989). Indians serve a longer portion of their sentence before parole release than non-Indians (Bynum and Paternoster, 1984). Green (1991) and Zatz, Lujan, and Snyder-Joy (1991) suggest that if a disproportionately higher number of American Indian persons is arrested in comparison to whites, this increases the likelihood that proportionately more Indians than whites will be subjected to the various agencies of the criminal justice system. This same comparison could also hold true for other nonwhite populations.

In contrast to the overrepresentation of racial and ethnic minority peoples as defendants in the criminal justice process, federal and state legislatures and administrative agencies are heavily staffed by white officials. Law enforcement remains a white-occupied field with white men comprising 78 percent and white women 5.6 percent of the full-time police population in 1990 (Reaves, 1992). Racial and ethnic minority peoples are cut off from the authority to make and the power to enforce the laws that govern their behavior. American Indians face the additional loss of power to create, maintain, and enforce the laws that regulate their own nations.

Other social, political, and economic factors may also contribute to the higher report rate of American Indian criminality and may be true as well for other racial and ethnic minority populations. Bachman (1992), French and Hornbuckle (1982), Peak (1989), and Peak and Spencer (1987) suggest that the high level of economic deprivation characteristic of some American Indian communities results in feelings of helplessness, powerlessness, and despair for some American Indians.[7] These feelings may result in increased violence, criminal activity, or the use and abuse of alcohol (Bachman, 1992; French and Hornbuckle, 1982; Peak, 1989; Peak and Spencer, 1987). Peak and Spencer (1987) report that 69.3 percent of the offenses investigated on or near reservations during 1982 were alcohol-related. French and Hornbuckle (1982) indicate that as much as 90 percent of American Indian homicides are alcohol-related.

Bachman (1992), Ivy et al. (1981), and Peak and Spencer (1987) note that the homicide rate for American Indians is much higher on-reservation than off-reservation. Bachman (1992) reports that the national homicide rate for American Indians is 9.6 per 100,000 population, but the rate may be over 100 per 100,000 population in some reservation counties.

The extant literature and current research brings into focus several of the issues surrounding higher rates of criminality among American Indians when compared with whites. These issues may also be relevant to the discussion of crime and criminality among African-Americans and people of Hispanic origin. Given the current findings, it is possible to suggest several directions for future research.

SUMMARY AND CONCLUSIONS

American Indians in the U.S.A. have disproportionately high rates of arrest and incarceration, and possibly longer prison terms than whites due to discretionary actions by criminal justice decision-makers. Further empirical research has been called for and remains a necessity in order to determine the extent to which discrimination is a factor as opposed to variables such as a prior criminal record and types of behavior while incarcerated (Bynum and Paternoster, 1984; Pommersheim and Wise, 1989; Zatz, Lujan, and Snyder-Joy, 1991). Future research must examine the entire criminal justice process to better understand how decisions made at the various stages in the process affect the outcome for American Indian defendants (Green, 1991; Zatz, Lujan, and Snyder-Joy, 1991). Discrimination may be cumulative rather than occurring at only one stage, such as arrest or sentencing.

If the research findings indicate the possibility of discriminatory behavior against American Indians at specific stages of the criminal justice system, administrative policies and practices need to target criminal justice professionals in those stages. Multicultural training for all criminal justice workers may be required to create greater awareness of diversity among employees. Intraagency task forces may be needed to formally sanction discriminatory practices among personnel.

In addition to systemic discrimination, future studies also need to focus on the social, economic, and political factors that may contribute to increased alcoholism and violence by American Indians and non-Indians alike. It is important to generate policy changes to alleviate the social problems prevalent in American Indian communities and for American Indians in off-reservation society.

Research on American Indian social problems (Bachman, 1992; Deloria and Lytle, 1983, 1984; Green, 1991; Szasz, 1977) has noted the need for greater American Indian self-determination and local control of programs and policies, reducing economic barriers, and providing for greater recognition of Indian cultures as a means of reducing social ills. More attention should focus on local control as a means of ameliorating the reservations' social problems, including violence and alcohol-related abuses among American Indians. American Indian–operated diversion and treatment programs must be examined to chart their impact on American Indian crime and social problems. Local control should also extend to tribal criminal jurisdiction on Indian lands. In this way, social control relevant to Indian cultures and concerns might be used to better address the social problems in Indian country.

NOTES

1. This chapter addresses issues for American Indians in the United States. Native peoples living in other parts of the Americas are not included in the discussion due to variation in the legal and political organizations among these peoples and the federal governments of their countries.

2. I deliberately refer to American Indian justice *systems* in the first sentence in recognition of the tribal and cultural diversity among American Indian peoples, while referring to the postintervention structure in the singular form. The actions taken by the federal and state governments often do not recognize the diversity of American Indian cultures and their related law ways.

3. In the Cherokee Nation v. Georgia decision of 1831, Chief Justice John Marshall referred to American Indian tribes as *domestic dependent nations.* He noted:

> They occupy a territory to which we assert a title independent of their will, which must take effect in point of possession when their right of possession ceases. Meanwhile, they are in a state of pupilage. Their relation to the United States resembles that of a ward to his guardian. (30 U.S. [5 Pet.] 1, 16 [1831])

4. The term *Hispanic origin* is used here only as it refers to the classification system used by the federal government as a means of determining ethnic identification.

5. The Federal Bureau of Investigation does not collect an overall count of persons of Hispanic origin. This information is provided on a state-by-state basis from those agencies collecting this information.

6. BJS noted that Hispanic origin is only reported for 55 percent of the probation population due to differences in report styles by the various agencies. Persons of Hispanic origin are also represented in the other racial categories.

7. Bachman (1992) notes that the unemployment rate on reservations ranges from an average of 50 percent to a high of nearly 90 percent.

REFERENCES

Bachman, R. 1992. *Death and Violence on the Reservation: Homicide, Family Violence, and Suicide in American Indian Populations.* New York: Auburn House.

Bynum, T. S., and R. Paternoster. 1984. "Discrimination Revisited: An Exploration of Frontstage and Backstage Criminal Justice Decision Making." *Sociology and Social Research* 69:90–108.

Canby, W., Jr. 1988. *American Indian Law,* 2d ed. St. Paul, Minn.: West Publishing Co.

Cohen, F. 1982. *Handbook of Federal Indian Law.* Charlottesville, Va.: Mitchie: Bobbs-Merrill.

Deloria, V., Jr., and C. M. Lytle. 1983. *American Indians, American Justice.* Austin: University of Texas Press.

———. 1984. *The Nations Within.* New York: Pantheon Books.

French, L. 1982. *Indians and Criminal Justice.* Totowa, N.J.: Allanheld, Osmun.

French, L., and J. Hornbuckle, 1982. "Indian Alcoholism" in L. French (ed.), *Indians and Criminal Justice.* Totowa, N.J.: Allanheld, Osmun.

Green, D. E. 1991. "American Indian Criminality: What do We Really Know?," in D. E. Green and T. V. Tonnesen (eds.), *American Indians: Social Justice and Public Policy*. Madison: University of Wisconsin System Institute on Race and Ethnicity.

Hall, E. L., and A. A. Simkus. 1975. "Inequality in the Types of Sentences Received by Native Americans and Whites." *Criminology* 13:199–122.

Hall, G. 1980. *Federal-Indian Trust Responsibility Filmstrip*. Washington, D.C.: Institute for the Development of Indian Law.

Ivy, S., C. Moelsworth, H. Stuler, and D. K. Hunter. 1981. *Crime in Indian Country: Final Report*. Washington, D.C.: SRI International.

LaFree, G. 1985. "Official Reactions to Hispanic Defendants in the Southwest." *Journal of Research in Crime and Delinquency* 22:213–37.

Lynch, M. J., and E. B. Patterson. 1991. *Race and Criminal Justice*. New York: Harrow and Heston.

MacLean, B., and D. Milovanovic. 1990. *Racism, Empiricism, and Criminal Justice*. Vancouver, Canada: Collective Press.

Peak, K. 1989. "Criminal Justice, Law, and Policy in Indian Country: A Historical Perspective." *Journal of Criminal Justice* 17:393–407.

Peak, K., and J. Spencer. 1987. "Crime in Indian Country: Another Trail of Tears." *Journal of Criminal Justice* 15:485–94.

Pommersheim, F., and S. Wise. 1989. "Going to the Penitentiary: A Study of Disparate Sentencing in South Dakota." *Criminal Justice and Behavior* 16: 155–65.

Prucha, F. P. 1984. *The Great Father: The United States Government and the American Indians*, volumes 1 & 2. Lincoln: University of Nebraska Press.

———. 1985. *The Indians in American Society*. Berkeley: University of California Press.

Reaves, B. 1992. *State and Local Police Departments, 1990*. Washington, D.C.: Bureau of Justice Statistics.

Shattuck, P., and J. Norgren. 1991. *Partial Justice: Federal Indian Law in a Liberal Constitutional System*. New York: Berg.

Snipp, C. M. 1986. "The Changing Political and Economic Status of the American Indians: From Captive Nations to Internal Colonies." *American Journal of Economics and Sociology* 45: 145–57.

Spohn, C., J. Gruhl, and S. Welch. 1987. "The Effect of Race on Sentencing: A Reexamination of an Unsettled Question." *Law and Society Review* 16:71–88.

Strickland, R. 1975. *Fire and the Spirits: Cherokee Law from Clan to Court*. Norman: University of Oklahoma Press.

Swift, B., and G. Bickel. 1974. *Comparative Parole Treatment of American Indians and Non-Indians at United States Federal Prisons*. Washington, D.C.: Bureau of Social Science Research.

Szasz, M. C. 1977. *Education and the American Indian: The Road to Self-Determination Since 1928*, 2d ed. Albuquerque: University of New Mexico Press.

————. 1990. "The Path to Self-Determination: American Indian Education, 1940–1990," in Sally Hyer (ed.), *One House, One Voice, One Heart: American Indian Education at the Santa Fe Indian School*. Santa Fe: Museum of New Mexico Press.

U.S. Department of Commerce, Bureau of the Census. 1992. *1990 Census of Population and Housing*. Washington, D.C.: U.S. Government Printing Office.

U.S. Department of Justice, Federal Bureau of Investigation. 1992. *Uniform Crime Report, 1991*. Washington, D.C.: U.S. Government Printing Office.

U.S. Department of Justice, Bureau of Justice Statistics. 1992. *Correctional Populations in the United States, 1990*. Washington, D.C.: U.S. Government Printing Office.

Wilbanks, W. 1987. *The Myth of a Racist Criminal Justice System*. Monterey, Calif.: Brooks/Cole.

Zatz, M. S. 1987. "The Changing Forms of Racial/Ethnic Biases in Sentencing." *Journal of Research in Crime and Delinquency* 24:69–92.

Zatz, M. S., C. C. Lujan, and Z. K. Snyder-Joy. 1991. "American Indians and Criminal Justice: Some Conceptual and Methodological Considerations," in M. Lynch and E. B. Patterson (eds.), *Race and Criminal Justice*. New York: Harrow and Heston.

CASES CITED

Cherokee Nation v. Georgia, 30 U.S. (5 Pet.) 1 (1831)

Duro v. Reina, 110 S.Ct. 2053 (1990)

Ex Parte Crow Dog, 109 U.S. 556 (1883)

Montana v. United States, 450 U.S. 544 (1981)

Oliphant v. Suquamish Indian Tribe, 435 U.S. 191 (1978)

Worcester v. Georgia, 31 U.S. (6 Pet.) 575 (1832)

ROLAND CHILTON
RAYMOND TESKE
HARALD ARNOLD

15

Ethnicity, Race, and Crime: German and Non-German Suspects 1960–1990

ANTICIPATED GERMAN AND AMERICAN PARALLELS

Interest in ethnicity and crime in the United States predates the 1931 Wickersham Commission on law observance and enforcement (National Commission). It is clear that the commission's discussion of the issue was, in part, a response to widely expressed concerns about crimes committed by foreign-born Americans.

In his 1938 book, *Culture Conflict and Crime*, Thorsten Sellin called attention to the commission's finding that foreign-born Americans came into contact with the law less frequently than native-born Americans. Nevertheless, Sellin pointed out that the term *foreign-born* is wide and that it is important to look at the data as they apply to specific foreign-born groups. He noted that the commission found higher than average arrest rates for some groups of people born outside the United States. Some groups identified as having high arrest rates in 1931 were Greeks, Lithuanians, Poles, Austrians, Italians, Mexicans, and Asians. Seeing some of these rates as the result of a conflict of conduct norms, Sellin cited differences in arrest rates for gambling, prostitution, weapons possession, and liquor law violations as findings that appeared to support such an interpretation. The laws of the United States on these matters, he suggested, were entirely different from those in the countries of origin of many American immigrants.

When the 1966–67 President's Commission on Law Enforcement and Administration of Justice reexamined these issues 28 years later, it relied heavily on a report submitted by Henry McKay and Solomon Kobrin. These authors shifted the discussion from parents to children. Rather than examine ethnicity in terms of country of origin, their analysis focused on the children of foreign-born parents. They noted that rates of delinquency were always high in the sections of cities occupied by new arrivals (1966). In relation to the Wickersham Commission's finding that different ethnic groups differed in their rates of crime, they cited Van Vechten's (1941) conclusion that the differences in rates among ethnic groups were largely a product of differences in age distribution. Nevertheless, McKay and Kobrin concluded that earlier studies of rates of delinquency in Chicago suggest that the children of foreign-born parents were more delinquent than the children of native-born parents.

They believed that these differences in delinquency rates were related to differences in the physical and economic conditions of urban communities. Their report says that delinquency rates for children of the foreign-born are low in attractive areas and high in less attractive areas. McKay and Kobrin concluded that rates of delinquency for specific ethnic groups varied considerably over time. They also found that when each major European immigrant group was concentrated in Chicago's high delinquency areas, it had high delinquency rates. Martin Killias (1989) suggests a parallel in contemporary western Europe, concluding that "the overrepresentation of young immigrants in the police statistics of many countries is not the result of discrimination against them; rather, some segments among the immigrant youths may be disproportionately involved in delinquent activities."

Focusing either on foreign birth or on the children of the foreign-born does not overcome a basic problem with the original comparisons of native-born and foreign-born Americans. That problem was the fact that a sizeable marginalized population, black Americans, was part of the native-born population. Analysis of arrest and adjudication trends for native-born Americans without concern for this distinction was certain to reduce the magnitude of differences between foreign-born and native-born Americans. Yet, the mechanisms of segregation and isolation make comparisons of native-white, native-black, and foreign-born areas impossible. It is not surprising that these issues were usually pursued separately.

Our analysis of German crime trends grew out of a belief that the social and economic position of non-German ethnic groups in Germany in recent decades might parallel that of black Americans in the United States for the same period. We reasoned that if there are substantial similarities in the social and economic situations of non-Germans in Germany and American blacks and Hispanics, we ought to find patterns in German crime trends that resemble some patterns found in the United States. Therefore we modeled our approach to the German crime data after approaches to race and crime that have been carried out in the United States (Chilton, 1986 and 1987). We are aware of the possibilities for misuse and misinterpretation of such a study. It is possible that an analysis of German and non-German crime trends may be just as controversial and disturbing for German criminologists and Germans in general as comparisons of white and nonwhite crime rates are for U.S. criminologists and other Americans.

In many ways, the overrepresentation of black citizens in U.S. prisons and jails is one of the most problematic facts in American criminology. In 1990, roughly one-half of the prisoners in state and federal prisons were black—when roughly 12 percent of the U.S. population was classified as black. Black Americans are also disproportionately arrested and charged with serious crime. Over the past 25 years, police reports have produced central city arrest rates for homicide and robbery that are six to nine times as high for the black populations as they are for the white populations of these cities (Chilton, 1987 and 1991). Arrest counts aggregated for all of the United States suggest that black Americans are disproportionately likely to be arrested and charged with predatory crimes in comparison with Americans in other racial categories (FBI, 1991).

The treatment of the this information by academic criminologists has varied from disinterest to disbelief. A few criminologists have suggested that crime statistics reflect only police activity, not the conduct of ordinary citizens (Kitsuse and Cicourel, 1963; McCleary et al., 1982). Many have examined a variety of data sets in an attempt to assess the discriminatory nature of various systems of justice. Yet for many years, most criminologists simply ignored the troublesome fact of race and imprisonment, and worked to develop strategies for dealing with crime in general or to develop and test psychological or social psychological theories of crime. More recently, other criminologists have examined the issue in great detail and several competing explanations for the discrepancies in rates by race have been developed (Sampson, 1987; Chilton, 1991; LaFree et al., 1992).

Analyses of arrest and court data generally fail to support suggestions that the overrepresentation of black Americans in prison is either a reporting artifact or the sole result of racial bias within the system of justice (Hindelang, 1978). Comparisons of information compiled by police agencies with victim survey results suggest that the higher rates of arrests for predatory crime of black people are the result of higher rates of involvement in victimizing activities by people classified as black (BJS, 1992). However, informal discussions with those studying racial discrimination in the system suggests that they are reluctant to examine or discuss such information because it can be used by others to support openly racist theories of crime. One fear is that any analysis of the rates by race will lead many to accept racially oriented biological explanations of crime. Another fear is that some will use the information to support suggestions that *black culture produces the observed differences. Similar concerns also may work against any analysis of German and non-German trends.*

However, the work of some criminologists who have examined race-specific rates suggests that structural explanations are more likely than biological or cultural theories to explain the divergent rates. Such analyses have focused on the impact of isolation, unemployment, family arrangements, and poverty on black and white crime rates (Sampson, 1987; Chilton, 1991). Race-specific analyses suggest that poverty and racial isolation increase the probability of vulnerable families, poor education, inadequate socialization, and criminal conduct.

As indicated above, this analysis of German and non-German crime trends begins with questions suggested by several earlier analyses of white and nonwhite arrest rates in the United States. To the extent that the economic and social situation of a large segment of the non-German population is similar to that of many black Americans, we anticipated finding higher predatory crime rates for non-Germans. In a 1987 study, Albrecht found that the 1982 rates of violent crime for foreign males in different age groups in Germany were considerably higher than those computed for their German counterparts. Rates of rape for foreign males were four to five times as high as age-specific rape rates for Germans. Homicide, robbery, and assault rates were two to four times as high for foreigners when compared with German rates for the same offenses. He concludes that if the rates could be adjusted for socioeconomic status and age composition, the differences he found would be reduced considerably.

We too were interested in the importance of a changing age composition for German and non-German suspect rates. Part of this interest came from our knowledge that changes in age composition of white and nonwhite Americans in central cities appeared to explain a substantial portion of increases of arrest for specific crimes (Chilton, 1986). Therefore, besides examining crime trends, we carried out a gender-, age-, and citizenship-specific analysis of suspect data for Germany. Although we did not expect this exploratory study to provide convincing support for any of the competing explanations for black and white differences in crime rates, it seemed useful to narrow the list of possible explanations for these divergent rates of predatory crime by shifting the focus from the United States to Germany and, in this way, from race to ethnicity.

METHOD

The most recent data for this analysis were provided by German statistical organizations, specifically the Federal Statistical Office (*Statistisches*

Bundesamt) and the Federal Police Office (*Bundeskriminalamt*). Basic population data are taken from the Statistical Yearbook (*Statistisches Jahrbuch*), a compendium of social, demographic, and economic data published annually by the Federal Statistical Office. The Statistical Office compiled the most recent data on the age and sex of foreigners in response to our request for this information. In addition, the office furnished us with recent information on nationality and income of foreigners. Full-scale population censuses are undertaken periodically in Germany and microcensuses are carried out on a regular basis. We have used projections of 1961, 1970, and 1987 census information to estimate population counts for the intercensal years. Social and economic measures are estimated from information provided in the microcensuses.

The Federal Republic of Germany has an additional resource for making population estimates, including estimates by sex, age, and nationality. Except for tourists, military personnel, diplomats, and persons in Germany for a short stay, all residents, whether temporary or permanent, must register with the local Residents Office (*Einwohnermeldeamt*). When people change their places of residence, they are required to notify the Residents Office at their former place of residence and to reregister at the new place of residence. Foreigners are registered in a central register for foreigners (*Ausländerzentralregister*). This information, combined with birth and death records, permits the creation of reasonably accurate population estimates by age, sex, and citizenship.

Changes in the age and sex composition of the German population are created by several types of immigration. Only some of these immigrants are classified as foreigners. Some are defined by law as Germans despite their entry into the Federal Republic from other countries. *Aussiedler* are Germans living in east European countries. They are considered German by law as people who were banished or exiled because of the world wars. Their families may have lived for generations in what are now parts of Poland or the former Soviet Union. Many, especially the younger ones, do not speak German. Their appearance and demeanor often resemble that of *regular* foreigners. Still, they are Germans by law. They enter Germany as Germans by definition. Hundreds of thousands of *Aussiedler* have settled in Germany since 1983 and have contributed to changes in the composition of the German population.

A second group of German immigrants came from the former German Democratic Republic before unification. Called *Zuwanderer (Übersiedler, Flüchtlinge)*, they too have always been considered German nationals by law. Some had permission to leave; others did not. German and non-German immigrants alike have had an impact on the age composition of the Federal Republic of Germany from 1978 to 1990.

For the years 1986 through 1990, immigration from Turkey and Yugo-slavia accounted for roughly 45 percent of the foreigners in Germany. By 1990, immigration from Italy, Greece, and Poland accounted for another 20 percent. Other countries with 2, 3, or 4 percent of the total in 1990 were Austria, Spain, and the Netherlands. The remaining 27 percent of the foreign population came from 30 different countries. In 1978, non-German men could be described as having average incomes 14 to 15 percent lower than German men. By 1990, the average income of foreign men was 17 to 18 per-cent lower than that of German men. In comparison with German women, fewer foreign women had their own income. Those foreign women who had their own income had an average income substantially lower than either German or foreign men.

Our data on persons suspected of criminal conduct in Germany are found in the publication Police Statistics, (*Polizeiliche Kriminalstatistik*) pub-lished annually by the Federal Police Office (*Bundeskriminalamt*) in Wiesba-den. We have taken counts of persons suspected of five specific types of crime and counts of persons reported as suspects for any not traffic-related crime at all. A suspect is someone who has been identified by the police. More than 80 percent of the incidents coming to the attention of the police come from victims who have identified the suspect. The police have specific information about the suspect's age, sex, and place of residence. Suspects may be arrested but, normally, this will happen only if they are considered dangerous, likely to flee, or may obstruct justice.

Except for 1983, when the system changed slightly, data have been col-lected and reported since 1978 by age, sex, citizenship, and offense. From 1971 through 1977, only the sex and nationality of suspects were recorded. From 1961 to 1970, aggregate data were recorded that distinguished suspects by nationality for most types of offenses. We selected the years 1978, 1984, and 1990 for detailed analysis and comparison, because 1978 was the first year that data were reported by age, sex, and nationality. In addition, 1990 is the year for which data are most recently available. Moreover, beginning in 1991, the statistics will be affected by reunification. Comparisons with the years before 1991 will be difficult. We selected 1984 as a midpoint because the way suspects are counted changed in 1983. Before 1983, a suspect was counted each time he or she was investigated for a separate offense. This and closely related procedures overestimated the number of different individuals involved. Since 1983, each suspect is counted only once during the calendar year, regardless of how many times that person was investigated that year.

Three of the five offense categories selected for analysis (aggravated assault, robbery, and theft) closely conform to offenses with the same names in the Uniform Crime Reports for the United States. Burglary of a home is comparable to burglary in the U.S.A. but more restricted in scope. Vehicle theft is comparable to the offense by the same name in the U.S.A. but it does not conform exactly (Teske and Arnold, 1982). As is true in the Uniform Crime Reporting Program, when the conduct involved in a single act violates several parts of the criminal code, only the most serious offense is counted. If the same incident involves independent actions that violate several paragraphs of the penal code, more than one offense will be counted.

As a first step in our analysis we plotted and examined trends in *suspect counts and rates* for 1960 to 1990. As part of the analysis we compared suspect trends for Germans and non-Germans living in Germany. Next, we focused on the contribution, if any, of a changing age structure in Germany over the period studied. The data available allowed us to carry out a twelve-year analysis consisting of two six-year periods, 1978–1984 and 1984–1990. An initial age-, gender-, and citizenship-specific analysis examined changes in suspect counts from 1978 to 1990. This early trend analysis suggested that it would be more useful to look at the impact of a changing age structure from 1984 to 1990. This emphasis on the second six-year period is justified in part because of the 1983 change in the procedure for counting suspects described above.

The underlying goal of the age-, gender-, and citizenship-specific analysis was to estimate the proportion of an observed increase or decrease in suspect counts that might be explained by the changing demographic composition of a population. The technique also provides more detailed information about the suspect rates and possible criminal activity of specific segments of the population. It also highlights changes in the populations used to compute specific crime rates.

FINDINGS

Figure 15.1 presents trends for the number of German and non-German suspects for five offenses combined as index offenses (the lines for 1972 to 1990). This measure was created by combining counts of aggravated assault, robbery, burglary, theft, and vehicle theft. The total suspect counts are the count of persons suspected for all reasons for 1961 to 1990. The lines without symbols show the trends when suspect counts from Germans and non-Germans are combined. An examination of the trends shown in Figure 15.1 suggests that the number of suspects for all offenses, Germans and non-Germans combined, increased steadily from 1963 to 1982. Following a decrease produced by a change in reporting procedures, such cases continued to increase from 1984 to 1990. Still, the number of Germans suspected for all offenses combined (total offenses) remained level or increased only slightly from 1984 to 1990, while comparable counts for non-Germans increased

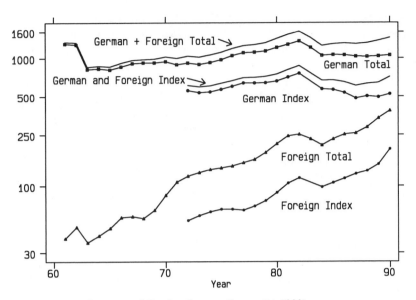

FIGURE 15.1 German and Foreign Suspect Counts (× 1000)

sharply for this period, producing most of the increase in the combined counts.

The number of Germans suspected of index offenses declined from 1984 to 1990 while the number of non-Germans suspected of index offenses increased at the same pace as that for total offenses. Over the 1963 to 1982 period, increases in the number of non-Germans suspected of index offenses exceeded those of Germans. Although the increases for non-Germans clearly had an impact on the trends for Germans and non-Germans combined, the combined counts reflect changes in the number of German suspects because there are relatively fewer non-Germans.

Figure 15.2 shows the trends in the number of persons suspected of index and total offenses when population counts are used to compare rates. Here we see that both the index and total suspect rates for non-Germans are much higher than similar rates for Germans. In 1963, the total suspect rate for non-Germans was over twice that of Germans. By 1990, it was over four times as high. Similar patterns are found for index offenses. In 1972, the index suspect rate for non-Germans was a little less than twice that of Germans. After a striking rise in index suspect rates from 1984 to 1990, the non-German index suspect rates were over four times those of Germans.

Clearly, something happened to either the composition or conduct of non-Germans or to the reporting procedure that sent these trends off in different directions after 1984. While the rates for non-Germans were always

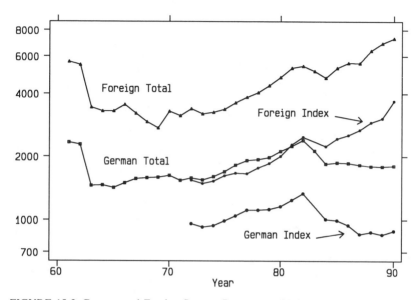

FIGURE 15.2 German and Foreign Suspect Rates (per 100,000)

higher than the rates for Germans, the lines begin to diverge sharply only after 1983. Such a shift could have been the result of demographic changes, a possibility we examine below. It also might have been the result of shifts in the policies and procedures of law enforcement agencies or changes in reporting practices, one of which has been identified above. Still, there is no obvious reason to suppose that the 1983 change described above would have, in itself, produced the increase in foreign suspects and the decrease in German suspects—although German citizens were more likely to be suspected more than once during a given year than foreigners. It is possible that these trends simply reflect changes in the conduct of both Germans and non-Germans.

The trends in Figure 15.3 suggest that the German and non-German larceny suspect rates converged from 1960 to 1970 before moving apart from 1970 to 1982. It shows them moving even further apart from 1984 to 1990. Assault suspect rates for non-Germans were generally higher, two and one-half times as high as those for Germans over the 30-year period, although they too diverge more sharply from 1984 to 1990.

These trends raise at least two questions. First, why are the non-German aggravated assault suspect rates consistently so much higher than the same rates for Germans? The German aggravated assault suspect rate remains under 100 per 100,000 Germans over a 30-year period. Simultaneously, the non-German assault suspect rate fluctuates between 300 and 400

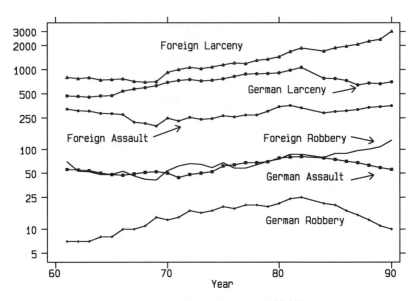

FIGURE 15.3 Larceny, Assault, Robbery Rates (per 100,000)

per 100,000 non-Germans. Although not so consistently different, the non-German larceny suspect rates remain higher than the German suspect rates for larceny, raising a similar question.

A second question raised by Figure 15.3 asks why the larceny and assault suspect rates for non-Germans diverged so sharply from those for Germans from 1984 to 1990. Changes in these specific rates, clearly influenced the trends for index and total suspect rates. Did Germans become even less assaultive and commit fewer larcenies from 1984 to 1990? Did non-Germans become more assaultive and engage in more larceny over the same period? If so, why?

AGE-, GENDER-, CITIZENSHIP-SPECIFIC ANALYSIS

From 1978 to 1990 the combined German and foreign population increased from 61.3 million to 63.7 million. Yet the combined population apparently decreased from 1978 to 1984. It then increased by 2.7 million from 1984 to 1990. The foreign population, from 1978 to 1984, increased by 320,000. It increased by another 900,000 from 1984 to 1990. Excluding the increase in the non-German population of Germany, the population of German nationals *decreased* by 1.7 million people from 1978 to 1984. It increased by 1.8 million from 1984 to 1990. Interestingly, the 1984 to 1990 increase in the German population appears to be the result of the variety of forms of immigration from East Germany and other east European countries. Nevertheless, at least 50 percent of the increase in the population of Germany from 1984 to 1990 was produced by an increase in the number of non-German immigrants.

Our examination of the impact of demographic changes may be confounded by the existence of these two different kinds of migration. One group of immigrants is classified as German. Another group is not. The immigrants classified as citizens will have some impact on the German suspect and population figures. Neither the size of the German immigrant population nor the conduct of its members will affect the data for foreigners.

Besides assessing the impact of demographic changes, the primary advantage of an age-, gender-, citizenship-specific analysis of suspect data for Germany is that it provides more information about the social location of those charged. For example, from 1984 to 1990, the number of suspects for all cases in Germany increased from 1.25 to 1.43 million. This increase, however, was not distributed evenly across all age, gender, and citizenship categories. The number of suspects who were German males under 18 decreased from 1984 to 1990 (141,357 to 107,015), while the number of suspects who were foreign males increased in this age category (30,771 to 50,099). The number of 18 to 29 year-old foreign men in the population increased by 40 percent over this period. Except for Germans—male and female—under 18, the population of other German age and gender categories also increased from 1978 to 1990.

In our analysis we use the 1984 suspect rates for each category to ask this question: If the rate for a specific category had remained constant from 1984 to 1990, how much of the increase in the number of suspects in that category might be attributed to an increase in the population in the category? The same question can be asked about the decrease in suspects in a specific category. However, in this analysis we have focused on the increase in the number of suspects from 1984 to 1990, and have ignored the decreases. What we want to consider are some possible explanations for increases in the suspect rates. Combining expected decreases for German suspects with expected increases for non-German suspects will produce a misleading summary figure that might suggest to some that age structure is not an important factor in the increase in the non-German suspect rates.

Focusing on these categories with increases and putting aside those with decreases, we find that the total increase in suspects was 228,725. To assess the impact of increases in the populations of specific categories, we estimate the number of suspects that would have been reported had the rate for a specific category remained the same. For example, in line 1 of Table 15.1, the 1984 rate for foreign males under 18 was 4,812 per 100,000 individuals in this category. Multiplying this rate (.04812) by the 1990 population, we find that if the rate had remained constant, we would have had about 33,105 suspects in this category in 1990. The expected change would have been an increase of about 2,334 suspects. Yet the actual number of suspects increased by 19,328. So only about 12 percent of the observed increase can be explained by the increase in the number of foreign males under 18 in this population. The remaining increase in the number of suspects must be attributed to changes in the conduct of foreign males under 18 or to changes in police activity. The rate for this group in 1984 was 4,812 per 100,000 foreign males under 18. This rate increased to 7,283 per 100,000 foreign males under 18 in 1990.

When this procedure is repeated for each line (each age-, gender-, citizenship-specific category) where there is an increase in suspects, it suggests a total observed increase of 228,725 suspects. When the expected increases for each category are totaled, limiting the expected increases for each category to the observed increases, it produces a total expected increase of 77,548. As shown in Table 15.1, this procedure suggests that about one-third (34 percent) of the total increase in suspects can be explained by changes in the age, gender, and citizenship categories. Conversely, this implies that two-thirds of the total observed increase was the result of increased suspect rates for specific age, gender, and citizenship categories.

Another advantage of this procedure is that it provides information on the size of the suspect rates for specific categories and shows how these specific rates have changed. For example, in 1984, the 18–29 year-old foreign male suspect rate for all offenses combined was 13,940 per 100,000 (about 14 percent), almost twice that of the German suspect rate for the same age group. By 1990, the foreign suspect rate for those in this age category was 20,125 per 100,000 (a 20 percent prevalence rate) in contrast with a German suspect rate of 5,303 (a 5 percent prevalence rate). In both time periods the lowest suspect rates were those of German women over 49 years old. All categories of German women had suspect rates lower than foreign women, German men, and foreign men.

When some numbers are recombined, Table 15.1 suggests that about 60 percent of the total observed increase from 1984 to 1990 was the result of increases in the number of foreign, male suspects. Another 15 percent was the result of increases in the number of foreign, female suspects. This means that three-quarters of the increase in suspects over this period were the result of increases in the number of non-German suspects—a fact also suggested by the trend analysis. Still, 44 percent of the increase in foreign male subjects and 28 percent of the increase in the number of foreign female suspects can be explained by increases in the number of people in these high-risk categories.

TABLE 15.1   Age-Specific Analysis by Citizenship and Gender of Total Suspects for Germany, 1984 to 1990.

Age, Citizen-ship, Gender*	1984 population	1984 arrests	1984 rate**	1990 population	1990 arrests	1990 rate**	Expected arrests	Expected change	Observed change
−18 FM	639400	30771	4812	687900	50099	7283	33105	2334	19328
18–29 FM	516700	72026	13940	723700	145645	20125	100881	28855	73619
30–49 FM	1017900	55285	5431	1043400	93750	8985	56670	1385	38465
50+ FM	325600	8683	2667	491000	14546	2963	13094	4411	5863
−18 FF	548100	7449	1359	604600	13211	2185	8217	768	5762
18–29 FF	413700	14450	3493	575200	32528	5655	20091	5641	18078
30–49 FF	701300	14720	2099	817800	27443	3356	17165	2445	12723
50+ FF	201000	4226	2102	298400	6361	2132	6274	2048	2135
−18 GM	5626700	141357	2512	5315500	107015	2013	133539	−7818	−34342
18–29 GM	5560600	302131	5337	5705600	302586	5303	304533	2402	455
30–49 GM	7740100	260818	3370	8030400	270733	3371	270600	9782	9915
50+ GM	7652900	87329	1141	8853400	115905	1309	101028	13699	28576
−18 GF	5432800	44092	812	5085300	33419	657	41272	−2820	−10673
18–29 GF	5397400	74257	1376	5471000	78396	1433	75270	1013	4139
30–49 GF	7714700	80249	1040	7814000	83679	1071	81282	1033	3430
50+ GF	11460500	56370	492	12208400	62607	513	60049	3679	6237
Total	61049400	1254213	2054	63725600	1437923	2256	1323070	68857	183710

Total observed increase 228725
Total expected increase*** 77548
Percent explained 33.9

*   FM Foreign Male, FF Foreign Female, GM German Male, GF German Female.
**   Number per 100,000 population.
*** To compute this total, the expected increase for a specific age group is limited to the observed increase for that group.

The complete analysis suggests that a changing age structure will explain about one-third of the increase in the total number of suspects from 1984 to 1990. Most of the increase must be attributed to increased suspect rates for non-Germans. These increases may be the result of increases in illegal activity by a segment of the non-German population. They also might point to a change in the ethnic composition of the non-German population. On the other hand, the higher counts and rates for non-Germans may reflect a change in recording procedures or a change in police activity. It is also possible that with fewer Germans committing crimes, the same amount of police activity and effort would produce increased attention to foreigners.

A similar analysis of persons suspected of aggravated assault suggests that a larger part (55 percent) of the increase in the number of suspects, from 1984 to 1990, can be attributed to changes in the age, gender, citizenship composition of the population. Careful analysis suggests that this is due in part to the very high 1984 aggravated assault suspect rates for foreign men. Although the number of Germans suspected of aggravated assault at both time periods is three and four times as large as the number of foreigners, their rates are lower at both time periods and the rates for Germans decreased from 1984 to 1990.

The results of an age-, gender-, citizenship-specific analysis of data for larceny suspects indicated that counts of theft suspects have so much impact on the five offense index we compiled that the results are very similar to those shown when the index suspect counts are examined. What stood out in this analysis was the sizeable increase in the suspect rate for 18–29 year-old foreign men from 1984 to 1990. It almost doubled, while the same rate for German men in this age category went down. Combined with the increase in the number of foreign men over this period, increases in suspect rates for larceny mean that most of the increase in larceny suspects from 1984 to 1990 was the result of increases in the number of foreign larceny suspects.

These analyses underscore the two questions raised earlier. Why are the foreign suspect rates so much higher than those for German nationals? Why did these rates increase from 1984 to 1990? However, the analyses also show the impact on suspect counts of relatively large increases in the number of non-Germans between 1984 and 1990.

DISCUSSION

As anticipated, this analysis of German and non-German suspects suggests some parallels with trends in arrests for white and non-white Americans. The economic circumstances of non-Germans are similar to those of non-white Americans—at least in the sense that the average income of foreigners is lower than that of Germans, with more foreigners described as not having incomes of their own. The status of foreigners as outsiders and marginalized people appears to persist. In this sense, the suspect or arrest rates of both countries are consistently higher for the most disadvantaged groups in both countries. And the gap between the levels of the rates appears to be increasing in both countries.

Changes in the composition of the German population by age, gender, and ethnicity from 1984 to 1990 appear to account for part of the increase in crime attributed to foreigners. Seventy-seven percent of the increase in suspects for all offenses combined from 1984 to 1990 grew out of situations involving foreign men or women. The contribution of non-Germans to the increases in suspects in what we have called index offenses (aggravated assault, robbery, burglary, theft, and vehicle theft) was 90 percent.

However, as we have seen, only part of these increases are explained by changes in the demographic composition of Germany. Sixty-two percent of the expected increase in arrests for all offenses can be attributed to increases in the number of foreigners in Germany from 1984 to 1990. This figure is 71 percent for index offenses, 82 percent for aggravated assault, 96 percent for robbery, 83 percent for burglary, and 79 percent for vehicle theft.

It is important to remember that the expectations used in this type of analysis start with the suspect rates for 1984 and explain 1990 counts by asking what would be expected if the 1984 rate had remained constant. We have seen that most rates for non-Germans did not remain constant but instead increased from 1984 to 1990. This raised two questions: Why were the rates for non-Germans so much higher than the rates for Germans in 1984? Why did the rates for non-Germans increase from 1984 to 1990?

One possible explanation would be the existence of widespread differences in the response of police officers to Germans and non-Germans. If, for example, the police in several large cities were more likely to charge a foreign suspect with aggravated assault, rather than simple assault, this would make the aggravated assault rates for non-Germans higher than the rates for Germans. The available data will not permit an examination of this possibility. Therefore, there is no evidence that would support or rule out such a possibility as a partial explanation of the differences in German and non-German suspect rates.

Another plausible explanation for some differences in suspect rates is the general economic and social situation of many non-Germans. The income information we examined does not suggest great inequity between Germans and non-Germans, but, as we have noted, all the data for Germans is a little misleading because of the number of immigrants classified by law as German. The possible parallel between the status of many black Americans in the U.S.A. and that of many foreign residents of Germany that triggered this analysis remains a plausible explanation for some of the differences in suspect rates and suspect trends.

The social and economic circumstances of many non-Germans are similar in several ways to that of many black Americans. These similarities include lower incomes and probably less secure employment, less formal education, language difficulties, and higher transiency. As Albrecht (1987) suggests, both groups may be marginal in other ways. They may be stigmatized and rejected by the majority. They may be perceived as endangering safety and stability. These negative reactions by other groups may be reinforced by competition for employment, housing, and education.

The similarity of the situations of many non-Germans in Germany to those of many black Americans is far from complete. There do not seem to be similar proportions of young people in poverty in Germany. The age groups contributing most to the suspect counts in Germany are slightly older than the groups contributing most to arrest counts in the United States. Of special importance is the possibility that the living arrangements of foreigners in Germany are sharply different from those found for many black Americans in the largest U.S. cities. Besides, even the urban concentration of the crime problem in the United States may be a way in which the two countries are different.

One striking difference between the response of Germans to non-German crime and the response of white Americans—and others exercising power in the United States—to increases in the arrests of black Americans stands out. The trends in incarceration rates are sharply different in the United States and Germany. Although there is no evidence to support it, it is possible that deportation and expulsion policies for non-Germans will offer a partial explanation for the failure of incarceration rates in Germany to increase as sharply as they have in the United States. It is also possible that the increases in incarceration rates in the United States, especially minority incarceration rates, are related to current policies calling for the incarceration of a wide variety of drug offenders.

In the U.S.A., incarceration rates roughly doubled from 1980 to 1990, without a similar increase in arrests or offenses known to the police. In Germany, total incarceration rates increased by 16 percent from 1978 to 1990 (55 per 100,000 to 64 per 100,00). For German men, the rate went from 113 to 116 per 100,000 (an increase of 3 percent). The incarceration rate for foreign men went up sharply from 1978 to 1990 (from 9 to 95 per 100,00). Still, it was lower than the German male incarceration rate in 1990. This comparison calls attention to a fundamental difference in the situation of black Americans and non-Germans in Germany. Black Americans are citizens entitled to all the rights of citizenship. Although these rights may not always be fully honored, citizens cannot be deported. As one possible explanation for the differences in incarceration rates, this suggestion needs additional investigation.

However, the parallels we have found suggest that ethnicity in Germany has much of the same impact on suspect rates as race has on arrest rates in the United States. In broad theoretical terms, it appears that any group of people occupying a marginal position in a society will be more likely to encounter the criminal justice system than groups with fewer disadvantages. The similarities in results in this comparison also suggest a more specific possibility. To the extent that a racial, ethnic, or culturally distinct group is disadvantaged economically, socially, and politically, its members will be more likely to engage in—and be charged with—criminal conduct. Such sweeping conclusions receive only limited support from this exploratory study. What we can say with confidence is that this analysis of data on ethnicity and suspicion of crime for Germany provides patterns similar to those produced when data on race and arrests are examined in the United States.

REFERENCES

Albrecht, Hans-Jörg. 1987. "Foreign Minorities and the Criminal Justice System in the Federal Republic of Germany." *Howard Journal* 26:272–86.

Chilton, Roland. 1986. "Age, Sex, Race, and Arrest Trends for 12 of the Nation's Largest Central Cities." Pp. 102–15 in *The Social Ecology of Crime,* James Byrne and Robert Sampson. (eds.) New York:Springer-Verlag.

———. 1987. "Twenty Years of Homicide and Robbery in Chicago: The Impact of the City's Changing Racial and Age Composition." *Journal of Quantitative Criminology* 3:195–214.

———. 1991. "Urban Crime Trends and Criminology Theory." *Criminal Justice Research Bulletin.* pp. 1–10 vol. 6, no. 3. Criminal Justice Center, Sam Houston State University, Huntsville, Texas.

Hindelang, M. J. 1978. "Race and Involvement in Common-Law Personal Crimes: A Comparison of Three Techniques." *American Sociological Review* 43:93–109.

Killias, Martin. 1989. "Criminality among Second-Generation Immigrants in Western Europe: A Review of the Evidence." *Criminal Justice Review* 14:13–42.

Kitsuse, J., and A. Cicourel. 1963. "A Note on the Use of Official Statistics." *Social Problems* 12:131–39.

LaFree, Gary, Kriss A. Drass, and Patrick O'Day. 1992. "Race and Crime in Postwar America: Determinants of African-American and White Rates, 1957–1988." *Criminology* 30:157–88.

McCleary, R., B. C. Nienstedt, and J. M. Erven. 1982. "Uniform Crime Reports as Organizational Outcomes: Three Time-Series Experiments." *Social Problems* 29:361–72.

McKay, Henry D., and Solomon Kobrin. 1966. "Nationality and Delinquency: A Study of Rates of Delinquents for Nativity, Nationality, and Racial Groups among Types of Areas in Chicago." Chicago: Institute of Juvenile Research, Department of Mental Health, State of Illinois. Unpublished Manuscript.

National Commission on Law Observance and Enforcement. 1931. *Report on Crime and the Foreign-Born.* Washington, D.C.: U.S. Government Printing Office.

Sampson, Robert J. 1987. "Urban Black Violence: The Effect of Male Joblessness and Family Disruption." *American Journal of Sociology* 93:348–82.

Sellin, Thorsten. 1938. *Culture Conflict and Crime.* New York: Social Science Research Council.

Teske, Raymond, and Harald Arnold. 1982. "Comparisons of the Criminal Justice Statistics of the United States and the Federal Republic of Germany." *Journal of Criminal Justice* 10:359–74.

U.S. Federal Bureau of Investigation. 1991. *Uniform Crime Reports: Crime in the United States.* Washington, D.C.: U.S. Government Printing Office.

U.S. Bureau of Justice Statistics. 1991. *Criminal Victimization in the United States: 1973–78 Trends.* Washington, D.C.: U.S. Government Printing Office.

U.S. President's Commission on Law Enforcement Administration of Justice. 1967. *Task Force Report: Crime and its Impact—An Assessment.* Washington, D.C.: U.S. Government Printing Office.

Van Vechten, C. C. 1941. "The Criminality of the Foreign Born." *Journal of Criminal Law and Criminology* 32:139–47.

PAMELA IRVING JACKSON

16

Minority Group Threat, Crime, and the Mobilization of Law in France

This study works toward a theory of the mobilization of law in response to ethnic threat. Its focus is on the actions of the majority group. The model investigated ties the visibility of ethnic minorities (their size and low socio-economic status) to social disorganization, differential cultural orientation, and competition for sociopolitical dominance. These conditions are seen to give rise to both crime and minority group threat, which is based on fear of crime and fear of loss of dominance. Social control efforts and resources are triggered, since greater control of minority group members and their deviance is viewed by the native population as necessary in preventing changes in their way of life and a loss of the majority's cultural dominance.

Recent work on the mobilization of law in response to ethnic and racial threat has focused on the majority group's collective commitment to social control in varying sociohistorical contexts of the United States (Jackson, 1985, 1986, 1989, 1992a, 1992b, 1992c; Jackson and Carroll, 1981). The problem has been seen to be peculiarly American, resulting from the heterogeneity and inequality of the society, in combination with its constitutionally provided creed of equal opportunity in the context of evident inequality. At this time, however, it makes sense to extend this work through investigation of nations on the continent of Europe.

Throughout the twentieth century, guestworkers have been both invited and tolerated as a permanent part of west European economies, despite the heterogeneity they have brought. Now, however, economic stagnation, urban decline, and the immigration resulting from the political upheavals in east Europe have strained the sociopolitical fabric of west European nations, undermining tolerance of difference. The rapid population growth involved is largely unwanted during this postindustrial period, and some types of heterogeneity have become politically more visible. In France, despite the onslaught of east European asylum seekers, the heterogeneity sparking fears of a loss of cultural dominance has come mainly from another source—Arab and African immigrants with their culturally distinct Muslim heritage.

This paper provides evidence suggesting that France has mobilized its law enforcement resources as a response to perceived minority threat—a threat engendered by the majority group's perceptions of unfair competition. Theories of internal colonialism (Hechter, 1975) and of the split labor market (Bonacich, 1972) present models wherein ethnic inequality, subordination, or class/economic disadvantage provide the backdrop for interethnic competition. In these contexts, Belanger and Pinard (1991:449) point out, even "objectively fair" competition will be perceived as unfair by the minority group because it occurs within structures perceived by them to be unfair. Belanger and Pinard (1991:446), in their recent effort to specify the missing links in the ethnic competition model (Barth, 1969; Hannan, 1979), add the two conditions addressed by the internal colonial and split labor market theory as necessary for ethnic mobilization. "Competition," they argue, "leads to mobilization only when competition is perceived as unfair and it occurs in a context of low ethnic interdependence."

Belanger and Pinard focus on the behavior of the ethnic minority groups, their propensity to separate or to initiate conflict. It is the contention of the present chapter that the dominant majority group's perceptions of unfair competition and segmented competitive relations may trigger mobilization of another sort: the mobilization of law, especially if the competition is over collective goods such as maintainance of the prevailing culture or a group's share of the labor market. The mobilization of law to protect the dominant cultural and economic groups can be seen in a number of societal areas: in sentencing and corrections, in policing and in immigration policy.

The sections below present the theoretical context of the chapter; an evaluation of the extent to which minority/majority competition in France is perceived (by the majority group) to be unfair; a discussion of the extent of segmentation in competitive relations between the groups; manifestations of the majority group's perceptions of minority group threat and crime; the actual level of minority criminal involvements; and evidence of the mobilization of law in response to perceived minority threat.

THEORETICAL BACKGROUND

In considering the development of Durkheim's *collective conscience* within a nation-state, Hechter (1975) discusses the importance of a collectivity's cultural, economic, and political integration. Identifiable differences in religion and language undermine cultural integration, and adherence to these differences retards the growth toward a national identity. Economic integration refers "to the evolution of substantially equal rates of social and economic development among the collectivities in a society" (Hechter, 1975: 19), as reflected in their per capita income, rates of literacy and infant mortality, as well as their political power. Finally, political integration occurs when the structural position of a group, rather than objective cultural factors, is most salient in formation of the group's political demands. The collective conscience that is the basis of national solidarity, Hechter points out, "may not be presumed to automatically cut across" groups that do not define their membership in the society as satisfactory (Hechter, 1975:20).

Hechter's focus is on the degree of dissatisfaction of the minority group. Meanwhile he describes the "crystallization of the unequal distribution of resources and power" between core and peripheral groups in the society. He notes that the "superordinate group, or core, seeks to stabilize or monopolize its advantages through policies aiming at institutionalization of the existing stratification system." He further explains that the development of a "cultural division of labor," which "contributes to distinctive ethnic identification in the two groups," is aided by "visible signs, or cultural markers, which are seen to characterize both groups." At this point, acculturation "does not occur because it is not in the interests of these institutions" (Hechter, 1975:9). With these points, Hechter addresses the perceptions of the majority group, and their use of existing resources to maintain their privileged position.

Bonacich (1972) brings us even closer to the problem at hand with her discussion of a three-way conflict as the basis for what she calls the ethnic antagonism that leads to exclusion movements and the development of caste systems. Noting that "economic processes are more fundamental than racial and ethnic cultural differences in the development of ethnic antagonism," Bonacich (1972:548–54) elaborates on the competing economic interests of what she refers to as the "white capitalist class," the "higher paid white labor group," and the cheaper labor group of ethnic workers. Ethnic antagonism, in the Bonacich scheme (1972, 549), does not emanate from one side only; it is often mutual, "the product of interaction." It has its roots in a labor market that is split along ethnic lines, containing at least two groups of workers "whose price of labor differs for the same work or would differ if they did the same work.'' The competition need not be direct; potential competition is as significant a threat as the actual competition. Citing Blalock's (1967) model of labor competition, Bonacich (1972:554) reasons that "when one ethnic group is decidedly cheaper than another, the higher paid worker faces more than the loss of his job; he faces the possibility that the wage standard in all jobs will be undermined by cheaper labor.''

The capitalist class, however, stands to gain significantly from the cheaper labor force, and to lose a great deal from their exclusion. (Their relegation to a caste would still allow their services to be exploited, but castes are no longer acceptable in most Western democracies.) The price of a labor force varies inversely with its political resources, Bonacich (1972:550) reminds us. By extension we must recognize that the cheapest labor forces are, therefore, the easiest to exclude, precisely because they have such limited resources. The more segmented the groups are—that is, the greater the number of cleavages separating the cheaper from the more highly paid labor group— the more likely it is that antagonism will develop.

Belanger and Pinard (1991:450) suggest that the lack of interdependence bred by such segmentation, especially when competition is over collective goods ("each group's share of the labor market," for example), gives rise to ethnic independence movements. But where one group is lopsidedly without resources, and where a three-way conflict exists between dominant group labor, cheaper ethnic group labor and capitalists, I argue that it is more likely that criminal justice control of the ethnic group will escalate and that exclusion movements of one form or another will develop.

A model linking public commitment to social control (through both the criminal justice system and immigration policy) with sociodemograhic and contextual characteristics of the unit of analysis appears below in Figure 16.1. The model guides the following analysis. I developed a rudimentary version of this model on the basis of U.S. data (Jackson, 1989). That model, however, evolved specifically to explain the mobilization of police resources in the United States. The expansion of its focus to the mobilization of law in general, and its incorporation of internal colonial and split labor market theories, allow it to direct investigation of the importance of structural segmentation and majority group perceptions of unfair competition. These elements of the sociocultural context were not investigated in earlier work on this topic.

SOCIOCULTURAL CONTEXT

Perceptions of unfairness. In the older industrial nations of Europe, immigration policy is tied to manpower policy. Until the late 1960s, France compensated for its long-term depopulation problem and (avoided significant responsiveness to negative public opinion about foreigners) with a laissez

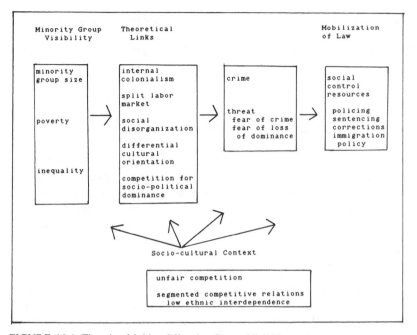

FIGURE 16.1 Theories Linking Minority Group Visibility and the Mobilization of Law

faire approach to immigration (Ogden and White, 1989). Immigrants, often encouraged by employers, entered the country during periods of labor shortage. Even before World War I, France's inability or unwillingness to "produce its own offspring" (Penin, 1986:148, cited in Ogden, 1989:39) was a catalyst to permissive immigration policies. After World War I, "immigration was seen as one of the few options open to France to make good its war losses" (Ogden, 1989:39). The aftermath of World War II brought an effort to encourage permanent settlement of easily assimilable groups. Even in the post–World War II era, however, "countries whose nationals were considered less desirable were allotted correspondingly fewer entry permits" (Freeman, 1989: 164).

Despite such attempts to control the racial and ethnic composition of immigration, Algerian, Moroccan, and Tunisian immigration climbed steadily in the postwar era, forming (with Turks) 13 percent of the foreign population of France in 1954, and 42 percent in 1982 (Ogden, 1989:44–49). The return en masse of French nationals (*pieds noirs*) in the 1960s and family reunification policies of the 1970s had a geometric effect on the number of foreign nationals in France. By 1982, "11% of births in France were to a foreign mother'' (Desplanques, 1985, cited in Ogden, 1989:50). Even though there has been a general decrease (as reflected in the 11 percent decline) in the employment of foreign workers beginning with the 1974 economic recession, they remain ''at the core of the economy,'' comprising in 1982 over 14 percent of the national work force in motor car and vehicle manufacture, 17 percent in building, and accounting for over 6 percent of the total labor force (Ogden, 1989:53–54).

The consistent importance of foreign labor to the French economy is not reflected in their housing and social conditions. Although their substandard housing conditions have regularly prompted public outcry, both from the residents of France and from officials of the sending nations, little has been done about them. Some have argued that the obvious explanation for the failure to eradicate these conditions is that improvements would reduce the attractiveness of foreign workers to employers by increasing their cost (Freeman, 1989:161).

Set apart from native French by history, religious tradition, and pigmentation, these immigrants are increasingly perceived as an unfair threat to the dominant Euro-Christian culture of the nation. Unfair, because to most French, they have no business in the country and no right to its services. This reaction has its contradictory aspects, in light of the nation's history of encouraging immigration to fuel its industrial economy. But the visibility of Arab and African immigrants and their *beur* descendants has increased, partly because their efforts to maintain their own religious and cultural heritage have attracted attention, and partly as a result of their persistently low skill and educational levels (*New York Times*, 1/24/92, A:4). In the current period of recession and high unemployment in France, these groups appear to native French to be competing for the scarce economic opportunities for unskilled workers in cities.

In a recent analysis of the degree and sources of ideological and structural racism in France, Michel Wieviorka outlines the extent to which the end of the industrial era and the decline of the trade union as a workers' movement have changed the social and political structure of French society and the public conception of immigrants. Immigrants once necessary to provide labor for industrial production, once perceived as exploited for their cheap labor and their substandard housing, are ''increasingly viewed as a problem, a source of worry'' (as translated from Wieviorka, 1992:28). Typical comments about immigrants, Wieviorka (1992:9–11) points out, include, ''they didn't come to France for nothing, they want to profit, and even to dictate. . . . They take jobs from us.'' In the context of the new urban questions raised by the simultaneous decline of industrial and manufacturing opportunities and the rapid growth of immigrant populations in cities, the National Front's linking of the themes of immigration, economic and political insecurity, and urban crime and delinquency has had, since the 1980s, broad appeal, reflecting "to a large extent the geography of immigrant settlement" (Ogden, 1989:57).

Segmentation. France is characterized by a crystalization of inequality in the distribution of resources and power, as well as by minority/majority segmentation. Despite its past history of absorption of minority populations within the culture, the economic and social forces of the postindustrial era have greatly changed the urban landscape of France, fostering the "dualization of French society" (translated from Wieviorka, 1992:31). More than a third of the population of French nationality is of foreign ancestry ("no more than three generations back," Ogden and White, 1989:2); the addition of foreign nationals brings this total to about 40 percent.

During the past twenty years, segregation in housing and schools has become noticeable and problematic, establishing a continuing spiral made all the more visible because of the social solidarity and persisting Islamic religious traditions of the lowest status groups, the North Africans. Their self-sufficient social networks reaffirm their distinctiveness and separate them even further from white, Catholic French. "In a climate increasingly dominated by economic recession and by anti-immigrant feeling," Philip Ogden (1989:52) notes, "much concern has been expressed in France, as in other European countries, about a second generation feeling neither fully part of the culture of their parents nor of French society in which they have been largely educated."

Philippe Robert and Jean-Marie Renouard (1991:197) refer (in their writings on deviance) to the "pluri-ethnic character" of French society. As Wieviorka describes, "industrial society was a powerful integrating factor, which, in disappearing, created an environment where cultural identities were redrawn first along national, community, and religious lines, and then, after that, along biological lines, indicating racism" (translated from Wieviorka, 1992:34). The changes wrought by postindustrialism have not created racism, Wieviorka (1989:39) points out, but they have opened the door to it. In addition, the cultural, economic, and political segmentation of native French and their Maghreb and Turkish immigrants is conducive to the development of conflict.

PERCEPTIONS OF MINORITY GROUP THREAT AND CRIME

In some areas of France, successive waves of foreign workers and their descendants now pose a significant threat to native populations, especially to the unskilled working class. Native members of the working class are in closest proximity to these (potential) ethnic workers in housing, schools, and in competition for employment. They have made their resentment clear at the polls and in the streets. They complain of the newcomers' crime, the smell of their neighborhoods, their failure to assimilate, and their drain on social welfare resources. Gradually, immigrants have come to be seen as the source of all the problems associated with postindustrial economic development and change.

Evident in the French situation is the mutuality that Bonacich (1972) indicates is characteristic of ethnic antagonism. North African ethnic groups, in France, concentrated in conditions of poverty that are conducive to the development of crime, are a source of fear and aggravation as a result of their criminal involvement and their riots. They have not fully assimilated, remaining apart in language, in culture—especially religion—and in their social networks. Wieviorka cites police impressions of the Maghrebins (immigrants from Algeria, Morocco, and Tunisia) "living as if they were in their own country," with stuffed lamb for Ramadan, and rabbits in the bathtubs. Minorities in Marseilles are described, again by police, as squabbling and divided, but united against the police; eight-year-old children are said to throw rocks at the police without any hesitation (Wieviorka, (1992:227–28).

The rise of ethnic enclaves in France's urban centers, populated by an underclass of visibly and culturally distinct Arab and African immigrants and their descendants, threatens the white Catholic core of French society. Statements by prominent French political figures evidence these perceptions of threat. Repatriation, implemented periodically, has again been raised in the current context as a solution to "the noise and smell" associated with the " 'overdose' of immigrants" (*New York Times*, 9/21/91, 6:49). The size and relative poverty of these culturally distinct groups contribute to the social disorganization of their neighborhoods and their continued differential cultural orientation.

These conditions do breed crime. However, the image of the immigrant population as the source of France's crime and drug trafficking problems is highly exaggerated among native French. Popular accounts assert unequivocally that 80 percent of the delinquent population in France is immigrant and North African in origin (Wieviorka, 1992:245). In fact, immigrants, about 8 percent of the population, account for roughly 15 percent of those charged with theft; about 13 percent of those charged with violent crimes; and 29 percent of those charged with violating drug laws and disturbing the peace (Direction Générale de la Police Nationale, 1990:125).

Their crimes are not distributed evenly throughout the country, however, but are clustered in the urban areas of their residence, enhancing the threat engendered by their presence. In the Paris department, for example, 40 percent of identified offenders are immigrants (Kania, 1989:12). Among the 95 departments (administrative units into which the country is divided) in

TABLE 16.1   Departments with Highest and Lowest Minority Crime Involvement: Level of *Étrangers*, Proportion of Criminal Suspects Who Are *Étrangers* and Overall Crime Rate for the Department, 1990.

Department	Etranger Level*	Percent Etrangers Suspects**	Crime Rate per 1,000 Residents***
Pyrénées-Orientales	4	49.56	96.61
Paris	5	40.53	136.95
Alpes-Maritimes	4	35.99˙	124.28
Seine-Saint-Denis	4	32.72	73.12
Hauts-de-Seine	5	31.06	69.76
Val-d'Oise	5	30.08	75.31
Val-de-Marne	5	28.27	80.53
Bouches-du-Rhone	4	25.79	97.35
Haut-Rhin	5	25.37	50.27
Sarthe	2	3.62	33.72
Cantal	1	3.46	24.85
Ille-et-Vilaine	1	3.36	36.72
Cotes d'Amor	1	3.33	40.07
Finistere	1	2.57	35.26
Charente-Maritime	2	2.31	51.67
Manche	1	2.30	31.37
Vendée	1	2.12	34.04
Morbihan	1	1.25	36.62

Source: Ogden, 1989:55. Codes: 1 = 1–.9% *étrangers;* 2 = 1–3.9%; 3 = 4–6.9%; 4 = 7–9.9%; 5 = greater than 10% *étrangers.*
**Source: Direction Générale de La Police Nationale, 1990:125, 128.
***Source: Direction Générale de La Police Nationale, 1990:32.

France, there is considerable variability in the overall proportion of foreigners, in the crime rate, and in the proportion of *étrangers* suspected of a criminal act. (*Etrangers,* foreigners, constitute the "minority" classification in French census records. While specific categories of etrangers are enumerated [for example, Moroccan, Algerian, or Portuguese], minorities are customarily not enumerated in other ways.) Rank ordered by the percent of delinquent *étranger* identified offenders, the eighteen departments with the highest and lowest levels are listed in Table 16.1. (The top and bottom nine are typically scrutinized in the official annual report of the Police Nationale.) Also shown are rankings indicating the relative size of the foreign population in the department, and the overall crime rate.

As is evident from Table 16.1, for those departments with a high proportion of *étrangers,* the level of foreign offenders sometimes noticeably exceeds what would be expected on the basis of the percentage of foreigners in the population. For example, less than 10 percent of the population of the department of Pyrénées-Orientales was *étranger,* yet about 50 percent of criminal suspects were *étrangers.* Similarly, in the departments of Alpes-Maritimes and Seine-Saint-Denis where the proportion of *étrangers* in the population was also less than 10 percent, the proportion of *étrangers* among those individuals *mises en cause* (suspects) was well over 30 percent.

Also apparent is the general lack of foreigner criminal justice involvement in departments with the lowest levels of foreign population. In departments with less than 1 percent foreign populations, such as Vendée, Cotes d'Amor, and Finistère, the proportion of identified offenders who are foreign was quite low (only about 2 or 3 percent), much more in line with the proportion foreign in the population. These departments lack the major urban centers of immigrant settlement characteristic of the departments mentioned earlier. That, their lower crime rates overall, and the low incidence of minorities in their overall population, may help to reduce minority visibility.

MOBILIZATION OF LAW

Until recently, despite the social and economic threat that foreign labor poses to native workers, immigration in France has been both permitted and encouraged by law. This has occurred in a seemingly haphazard, semipublic manner, ostensibly, as discussed above, to protect the nation's "fragile rate of population increase over the last two centuries" (Ogden and White, 1989: 5). It can be argued, however, that official tolerance of the immigration of actual or potential foreign labor pools serves to protect the capitalist class by creating a secure source of cheap labor. It also thereby sets up the three-way conflict described by Bonacich (1972).

Similarly, government sponsored efforts in France to facilitate integration and to stem the tide of *xenophobic nationalism* can also be seen as protecting and preserving (untintentionally or not) the cheap foreign labor pool. These efforts have met with resistance at several levels. For example, a plan by the French socialist government to "withhold national budget revenues from rich communities and give it to poor towns" to facilitate efforts to improve substandard schools and housing was condemned "by conservatives as a misguided Robin Hood scheme" (*New York Times* Index to 3/24/91:I:6) despite the recent report of the nation's newly created Council on Integration in France. The council had argued that "integration of third world immigrants into French society is the proper answer to concern among the French population that immigrants are 'taking over.' " The group had further warned that "integration means guaranteeing equality of rights and duties for everyone rather than reinforcing segregation of immigrants by treating them as special communities or minorities. . . . [and that] new measures . . . [are] needed to integrate Arabs, Africans, and Asians now crowding French schools, housing complexes, and hostels'' (*New York Times*, Index to 3/24/91, I:3).

The climate may now be right for native labor groups to be successful in their struggle to mobilize the law to protect their advantaged position: more unskilled labor may not be needed in Europe in general, or in France in particular, at this time. In their recent analysis of international migration in the European community, Muus and Cruijsen conclude:

> There is at the moment in the EC region no big need for importing low-skilled people. The presence of an enormous reservoir of often un-skilled and semi-skilled labor may at least in the short run, block a massive inflow of low(er) skilled persons. Just for certain specific, high-qualified areas, labour force shortages seem to exist.'' (Muus and Cruijsen, 1991: 63)

Perhaps in response to this reality, efforts to mobilize law to protect the advantages of the native working class have taken two forms: an escalation of minority crime control and repatriation policies.

Minority crime control. ''Get-tough'' policies on immigrants have emerged (*New York Times*, 9/21/91, VI:33), in the face of continuing popularity of Jean-Marie Le Pen as leader of the ''xenophobic and anti-Semitic National Front'' (*New York Times*, 9/21/91, VI:49). (In national opinion polls, he captures about 15 percent of the vote overall, but closer to 30 percent in southern departments with the heaviest immigrant population.) Indeed a careful look at the relationship between growth in the foreign population, increases in the rate of *étranger* suspects, and changes in the proportion of *étrangers* incarcerated provides some support for the conclusion that justice systems in France have responded in recent years in line with the current ''get tough policy'' toward foreigners.

For the 1970–80 decade the figures in Table 16.2 indicate a greater rate of growth in the size of the minority population than in their representation in the criminal justice system. But during the next decade the situation was reversed. Between 1970 and 1980 the proportion of immigrants increased from 5 percent to 7 percent of the population, a growth of 2 percent in the overall population, and of 40 percent of the original 1970 figure. The rate of foreign suspects grew from 20 to 24 per thousand *étrangers* population, a figure 20 percent higher in 1980 than in 1972 (the earliest year for which this measure is available). The proportion of those incarcerated who were immigrants increased from 15.1 percent to 19.8 percent. This 4.7 percent increase represented a 31 percent growth rate during the decade.

TABLE 16.2　France: Percent *Étranger, Étranger* Suspects per Thousand *Étranger* Population, Percent Incarcerated Who Were *Étrangers*, 1970–1990.

Year	Percent Etranger*	Etranger Suspects per 1,000 Etrangers**	Percent Incarcerated Who Were Etrangers***
1990	7.9	28	29.7
1980	7.0	24	19.8
1970	5.0	20	15.1

Source: Ogden, 1989: 40; Direction Générale de la Police Nationale, 1990:125.

**Source:* Direction Général de la Police Nationale, 1990:125; Tournier and Robert, 1991:67–68. (Since 1972 is the earliest year for which this calculation is available, it is used as the base line in this column.)

***Source:* Tournier and Robert, 1991:103.

In the next decade, however, the proportion *étranger* changed by less than 1 percent growing from 7.0 percent in 1980 to 7.9 percent in 1990. This represented only a 12.8 percent increase during the decade. The proportion of immigrants identified as offenders, however, grew by 16.6 percent, rising to 28 per thousand *étrangers*, from 24 per thousand. The proportion incarcerated who were *étrangers* experienced a 50 percent increase, growing from 19.8 percent of the incarcerated population in 1980 to 29.7 percent in 1990. It appears that in the 1980–90 decade both police and corrections officials stepped up their efforts to control minority group members and their deviance.

France has also moved in the direction of escalating resources for social control, especially in the areas of greatest ethnic visibility (*Le Monde*, 9/10/91: 12). The Centre de Recherches Sociologiques sur le Droit et les Institutions Pénales (CESDIP) documents the costs of crime control to the nation as a whole in three categories: public costs for repression, public costs for prevention, and private costs for protection. Costs for repression (CESDIP's term) include officer time devoted to apprehension of those who have violated the law. Prevention includes police patrol activities in a narrow sense; and in a larger sense, all activities not specifically devoted to repression or administrative work (Godefroy and Laffargue, 1989:27).

Public costs include those for the Police Nationale (responsible for policing cities of 10,000 or more population); the Gendarmerie (which polices all other areas of France, the less populated and rural locations); the Ministère public et juridictions (costs for courts and related services); Administration pénitentiaire (costs related to imprisonment); Education surveillée (expenses related to delinquent youth); and Casier Judiciaire (expenses related to the national judiciary). Private costs are those for alarm and other security systems, as well as insurance and legal costs. All three categories of

TABLE 16.3   France: Public and Private Costs for Crime Repression and Prevention, and Private Costs for Protection from Crime, 1980–87 (in millions of francs).

Year	Public Cost Repression*	Public Cost Prevention**	Private Cost Protection***
1980	5789	10140	15013
1981	7210	11836	17139
1982	7963	13947	19084
1984	9178	16785	25963
1985	9395	17636	27949
1986	9842	18600	30003
1987	10175	19194	33845

Sources: Godefroy and Laffargue, 1984: 53, 54; 1989: 95. (1983 figures were not available for any category.)
**Sources:* Godefroy and Laffargue, 1984: 54; 1989: 96.
***Sources:* Godefroy and Laffargue, 1984: 54; 1989: 97.

expenses (public costs for crime repression, public costs for crime prevention, and private costs for protection from crime) are depicted in Table 16.3 for the years 1980–1987.

In this seven-year period there has been about a 43 percent increase in the costs defined as repression of infractions (these costs, in millions of francs, increased from 5,789 to 10,175); a 47 percent increase in prevention costs (which grew from 10,140 million francs in 1980 to 19,194 in 1987); and a 56 percent increase in private protection costs (from 15,013 to 33,845 million francs). Even with adjustments for inflation over the seven years, the increases are notable, suggesting greater reliance on both criminal justice agencies and private surveillance during this period.

Other analyses confirm this impression. Wieviorka (1992: 230) describes public reliance on police as "the last rampart" (translated from Wieviorka, 1992: 230) preventing the engulfment of traditional French society. He notes that this reflects, and may well exacerbate what he (1992:230–42) has termed an institutional malaise and a crisis of justice and the social order. Overreliance on justice agencies to solve the economic and institutional dislocations of the transition to postindustrialism, he argues, has paved the way for the growth of racism among criminal justice officers.

Charges of police racism, officers argue, are excessive and unjust. Yet they admit that the anti-French, antipolice hostility that they experience on a daily basis triggers resentment. One consequence of their real life experience, "professional and familial," they point out, is the development of "anti-Arab, anti-black, anti-Turk . . . anti-gypsy" racism (translated from Wieviorka, 1992:230). Police become racist; and they are paralyzed in sections of many cities, sections that resemble a "jungle" (Wieviorka, 1992:228). Line officers feel isolated, and begin to rely only on each other. They also feel unsupported by the hierarchy above them. Without their weapons, they point out, they are inferior to those they must control. They play cards instead of patrolling the streets during the evening hours in some sections of Marseilles, they confess, because of the danger involved on those streets. The institution of policing is developing a racist normative structure as police collectively accept their isolation in controlling the immigrant underclass (Wieviorka, 1992:264).

Three incidents in the spring of 1993 epitomized this problem. They were highly publicized by both French and foreign mass media. In the most widely discussed case (on April 6), 17-year old Nakome M'Bowole, a Zairean immigrant under interrogation at a police station in Paris for stealing a package of cigarettes, was shot in the face and killed by a police officer. This case was followed one day later by the serious wounding of Rachid Ardjouni, 18-year-old son of an Arab immigrant. He was shot in the head by police while being pursued for disturbing the peace in Wattrelos, near Lille. On the same night, in Arachon (in the west of France near Bordeaux), Pascal Tais, a drug addict of Moroccan ancestry, was found dead in a police cell, having suffered a ruptured spleen, broken ribs, and a punctured lung (*New York Times*, 4/9/93, A:2).

The fact that these incidents came one week after the selection of Charles Pasqua—a hardliner—to the post of Interior Minister, suggests to many in France that police sense a lifting of restraints on their behavior toward immigrants and their descendants. In a letter to Mr. Pasqua (dated April 8), several community associations complained that since he assumed the post "some police have the feeling that they are protected, no matter what they do." The letter also complained of racist and physical abuses during police sweeps of the neighborhood (*New York Times*, 4/9/93, A:2). A human rights group, SOS-Racisme, called a protest meeting over this issue.

Immigration policy. Through immigration policy the most effective forms of control over the immigrant underclass can be imposed—exclusion and repatriation. France has undergone several waves of repatriation, especially affecting its African and Arab immigrants. During the latter part of the 1960s many factors came together triggering a major shift in government attitudes concerning the "benefits from an uncontrolled flow of workers" into the country (Freeman, 1989:165). Strikes and demonstrations in the spring of 1968 brought the matter to public attention. There was some immigrant involvement, and many immigrants were expelled as a result.

But the issues that led to France's protection of the native labor market were longer-term in nature. Freeman (1989:165) lists the following as being most important: the scandalous living conditions in immigrant communities; racial and ethnic tensions; extremist nationalism; the discouragement of productivity enhancing capital intensification caused by the abundance of cheap labor sources; the recognition that "supposedly temporary workers were not, in fact temporary after all and, perhaps most importantly, the striking shift in the sources of immigration to non-European countries." As immigrants began to threaten French society by their character, culture, and place in the economic system, immigration policy was revised to restrict their flow.

By the summer of 1968 France placed significant limitations on Algerian immigration, and in 1974, faced with the recession resulting from the OPEC oil embargo, the French "closed the door to new immigration for work as tightly as they could" (Freeman, 1989:166) suspending all immigration for work from sources outside the European Economic Community. In 1977 an assisted repatriation plan was put forward, but was not successful in convincing the targeted group (North African immigrants) to leave. Despite the severe restrictions on immigration of foreign workers, reunification of family members and the regularization of the official status of immigrants who had been in the country for many years have masked resulting reductions in the overall flow of immigrants. However, current immigration policy in France continues to be restrictive.

A wave of involuntary deportations resulted from the 1986 "Pasqua Act," named for its author, then Minister of the Interior (from 1986 to 1988). Oficially entitled the Loi Relative aux Conditions d'Entrée et de Sejour des Etrangers en France, the act allowed officials to stop foreigners for examination of their documents and, where those papers were not in order, give them "just 24 hours to exit Paris or face arrest and involuntary deportation." Special planes handled the deportations, largely of "Middle Eastern and African laborers who often lacked legal work permits" (Kania, 1989:16). Critics (Hunter, 1989:44) argued that the "anti-terrorist law subtly was converted into an anti-minorities law" (Kania, 1989:16).

The 1993 parliamentary elections in France seemed to assure the success of exclusion efforts in France. The final results, a stunning conservative victory, were attributed to French frustration with unemployment and the changing character of France's immigrant neighborhoods (*New York Times,* 3/22/93, A:1; 4/4/93, IV:4). One of the first acts of the new administration was to revise the nationality code, symbolically undermining the citizenship rights of French-born children of foreigners by requiring that they officially request citizenship between the ages of 16 and 21 rather than receive it automatically as had been the case. This legislation has been seen as the harbinger of "much tougher measures" (*New York Times,* 5/16/93, IV: 2) intended to retain the cultural and religious core of the nation and to protect the economic advantages of native French.

DISCUSSION AND CONCLUSIONS

The economic changes triggered by the Western world's shift from manufacturing to service-based economies have increased the pressure on the working class, sharply reducing their employment opportunities. Segmentation within the working class, especially where it overlays racial, ethnic, and cultural divisions becomes critical, as the competition between segments for scarce employment escalates. As conditions worsen in the lowest groups, crime and other social problems spiral in their communities, increasing the visibility of these groups and the perceived importance of their cultural and physical differences from members of the dominant working class. This triggers dominant workers' pressure for both control and exclusion of the highly visible racial and ethnic workers with whom they are in (actual or perceived) competition.

In the current postindustrial economic context where the dominant working classes contain sufficient surplus labor, resistance by the capitalist class to control and exclusion of subordinate working class members is likely to be too weak to block minority exclusion and control efforts. Eventually, in capitalist Western democracies that pressure is likely to succeed in achieving the mobilization of social control resources to police, exclude or otherwise control the threatening groups. (See Rueschemeyer et al., 1992, on the extent to which capitalism strengthens the political position of the working classes.)

The mobilization of law sought by majority workers to protect their labor market advantages vis-à-vis minority workers or to safeguard their way of life is not always successful: legal mechanisms may not be effective in containing the (actual or perceived) threat. As is evident in the case of France (and currently being demonstrated in the United States), the pushes and pulls of human migration and the complications of the social disorganization associated with poverty defy legal control.

Despite efforts to restrict immigration and to encourage repatriation of ethnic minorities, criminal justice agencies in France are increasingly being expected to handle the problems of inner-city disorganization resulting from the growth of minority populations in a stagnant economy. There is no evidence that they will be able to do this in the absence of social policies that improve the now criminogenic living conditions in minority communities, and in the absence of national economic policies that reduce the potential threat of these groups to native workers.

The problems that criminal justice agencies are being asked to control in France are, like those in the United States, significantly beyond their best efforts; and their potential for violence has been demonstrated by recent incidents. The current problems have at their root economic dislocations that exacerbate cultural divisions in the population. The broad scope of the determinants of crime and social threat diagramed in Figure 16.1 and illustrated in France suggest that reductions of both ethnic antagonism and crime require greater breadth in policy formulation than a delimited law enforcement approach can provide.

NOTE

This paper could not have been written without the resources provided by the Groupe Européen de Recherche sur les Normativités (GERN), the Centre de Recherches Sociologiques sur le Droit et les Institutions Pénales, and the Faculty Research Committee of Rhode Island College. Special thanks are owed to Madam Lopez at GERN for her assistance.

REFERENCES

Barth, Fredrik. 1969. "Introduction." Pp. 9–38 in *Ethnic Groups and Boundaries: The Social Organization of Culture Difference,* Boston: Little, Brown. Fredrik Barth (ed).

Belanger, Sarah, and Maurice Pinard. 1991. "Ethnic Movements and the Competition Model: Some Missing Links." *American Sociological Review* 56:446–57.

Blalock, Hubert M. 1967. *Toward a Theory of Minority Group Relations.* New York: John Wiley.

Bonacich, Edna. 1972. "A Theory of Ethnic Antagonism: The Split Labour Market." *American Sociological Review* 37:547–59.

Desplanques, G. 1985. "Nuptialité et fécondité des étrangeres." *Economie et Statistique* 179:29–46.

Direction Générale de la Police Nationale. 1990. *Aspects de la Criminalité et de la Delinquance Constatées en France en 1990.* Paris: Documentation française.

————. 1989. *Aspects de la Criminalité et de la Delinquance Constatées en France en 1989.* Paris: Documentation française.

Freeman, Gary P. 1989. "Immigrant Labour and Racial Conflict: The Role of the State." Pp. 160–76 in *Migrants in Modern France,* Philip E. Ogden and Paul E. White (eds.). London: Unwin Hyman.

Godefroy, Thierry, and Bernard Laffargue. 1989. *Les Coûts du Crime en France: Données 1984, 1985, 1986 et 1987. Etudes et Données Pénales.* Paris: Centre de Recherches Sociologiques sur le Droit et les Institutions Pénales.

————. 1984. *Les Coûts du Crime en France: Données 1980, 1981 et 1982.* Etudes et Données Pénales. Paris: Centre de Recherches Sociologiques sur le Droit et les Institutions Pénales.

Hannan, Michael T. 1979. "The Dynamics of Ethnic Boundaries in Modern States." Pp. 253–75 in *National Development and the World System: Educational, Economic and Political Change, 1950–1970.* John W. Meyer and Michael T. Hannan (eds.). Chicago: University of Chicago Press.

Hechter, Michael. 1975. *Internal Colonialism.* Berkeley: University of California Press.

Hunter, Mark. 1989. "Visa La Différence." *Paris Passion* 59 (January/February): 44–45.

Jackson, Pamela Irving. 1985. "Ethnicity, Region, and Public Fiscal Commitment to Policing." *Justice Quarterly* 2 (2):167–94.

———. 1986. "Black Visibility, City Size, and Social Control." *Sociological Quarterly* 27 (2):185–203.

———. 1989. *Minority Group Threat, Crime and Policing: Social Context and Social Control.* New York: Praeger.

———. 1992a. "Minority Group Threat and Social Control: Twenty Years of Investigation." Pp. 209–21 in *Research in Inequality and Social Conflict,* vol. 2, Michael Dobkowski and Isidor Walliman (eds.). Greenwich, Conn.: JAI Press.

———. 1992b. "Minority Group Threat, Social Context, and Policing." Pp. 89–102 in *Social Threat and Social Control,* Allen E. Liska (ed.). Albany: State University of New York Press.

———. 1992c. "The Police and Social Threat: Urban Transition, Youth Gangs, and Social Control." *Policing and Society* 2:193–204.

Jackson, Pamela Irving, and Leo Carroll, 1981. "Race and the War on Crime: The Sociopolitical Determinants of Municipal Police Expenditures in 90 U.S. Cities," American Sociological Review 46:290–305.

Kania, Richard R. E. 1989. *The French Crime Problem—How Bad Is It?"* Unpublished paper, Guilford College, N.C.

Le Monde. 9/10/91. "Le Projet de Loi Sur la Securité Intérieure est Reporté," p. 12.

Muus, Philip, and Harri Cruijsen. 1991. "International Migration in the European Community." Unpublished paper presented at the International Conference on Human Resources in Europe at the Dawn of the 21st Century. Luxembourg, November 27–29, 1991.

New York Times. 3/24/91. Section I:3.

———. 3/24/91. Section I:6.

———. 9/21/91. "Strangers at the Gate: Europe's Immigration Crisis." VI:33–86.

———. 1/24/92. "Europe's Homebred Imams, Preaching Tolerance." Section A:4.

———. 3/22/93. "Strong Conservative Vote Stuns Mitterrand and French Socialists." Section A:1.

———. 4/4/93. "France Goes to the Right, by Default." Section IV:4.

———. 4/9/93. "France Takes Tough Stance on Crime and Immigration." Section A:2.

———. 5/16/93. "Marie France and Illegal Immigrants." Section IV:2.

Ogden, Philip E. 1989. "International Migration in the Nineteenth and Twentieth Centuries." Pp. 34–59 in *Migrants in Modern France*, Philip E. Ogden and Paul E. White (eds.). London: Unwin Hyman.

Ogden, Philip E., and Paul E. White. 1989. *Migrants in Modern France*. London: Unwin Hyman.

Penin, M. 1986. "Les Questions de Population au tournant du siècle à travers l'oeuvre de Charles Gide (1847–1932)." *Histoire, Economie et Société* 5, 137–58.

Robert, Philippe, and Jean-Marie Renouard. 1991. "Bilan des Connaissances en France." Pp. 191–205 in *Les Politiques de Prévention de la Delinquance*, under the direction of Philippe Robert, Paris: L'Harmattan.

Rueschemeyer, Deitrich, Evalyne Huber Stephens, and John D. Stephens. 1992. *Capitalist Development and Democracy*. Chicago: University of Chicago Press.

Tournier, Pierre, and Philippe Robert. 1991. *Etrangers et Delinquances*. Paris: L'Harmattan.

Wieviorka, Michel. 1992. *La France Raciste*. Paris: Seuil.

Contributors

HARALD ARNOLD received a diploma in psychology in 1978 from the University of Freiburg, Federal Republic of Germany. Since then he has been a member of the criminological research group at the Max Planck Institute for Foreign and International Penal Law at Freiburg. In addition, starting this year, he is assisting the law faculty of the University of Konstanz. He has published articles in national and international journals on juvenile delinquency, victim surveys, comparative research, and methodology. His current research focus is on cocaine, drug law enforcement, and organized crime.

E. M. BECK is professor of sociology and head of the department at the University of Georgia. His interest is on the political economy of racial violence, in particular the relationship between economic changes in the status of the white lower class and violence against blacks. His current research focuses on the economic and organizational factors associated with contemporary racial violence in the American south.

M. CRAIG BROWN teaches on an adjunct basis with the department of sociology and the schools of Criminal Justice and Social Welfare at SUNY, Albany. In addition to continuing his work with Barbara Warner on politics, ethnicity, and crime, his research interests include the emergence of machine politics in U.S. cities, and the expansion and contraction of public institutions serving the mentally disabled.

After teaching at numerous universities in the United States and abroad including the Universities of Washington, California-Santa Barbara, Delaware, Stockholm, Norway, Ibadan, Cardiff, and Zambia, WILLIAM CHAMBLISS stopped for a spell at the George Washington University. Between traveling and teaching he has written and edited over fifteen books and numerous articles. His main interests have been the intersection of politics, law, and crime. With Robert Seidman he authored *Law, Order and Power* (1971, revised 1982). He published two books (*Boxman: A Professional Thief's Journey* with Harry King and *On the Take: From Petty Crooks to Presidents*) on the basis of ten years of participant observation research on organized crime in Seattle, Washington. His most recent book *Making Law: The Law, State and Structural Contradictions* (edited with Marjorie Zatz) applies his theory of lawmaking to a wide range of legal phenomenon from state criminality to immigration laws. He is past president of the American Society of Criminology (1988–1989) and the Society for the Study of Social Problems (1992–1993). In 1985 he received the Bruce Smith Sr. Award from the Academy of Criminal Justice Sciences for outstanding contributions to criminal justice. He received also the Lifetime Award for Outstanding Achievement from the American Sociological Association's Criminology Section. Chambliss is a fellow of the American Society of Criminology and an Augustus Scholar at the National Institute for Alternatives to Prison.

ROLAND CHILTON, professor of sociology at the University of Massachusetts at Amherst, has published articles on crime and delinquency in a variety of social science journals. He has been executive secretary of the American Society of Criminology and, for 1993–1994, will chair the crime, law, and deviance section of the American Sociological Association. Recent articles have examined the theoretical implications of trends suggested by police reports for specific U.S. cities of the age, race, and gender of persons arrested.

THEODORE G. CHIRICOS is professor of criminology at Florida State University. His earlier research involved deterrence and sentencing. His current interests are primarily political economy, crime and punishment, with a particular focus on labor markets and race.

CHARLES E. CRAWFORD received his B.A. in criminal justice from the University of Florida and is currently a doctoral candidate in criminology at Florida State University. He is a former Delores Auzenne and Patricia Roberts Harris fellow. His research interests include political economy and punishment, and minority issues in criminal justice.

ROBERT CRUTCHFIELD is an associate professor of sociology and the director of the Institute for Ethnic Studies in the United States at the University of Washington. He received his Ph.D. from Vanderbilt University in 1980. He has done research on racial disparities in the criminal justice system, delinquency, and urban crime patterns. His current research interest focuses on the relationship between economic and social dislocations and urban crime.

DARNELL F. HAWKINS is a professor of African-American studies and sociology at the University of Illinois at Chicago. He received his Ph.D. in sociology from the University of Michigan in 1976, and a J.D. from the University of North Carolina at Chapel Hill in 1981. He has conducted research on racial disproportinality in the nation's prison system, homicide trends, and public perceptions of crime and punishment. He is editor of *Homicide Among Black Americans* (1986). His current research projects include a history of state prisons in North Carolina from 1870 to 1957.

JAMES A. INCIARDI, Ph.D., is director of the Center for Drug and Alcohol Studies at the University of Delaware; professor in the department of sociology and criminal justice at Delaware; adjunct professor in the department of epidemiology and public health at the University of Miami School of Medicine; a distinguished professor at the State University of Rio de Janeiro; chair of the NIDA/NIH AIDS Research Review Committee; and a member of the AIDS Research Committee of the Institute of Medicine, National Academy of Sciences. Dr. Inciardi received his Ph.D. in sociology at New York University and has research, clinical, field, and teaching experience in the areas of AIDS, substance abuse, and criminal justice. He has done extensive consulting work nationally and internationally, and has published some thirty books and more than 150 articles and chapters in the areas of substance abuse, criminology, criminal justice, history, folklore, social policy, AIDS, medicine, and law.

PAMELA IRVING JACKSON, professor of sociology and director of the Justice Studies Program at Rhode Island College, holds a Ph.D. from Brown University. She recently served a three-year stint as associate editor of the *American Sociological Review* and has published a book on the bases of collective support for social control, *Minority Group Threat, Crime and Policing: Social Context and Social Control.* Her research articles have appeared in the *American Sociological Review, Criminology, Justice Quarterly, Policing and Society,* and other scholarly journals. Currently her research centers on comparative investigation of crime rates and social control efforts in France, Germany, and the United States.

GARY LAFREE is professor and chair of sociology at the University of New Mexico. He is also the director of the New Mexico Statistical Analysis Center. He received his Ph.D. in sociology from Indiana University in 1979. He has published articles in sociology and criminology journals and law reviews on a wide range of topics, including the official processing of rape cases, discrimination in the application of the law, and cross-national trends in rates of crime. His book, *Rape and Criminal Justice* was published by Wadsworth Press in 1989. He spent the past year on a fellowship from the Harry Frank Guggenheim Foundation, preparing a book on race and crime trends in the post-World War II United States.

DOROTHY LOCKWOOD is an associate scientist with the Center for Drug and Alcohol Studies at the University of Delaware. She is the project director for a NIDA-funded research demonstration grant. Dr. Lockwood also conducts program evaluations of various juvenile and adult offender programs. Her research interests include juvenile delinquency, women and drug use, drug abuse treatment, and criminal justice policy.

CORAMAE RICHEY MANN, professor of criminal justice at Indiana University, Bloomington, received undergraduate and graduate degrees in clinical psychology from Roosevelt University in Chicago and her Ph.D. in sociology (criminology) from the University of Illinois, Chicago Circle. Her research has been directed toward those oppressed by the juvenile and criminal justice systems: youth, women, and racial/ethnic minorities. Professor Mann is the author of numerous scholarly articles and chapters on these topics and two books: *Female Crime and Delinquency* and *Unequal Justice: A Question of Color*. She recently completed her third book, *Women Murderers: Deadliest of the Species*.

JOAN MCCORD, professor of criminal justice at Temple University, received a Ph.D. in sociology from Stanford University. She has served as vice-chair of the National Research Council Committee on Law and Justice since 1991, on the Scientific Commission of the International Society for Criminology since 1990, president of the American Society of Criminology, 1988–1989, and fellow of the ASC and of the International Society for Research on Aggression. Her publications include work on causes of crime, alcoholism, psychopathy, intervention programs, and theory.

ERIC H. MONKKONEN is a professor of history at UCLA, specializing in the history of American cities and urban problems, especially crime and poverty. He holds a Ph.D. from the University of Minnesota. Since 1975, his research has focused on the larger issues of American urbanization. These broad interests are reflected in his most recent book, *America Becomes Urban: The Development of U.S. Cities and Towns, 1790–1980* (1988). Monkkonen has written several other books and over thirty research articles. Books include *The Dangerous Class: Crime and Poverty in Columbus, Ohio, 1860–1920* (1975); *Police in Urban America, 1860 to 1920* (1981). Some recent articles include "Police History: An Overview of Recent Research," in *Crime and Justice: Annual Review of Research* 15 (1992); "Origins of Urban Institutions for the Underclass," in Michael Katz, ed., *The "Underclass" Debate* (Princeton University Press, 1993); "The American State from the Bottom Up: Of Homicides and Courts," *Law and Society Review* (spring 1990); "Diverging Homicide Rates, England and the United States, 1850–1875," in Ted Robert Gurr, ed., *Violence in America* (1989).

MARTHA A. MYERS is professor of sociology at the University of Georgia. She is a member of the editorial boards of *Criminology, Law and Society Review,* and *Journal of Quantitative Criminology.* Her research examines the relationship between social control and various dimensions of inequality. She is currently working on a book that specifies the ways in which economic and demographic changes shaped late nineteenth and early twentieth century punishment. Of particular interest are trends in black and white admissions to the southern penitentiary, and in the length and actual duration of penitentiary sentences.

ANNE E. POTTIEGER is a scientist with the Center for Drug and Alcohol Studies at the University of Delaware, where she is a co-principal investigator on two treatment demonstration projects funded by the National Institute on Drug Abuse. She was the project director of the Crack Abuse Patterns and Crime Linkages study described in this book. Her publications are in the areas of crime, delinquency, and substance abuse. She received her Ph.D. in sociology from the University of Delaware.

THOMAS A. REGULUS, Ph.D., received his degree in sociology and social work from the University of Michigan in 1982. His research includes the study of delinquency, gangs, prison violence, and crime control policies. He is currently completing a collaborative evaluation of drug house abatements in Cook County, Illinois. He was the principal investigator of *From State-school to Stateville,* a study of criminal prosecutions of juveniles in Cook County, Illinois. He contributed to the NIJ sponsored National Youth Gang Suppression and Intervention study (1992) and the National Study of Collective Actions and Civil Disturbances (1980).

ZOANN SNYDER-JOY, assistant professor of sociology at Western Michigan University, recently received her Ph.D. in justice studies at Arizona State University. Her research and publications focus on self-determination, local control, and justice issues as they pertain to American Indians. Dr. Snyder-Joy is currently working on the integration of multicultural perspectives into criminal justice education.

RAYMOND TESKE, JR., is a professor of criminal justice at Sam Houston State University. His areas of interest are victimization, survey research, and comparative research, with particular emphasis on the German criminal justice system. Professor Teske is a former Alexander von Homboldt scholar and has authored articles on comparative police statistics, prosecution and sentencing in Germany, and on victims' rights in Germany.

STEWART TOLNAY is professor of sociology and director of the Center for Social and Demographic Analysis at the State University of New York at Albany. His research has been concentrated in two general areas. With E. M. Beck he has authored a number of papers on lynching in the American south between 1880 and 1930. They are also co-authors of *A Festival of Violence:*

An Analysis of the Lynching of Blacks in the American South, 1882 to 1930 (forthcoming from University of Illinois Press), which won the 1992 President's Book Award from the Social Science History Association. His other research interest concerns the historical fertility of African-Americans in the United States. He is currently working on an NSF-supported project investigating rural black fertility in the south between 1910 and 1940.

BARBARA D. WARNER is assistant professor of sociology at the University of Kentucky. Her research examines the macrosociological causes of variations in both crime and crime control. Her ongoing research on crime control focuses on variables such as the reporting of crime, political structure, and definitions of crime that may mediate social structure and formal responses to crime. Some of her recent publications have appeared in the *American Sociological Review, American Journal of Sociology* and *Criminology*.

Subject Index

A

Author Index

A

Abbott, G., 69, 79
Adlaf, Edward, 215, 232
Ageton, Suzanne S., 46, 61
Aidala, Angela A., 216, 232
Aitkin, Murray, 140n.17, 141
Akiyama, Yoshio, 178, 187nn.2–3, 188
Albrecht, Hans-Jorg, 326, 338–39
Allen, Walter, 1, 8
Ames, Jessie, 138n.3, 141
Anderson, Dorothy, 140n.17, 141
Anderson, Margo, 108, 119
Andrew, June, 48, 60
Anglin, M. Douglas, 215, 232
Arnold, Harald, 323–40
Auletta, Ken, 195–96, 210
Austin, Gregory A., 215, 232, 234
Austin, James, 252, 256, 304
Austin, Roy L., 289, 306
Austin, Thomas L., 285, 292, 304
Axinn, J., 69, 79

B

Bachman, R., 316, 318–20, 320n.7
Bachman, Jerald G., 215, 232, 234
Baker, Ralph, 215, 234
Bakkestrom, Eskild, 48, 65
Bales, William D., 286, 288, 304
Ball, John, 215, 232
Baltzell, E. D., 70, 79
Banfield, Edward, 195, 208, 210

Banks, Enoch M., 160, 163
Barr, Helen M., 55, 64
Barrera, Mario, 187n.1, 188
Barrett, Peter, 55, 63
Barrow, L. C., 270–71, 276
Barth, Fredrik, 342, 357
Barth, G., 79
Beck, E. M., 4, 5, 7, 121–44, 147, 150, 162–63, 163n.1, 165
Becker, Howard, 39, 42
Belanger, Sarah, 342, 344, 357
Belenko, S., 272, 276
Bell, D., 70, 79
Bell, Derrick, 262, 265, 276
Belluci, Patricia A., 213, 232
Benedict, Ruth, 23, 42
Bennett, Steve, 140n.17, 141
Benson, Michael, 83, 94, 97
Bentler, Peter M., 215, 233
Berger, Peter, 31, 42
Berk, Richard, 300, 304
Bernstein, Ilene, 118n.3, 119, 293, 304
Bernstein, Iver, 118n.3, 119
Bickel, G., 317, 322
Billingsley, A., 266, 276
Bishop, John, 184, 188
Black, Donald, 173, 188
Blalock, Hubert, 83–84, 96, 132–33, 141, 146, 150, 160, 164, 286–87, 304, 344, 357
Blau, Judith, 185, 188, 269, 276
Blau, Peter M., 185, 188, 269, 276
Blauner, Robert, 286, 304
Block, Richard, 173, 188

375

**NATIONAL UNIVERSITY
LIBRARY**

NATIONAL UNIVERSITY
LIBRARY SACRAMENTO